Mary: Adept, Queen, Mother, Priestess

By the Same Author

Quest for the Soul (2004)

The Soul and Its Destiny (2004)

Christianity: the One, the Many, vols. I and II (2007)

The Sacramental Church (2011)

Mary: Adept, Queen, Mother, Priestess (first online edition, 2020; second online edition 2021).

For additional information on the author's publications see http://uriel.com/index.html.

Mary: Adept, Queen, Mother, Priestess

John F. Nash

Palmetto Publishing Group
2837 Rivers Avenue
North Charleston, SC 29405

First print edition

Paperback ISBN: 978-1-68515-463-9
eBook ISBN: 978-1-68515-464-6

November 21, 2021

**Copyright © 2021, John F. Nash
All rights reserved.**

No part of this publication may be reproduced, distributed, or transmitted in any form or by any means, including photocopying, recording, or other electronic or mechanical methods, without the prior written permission of the publisher, except in the case of brief quotations embodied in critical reviews and certain other noncommercial uses permitted by copyright law.

Originally published online: http://uriel.com/Mary/index.html. First edition March 25, 2020; second edition September 8, 2021.

Cover picture: Based on *Head of a Woman* (c.1507) by Leonardo da Vinci.

Nash, John F., http://uriel.com/index.html

Dedicated to
the Right Reverend Brian Lee Cole,
Bishop, Episcopal Diocese of East Tennessee, USA.

My soul doth magnify the Lord,
And my spirit hath rejoiced in God my Savior.
For he hath regarded the low estate of his handmaiden: for, behold, from henceforth all generations shall call me blessed.
For he that is mighty hath done to me great things; and holy is his name.
And his mercy is on them that fear him from generation to generation.

(Luke 1:46-50)

"I was Miriam, the Mother of Jesus, and now hold the Office of World Mother. I knew you in that life and befriended you. I have given you messages in this life. Could you not collect all your writings of Me and publish them as an aid to My cause amongst men?"

Her shining blue aura seemed to enfold me for a moment, and its light to fill the room. A still peace pervaded me from the highest levels down to the physical. This experience seems like an answer to an unspoken wish, that I might again have contact with Her and receive direct assurance of the correctness of the teachings concerning Her. I now feel utterly sure and re-dedicate my life to Her service.

(Geoffrey Hodson's spiritual diary.
Entry dated January 28, 1945.)

Contents

Chapter	Title	Page
	Illustrations	viii
	Preface	ix
	Introduction	1
1	Mary in Scripture	13
2	Mary According to Anne Catherine Emmerich	49
3	Mary in Early Christian Writings	75
4	Marian Doctrine and Beyond	113
5	Marian Devotion and Intercession	157
6	Mary Reveals Herself to the World	203
7	Mary in Esoteric Teachings	247
8	Mary and the Feminine Face of God	285
9	Synthesis and Reflections: the Historical Mary	327
10	Synthesis and Reflections: the Celestial Mary	373
	Epilogue	415
	Glossary	419
	Index	433

Illustrations

Figure	Caption	Page
1.1	*The Adoration of the Shepherds* (detail) by Guido Reni (c.1640).	28
3.1	Centerpiece of an early third-century fresco in the Priscilla Catacombs, Rome.	93
4.1	*The Virgin Adoring the Host* (1852) by Jean Auguste Dominique Ingres (detail).	138
5.1	*Madonna della Pace* ("Madonna of Peace") detail, by Bernardino di Pinturicchio (c.1452).	166
5.2	*Mary Theotokos of Yaroslavl*, Russia (c.1114).	189
6.1	*Our Lady of Lourdes.* Representation of the Marian apparition in the grotto in 1858.	211
8.1	Twelfth-century fresco of the Trinity in the Chapel of St James, Urschalling, Upper Bavaria, depicting the Holy Spirit as female.	298
9.1	*Theotokos of Vladimir.* One of several portraits of Mary claimed to have been painted by Luke the Evangelist.	331
9.2	Mary, flanked by archangels, blessing her followers. Detail from an illustration in the *Rabbula Gospels* (sixth century).	351
10.1	*Madonna del Magnificat* ("Madonna of the Magnificat"), detail, by Sandro Botticelli (1481).	381
10.2	*Le sacerdoce de laVierge* ("Priesthood of the Virgin"). School of Amiens, France. Early fifteenth century.	388

Preface

Mary: Adept, Queen, Mother, Priestess is addressed to ordinary people: laypersons, clergy, esotericists, Christians, members of other world religions, or anyone else who feels drawn to Mary, wants to learn more about her, or wants to serve her.

Parts of this book reflect traditional Christian teachings and practices; other parts draw upon modern esoteric teachings. Every author's dream is that people will read a book from cover to cover. More often readers go first to the chapters or sections with most immediate appeal; later their interest may be piqued to explore the rest of the book. *Mary: Adept, Queen, Mother, Priestess* lends itself to selective reading. Each chapter is largely self-contained, allowing readers to begin "on safe ground" of their choosing, before venturing into more challenging territory. Eventually we trust that readers will find the whole book informative and rewarding.

Two online editions of the book were published on the webpage http://uriel.com/Mary/index.html, the first in March 2020, the second in September 2021. Popular demand, along with a desire to ensure the book's continued availability, led to the decision to publish a print edition.

This print edition is based on, but is not identical to, the second online edition. Some revisions have been made to content, and the change of format has substantially altered pagination.

Whether to retain the full-color images from the online editions was a hard decision. In the end the choice focused on the book's retail price; the price would be doubled if the book contained color images. The author trusts that readers will accept the grayscale images in return for greater price accessibility. All images can be viewed in full color on the Internet.

The online editions will remain on the website for the foreseeable future. They may have intrinsic value; some readers may find them more accessible; or they may serve as a baseline to show how the story of Mary evolved from March 2020 onward.

The author is indebted to Spring ("Malone") Brooks, Virginia ("Ginger") Oaks, and Dr Glynda Ramsey, members of an ongoing study group that provided valuable feedback on the second online edition, and in turn contributed greatly to this print edition.

Numerous others in the traditional Christian and esoteric communities offered helpful suggestions and constructive criticism. Most of all they offered encouragement and reassurance that the book was necessary and timely.

The author is indebted, for her unwavering support of the project, to the Rev'd Canon SuzeAnne Silla, Interim Rector of St John's Episcopal Church, Johnson City, Tennessee, from early 2018 through November 2020.

The book is dedicated to the Right Rev'd Brian L. Cole, Episcopal Bishop of East Tennessee, respected and loved throughout his diocese and beyond. Bishop Cole's sensitive pastoral care extends not only to the faithful sheep but also to the goats who get through the fence, climb up on things, and eat the flowers!

John F. Nash
November 21, 2021
Feast of the Presentation of Mary in the Temple

The author's website: http://uriel.com/index.html.

Introduction

This book is about Mary, the mother of Jesus. Who was Mary? What do we know about her? How have Christians and others related to her over the centuries? Has she communicated with us—and, if so, in what ways? Can we communicate with her? Where is Mary now? Does she continue to play a role in the church, humanity, and the world? This book addresses these and a myriad of other questions.

Mary: Adept, Queen, Mother, Priestess is Mary's story, gleaned from scripture, early Christian writings, mainstream Christian doctrine and devotional practices, modern esoteric teachings, and information from visions, apparitions, and other contacts. In a few cases we have Mary's own words. Material from these various sources coalesces into a remarkably coherent account of Mary's life in Palestine, her role in the Redemption, her present position, and her ongoing ministry. The picture of Mary that emerges amply justifies the fourfold accolade proclaimed in the book's title.

Background and Objectives

Mary: Adept, Queen, Mother, Priestess is addressed to Christians of all traditions and to students of modern esotericism—not necessarily separate groups of people, but distinguished to a greater or lesser degree by the sources of truth on which they rely. For many years the author has tried to build bridges between Christianity and esotericism, and the story of Mary provided a rich opportunity to pursue that mission. Writing the book has also been a great privilege and learning experience.

The author is a practicing member of the Episcopal Church, the national province of the Anglican Communion in the United States. He is indebted to fellow members and clergy, at the parish and diocesan levels, for their generous support and encouragement.

The book does not attempt to present or defend an "Anglican position" on Mary, however. Indeed there may be as many positions as there are Anglicans! This is a personal testimony in which the opinions expressed are the author's alone. Frequently the discussion draws upon Roman Catholic or Eastern Orthodox traditions which focus more strongly on Mary.

Significant events occurred over many years preceding any conscious notion on the author's part to write this book. There were many dots, but they remained unconnected. Things began to come together in 2018, and early in 2019 the author received a directive to "Write down everything you know about Mary." In reality a considerable amount of new research was required, in addition to what was on hand and previously published;[1] but the first edition came together remarkably quickly, then a second online edition, and now this print edition.

The book's title was borrowed from the author's article: "Adept, Queen, Mother, Priestess: Mary in the writings of Geoffrey Hodson," published in the Winter 2019 issue of *The Esoteric Quarterly*. As will be seen, Hodson's esoteric diary was one of the most important sources in the present study.

Target Readership

Mary: Adept, Queen, Mother, Priestess is not a devotional text, an attempt to write an accurate history of events that occurred two millennia ago, or a critical analysis of Marian literature. It is Mary's *story*.

The book is addressed to ordinary people: laypersons, clergy, esotericists, Christians, members of other world religions, or anyone else who feels drawn to Mary, wants to learn more about her, or wants to serve her. It is not intended to contribute to, or intrude upon, the professional literature of theology, academic religious studies, church history, biblical studies, or textual analysis—though individuals in those disciplines are most welcome to read the book and offer comments or suggestions.

The author is indebted to scholars in the academic fields whose research provided much of the source material. The book is written by a generalist, whose goal is the integration of knowledge rather than detailed analysis, building bridges and seeing connections rather than dwelling upon minutiae. Every effort has been made to verify facts. But generalists inevitably face criticism from specialists, each of whom insists that his or her field is more complicated and nuanced than the generalist takes it to be.

The book *is* intended to contribute to the literature of modern esotericism, where informed discussion of Mary is woefully lacking. The author will gladly respond to challenges on points of detail from the esoteric community.

Who Was, and Is, Mary?

Mary was an historical figure, a Jewish woman who lived in her native Palestine at the dawn of the Common Era. She was the mother of Jesus. After her earthly death Christianity created a new Mary, whom we call the "celestial Mary." During its 2,000-year history, peasants, educated laypeople, theologians, and ecclesiastical authorities projected onto the celestial Mary the most cherished values of their time and culture, elevating her to near-divine heights. In some cultures she took the place of pre-Christian goddesses in the popular consciousness. Other people reacted to her, as far as scripture and tradition would allow, with indifference or even hostility.

Feminist theologians have been ambivalent about Mary. The quest for a goddess to satisfy the hunger left by centuries of religious patriarchy took them first to Sophia, revered in late-biblical Judaism, Gnosticism, and Eastern Orthodox Christianity. By contrast, Mary was seen as the embodiment of passive submission, unworthy to inspire newly empowered women.[2] We now know that the passive, submissive persona was a creation of the patriarchal church; the historical Mary was an assertive woman who played a prominent role in nascent Christianity. Finally a number of feminists are becoming her champions.

Esotericists too have been ambivalent about Mary. Some recognize in her the supreme expression of feminine humanity, holding a high position in the inner governance of the planet and expressing the Feminine Aspect of Deity. Others prefer to discuss the Shekinah, Sophia, Tara, or Kuan Yin, giving the impression that Mary lies below the level of useful discourse. In some esoteric writings Mary is reduced to a symbol of the material world.

One wonders why Mary, represented in every manger scene and acclaimed in numerous Christmas carols, became such a controversial figure! Recognizing the conflicting attitudes, she might have retired into obscurity. Fortunately for us Mary refused to go away. Indeed, she now seems eager to reveal more of herself and to communicate more directly with humanity. Through visitations, apparitions, locutions, and other means Mary speaks of herself, her concerns for all lives on the planet, and her ongoing work for peace.

Mary's own revelation and communication come at a time when modern scholarship is revealing a clearer picture of her historical life in Palestine. The traditional narrative, based on the gospels, is that she gave birth to Jesus, watched him grow to manhood and take up his ministry, and stood in sorrow as he died on the cross.[3] *Acts* records one last appearance in the upper room at Pentecost.[4] In the expanded narrative now emerging, Mary continued Christ's ministry after the Ascension. She taught, counseled Jesus' disciples, baptized converts, and healed the sick. We believe that she even served in a priestly role in the emerging liturgy of the Eucharist.

Our story of Mary draws upon multiples sources, including canonical and extracanonical scripture, early Christian writings, mainstream Mariology and Marian devotion, visions of the mystics, information communicated during apparitions and more extended contacts, and modern esoteric teachings. Wherever possible sources are allowed to speak for themselves through direct quotes. Most valuable are Mary's own words.

One might expect that such diverse traditions would yield incompatible depictions of Mary. To be sure, there are differences in emphasis, and in a few cases what appear to be deliberate efforts to obscure the real Mary. But a remarkable consensus emerges, even in terminology, which so often poses a stumbling block to synthesis from different sources. The coherence of the composite picture of Mary—a rich mosaic created from pieces that could never have been expected to fit together so well—gives the story credence and supports its relevance. This is a story that needed to be told.

This book presents Mary as Adept, Queen, Mother and Priestess. The notion of Mary as Priestess comes from early Christian writings, the commentaries of nineteenth-century churchmen, and modern esoteric teachings. The notion of Mary's Queenship comes from traditional Mariology, Marian devotion, the pronouncements of recent popes, and esoteric teachings. Mary's role as Mother, not "just" of Jesus—or even of God—but of humanity is supported by age-old devotions, recent papal pronouncements, and the long tradition of the Divine

Introduction

Mother in the religions of South Asia. Adeptship, perfection of the human condition, is primarily an esoteric concept, but it bears a strong resemblance to the Eastern Orthodox doctrine of *theosis*, or "deification." The broader concept of initiation has parallels in sacraments like baptism and holy orders, in beatification and sainthood, and in Freemasonry.

The book presents the unfolding story of an individual, already of significant spiritual stature when she bore Jesus, who rose to ever-higher levels of authority and responsibility in service to humanity and the planet. It presents an individuality supremely relevant to our time, one revered in Christianity—and Islam—but who transcends sectarian divisions to address the spiritual and practical concerns of the twenty-first century. The book presents a feminine figure who can inspire women and men and connect us all in new ways to God.

Outline of the Book

Mary: Adept, Queen, Mother, Priestess is divided into ten chapters, plus this introduction, a brief epilogue, and a glossary and index:

1. Mary in Scripture
2. Mary According to Anne Catherine Emmerich
3. Mary in Early Christian Writings
4. Marian Doctrine and Beyond
5. Marian Devotion and Intercession
6. Mary Reveals Herself to the World
7. Mary in Esoteric Teachings
8. Mary and the Feminine Face of God
9. Synthesis and Reflections: the Historical Mary
10. Synthesis and Reflections: the Celestial Mary

The first eight chapters present knowledge of Mary from the various sources. The ninth and tenth chapters synthesize and reflect upon that knowledge to offer as complete a picture as possible of Mary: who and what she was, and is, and what her current mission appears to be.

Chapter 1 presents the scriptural record of Mary's life in Palestine and its immeasurable contribution to humanity: the birth of Jesus and witness to the Crucifixion. It reaches beyond the New Testament to include a number of extracanonical texts, particularly the *Infancy Gospel of James*, which provides important details of Mary's birth and childhood. Mary is also mentioned multiple times in the *Qur'an*; and a few quotes are included to facilitate interesting comparisons—and to provide insights into reverence for Mary and Jesus in early Islam .

Chapter 2 presents a description of Mary's life from the visions of Anne Catherine Emmerich, an eighteenth-century German nun. The placement of this chapter could be questioned; the case could be made that Emmerich's account should be grouped with the Marian communications in Chapter 6. But the flow of information suggested otherwise. After receiving the stigmata, open wounds on her body corresponding to those suffered by Jesus on the cross, Emmerich acquired the ability to travel back in time and view historical events. Her extensive and detailed descriptions of events in the lives of Jesus and Mary read almost like scripture. Accordingly, the decision was made to place the chapter next to the scriptural record, to permit parallel comparisons and contrasts.

Chapter 3 plays a vital role in building the picture of the historical Mary. It summarizes relevant Christian writings from the fourth to the tenth centuries (and beyond), many of which have only recently come to light. Modern textual scholarship, and examination of artifacts from the period, reveal an image of Mary contrasting sharply with the demure, passive, self-sacrificial image familiar in Marian devotion.

Early Christians remembered or envisioned Mary as a strong, assertive woman, actively engaged in the work of the church. Texts describe Mary teaching, baptizing converts to Christianity, and blessing and counseling Jesus' disciples. A combination of writings and artwork testifies that she engaged in liturgical ritual and celebrated the Eucharist. The Dormition literature offers a dramatic, if not always coherent, account of the arrival of the disciples, and then Christ, at her deathbed.

Chapters 1–3 provide overlapping accounts of Mary's Palestinian life, offering a rich description of a woman chosen to give birth to Jesus, to support and continue his ministry, and to develop her own distinctive ministry after Pentecost. We find disagreements over points of detail, and writers betray limitations in their knowledge of events as well as their own perspectives and biases. Yet the picture that emerges—far richer than the canonical scriptural record alone—gives us a clearer image of who Mary was and sets the stage for the discussion of who she is now and the mission she has undertaken.

Chapters 4 studies Christian doctrine relating to Mary. *Mariology* is a recognized branch of theology. Two Marian dogmas were defined in the early church: that Mary is the mother of God, and that she was a virgin when she gave birth of Jesus. More recently the Church of Rome has issued two more dogmatic pronouncements: her Immaculate Conception, and her Assumption into heaven at the end of her earthly life. Mariologists have explored Mary's queenship and her role in the Redemption, though no new dogmatic pronouncements seem likely in the foreseeable future.

Two other major topics in Mariology are summarized in Chapter 4. One is the notion of Mary's preordination, or predestination, to be the mother of Christ—a notion that emerged as a corollary of the doctrine of the absolute primacy of Christ. The other is Mary's priestly role; influential churchmen declared that when she stood at the foot of the cross Mary earned the right to be called the priestess for all humanity.

Chapter 5 examines traditional expressions of Marian devotion and intercession. Devotion to Mary, often accompanied by pleas to intercede with her son to grant favors, expanded rapidly in the Middle Ages and continued after the Reformation in the Church of Rome and the Eastern Orthodox Churches. In a few cases devotion rose to the level of adoration or worship.

By contrast, the Protestant churches were indifferent or even hostile to any type of Marian devotional practice—contributing to their own spiritual impoverishment. Traditions like Anglicanism that sought a middle way between Roman Catholicism and Protestantism have taken small steps toward reinstating Marian devotion into their religious practices.

Chapter 5 ends with a discussion of Marian devotion as it has been, and continues to be, expressed through the arts, including the visual arts, music, and dance.

Chapter 6 explores Mary's communications with humanity through apparitions, locutions, and other contacts with individuals and groups. The frequency of apparitions has increased, and more people—and a greater diversity of people—are testifying to seeing her or hearing her speak. In addition to the best-known apparitions, like those at Guadalupe and Lourdes, two series of apparitions command special attention. One, in Zeitoun, Egypt, extended over a period of years, witnessed by millions of people, many of them Muslims. The other, in Medjugorje, Bosnia–Herzegovina, involved six witnesses and has continued for nearly four decades. The Medjugorje apparitions include messages that Mary wished to be shared with the world.

Chapter 6 also examines more detailed communications with individuals who served as Mary's scribes and were charged with publishing her words. The work of three scribes is examined: Bridget of Sweden, from the fourteenth-century, and Theosophist Geoffrey Hodson and spiritual teacher Anna Raimondi in our own times. Mary's communications to all three include commentary on a variety of important topics.

Chapter 7 presents modern esoteric teachings on Mary, primarily but not exclusively by members of the Theosophical Society. Often these teachings were dictated to scribes: in Hodson's case occasionally by Mary herself, in other cases by masters or archangels. In almost every instance esoteric teachings concerning Mary are supported by, or build upon, assertions from traditional Christianity. The major strength of esoteric teachings lies in their intellectual merit and esotericists' commitment to integrate new concepts into a larger, self-consistent body of knowledge. The Mariology of the future could ill-afford to ignore relevant teachings.

The Church of Rome uses rigorous procedures to identify apparition reports that may have relevance beyond the individual's own spiritual experience. Comparable criteria have evolved within the esoteric community for evaluating the authenticity of alleged communications from higher beings. In each case, only a small fraction of claims meet applicable standards.

Chapter 8 explores our perception of the Feminine Face of God. The purpose is to see whether Mary can be viewed as an expression of the Divine Feminine. If she can that would provide important context for her ministry and responsibilities. Esoteric teachings draw upon Vedantic Hindu precedents to affirm the emergence of a Feminine Principle from the highest levels of the Godhead. Judeo-Christianity os-

Introduction

tensibly affirms a masculine Deity, but people's hunger for the Divine Feminine has been apparent since the time of Abraham.

In biblical Judaism Goddess worship was sufficiently common and enduring to require continual condemnation by the prophets. In addition to traditional goddesses like Asherah, Judaism gave us *Ruach ha-Kodesh* ("the Holy Spirit"), the *Shekinah* (the indwelling presence of God), and *Chokmah/Sophia* ("Wisdom")—all three considered feminine. A masculinized Ruach ha-Kodesh eventually became the Third Person of the Christian Trinity, but not without "competition" from Sophia. Efforts to reintroduce a feminine element into the Trinity have continued to the present.

Chapters 9 and 10 offer a synthesis of the material presented in the previous chapters and reflections on what has been learned. Information from the various sources comes together to produce a rich picture of Mary; to tell a compelling story of her life in Palestine and her continuing presence in the world today.

Chapter 9 focuses on the historical Mary. She was a Middle Eastern woman, a woman of her time who remained true to Judaic tradition throughout her life. Mary gave birth to Jesus and raised him to manhood, saw him take up his ministry; participated in the Sacrifice of the Cross; and reportedly had a vision of his Resurrection. Present with the disciples at Pentecost, Mary went on to pursue her own ministry in the Christian community of Jerusalem. From the Dormition literature we learn of Mary's last days and the appearance of Christ to take her soul to Paradise.

The belief that the historical Mary was a member of the human family is defended against suggestions that she was the manifestation of a divine being. But Mary did make extraordinary progress on the spiritual path. Most likely she was already a third-degree initiate when she was born in Palestine, primed over multiple lifetimes to give birth to Jesus. She progressed on the initiatory path toward "human perfection." Mary probably received the crown of adeptship, the fifth initiation, on her deathbed.

Chapter 10 focuses on the "celestial" Mary, the exalted personage envisioned both by Christian doctrine and devotion and by modern esoteric teachings. Further insights have been gained from her apparitions and communications with favored individuals. Upon her attainment of adeptship we believe that Mary became a powerful member of the Hierarchy of Masters, exercising a unique, feminine role in the inner life of the planet, and serving as an expression of the Feminine Aspect of Deity.

Mary pursues an active ministry of peace and healing, with special concern for women and children. She merits the high status to which her Christian devotees have raised her; concerns about "Marian excess" are unwarranted. Mary does not compete with Christ; in her messages and communications she always defers to her son. Similarly, there need be no conflict in our respective relationships with her and Christ. In Christ we see the Masculine Face of God; in Mary we see the Feminine Face.

We affirm that the historical Mary evolved into the celestial Mary. Claims that a "celestial Mary" existed before the historical Mary was born—even that she was present at the dawn of creation—are dismissed. Where such claims cannot simply be attributed to pious hyperbole, they can be explained by the projection of Mary's identity onto a different entity. Suggestions are made as to who that entity might have been.

The Epilogue offers some final thoughts on Mary, her spiritual status, and her relationship with Christ and God the Father. It includes two quotes from early Christian writings in which Christ offered Mary his blessing and praise.

Copious endnotes are provided at the end of each chapter. Most of them are references to the literature, provided to readers in the belief that even ordinary people—to whom the book is primarily addressed—may be interested to know where quotes came from, to verify their accuracy, or to explore the context in which they were made. Some of the endnotes offer additional information or clarification concerning topics discussed in the body of the text.

The glossary offers definitions or explanations of technical terms used in the book. It should provide a useful reference for traditional Christians encountering the terminology of esoteric teachings for the first time, and for esotericists who may not be familiar with terms pertaining to Christian doctrine, practices, or institutional structures. The glossary also defines how the terms are used in this book in cases where their meaning in the general literature may be ambiguous.

Introduction

An index lists internal references to the most important Marian-related words and phrased used in the traditional Christian literature and in modern esoteric teachings. Referenced persons include authors of source material as well as characters who play significant roles in Mary's story.

---

[1] John F. Nash, "The World Mother: Teachings of Helena Roerich and Geoffrey Hodson," *The Esoteric Quarterly* (Winter 2006), 35-46; "Mary: Blessed Virgin and World Mother," *The Esoteric Quarterly* (Winter 2010), 19-39; "Adept, Queen, Mother, Priestess: Mary in the Writings of Geoffrey Hodson," *The Esoteric Quarterly* (Winter 2019), 37-65; Review of *Conversations with Mary: Messages of Love, Healing, Hope and Unity for Everyone* by Anna Raimondi, *The Esoteric Quarterly* (Summer 2019), 84-88. Mary is also mentioned in *Christianity: the One, the Many* (2007), and *The Sacramental Church* (2011).

[2] Mary is not even listed in the indexes of influential works by Merlin Stone, *When God was a Woman*, Dorset Press, 1976; and *Ancient Mirrors of Womanhood*, Beacon, 1979. Sherry Ruth Anderson's and Patricia Hopkins' *The Feminine Face of God*, Bantam, 1991, contains a single reference to Mary, acknowledging simply that she may be beloved but is "never mistaken for God."

[3] Only *Luke* offers any details of the Annunciation and Nativity, and only *John* identifies her as being at the Crucifixion. None of the gospels lists Mary as a witness to the Resurrection—or acknowledges that she ever saw the risen Christ.

[4] *Acts* 1:14.

Mary: Adept, Queen, Mother, Priestess

Chapter 1
Mary in Scripture

The first three chapters present the quest for the historical Mary. Chapter 1 examines the scriptural record of Mary's life in Palestine, 2,000 years ago, from the time of her conception and birth, through the end of her earthly life. It draws upon the canonical New Testament, extracanonical texts, and the *Qur'an*. While the extracanonical gospels, epistles, and other writings may not carry the authority of the New Testament, they contribute important details to our story. Mary features prominently in the *Qur'an*, and both she and Jesus were highly regarded in early Islam.

Introduction
The Scriptural Record

Our quest for the historical Mary begins with scripture. Scripture is the testimony of believers. It may refer to historical events, perhaps accurately, but the authors' foremost concern was to affirm their faith. That concern influenced what they recorded, how they presented it, and the significance they attached to it.

In some instances the authors of scripture were eye witnesses to the events they described. In many cases they were not;[1] rather, they recorded stories circulating in their communities. Stories grow in complexity over time; interesting—but not necessarily factual—details are added, and new interpretations are suggested. Alternatively, storytellers may omit material they disagree with or do not understand, or which their audiences might not want to hear. Storytelling is an organic process with continual expansion and contraction, and continual interaction between speakers and listeners.

The expansion and contraction of stories relating to Jesus, his ministry, and those around him was taking place before and while the scriptural texts were being written. The final chapter of *Mark* originally ended with verse 8; verses 9–20 were added later. The process has continued down the ages in interpolations or redactions to sacred texts, in translators' choice of words or phraseology,[2] and in the evolution of beliefs about the events and people described. The beliefs that Eve ate an apple, three kings rode camels to Bethlehem, Paul fell off his horse on the way to Damascus, and Satan wields a pitchfork do not come from scripture; they come from piety, art and fiction.

Jesus made use of allegory, metaphor and parable in his teaching. Nobody would take "I am the vine, ye are the branches"[3] literally. And Jesus may not have had a particular farmer in mind when he said: "A sower went out to sow his seed."[4] Some scriptural passages clearly were intended to be allegorical, or to be read on multiple levels. The modern quest for "biblical literalism" is undermined, not only by inconsistencies among parallel scriptural accounts, but by the recognition that few people wrote with that intent two millennia ago. On the other hand, overemphasis on allegory and symbolism can rob the texts of any sense of validity; a scriptural passage can mean anything we want it to mean.

Some of the later texts take the form of hagiographies, and their factual basis is even less secure. But even if hagiographies tell us little about their heroes and heroines, they tell us much about the status those individuals enjoyed in the particular culture.

As we read the scriptural records we should try to see Mary through the eyes of the writers: who they were and what they knew, believed or imagined. Mary was obviously very significant to them, and what they wrote can become equally significant to us.

Canonical and Extracanonical Texts

In 367 CE, Athanasius, Patriarch of Alexandria, wrote his thirty-ninth Festal Letter to churches and monasteries within his jurisdiction. Its ostensible purpose was to fix the date of Easter, but the letter is best-remembered because it listed the twenty-seven books of the canonical New Testament. Athanasius' list, the first from a senior church official, included the then-controversial *Book of Revelation* but omitted other contenders, like the *Shepherd of Hermes* and the two *Epistles of Clement*.

The institutional church agreed that the twenty-seven books had a quality that distinguished them from other texts of the period: the books were believed to be divinely inspired. Athanasius' New Testament canon was confirmed in 382 by Pope Damasus I and by later

Chapter 1. Mary in Scripture

regional synods and individual denominational authorities. But it was never confirmed by an ecumenical council and never attained universal recognition. Martin Luther doubted the legitimacy of *James*, *Hebrews*, *Jude* and *Revelation* and placed them in an appendix to his Bible.[5] Otherwise, and perhaps most importantly, the canon has stood the test of time; few people today could imagine it being different.

The canonical New Testament resulted from a desire, on the part of the institutional church, to compile from the available writings a record of Christ's most important sayings and actions and an account of the church's origins. Total coherence was not possible, but the selected writings have served the church's purposes well.

At the time Athanasius made his selection, many other texts were circulating in the Christian world. Now referred to as "extracanonical texts," they included gospels, epistles, "acts" of various apostles, and miscellaneous writings. Athanasius ordered that all such texts in Christian libraries in the Alexandria patriarchate be burned. He considered them heretical and dangerous; they could mislead even sincere members of the church. The trove of manuscripts discovered in 1945 at Nag Hammadi, Egypt, may have been buried to protect them from Athanasius' wrath.[6]

Even if the extracanonical texts were not destroyed, many were probably lost, and some are known only through references in surviving texts. On the other hand previously unknown texts have been discovered quite recently, as were the Nag-Hammadi Library and the Dead Sea Scrolls. Other important texts may await future discovery.

This book pays special attention to the biblical accounts, as befits their place in Christian tradition. Every significant reference to Mary in the New Testament is cited and discussed. But the scriptural record is sparse. Mary speaks only four times in the gospels. She is mentioned by name twelve times in *Luke*, five times in *Matthew*, once in *Mark*, and once in *Acts*. *John* never names her, though it describes three incidents in which she was involved. The epistles in their entirety contain only one verse even obliquely referring to Mary.[7]

Faced with the paucity of information we turn to the extracanonical texts to build our story of Mary. A text of particular importance and relevance is the *Infancy Gospel of James*, also known as the *Protoevangelium of James*. Like the canonical gospels, it was originally written in Greek, probably in about 145 CE. For comparison, *John* was probably written shortly before 100 CE.

In many cases, there is little internal evidence of the inferiority of the extracanonical texts; their authors, like the evangelists, wrote as though they had first-hand knowledge of the events they described. The argument is sometimes made that the extracanonical texts stand out because of implausible or fanciful content. But plausibility is subjective, and a comparison of canonical and extracanonical texts on that basis might not yield a clear distinction.

The institutional church has not ignored the extracanonical texts altogether. The Church of Rome frequently appealed to "tradition" to support a doctrine or liturgical observance, and in some cases that tradition can be traced to particular texts. For example, the feast of the Presentation of Mary in the Temple (November 21)—also observed in the Eastern Orthodox churches—is based on an account in the *Infancy Gospel of James*. The doctrine of Mary's Assumption into heaven is based entirely on texts written after the fourth century.

The *Qur'an*

A few quotes from the *Qur'an* are included for comparison with Christian sources. The *Qur'an*, which dates from the seventh century, drew upon canonical and extracanonical Christian texts, and possibly on independent traditions, for its descriptions of Jesus and Mary. Early Islam showed great reverence to both, regarding Jesus as the latest of the prophets and precursor of Muhammad, and giving Mary more "coverage" than the New Testament does.[8] Mary is the single most prominent female figure in the *Qur'an* and the only woman mentioned by name. She is equated in importance to the male prophets.

Was Mary revered more in Islam than in Christianity? No, the difference in emphasis was probably the product of time. By the seventh century Mary was receiving more attention in Christianity than she did in the first century, and Islam was born in that new environment. Had the canonical gospels been written later, Mary would have featured more prominently there too.

All ancient scriptures are sacred to the extent that people throughout the ages have invested faith and trust in them; we revere them and are blessed by them. In some instances the accounts of Mary in the various texts seem to have historical value; in others they come across as

Chapter 1. Mary in Scripture

allegorical, hagiographical, or devotional in nature. Factual credibility can be assessed as the narrative unfolds.

Divine Revelation

The Bible is said to have been inspired by the Holy Spirit. Christians regard the Old and New Testaments as foundational documents on which Christianity was built. They affirm, as an article of faith, that the canonical scriptures represent revealed truth: the word of God. The Lutheran and Calvinist reformers went farther to declare that the Bible represents the *only* source of truth, dispensing with tradition, which the Roman Church interpreted as the consensus teachings of the bishops, and human reason.[9]

The Protestant reformers asserted that the Bible is self-authenticating: its content proves that it was inspired. Whether or not that assertion involves circular reasoning, certain passages do claim divine inspiration: "All scripture is given by inspiration of God, and is profitable for doctrine ... for instruction in righteousness,"[10] and "Knowing this first, that no prophecy of the scripture is of any private interpretation. For the prophecy came not in old time by the will of man: but holy men of God spake as they were moved by the Holy Ghost."[11] Those passages referred to the Old Testament; the four gospels of the New Testament had not yet been written, or at least had not yet attained the status of scripture.[12]

The evangelists no doubt were inspired—as were many other writers before and since. But, except perhaps in the preamble to *John*, the evangelists themselves made no such claim or indicated in any way that they were being guided from above. Rather, they seemed to take responsibility for what they wrote. The argument for self-authentication is weak.

Most Christian denominations teach that the Bible represents the only authentic source of divine revelation: a deposit of faith that will suffice until the end of the age. Yet the Church of Rome acknowledges that information supporting that deposit of faith has been communicated to certain individuals by Christ, Mary, saints or angels during apparitions or visions. Chapter 6 will examine information received in Marian apparitions.

Esotericists and others insist that revelation is ongoing and that important new knowledge has been revealed during the last 150 years. Some modern esoteric writers claim to have received teachings from higher beings, by telepathy, dictation, or other means. Sources include *masters*—human beings alleged to have achieved perfection and no longer restricted by physical embodiment—and archangels. Examples of such teachings will be examined in Chapters 6 and 7.

The church struggled to determine which texts were divinely inspired. Similarly, individuals and groups inside and outside the church struggle to assess the authenticity of more recent communications. Absolute certainty is unattainable. The goal is to strike a reasonable balance between closed-mindedness and gullibility; the one extreme would deny us knowledge and wisdom that higher beings may be offering us, while the other would undermine a responsible commitment to truth.[13] The church and the esoteric community both take the matter seriously and have developed criteria to help sift through the large number of claims to identify communications—typically a small fraction—that may be trustworthy and relevant. Those pertaining to Mary make a valuable contribution to our story and will be discussed later in the book.

Mary's Birth and Childhood

Mary's first appearance in the New Testament is in the Annunciation stories of *Matthew* and *Luke*. But the gospels tell us nothing about Mary's background or her earlier life. Neither do they tell us how she came to be betrothed to Joseph.

Fortunately, the extracanonical *Infancy Gospel of James* fills in valuable details. The text tells us that Mary was the daughter of Joachim and Hannah. Joachim is described therein as "a man exceedingly rich"; but wealth brought the couple little joy because they were childless.[14]

Hannah was advanced in age, and both she and Joachim offered sacrifices and prayed daily that they might be blessed with a child, as the Old Testament Sarah was in her old age. In due course an angel appeared to Hannah to announce: "the Lord hath heard thy prayer, and thou shalt conceive, and shall bring forth; and thy seed shall be spoken of in all the world."[15] To which Hannah replied: "As the Lord my God liveth, if I beget either male or female, I will bring it as a gift to the Lord my God; and it shall minister to Him in holy things all the days of its life."[16]

The angel brought the same good news to Joachim, who was away fasting in the desert.[17] Joachim returned with his flocks, and the happy couple rejoiced and gave thanks. Nine months later Hannah gave birth to a girl, whereupon Hannah exclaimed. "My soul has been magnified this day."[18]

The child was duly named Mary. The name has a long etymological history. The earliest form was the Hebrew *Miryam*, possibly based on the Egyptian word *mir*, meaning love. Mary was probably known to her family and community by the Aramaic form *Maryam*. Later forms were the Greek *Mariam* and the Latin *Maria*, from which "Mary" and its variants in the modern European languages are derived.

An earlier bearer of the name was Miriam the Prophetess, sister of Moses and Aaron.[19] Significantly, the *Qur'an* traces Mary's maternal lineage back to Moses and Aaron.[20] *Luke* 1:5 provides at least indirect support for that assertion in its statement that Mary's cousin Elizabeth "was of the daughters of Aaron." The male descendents of Aaron, the *kohanim*, were accorded priestly status in biblical Judaism; whether the female descendents could claim any such status will be discussed later in the book.

Mary was probably born in about 22–20 BCE.[21] From the very beginning Mary was recognized as a special child. Remembering Hannah's promise to the angel, she and Joachim offered to present Mary to the temple when she was only a few months old. But the parents were persuaded to wait until the child was three. When Mary was presented to the temple,

> the priest received her, and kissed her, and blessed her, saying: The Lord has magnified thy name in all generations. In thee, on the last of the days, the Lord will manifest His redemption to the sons of Israel. And he set her down upon the third step of the altar, and the Lord God sent grace upon her; and she danced with her feet, and all the house of Israel loved her.[22]

King Herod of Judaea was rebuilding the temple during that general period. But the main temple buildings were completed and dedicated by 18 BCE. Moreover, temple ritual continued throughout the whole period of reconstruction.

Mary lived in the temple "as if she were a dove that dwelt there, and she received food from the hand of an angel."[23] The *Qur'an* relates that Mary's upbringing in the temple was entrusted to Zachariah, later to become the father of John the Baptist. "Whenever Zachariah entered in upon her in the sanctuary, he found food by her side. He said: 'Mary, from where do you have this?' She said: 'It is from Allah. Allah provides for whomever He wills, without beckoning."[24]

The *Infancy Gospel of James* tells us that, when Mary was twelve, the priests decided that she could no longer live in the temple "lest perchance she defile the sanctuary of the Lord." Presumably they were afraid that she would menstruate.[25] The priests resolved to find Mary a husband. No consideration seems to have been given to whether Mary wanted to marry, or whom she might have preferred; she was the property of the temple, to be disposed of as the priests saw fit.

An angel told Zachariah, the high priest to "go out and assemble the widowers of the people, and let them bring each his rod; and to whomsoever the Lord shall show a sign, his wife shall she be. And the heralds went out through all the circuit of Judaea."[26] Among the widowers from Judaea was Joseph. The reference to Joseph's location is interesting because *Luke* would soon place Joseph in Galilee, to the north.[27]

The *Infancy Gospel of James* testifies: "[B]ehold, a dove came out of the rod, and flew upon Joseph's head. And the priest said to Joseph, Thou hast been chosen by lot to take into thy keeping the virgin of the Lord."[28] Joseph protested: "I have children, and I am an old man, and she is a young girl. I am afraid lest I become a laughing-stock to the sons of Israel."[29]

The high priest managed to persuaded him, whereupon Joseph "took her into his keeping." He gave Mary his pledge: "Behold, I have received thee from the temple of the Lord; and now I leave thee in my house, and go away to build my buildings, and I shall come to thee. The Lord will protect thee."[30] Whether Joseph's house was in Judaea or Galilee remains in doubt. In either case we assume that servants, and probably other family members, were there to care for Mary, and she was not left alone.

The Nativity Narrative

The Annunciation

Matthew, probably written around 80 CE, offers an abbreviated Annunciation story with the terse beginning: "Now the birth of Jesus Christ was on this wise: When as his mother Mary was espoused to

Chapter 1. Mary in Scripture

Joseph, before they came together, she was found with child of the Holy Ghost."[31]

Luke, written a few years later, is more elaborate. The angel Gabriel had already appeared to Zachariah to announce that his wife Elizabeth would bear a son, the future John the Baptist. And when Elizabeth was six-months pregnant,

> Gabriel was sent from God unto a city of Galilee, named Nazareth, To a virgin espoused to a man whose name was Joseph, of the house of David; and the virgin's name was Mary. And the angel came in unto her, and said, Hail, thou that art highly favored, the Lord is with thee: blessed art thou among women. And when she saw him, she was troubled at his saying, and cast in her mind what manner of salutation this should be.[32]

Luke speaks of the "city" of Nazareth, but archeologists believe that it was actually a tiny village at that time, one of several within a few miles of Sepphoris, the capital of Galilee.[33] It did not become a city of any appreciable size until more recent times.

The angel Gabriel responded to Mary in words that would become immortalized in the liturgy of Christmas:

> Fear not, Mary: for thou hast found favor with God. And, behold, thou shalt conceive in thy womb, and bring forth a son, and shalt call his name Jesus. He shall be great, and shall be called the Son of the Highest: and the Lord God shall give unto him the throne of his father David: And he shall reign over the house of Jacob for ever; and of his kingdom there shall be no end.[34]

Not surprisingly, Mary was startled by suggestions of pregnancy: "How shall this be, seeing I know not a man?" But Gabriel explained that this would be no ordinary child: "The Holy Ghost shall come upon thee, and the power of the Highest shall overshadow thee: therefore also that holy thing which shall be born of thee shall be called the Son of God."[35]

The angel went on to announce that Mary's cousin Elizabeth "hath also conceived a son in her old age: and this is the sixth month with her, who was called barren. For with God nothing shall be impossible." Mary duly consented to Gabriel's request: "Behold the handmaid of the Lord; be it unto me according to thy word. And the angel departed from her."[36]

Mary: Adept, Queen, Mother, Priestess

The Annunciation story in the *Infancy Gospel of James* resembles *Luke*'s, but there are interesting differences in detail. The context for the whole story was a project to weave a new veil for the temple. The work was divided among several young women known to the priests, and Mary was assigned to weave the "true purple and the scarlet."[37] She returned home with the materials and set to work.

Shortly thereafter, Mary went out of the house to fetch a pitcher of water, when she heard a voice: "Hail, thou who hast received grace; the Lord is with thee; blessed art thou among women!"[38] The disembodied voice was not necessarily Gabriel's. Some modern writers have suggested that it may have been the "Voice of God," the *Bath Kol* of Judaic tradition.

Mary returned home trembling. Only then did the angel appear to her and proclaim: "Fear not, Mary; for thou hast found grace before the Lord of all, and thou shalt conceive, according to His word." Mary "reasoned with herself, saying: Shall I conceive by the Lord, the living God? And shall I bring forth as every woman brings forth?" Whereupon, the angel replied: "Not so, Mary; for the power of the Lord shall overshadow thee."[39] Mary agreed, as recorded in *Luke*.

The Annunciation story in the *Infancy Gospel of James* ends when Mary completes her portion of the temple veil: "[S]he made the purple and the scarlet, and took them to the priest. And the priest blessed her, and said: Mary, the Lord God hath magnified thy name, and thou shall be blessed in all the generations of the earth."[40] In this account, the priests were in touch with Mary, and she made at least two trips to the temple, suggesting that she lived close to Jerusalem; the journey from Nazareth would have taken several days.

The *Qur'an* records the Annunciation. The "angels"—plural in this instance—addressed Mary: "'O Mary, Allah has chosen you, made you pure and chosen you above all the women of the world.'"[41] They prophesied that Mary would bear a son, the Messiah, who would be "greatly honored in this world and the next, and among those drawn nearest to God."[42]

In another *surah*, or chapter, of the *Qur'an*, God himself spoke first, addressing the reader: "We sent her Our Spirit, which appeared before her as an immaculate human."[43] Uncertain who this being might be, Mary invoked divine protection: "I take refuge in the All Merciful from you, if you fear Allah." The familiar dialog with Gabriel then ensued:

> He [Gabriel] said: "I am but a messenger from your Lord, to bestow upon you a son most pure." She said: "How can I have a son when no man has ever touched me, nor am I an adulteress?" He said: "Thus did your Lord speak: 'It is a matter easy for Me. We shall make him a wonder to mankind and a mercy from Us—a decree ordained.'" So she conceived him and withdrew with him to a distant place.[44]

The Visitation

Luke's account of the Annunciation included the angel's news that Mary's older cousin Elizabeth was pregnant. Whereupon "Mary arose in those days, and went into the hill country with haste, into a city of Juda."[45] From Byzantine times, the "city of Juda" has been identified as the village of Ein Kerem, five miles southwest of Jerusalem. A major pilgrimage destination, it is the site of two major Christian churches: the Church of St John the Baptist and the Church of the Visitation.

We are not told who went with Mary. Presumably others accompanied her because it would have been dangerous for woman—a pregnant teenager—to travel alone, especially if as *Luke* asserts she was traveling from Nazareth. In any event, Mary "entered into the house of Zachariah, and saluted Elizabeth."[46] Both Elizabeth and her fetus immediately recognized that something incredible had happened; Mary was to bear the Messiah:

> And it came to pass, that, when Elizabeth heard the salutation of Mary, the babe leaped in her womb; and Elizabeth was filled with the Holy Ghost: And she spake out with a loud voice, and said, Blessed art thou among women, and blessed is the fruit of thy womb. And whence is this to me, that the mother of my Lord should come to me? For, lo, as soon as the voice of thy salutation sounded in mine ears, the babe leaped in my womb for joy. And blessed is she that believed: for there shall be a performance of those things which were told her from the Lord.[47]

Mary responded with the ecstatic prayer now known as the canticle of the *Magnificat*:

> My soul doth magnify the Lord, and my spirit hath rejoiced in God my Savior. For he hath regarded the low estate of his handmaiden: for, behold, from henceforth all generations shall call me blessed. For he that is mighty hath done to me great things; and holy is his name. And his mercy is on them that fear him from generation to generation.[48]

She continued with a strong social message:

> He hath shewed strength with his arm; he hath scattered the proud in the imagination of their hearts. He hath put down the mighty from their seats, and exalted them of low degree. He hath filled the hungry with good things; and the rich he hath sent empty away. He hath helped his servant Israel, in remembrance of his mercy; as he spake to our fathers, to Abraham, and to his seed for ever.[49]

The *Magnificat* is by far Mary's longest utterance recorded in the New Testament. The first line may have been inspired by (or, given the order in which the gospels were written, may have inspired) Hannah's alleged exclamation upon Mary's birth. Mary's canticle also has parallels with a passage in *1 Samuel*—interestingly exclaimed by another Hannah: "My heart rejoiceth in the Lord, mine horn is exalted in the Lord: my mouth is enlarged over mine enemies; because I rejoice in thy salvation."[50]

Clearly the *Magnificat* was addressed to an audience larger than just Elizabeth, and, by divine decree or otherwise, it came to be recorded in scripture. It was a remarkable utterance for a young teenage woman. The latter part was a courageous protest against the social, economic and political inequalities of her time, suggesting that Mary's active ministry began even before the birth of Jesus.

The Visitation story in *Luke* ends with the news that "Mary abode with her [Elizabeth] about three months, and returned to her own house."[51] In the *Infancy Gospel of James* it ends thus: "And she abode three months with Elizabeth, and day by day her womb grew: and Mary was afraid and departed unto her house and hid herself from the children of Israel. Now she was sixteen years old when these mysteries came to pass."[52] Later writings stated that she was fifteen or even younger.

Chapter 1. Mary in Scripture

Discovery of Mary's Pregnancy

The circumstances and timing of Joseph's discovery of his betrothed wife's pregnancy call for comment. *Matthew* simply states that, before Joseph and Mary "came together, she was found with child of the Holy Ghost."[53] Her pregnancy obviously would shame a respectable older man associated with the temple, but an unnamed angel appeared to Joseph and persuaded him not to put Mary away. The angel reiterated that the child was of the Holy Ghost, adding: "she shall bring forth a son, and thou shalt call his name Jesus: for he shall save his people from their sins."[54]

The author of *Matthew*, always eager to establish continuity between Hebrew tradition and the new Jesus movement, quoted from *Isaiah*: "Now all this was done, that it might be fulfilled which was spoken of the Lord by the prophet, saying, Behold, a virgin shall be with child, and shall bring forth a son, and they shall call his name Emmanuel, which being interpreted is, God with us."[55] Issues surrounding this passage will be discussed later.

Although *Matthew* does not actually state that Mary told Joseph of her pregnancy, we get the impression that he became aware of her condition and received the angel's reassurance soon after the Annunciation. But the *Infancy Gospel of James* suggests otherwise. Its story is vivid and dramatic.

Joseph, we are told, returned home from what must have been an extended period in which he plied his building trade. He found Mary "in her sixth month ... big with child."[56] Presumably this was after the Visitation, which had taken place during his absence. Joseph erupted in rage, blaming some unknown assailant and Mary herself:

> And he smote his face, and threw himself on the ground upon the sackcloth, and wept bitterly, saying: With what face shall I look upon the Lord my God?.... Who has done this evil thing in my house, and defiled the virgin?.... [W]hy hast thou done this and forgotten the Lord thy God? Why hast thou brought low thy soul, thou that wast brought up in the holy of holies, and that didst receive food from the hand of an angel?[57]

Mary defended herself as best she could, and Joseph withdrew to consider his next step. It was then that an angel of the Lord appears to him in a dream, saying: Be not afraid for this maiden, for that which is in her is of the Holy Spirit; and she will bring forth a Son, and thou shall call His name Jesus, for He will save His people from their sins. And Joseph arose from sleep, and glorified the God of Israel, who had given him this grace; and he kept her.[58]

The *Infancy Gospel of James* relates that Joseph still had to face the high priest. The latter had Mary arrested and brought before a tribunal. After interrogation and Mary's continued protest of innocence, both Mary and Joseph were sentenced to trial by ordeal.[59] They successfully passed the test, and the high priest finally gave them his blessing.[60]

Nowhere in scripture do we learn of Mary's and Joseph's wedding. For that we must wait to hear from other sources.

The Birth of Jesus

The account of the Nativity in *Matthew* is terse: "Jesus was born in Bethlehem of Judaea in the days of Herod the king."[61] It then turns immediately to the story of the Magi, which will be discussed in its turn.

The account in *Luke* is more elaborate and differs in essential details. It explains that Joseph and Mary traveled from Nazareth to Bethlehem, a journey of at least four days, in response to a tax census:

> And it came to pass in those days, that there went out a decree from Caesar Augustus that all the world should be taxed.... And Joseph also went up from Galilee, out of the city of Nazareth, into Judea, unto the city of David, which is called Bethlehem; (because he was of the house and lineage of David): to be taxed with Mary his espoused wife, being great with child.[62]

While there, Mary went into labor: "[S]he brought forth her firstborn son, and wrapped him in swaddling clothes, and laid him in a manger; because there was no room for them in the inn."[63]

The *Infancy Gospel of James* concurs with *Luke* that Joseph and Mary traveled to Bethlehem for the census but adds that Joseph also brought with him two of his grown sons.[64] Mary rode on a donkey, and she went into labor before they reached their destination. "Mary said to him: Take me down from off the ass, for that which is in me presses to come forth. And he [Joseph] took her down from ... the ass,

Chapter 1. Mary in Scripture

and said to her: Whither shall I lead thee ... for the place is desert."[65] In the fifth century a Byzantine church, the *Kathisma Theotokos* ("Seat of the Theotokos"), was built at the location where Mary is believed to have dismounted and rested.[66]

Joseph found a cave in the desert, and leaving Mary in his sons' care, went looking for a midwife. Joseph came across a woman in the hill country and told her: "I am seeking an Hebrew midwife. And she answered and said unto me: Art thou of Israel? And I said to her: Yes. And she said: And who is it that is bringing forth in the cave? And I said: A woman betrothed to me. And she said to me: Is she not thy wife?"[67]

Joseph tried to explain as they proceeded to the cave where Mary lay. Upon their arrival all suspicions in the woman's mind were dispelled:

> And they stood in the place of the cave, and behold a luminous cloud overshadowed the cave. And the midwife said: My soul has been magnified this day, because mine eyes have seen strange things—because salvation has been brought forth to Israel. And immediately the cloud disappeared out of the cave, and a great light shone in the cave, so that the eyes could not bear it. And in a little that light gradually decreased, until the infant appeared, and went and took the breast from His mother Mary.[68]

Did Mary experience labor pains? After Adam and Eve ate the forbidden fruit God cursed Eve and her descendents: "I will greatly multiply thy sorrow and thy conception. In sorrow thou shalt bring forth children."[69] But Jewish tradition taught that certain women had been spared the pain of childbirth, notably Jochebed, the mother of Moses.[70] Early Christians believed that Mary was similarly favored. Later, the doctrine of the Immaculate Conception was invoked to protect her, because labor pain was linked to inherited original sin.

Islamic tradition did not spare Mary. In the *Qur'an* we read: "[T]he pains of childbirth drove her to the trunk of a palm tree." But Jesus, still in the womb, "called her from below her, 'Do not grieve; your Lord has provided beneath you a stream. And shake toward you the trunk of the palm tree; it will drop upon you ripe, fresh dates'"[71]

That was not the only time the fetus or infant Jesus is alleged to have addressed his mother. Another incident reported in the *Qur'an* will be cited shortly. A third incident is recorded in the extracanonical *Arabic* (or *Syriac*) *Gospel of the Infancy of the Savior*. According to that text

Mary: Adept, Queen, Mother, Priestess

Jesus spoke from the cradle, saying: "I am Jesus, the Son of God, the Logos, whom thou hast brought forth, as the Angel Gabriel announced to thee; and my Father has sent me for the salvation of the world."[72] Whether or not we believe that the baby Jesus could talk, the theological language attributed to him was not formulated for another one-hundred years.

Figure 1.1. *The Adoration of the Shepherds* (detail) by Guido Reni (c.1640). As was common in Renaissance and Baroque art, Reni showed the child Jesus bathed in light. Mary is depicted in the customary devotional pose of the period.

Luke relates that shepherds were keeping watch over their flocks nearby. And, in a passage immortalized in George Frideric Handel's *Messiah*, angelic beings alerted them—and the world—to Jesus' birth:

And, lo, the angel of the Lord came upon them, and the glory of the Lord shone round about them: and they were sore afraid. And the angel said unto them, Fear not: for, behold, I bring you good tidings of great joy, which shall be to all people. For unto you is born this day in the city of David a Savior, which is Christ the Lord.... And suddenly there was with the angel a multitude of the heavenly host praising God, and saying, Glory to God in the highest, and on earth peace, good will toward men.[73]

The shepherds "came with haste, and found Mary, and Joseph, and the babe lying in a manger."[74] The shepherds' adoration of Jesus has inspired thousands of works of art, One from the seventeenth century, shown in Figure 1.1, is particularly successful in capturing the sense of awe and excitement.[75]

The shepherds spread word of Jesus' birth to surrounding communities: "[W]hen they had seen it, they made known abroad the saying which was told them concerning this child. And all they that heard it wondered at those things which were told them by the shepherds."[76]

After eight days Joseph and Mary took the infant Jesus to Jerusalem to be circumcised according to Jewish law. They offered sacrifice in the temple, and while there they met Simeon and Anna.

Simeon was "a devout man," who had yearned to see the messiah before he died. Upon seeing the holy family he uttered what is now known as the canticle *Nunc Dimittis*: "Lord, now lettest thou thy servant depart in peace, according to thy word: for mine eyes have seen thy salvation, which thou hast prepared before the face of all people; a light to lighten the Gentiles, and the glory of thy people Israel."[77]

Simeon blessed the parents and said to Mary: "Behold, this child is set for the fall and rising again of many in Israel; and for a sign which shall be spoken against; yea, a sword shall pierce through thy own soul also, that the thoughts of many hearts may be revealed."[78]

Also at the scene was Anna, "a prophetess ... of great age [who] departed not from the temple, but served God with fastings and prayers night and day." She gave thanks for Jesus' birth "and spake of him to all them that looked for redemption in Jerusalem."[79] Unfortunately her words were not recorded.

Luke relates that Joseph and Mary then "returned into Galilee, to their own city Nazareth."

Matthew does not mention the shepherds or the presentation of Jesus in the temple. Instead it reports: "there came wise men from the east to Jerusalem, saying, Where is he that is born King of the Jews? for we have seen his star in the east, and are come to worship him."[80] The Magi stopped in Jerusalem to inquire of the child's whereabouts. This caused great consternation, and Herod, fearing that a new King of the Jews would threaten his own position, entreated the men to report back to him when they found Jesus "that I may come and worship him also."[81] Clearly, the duplicitous Herod had no such plan in mind.

The Magi reached "the house ... where the young child was," fell down in adoration, and presented their gifts of gold, frankincense and myrrh. Their mode of transportation is not mentioned in *Matthew*. We are not even told how many Magi there were! The tradition of "Three Wise Men," in later Christian writings, was inferred solely from the number of gifts. Furthermore, the identification of the Magi as "kings" was probably inspired by a passage in *Psalms*: "Yea, all kings shall fall down before him."[82] Based on the fact that they observed the heavens, we can conclude that they were astronomers or astrologers. *Magi* (singular *magus*) means "magicians."

According to *Matthew*, the Magi were warned in a dream not to return to Jerusalem; instead they "departed into their own country another way."[83] The Magi took a different route home to avoid Herod. But perhaps this passage also means that their experience of visiting the Christ Child and Mary was powerfully transformative.

When Herod learned that the Magi had not complied with his request, he was enraged and ordered the Massacre of the Innocents. But the Holy Family escaped to Egypt and remained there until after Herod's death.[84] Only then did they return to Palestine, avoiding Bethlehem and proceeding to "a city called Nazareth: that it might be fulfilled which was spoken by the prophets, He shall be called a Nazarene."[85] This last statement might suggest—contrary to *Luke*—that Mary and Joseph were going there for the first time.

The extracanonical *Infancy Gospel of Matthew*, sometimes called the *Gospel of Pseudo-Matthew*, offers a more detailed account of the flight to Egypt. It asserts that, on the way to Egypt, the Holy Family rested near a cave, only to be dismayed by what rushed out:

> Mary dismounted from her beast, and sat down with the child Jesus in her bosom.... And lo, suddenly there came forth from the

cave many dragons.... Then Jesus went down from the bosom of His mother, and stood on His feet before the dragons; and they adored Jesus, and thereafter retired. Then was fulfilled that which was said by David the prophet, saying: Praise the Lord from the earth, ye dragons; ye dragons, and all ye deeps.[86]

That was not all; "Lions and panthers adored Him likewise, and accompanied them in the desert."[87] On another occasion, when Mary was thirsty, a palm tree bent down so she could pick the fruit.[88] This story may have inspired the one in the *Qur'an*, in which a palm tree offered its dates during Jesus' birth.

Upon their arrival in a city in Egypt, Mary took Jesus into the pagan temple, probably not anticipating what would happen next:

And it came to pass, when the most blessed Mary went into the temple with the little child, that all the idols prostrated themselves on the ground, so that all of them were lying on their faces shattered and broken to pieces; and thus they plainly showed that they were nothing. Then was fulfilled that which was said by the prophet Isaiah: Behold, the Lord will come upon a swift cloud, and will enter Egypt, and all the handiwork of the Egyptians shall be moved at His presence.[89]

Betraying a late date of composition, or a late interpolation, the *Infancy Gospel of Matthew* notes: "Then all the people of that same city believed in the Lord God through Jesus Christ."[90]

It is interesting that, across the various Nativity stories, the location of Jesus' birth varies from a manger (a feeding trough, which we assume to be in a stable), to a house, a cave, and finally the shade of a palm tree. Only the *Infancy Gospel of James* includes a donkey, a staple of every modern crèche; nowhere in scripture do we find any mention of camels. Tradition has filled in many of the details we now associate with the Nativity scene. Conspicuously absent from every modern crèche are Joseph's two sons from his previous marriage!

Mary's Virginity

Paul's epistles, the earliest of the New Testament texts, do not mention Mary.[91] And *Mark*, the earliest gospel, does not record the Nativity. The first reference to the Mary's virginity appears in *Matthew*, which biblical scholars believe was probably written between 73 and 80 CE—three or more generations after Mary gave birth to Jesus.

Mary: Adept, Queen, Mother, Priestess

Matthew claims that Jesus' birth fulfilled a prophecy in *Isaiah*: "Behold, a virgin [Hebrew: *almah*] shall conceive, and bear a son, and shall call his name Immanuel."[92] Yet it is by no means clear that the Old Testament passage had any relevance to a coming messiah. Furthermore, *almah* generally meant "a young woman;" the more specific word for a virgin was *bethulah*. In the Greek Septuagint, from which the gospel writers drew most of their quotes,[93] *almah* became *parthenos*, which could mean "an independent woman" of any age, celibate or otherwise. In Latin it became *virgo*. When Romans of the classical period wanted to speak of a woman without sexual experience they used *virgo intacta*.

The author of *Matthew* clearly attached great importance to Mary's virginity. Possibly an effort was being made to associate Mary with the Jewish people, collectively personified as the "virgin [*bethulah*] of Israel"[94] But the main emphasis was on Mary's physical virginity. *Matthew* asserts that Joseph "knew her not till she had brought forth her firstborn son."[95] The *Infancy Gospel of James* goes so far as to record that a midwife conducted a post-partum examination:

> Then said Salome: As the Lord my God liveth, unless I thrust in my finger, and search the parts, I will not believe that a virgin has brought forth. And the midwife went in, and said to Mary: Show thyself; for no small controversy has arisen about thee. And Salome put in her finger, and cried out, and said: Woe is me for mine iniquity and mine unbelief, because I have tempted the living God; and, behold, my hand is dropping off as if burned with fire.[96]

This and earlier passages in the *Infancy Gospel of James* may have inspired a comment in the Nag Hammadi text *The Testimony of Truth*: "John was begotten by means of a womb worn with age, but Christ passed through a virgin's womb. When she had conceived, she gave birth to the Savior. Furthermore, she was found to be a virgin again."[97] Another scriptural passage sometimes cited in support of Mary's virginity is from *Ezekiel*: "This gate shall be shut, it shall not be opened, and no man shall enter in by it; because the Lord, the God of Israel, hath entered in by it."[98]

The *Qur'an* also refers to Mary's virginity. Responding to the angel's announcement of her conception, she declared: "no man has ever touched me, nor am I an adulteress."[99] The divine narrator added: "Mary, daughter of Imran [Joachim], she who guarded her chastity, and We breathed into her of Our spirit, and the reposed her trust in the words of her Lord… and was devout in worship."[100]

Mary's virginity continued to be questioned after the Nativity, focusing both on her fidelity to Joseph and on Jesus' legitimacy. According to the *Qur'an*, people exclaimed: "O Mary, you have certainly done a thing unprecedented. O sister of Aaron, your father was not a man of evil, nor was your mother unchaste." But Jesus addressed them from the manger: "Indeed, I am the servant of God. He has given me the Scripture and made me a prophet. And He has made me blessed.... Peace be upon me the day I was born, the day I die, and the day I am resurrected."[101]

In the canonical gospels the issue of Jesus' legitimacy was raised during his ministry. When the people in the temple asked: "Is not this the carpenter, the son of Mary,"[102] they were intentionally using her name because his father's identity was in question. In another incident the Jews reportedly taunted Jesus when he was teaching in the temple: "We be not born of fornication,"[103] implying "but you were."

Matthew, *Luke*, and the *Infancy Gospel of James* all declare that Mary conceived by the Holy Spirit (or Holy Ghost). When the scriptures were written, the Holy Spirit was still understood, as it had been in Judaism, as an impersonal force or activity, the "breath of God;" moreover, it was grammatically feminine. Personalization and incorporation into the Trinity was not completed until the end of the fourth century, and grammatical masculinity was not achieved until "Holy Spirit" was translated into Latin.

The comment in *Matthew* that Joseph "knew her not till she had brought forth her firstborn son" could be interpreted to mean that he and Mary enjoyed a normal conjugal life after the birth of Jesus. Judaic tradition favored large families and attached little merit to celibacy.[104]

Matthew and *Mark* both suggest that Jesus had siblings. The people in the synagogue asked: "Is not this the carpenter, the son of Mary, the brother of James, and Joses, and of Juda, and Simon? and are not his sisters here with us?"[105] The simplest interpretation of that passage is that Jesus had at least six brothers and sisters, and Mary was their mother; they were identified as a family.

Setting aside that interpretation, Christian apologists from the fourth century onward insisted that Mary remained a virgin for the rest of her life. They argued that the alleged siblings were either Joseph's children from a previous marriage or cousins.[106] The suggestion that they were Joseph's children is plausible but faces challenges. The *Infancy Gospel of James* depicts two of them as adults at the time of Jesus' birth, and all would have been considerably older than Jesus. Yet the canonical gospels do not comment on an age difference.

The suggestion that the alleged siblings were actually cousins can also be justified; "brother" (Greek: *adelphos*) could mean a member of an extended family, even of a community.[107] On the other hand, James is described as the "brother of Jesus" elsewhere in the New Testament,[108] as well as in early Christian writings. Neither suggestion explains the close familial connection that seemed to exist between the siblings and Mary; the gospel writers made no effort to identify the siblings' mother as anyone other than Mary. Significantly, they did not even mention Joseph.

The strongest argument for Mary's perpetual virginity might be Joseph's age. If the *Infancy Gospel of James* is correct that Joseph was "an old man" at the time of his betrothal to Mary, his ability to father six more children could be questioned. Or perhaps Mary simply chose, in the face of Judaic tradition, to remain celibate.

Scripture does not provide clarity concerning the conjugal relationship between Joseph and Mary and the alleged siblings of Jesus. Mary's perpetual virginity is essentially a matter of faith. The broader implications of Mary's virginity will be discussed later in the book.

Mary During Jesus' Lifetime

Mary and Joseph Find Jesus in the Temple

When Jesus was twelve years old he accompanied Mary and Joseph on their annual trip to Jerusalem for the feast of the Passover. It was there that Jesus got lost. *Luke* explains:

> And when they had fulfilled the days, as they returned, the child Jesus tarried behind in Jerusalem; and Joseph and his mother knew not of it. But they, supposing him to have been in the company, went a day's journey; and they sought him among their kinsfolk and acquaintance. And when they found him not, they turned back again to Jerusalem, seeking him. And it came to pass, that after

three days they found him in the temple, sitting in the midst of the doctors, both hearing them, and asking them questions.[109]

When Mary and Joseph saw their precocious son "they were amazed." Mary spoke first: "Son, why hast thou thus dealt with us? Behold, thy father and I have sought thee sorrowing. And he said unto them, How is it that ye sought me? Wist ye not that I must be about my Father's business?"[110] Not surprisingly, "they understood not the saying which he spake unto them."

The *Infancy Gospel of Thomas*, an extracanonical text possibly contemporary with the *Infancy Gospel of James*, provides a version of the encounter in the temple in which "the scribes and the Pharisees said: Art thou the mother of this child? And she said: I am."[111] The scribes and Pharisees then congratulated Mary on her son's performance, borrowing a phrase from Elizabeth's greeting at the Visitation: "And they said to her: Blessed art thou among women, for God hath blessed the fruit of thy womb; for such glory, and such virtue and wisdom, we have neither seen nor heard ever."[112] Interestingly, the priests addressed their remarks to Mary rather than to Joseph. Perhaps Joseph was not with her, though it is hard to imagine that an adult woman would enter the temple unaccompanied by her husband.

After the exchange with his parents in the temple, *Luke* records that Jesus "went down with them, and came to Nazareth, and was subject unto them: but his mother kept all these sayings in her heart."[113]

Other Incidents

Some of the extracanonical texts describe mischievous activities in which the child Jesus experimented with his supernatural powers. For example, the *Arabic Gospel of the Infancy of the Savior* reports that Jesus turned a group of children into goats that "began to dance round Him."[114] Fortunately, he changed them back. The *Infancy Gospel of Thomas* describes a number of miracles, including bringing clay sparrows to life. And in once instance he raised a friend from the dead.[115]

The first miracle recorded in the canonical New Testament took place at the Marriage Feast of Cana, after Jesus had begun his public ministry. The story appears in *John*. The miracle was performed at Mary's prompting, though she is not mentioned by name:

> [T]here was a marriage in Cana of Galilee; and the mother of Jesus was there: and both Jesus was called, and his disciples, to the mar-

riage. And when they wanted wine, the mother of Jesus saith unto him, They have no wine. Jesus saith unto her, Woman, what have I to do with thee? Mine hour is not yet come. His mother saith unto the servants, Whatsoever he saith unto you, do it.[116]

Jesus duly turned water into wine. Two statements in this passage from *John* are puzzling. Jesus' assertion that his hour had not yet come was immediately contradicted by his performance of the miracle. And the remark "Woman, what have I to do with thee?" sounds disrespectful. Recent commentators have tried to explain away Jesus' remark, and some modern translations soften it to "in what way does that concern us?"

On another occasion, recorded in all three synoptic gospels, Jesus seemed to snub his mother and "brethren":

There came then his brethren and his mother, and, standing without, sent unto him, calling him. And the multitude sat about him, and they said unto him, Behold, thy mother and thy brethren without seek for thee. And he answered them, saying, Who is my mother, or my brethren? And he looked round about on them which sat about him, and said, Behold my mother and my brethren! For whosoever shall do the will of God, the same is my brother, and my sister, and mother.[117]

If it seems that Mary had a challenging relationship with her son, she enjoyed the greatest respect from his disciples. A significant example is described later in this chapter.

Mary at Calvary and Beyond

John places Mary and other women at the Crucifixion. Speaking from the cross, Jesus commended his mother into the hands of the beloved disciple:

Now there stood by the cross of Jesus his mother, and his mother's sister, Mary the wife of Cleophas, and Mary Magdalene. When Jesus therefore saw his mother, and the disciple standing by, whom he loved, he saith unto his mother, Woman, behold thy son! Then saith he to the disciple, Behold thy mother! And from that hour that disciple took her unto his own home.[118]

The synoptic gospels are more ambiguous concerning who was present at the Crucifixion. In *Mark* we read: "There were also women

Chapter 1. Mary in Scripture

looking on afar off: among whom was Mary Magdalene, and Mary the mother of James the less and of Joses, and Salome."[119] In *Matthew*: "[M]any women were there beholding afar off ... among which was Mary Magdalene, and Mary the mother of James and Joses, and the mother of Zebedees [sic] children."[120] Biblical exegetes have often identified the "mother of James and Joses" with *John*'s "wife of Cleophas."[121]

It is worth noting that *John* describes the intimacy of a conversation between Jesus, Mary and John. By contrast, the synoptic gospels—including *Luke*, which does not name them[122]—place the women "afar off," clearly out of earshot of the crucified Jesus.

More importantly, a first reading of the passages in *Mark* and *Matthew* would lead to the conclusion that Mary the mother of Jesus was not present at the Crucifixion. But a closer examination might suggest otherwise. Comparison with *Mark* 6:3 and *Matthew* 13:55-56, respectively, could imply that "Mary the mother of James and Joses" was also the mother of Jesus. Why would the authors of the two gospels fail to mention so important a fact? Perhaps the authors, or later copiers or translators, wanted to downplay any suggestion that Jesus had siblings, in order to defend the assertion of Mary's perpetual virginity. Yet *John*'s statement that Jesus entrusted the care of his mother to a disciple would seem to confirm that Mary had no other children; care would normally be the responsibility of her own family.

Mary is not counted among the women who went to the tomb on the first Easter Sunday. Mary Magdalene, not Mary the mother of Jesus, is named as first witness to the Resurrection. Indeed, the canonical scriptures do not record that the risen Christ ever appeared to his mother.

Mary at Pentecost

The *Acts of the Apostles* records that Mary was present, along with other women and Jesus' disciples in the upper room at Pentecost:

> Then returned they [the disciples] unto Jerusalem from the mount called Olivet, which is from Jerusalem a sabbath day's journey. And when they were come in, they went up into an upper room.... These all continued with one accord in prayer and supplication, with the women, and Mary the mother of Jesus, and with his brethren.[123]

37

Christ had promised great blessings to those present:

> [B]ehold, I send the promise of my Father upon you: but tarry ye in the city of Jerusalem, until ye be endued with power from on high.[124]
>
> [T]he Comforter, which is the Holy Ghost, whom the Father will send in my name, he shall teach you all things, and bring all things to your remembrance, whatsoever I have said unto you.[125]
>
> [W]hen he, the Spirit of truth, is come, he will guide you into all truth ... he will shew you things to come.[126]

While the group was in the upper room: "[S]uddenly there came a sound from heaven as of a rushing mighty wind, and it filled all the house where they were sitting. And there appeared unto them cloven tongues like as of fire, and it sat upon each of them. And they were all filled with the Holy Ghost."[127] Filled with the Holy Ghost and with new-found courage the disciples preached to the crowds outside. They "began to speak with other tongues, as the Spirit gave them utterance."[128]

We often forget that Mary was there when the Holy Spirit descended and was a recipient of all the powers that flowed from its blessing. She may not have preached in public. But Paul listed other gifts of the Spirit:

> For to one is given by the Spirit the word of wisdom; to another the word of knowledge by the same Spirit; to another faith by the same Spirit; to another the gifts of healing by the same Spirit; to another the working of miracles; to another prophecy; to another discerning of spirits; to another divers kinds of tongues; to another the interpretation of tongues.[129]

Mary put several of the gifts to good use. Many of Jesus' disciples went to distant places to proclaim Christ's message. But a vibrant community remained in Jerusalem. And later writings indicate that Mary pursued an active ministry in and around the city, serving as a counselor and "mother figure" to the disciples and nurturing what eventually would become known as Christianity.

James the Just (or the Righteous) served as the community's leader, at least after Peter's departure. An important reference is found in the extracanonical *Gospel of Thomas*: "The disciples said to Jesus, 'We know that you will depart from us. Who is to be our leader?' Jesus said to them, 'Wherever you are, you are to go to James the righteous, for whose sake heaven and earth came into being.'"[130]

Most scholars identify James the Just as the "brother" of Jesus, or "brother of the Lord," mentioned in *Mark* 6:3, *Matthew* 13:55-56, and *Galatians* 1:19. Additionally, or alternatively, he may have been James the Less: one of Jesus' twelve disciples, son of Alphaeus, and possibly the brother of Matthew.[131] Least likely, but not entirely out of the question, he may have been James the Greater: another disciple, son of Zebedee and brother of John the Apostle.

The canonical *Acts of the Apostles* describes the Council of Jerusalem (c.50 CE), at which James spoke on behalf of the local church to affirm the legitimacy of Paul's and Barnabas' mission to the Gentiles.[132] On Paul's subsequent visit to Jerusalem, "the brethren received us gladly. And the day following Paul went in with us unto James; and all the elders were present."[133]

Mary's ministry will be discussed in Chapters 2 and 3. But one incident is worthy of note here. According to the extracanonical *Gospel of Bartholomew* it took place sometime "after the Resurrection." The disciples wanted to know how Mary managed to give birth to so great a personage as Jesus:

> Bartholomew came near unto her with a cheerful countenance and said to her: Thou that art highly favored, the tabernacle of the Most High, unblemished we, even all the apostles, ask thee to tell us how thou didst conceive the incomprehensible, or how thou didst bear him that cannot be. But Mary said unto them: Ask me not concerning this mystery. If I should begin to tell you, fire will issue forth out of my mouth and consume all the world.[134]

We shall see shortly that her warning was to be taken seriously.

The disciples then pressed Mary to lead them in prayer, commenting: "In thee did the Lord set his tabernacle, and it was his good pleasure that thou shouldest contain him." Clearly the disciples were showing reverence to Mary and acknowledging her leadership role. Mary stood up before them and spread out her hands toward the heaven" and began to speak thus:

> O God the exceeding great and all-wise and king of the ages, that art not to be described, the ineffable, that didst establish the greatness of the heavens and all things by a word, that out of darkness

Mary: Adept, Queen, Mother, Priestess

> didst constitute and fasten together the poles of heaven in harmony ... didst part the misty darkness from the light, didst establish in one place the foundations of the waters, thou that makest the beings of the air to tremble, and art the fear of them that are under the earth, that didst settle the earth and not suffer it to perish, and filledst it, which is the nourisher of all things, with showers of blessing: Son of the Father, thou whom the seven heavens hardly contained, but who wast well-pleased to be contained without pain in me, thou that art thyself the full word of the Father in whom all things came to be: give glory to thine exceeding great name, and bid me to speak before thy holy (?).[135]

Mary then told the disciples of an ecstatic experience she had had as a child, while living in the temple. It began with the appearance of an angelic figure:

> When I abode in the temple of God and received my food from an angel, on a certain day there appeared unto me one in the likeness of an angel, but his face was incomprehensible.... And straightway the veil of the temple was rent and there was a very great earthquake, and I fell upon the earth, for I was not able to endure the sight of him. But he put his hand beneath me and raised me up, and I looked up into heaven and there came a cloud of dew and sprinkled me from the head to the feet, and he wiped me with his robe. And said unto me: Hail, thou that art highly favored, the chosen vessel, grace inexhaustible.[136]

Mary's ecstatic experience continued with a prophecy of the Eucharist:

> And he [the angelic figure] smote his garment upon the right hand and there came a very great loaf, and he set it upon the altar of the temple and did eat of it first himself, and gave unto me also. And again he smote his garment upon the left hand and there came a very great cup full of wine: and he set it upon the altar of the temple and did drink of it first himself, and gave also unto me. And I beheld and saw the bread and the cup whole as they were.[137]

The angel also prophesied that Mary—at that time still a temple virgin—would bear the Savior:

> And he said unto me: Yet three years, and I will send my word unto thee and then shalt conceive a son, and through him shall the whole creation be saved. Peace be unto (?). And when he had so

Chapter 1. Mary in Scripture

said he vanished away from mine eyes, and the temple was restored as it had been before.[138]

The *Gospel of Bartholomew* adds that, as Mary related the latter prophecy to the disciples, "fire issued out of her mouth; and the world was at the point to come to an end." But Jesus appeared "and laid his hand upon her mouth and said unto Mary: Utter not this mystery, or this day my whole creation will come to an end."[139]

The Woman in *Revelation*

Revelation, the concluding book of the canonical New Testament, speaks of "a woman clothed with the sun, and the moon under her feet, and upon her head a crown of twelve stars."[140] The story continues:

> And she being with child cried, travailing in birth, and pained to be delivered. And there appeared another wonder in heaven; and behold a great red dragon, having seven heads and ten horns, and seven crowns upon his heads. And his tail drew the third part of the stars of heaven, and did cast them to the earth: and the dragon stood before the woman which was ready to be delivered, for to devour her child as soon as it was born. And she brought forth a man child, who was to rule all nations with a rod of iron: and her child was caught up unto God, and to his throne.[141]

After that frightful incident, "the woman fled into the wilderness, where she hath a place prepared of God, that they should feed her there a thousand two hundred and threescore days."[142] But she was still not safe. Michael and his angels drove the dragon out of heaven, whereupon once more he pursued the woman:

> [W]hen the dragon saw that he was cast unto the earth, he persecuted the woman which brought forth the man child. And to the woman were given two wings of a great eagle, that she might fly into the wilderness, into her place, where she is nourished for a time, and times, and half a time, from the face of the serpent. And the serpent cast out of his mouth water as a flood after the woman, that he might cause her to be carried away of the flood.[143]

The one quote states that the woman spent "a thousand two hundred and threescore days" in the wilderness. The other describes her stay as "a time, and times, and half a time."[144] Based on the Babylonian calendar of 360 days in the year, we find that $(1 + 2 + 0.5) \times 360$

again equals 1,260. It appears that the woman spent 1,260 days, forty-two months, or three-and-a half years in the wilderness.

Revelation never identifies the woman in the story. She was given the wings of an eagle, though they did not enable her to escape from the earth. On the other hand, being "clothed with the sun, and the moon under her feet, and upon her head a crown of twelve stars" would seem to give her celestial status.

Christianity identified the woman as Mary, pointing to the deliverance of her child in the face of great danger—the Massacre of the Innocents—and Satan's desire to prevent the Redemption. "Clothed with the sun" provided a scriptural basis for the glorification of Mary as Queen of Heaven. But it is not out of the question that the woman was meant to be a symbol of the Jewish people.[145] Or she might have been Sophia ("Wisdom") of Hellenic Judaism.

Controversy continues over whether Mary spent her last years in Bethlehem, Jerusalem or Ephesus. Her death is not recorded in scripture.

---

[1] For example, all four evangelists describe the Crucifixion, but only John claims to have been there. None of the evangelists was present at the Nativity, but the authors of *Matthew* and *Luke* confidently described it.

[2] The fact that each Christian denomination has its favored translation of the Bible is telling.

[3] *John* 15:5. Unless stated otherwise all biblical references in this book are from the King James Bible.

[4] *Luke* 8:5.

[5] Luther had reason to exclude the *Epistle of James* because it undermined his assertion that good works have no value in securing salvation: "Ye see then how that by works a man is justified, and not by faith only.... For as the body without the spirit is dead, so faith without works is dead also" (*James* 2:24, 26).

[6] The 52 texts of the Nag Hammadi Library are often referred to as the "Gnostic Gospels," largely as a result of Elaine Pagels' landmark book *The Gnostic Gospels* (1979). But many scholars feel that the term "Gnostic" is overly broad and difficult to distinguish from early "mainstream" Christianity. Even given breadth of meaning, some of the Nag Hammadi texts lie outside the boundaries of any reasonable definition of Gnosticism. For example, the *Gospel of Thomas* promotes concepts, like the reality and sanctity of incarnate life, antithetical to Gnostic teachings. One

of the 52 texts in the Nag Hammadi Library is an edited version of Plato's *Republic*.
7   Paul mentioned that Jesus was "born of a woman" (*Galatians* 4:4).
8   Mary is mentioned 34 times in the *Qur'an*. An entire *surah*, or chapter, is named for her, and significant references appear elsewhere.
9   Anglicanism also affirms a "three-legged stool" of scripture, tradition and reason.
10 *2 Timothy* 3:16.
11 *2 Peter* 1:20-21.
12 Traditionally attributed to the Apostle Peter, who was martyred 64-68 CE, *2 Peter* may actually have been written by an anonymous author sometime in the latter half of the first century. *Second Timothy* was traditionally attributed to Paul, martyred 64-68 CE; but it is now generally believed to have been written by an anonymous author, sometime between 90 and 140 CE. For comparison, the gospels later anointed as "canonical" were written between 70 and 95 CE, and they may not have received widespread circulation until the latter part of the second century.
13 Skeptics are quick to capitalize on incidents where gullible audiences are deceived by hoaxes or other questionable claims.
14 *Infancy Gospel of James* 1-3 (transl.: A. Roberts & J. Donaldson), *Early Christian Writings*. In citations from this translation "Anna" is replaced by the more common "Hannah."
15 Perhaps we can detect here an echo of God's promise to Sarah's husband Abraham: "I will make thy seed as the dust of the earth: so that if a man can number the dust of the earth, then shall thy seed also be numbered" (*Genesis* 13:16).
16 *Infancy Gospel of James* 4.
17 If Joachim was still away when Hannah conceived, the implication would be that Mary—like her son—was the outcome of a virgin birth.
18 *Infancy Gospel of James* 5.
19 "Miriam the prophetess, the sister of Aaron, took a timbrel in her hand; and all the women went out after her with timbrels and with dances." *Exodus* 15:20.
20 Abla Hasan, "The Quranic Story of Mary," *International Journal of Islamic Studies* (June 2016), 189-204. See also Michael Pregill, "Mary in the Qur'an." Online:
https://www.bibleodyssey.org:443/en/people/related-articles/mary-in-the-quran. Last accessed Nov. 16, 2019.
21 Jesus allegedly was born during the reign of King Herod, whom historians believe died in 4 BCE. The consensus of biblical scholars is that Jesus was born in about 6 or 5 BCE, when Mary was fifteen or sixteen years old.
22 *Infancy Gospel of James* 7.

Mary: Adept, Queen, Mother, Priestess

---

[23] *Ibid.* 8.
[24] *Qur'an* 3:37 (transl: T. Khalidi), Viking Press, 2008. "Allah" is restored to conform to other translations. It should be noted that Arabic-speaking Christians also refer to God as Allah.
[25] Any human blood was abhorrent to Jewish priests, and menstrual (or post-puerperal) blood was considered particularly abhorrent.
[26] *Infancy Gospel of James* 8.
[27] According to *Luke* Joseph and Mary set off from Nazareth to Bethlehem, where Jesus would be born. *Matthew* 2:22-23 suggests that the Holy Family might have settled in Nazareth only after their return from Egypt.
[28] *Infancy Gospel of James* 9.
[29] *Ibid.* According to later sources, Joseph was a widower whose late wife Escha had borne him four sons and two daughters. See https://www.biblicalcyclopedia.com/P/perpetual-virginity-of-mary.html. Last accessed May 17, 2020.
[30] *Infancy Gospel of James* 9.
[31] *Matthew* 1:18.
[32] *Luke* 1:26-29.
[33] James A. Tabor, *The Jesus Dynasty*, Simon & Schuster, 2006, 17-18. Tabor estimated Nazareth's population to be around 200. Today, Nazareth is a large city, and Sepphoris is little more than an archeological site.
[34] *Luke* 1:30-33.
[35] *Ibid.* 1:34-35.
[36] *Ibid.* 1:36-38.
[37] *Infancy Gospel of James* 10. We are not told whether this was the same veil that was rent when Jesus died on the cross. But the emphasis placed on it in the *Protoevangelium*—as part of a story so closely related to the Incarnation—might encourage that conclusion.
[38] *Ibid*, 11.
[39] *Ibid.*
[40] *Ibid.*, 12.
[41] *Qur'an* 3:42.
[42] *Ibid.* 3:45.
[43] *Ibid.* 22:17. Other translations have "well-formed human."
[44] *Ibid.* 22:18-22. In the *Qur'an* Gabriel is known as Jibril.
[45] *Luke* 1:39.
[46] *Ibid.* 1:40.
[47] *Ibid.* 1: 41-45.
[48] *Ibid.* 1: 46-50.
[49] *Ibid.* 1:51-55.
[50] *1 Samuel* 2:1. See also verses 2–10.
[51] *Luke* 1: 56.

Chapter 1. Mary in Scripture

---

52 *Infancy Gospel of James* 12.
53 *Matthew* 1:18.
54 *Matthew* 1:20-21.
55 *Ibid.* 1:22-23.
56 *Infancy Gospel of James* 13.
57 *Ibid.*
58 *Ibid.* 14.
59 The precise nature of the ordeal is disputed. The *Infancy Gospel of James* describes it thus: "[T]he priest took the water, and gave Joseph to drink and sent him away to the hill-country; and he returned unhurt. And he gave to Mary also to drink, and sent her away to the hill-country; and she returned unhurt" (§16). By contrast, the *Infancy Gospel of Matthew* declares: "And when any one that had lied drank this water, and walked seven times round the altar, God used to show some sign in his face." (§12).
60 *Infancy Gospel of James.* 15-16.
61 *Matthew* 2:1.
62 *Luke* 2:1-5. Parenthesis in translation.
63 *Ibid.* 2:7.
64 It is interesting that *Luke* invokes Joseph's ancestry to link him to Bethlehem, whereas the *Infancy Gospel of James* suggests that he had once lived in Judaea and may even have been born there. On the other hand, the *Infancy Gospel*'s description of the journey to Bethlehem implies that Joseph and Mary traveled some distance, so they may have been living in Nazareth when the census was called.
65 *Infancy Gospel of James* 17.
66 Stephen J. Shoemaker, *Ancient Traditions of the Virgin Mary's Dormition and Assumption*, Oxford Univ. Press, 2002, 79-82. The church fell into ruins, and now at least two archeological sites claim to be the Kathisma Theotokos. Mary's title of *Theotokos* ("God bearer," or "Mother of God") will be discussed in Chapter 4.
67 *Ibid.* 19.
68 *Ibid.*
69 *Genesis* 3:1.
70 This belief was noted by the Roman–Jewish historian Titus Flavius Josephus (37–c.100 CE).
71 *Qur'an* 19:23-26.
72 *Arabic Gospel of the Infancy of the Savior* §1. Wesley Center for Applied Theology. Online: https://web.archive.org/web/20040927133541/http://wesley.nnu.edu/biblical_studies/noncanon/gospels/infarab.htm. Last accessed June 9, 2021.
73 *Luke* 2:9-14.
74 *Ibid.* 2:16.

[75] *The Adoration of the Shepherds* by Guido Reni (c.1640) is exhibited at the Certosa di San Martino, a former monastery and now a museum, in Naples, Italy.
[76] *Luke* 2:17-18.
[77] *Ibid.* 2:29-32.
[78] *Ibid.* 2:34-35.
[79] *Ibid.* 2:36-38.
[80] *Matthew* 2:1-2.
[81] *Ibid.* 2:8.
[82] *Psalm* 72:11.
[83] *Matthew* 2:11-12.
[84] *Ibid.* 2:13-20.
[85] *Ibid.* 2:23.
[86] *Infancy Gospel of Matthew* 18 (transl.: A. Roberts, et al.), Gnostic Society Library.
[87] *Ibid.* 19.
[88] *Ibid.* 20.
[89] *Ibid.* 23.
[90] *Ibid.* 24. The *Infancy Gospel of Matthew* contains earlier material, but it may not have taken its final form until the seventh century.
[91] An oblique reference to Mary—c.44 CE—is found in *Galatians* 4:4: "God sent forth his Son, made of a woman, made under the law." Paul commented extensively on the significance of Jesus' death. But he seems to have been uninterested in Jesus' birth and may have been unaware of the developing narrative of the virgin birth.
[92] *Isaiah* 7:14. It is worth noting that *almah* is connected with the definite, not the indefinite, article in the Hebrew text, suggesting that Isaiah may have been referring to a specific young woman of his own time.
[93] The gospel writers drew most of their quotes from the Septuagint, the Greek version of the Hebrew Bible, which dates from the third or second century BCE.
[94] *Deuteronomy* 22:19; *Jeremiah* 31:4. In the Septuagint *bethulah* is translated as *parthenos*.
[95] *Matthew* 1:25.
[96] *Infancy Gospel of James* 19-20,
[97] *The Testimony of Truth* (transl.: S. Giversen & B. Pearson), The Nag Hammadi Library.
[98] *Ezekiel* 44:2.
[99] *Qur'an* 19:20.
[100] *Ibid.* 66: 12. Al 'Imran was the Arabic name of Mary's family.
[101] *Ibid.* 19:27-33
[102] *Mark* 6:3. Joseph is named in *Matthew* and *John*.: "Is not this the carpenter's son? is not his mother called Mary?" (*Matthew* 13:55); "And they

Chapter 1. Mary in Scripture

[103] *John* 8:41.
[104] Celibacy was not even one of the specific vows taken in the ascetic Nazarite sect, to which John the Baptist may have belonged.
[105] *Mark* 6:3; *Matthew* 13:55-56. See also *Mark* 15:40, but note that in this case the identity of "Mary" is in doubt.
[106] James Tabor offered a third possibility: Joseph died and Mary married his younger brother "Clophas," who fathered the six children. *The Jesus Dynasty*, 75-77, 291.
[107] We retain a similar usage in speaking of a fraternity brother.
[108] *Galatians* 1:19.
[109] *Luke* 2:43-46.
[110] *Ibid.* 2:48-49.
[111] *Infancy Gospel of Thomas* §XIX, (transl.: A. Roberts & J. Donaldson), Early Christian Writings.
[112] *Ibid.*
[113] *Luke.* 2:50-51.
[114] *Arabic Gospel of the Infancy of the Savior* §40.
[115] *Infancy Gospel of Thomas* §IX.
[116] *John* 2:1-5. *John* never mentions Mary by name.
[117] *Mark* 3:31-35. The same incident is recorded in *Matthew* 12:46-50 and *Luke* 8:19-21.
[118] *John* 19:25-27. Assuming that "his mother's sister" refers to "Mary the wife of Cleophas," one wonders why two sisters would have the same name. In Chapter 2 we learn that Mary Cleophas may have been our Mary's aunt.
[119] *Mark* 15:40.
[120] *Matthew* 27:55-56. Luke, normally the main source of information about Mary, merely wrote "women that followed him from Galilee, stood afar off, beholding these things" (*Luke* 23:49).
[121] As noted, James Tabor suggested that Cleophas was Mary's second husband.
[122] *Luke* 23:49.
[123] *Acts* 1:12-14.
[124] *Luke* 24:49.
[125] *John* 14:26.
[126] *John* 16:13.
[127] *Acts* 2:2-4.
[128] *Ibid.* 2:4.
[129] *1 Corinthians* 12:8-10.
[130] *Gospel of Thomas* (transl.: T. O. Lamdin), Saying 12. Nag Hammadi Library. The *Gospel of Thomas* may have been a product of the church of

(Note: footnote text at top continues from previous page: said, Is not this Jesus, the son of Joseph, whose father and mother we know?" (*John* 6:42).)

Jerusalem. It is dated to, or may contain material dated to, as early as 40 CE.

[131] *Mark* 2:14 and *Luke* 5:27 identify the tax collector Levi as the son of Alphaeus, and Levi customarily is equated with Matthew. But the gospels do not explicitly state that Matthew was Alphaeus' son.

[132] *Acts* 15:13-21.

[133] *Acts* 21:17-18.

[134] *Gospel of Bartholomew* II:4-5 (transl.: M. R. James), Gnostic Society Library. This gospel was included in James' *The Apocryphal New Testament*, Clarendon Press, 1924, 170ff.

[135] *Ibid.* 13. The last word in this portion of the manuscript is illegible.

[136] *Ibid.* 15-18.

[137] *Ibid.* 18-19.

[138] *Ibid.* 20-21.

[139] *Ibid.* 22.

[140] *Revelation* 12:1.

[141] *Ibid.* 12:2-5.

[142] *Ibid.* 12:5.

[143] *Ibid.* 12: 13-15.

[144] Similar references can be found elsewhere in *Revelation* and in *Daniel*.

[145] See for example the discussion in Geoffrey Ashe, *The Virgin: Mary's Cult and the Re-Emergence of the Goddess*, Arkana, 1976/1988, 121-122.

Chapter 2
Mary According to Anne Catherine Emmerich

This chapter examines the story of Mary's life told by Anne Catherine Emmerich, a Roman Catholic nun whose life spanned the late eighteenth and early nineteenth centuries. Emmerich's clairvoyant visions provide a parallel narrative, not independent of scripture, but filling in sometimes-minute details of life in first-century Palestine and offering new insights into Mary's own life and mission.

Introduction

Anne Catherine Emmerich (1774–1824) was born in a poor farming community in Westphalia, northwest Germany. From an early age she displayed exceptional piety; she had visions of the souls in purgatory, talked to Jesus, and saw the Trinity in symbolic form. At the age of twenty-nine she professed religious vows at the Augustinian convent of Agnetenberg in Dülmen. In 1812 the convent was suppressed, and she found lodgings in a widow's home. By then Emmerich was in ill health and severe pain, due at least in part to the ascetic practices she had practiced. The following year she received the stigmata: open wounds on her body corresponding to those suffered by Jesus on the cross. The wounds lasted for the rest of her life, causing her great pain, particularly on days like Good Friday.

Emmerich had clairvoyant visions that enabled her to travel to remote locations and times, and to report back in great detail what she saw. In particular she was able to view biblical scenes, as far back as *Genesis*. From 1819 until Emmerich's death in 1824, German poet and novelist Clemens Wenzeslaus Brentano served as her scribe, writing down, editing and compiling what Emmerich told him.

Anne Catherine Emmerich was not the only person to have that ability. Medieval mystics Bridget of Sweden (c. 1303–1373) and Margery

Kempe (c.1373–c.1438), and contemporary stigmatic Judith von Halle (1972–) also observed and reported on biblical scenes. But Emmerich's descriptions are the most complete and provide almost a parallel scriptural record. They are vivid and have a sense of immediacy not found elsewhere.

Emmerich's narrative is not independent of real scripture. The story she told clearly was colored by her knowledge of the Bible as well as by tradition, Christian doctrine, and her own religious piety. "Tradition" in many cases consisted of legends that are recorded in, or may have originated from, the extracanonical texts examined in Chapter 1 or from the later texts discussed in Chapter 3.

Where they overlap, Emmerich's account of the life of Mary is in general agreement with scripture. But it provides additional detail—often minute detail, like the arrangement of furniture in a room, the fabric and style of clothing, or the color of someone's eyes. The larger story may be more important; yet detail adds context, helping us relate to an environment very different from our own.

Emmerich's account also fills in gaps in the scriptural record. She named individuals and places that, with her limited education, she could not possibly have known. She pronounced names in Wesphalian dialect, and Brentano translated them into standard German. The spelling was his, but in a number of instances scholars verified that the basis of the names was historically or linguistically correct. What we have now is the English translation of Brentano's German: four volumes relating to Jesus Christ—including an almost day-by-day log of his travels through Galilee and Judaea—and one volume relating specifically to Mary.[1]

Not surprisingly Emmerich had her detractors. Both she and Brentano were accused of fraud. What Emmerich reported may have been nothing but fantasy, or perhaps her scribe wrote a work of fiction and attributed it to Emmerich to give it an aura of credibility. Doubts will never be settled one way or the other. When Emmerich was beatified in 2004, a step toward possible sainthood, her writings were not considered as supporting evidence. Nevertheless, Emmerich deserves a voice, and her story of Mary has a compelling force—as does her longer story of Jesus which can be read elsewhere.

This chapter cites and comments on a small sample of Anne Catherine Emmerich's clairvoyant visions of Mary and those closest to her. Together with the scriptural records summarized in Chapter 1 and the early Christian writings examined in Chapter 3, they help create a picture of Mary's Palestinian life. This picture, in turn, provides context for the discussion of Marian doctrine and devotion. It also provides a backdrop for insights—shared in recent times by high-ranking churchmen and by esotericists—into Mary's ongoing ministry to humanity and the planet.

Mary's Early Life

Mary's Family

Anne Catherine Emmerich traced Mary's ancestors back to her maternal great-grandparents, whom she named as Stolanus and Emeron. The latter was an Essene devoted to Arkas, a spiritual leader who resided on Mount Carmel. Arkas prophesied that Emeron would "bear a child marked with a sign"—an *M*—"who was chosen out as a vessel of election in preparation for the coming of the Savior."[2] Emmerich did not reveal what form the sign would take: something readily visible, like a birthmark, or something more ethereal, seen only by the parents, priests, or other favored persons.

Stolanus and Emeron's second daughter Ismeria bore the sign, and in turn Ismeria bore Mary's mother, Hannah. Within the same extended family, according to a family tree based on Emmerich's visions, we find John the Baptist, Mary Salome, Mary Cleophas, and the apostles James, John, Matthew, Jude Thaddeus, Simon the Zealot, and James the Less.[3]

The *Infancy Gospel of James* describes Mary's father Joachim as exceedingly rich. Emmerich agreed that he amassed great wealth in livestock late in life, but commented that he was poor at the time he married Hannah.

Emmerich disputed the assertion, found in the *Infancy Gospel of James*, that Joachim and Hannah were childless. Rather, she testified, they had a daughter, Maria Heli, early in their marriage, but the child did not carry the hoped-for sign. Maria Heli grew up to marry Cleophas, and the couple became the parents of Mary Cleophas.[4] *John* mentions Mary Cleophas as one of the women present at the Crucifixion.[5] Both *John* and the *Infancy Gospel of Matthew* identify Mary Cleophas as the sister of Mary the mother of Jesus, raising the question of why two sisters would have the same name. In Emmerich's

51

account that question is resolved; the two women were of similar age but Mary Cleophas was our Mary's aunt.

Mary's Conception and Birth

Another nineteen years went by, while Joachim and Hannah yearned for the promised child. At last, when Emmerich believed Hannah was forty-three years old, an angel visited her to announce that their time had come. The angel also visited Joachim who was away with his flocks in the wilderness. Joachim and Hannah were told to proceed separately to the temple during the feast of Tabernacles. After ritual preparation they met in a passageway—elsewhere a subterranean hall—under the Golden Gate of the temple.

Joachim, Emmerich reported, "was met by Hannah, radiant with happiness. They embraced each other with holy joy, and each told the other their good tidings. They were in a state of ecstasy and enveloped in a cloud of light."[6] And: "I saw Joachim and Hannah encompassed by a host of angels with heavenly light. They themselves shone and were as pure as spirits in a supernatural state, as no human couple had ever been before them."[7] It was there that Mary was conceived.

The tradition of the Immaculate Conception was well-established when Emmerich had these visions, even though the Roman Catholic dogma had not yet been proclaimed. Furthermore, the legend of Joachim and Hannah meeting at, or under, the Golden Gate was not new; it was the subject of two famous works of art: a painting by the German artist known as the Master of the Bamberg Altarpiece (c.1420–1440), and a woodcut by fellow German Albrecht Dürer (1471–1528). We do not know whether Emmerich was familiar with those artworks.

When Hannah was "seventeen weeks and five days" into her pregnancy, she had an ecstatic experience in which her womb opened "to enclose a shining little virgin from whom man's whole salvation was to spring." Emmerich, who observed the scene, reported: "It was made known to me that the Blessed Virgin's soul was united to her body five days earlier than with other children, and that her birth was twelve days earlier."[8] Significantly, Emmerich did not date the union of body and soul to the time of conception.

In Emmerich's account Hannah's older daughter Mary Heli, already married and a mother herself, "looked after the house" but was not

Chapter 2. Mary According to Anne Catherine Emmerich

present at the birth. Instead, three cousins served as midwives. When the baby was laid in Hannah's arms:

> I [Emmerich] saw that at the same time the child was presented in Heaven in the sight of the Most Holy Trinity, and greeted with unspeakable joy by all the heavenly host. Then I understood that there was to be made known to her in a supernatural manner her whole future with all her joys and sorrows. Mary was taught infinite mysteries, and yet was and remained a child.[9]

Emmerich described Mary's festive naming ceremony, which took place in Hannah's home:

> In the middle of the room was an altar covered with red and white, and a stand upon which scrolls were laid.... Enue, Elizabeth's sister, brought the infant Mary swathed ... in red and transparent white, and gave her to Joachim. The priests approached the altar, the attendants bearing the chief priest's train, and prayed from the scrolls. Joachim placed the child on the arms of the chief priest, who held her aloft, prayed for awhile, and then laid her in the little cradle on the altar.[10]

Emmerich offered the following description: "Mary is very delicately formed, and has reddish-fair hair, smooth but curly at the ends."[11]

While the gospels might leave some uncertainty regarding Mary's whereabouts at this time—even until the return from Egypt—Emmerich placed the child Mary firmly in Nazareth, where she played with Mary Cleophas and others.

Presentation in the Temple

Anne Catherine Emmerich witnessed the presentation of Mary to the temple at three years of age. It is doubtful whether Emmerich had ever read the *Infancy Gospel*, which also contains the story, but the associated feast day—the only one in the liturgical calendar to be based on an extracanonical gospel—had long been celebrated in the Roman and Orthodox churches.

According to Emmerich, preparations began in Mary's home in Nazareth. Priests were invited to a ceremony at which Mary was questioned about many things relating to her forthcoming life in the temple. Mary changed attire three times during the ceremony. Before the final part of the ceremony in which she stood before an altar which had been erected in their home, she wore

> a violet-blue dress woven with a pattern of yellow flowers; over this was a bodice or corset embroidered in different colors ending in a point and fastening under the arms, where it gathered and held the fullness of the dress. Above this was a violet-blue robe, fuller and grander than the other ones, and ending in a short, rounded train. Down each side of the front were embroidered silver stripes with what seemed to be little gold rose buds strewn between them; the robe was open down to the lower edge of the bodice, and formed two pockets at the sides in which the arms rested.[12]

Mary also wore a veil crowned with metal bands and adorned with silk roses and pearls or precious stones. Such was the level of detail Emmerich saw and reported in her visions.

Then began the long journey to Jerusalem. Upon their arrival they stayed at the home of Zachariah and Elizabeth, the parents of John the Baptist. Finally, the party proceeded to the temple. Mary's father Joachim and Zachariah went first.

> Afterwards Mary was taken there by her mother Hannah in a festal procession. First came Hannah and her elder daughter Mary Heli, with the latter's little daughter Mary Cleophas, then the holy child Mary followed in her sky-blue dress and robe with wreaths round her arms and neck; in her hand she held a candle or torch entwined with flowers. Decorated candles like this were also carried by three maidens on each side of her, wearing white dresses, embroidered with gold.[13]

After the formal induction ceremony, Mary danced with the other temple virgins:

> They stood opposite each other in pairs, and danced in various figures and crossings.... [I]t was like a minuet. Sometimes there was a swaying, circular motion of the body, like the movement of the Jews when they pray. Some of the young girls accompanied the dancing with flutes, triangles, and bells.[14]

Another musical instrument, with both strings and pipes, "sounded particularly strange and delightful." The player held the instrument on the knee, plucking the strings with one hand and pressing keys with the other, which "sent the air through several pipes."[15] Emmerich mentioned bellows, and these were probably pumped by the arm, as in the *portativ* organs of a later era.

Mary's life in the temple consisted largely of "prescribed Temple-prayers" and private devotions. But she had a teacher, Noemi, "sister of Lazarus' mother," fifty years old, and an Essene. Noemi taught Mary to knit and weave. Like other temple virgins, Mary learned "embroidery and other forms of decoration of carpets and vestments."[16] The virgins also did mundane tasks like washing pots and pans, washing the priests' clothes and vessels used during animal sacrifices, and preparing food, some of which came from sacrificed animals. Emmerich commented that Zachariah occasionally visited her and that Simeon "was also acquainted with her."[17] But no contacts with her mother were mentioned.

Marriage to Joseph

In Anne Catherine Emmerich's account, Mary remained at the temple until she was fourteen,[18] whereupon the priests resolved to find her a suitable husband. Emmerich's description of the selection process was generally similar to that in the *Infancy Gospel of James*. Eligible men "of the line of David" were brought in, and the priests asked for a sign from God indicating which one should marry Mary.

The first round of candidates included a suitor: "a devout youth from the region of Bethlehem" who had "an ardent longing in his heart to become Mary's husband."[19] Alas, that was not to be; neither he nor any of the other men received the requisite sign.

The second round included "six brothers registered in Bethlehem," and Joseph located "not far from Samaria in a place beside a little stream, where he lived alone by the water."[20] This information about Joseph's location is interesting. The brothers' presence near Bethlehem suggests that Joseph grew up there, as noted in Chapter 1. But Joseph had moved north to the vicinity of Samaria—presumably the city as distinct from the province of the same name; importantly, Emmerich did not place him in Galilee.

Emmerich described Joseph's difficult childhood, tormented by five brothers; but she said nothing of his adult life. By contrast with scriptural assertions that he was a widower, she commented: "I never saw that he was married before; he was very retiring and avoided women."[21] The suggestion that Joseph was not previously married narrows down the possible identities of Jesus' "brothers and sisters." If true, it would mean that the alleged siblings were either cousins or Mary's own children.

According to Emmerich, each man held a branch in his hand, and as Joseph laid his hand on the altar before the Holy of Holies, "a white flower like a lily blossomed out of the top of [Joseph's branch], and I saw over him an appearance of light like the Holy Ghost. Joseph was now recognized as appointed by God to be the bridegroom of the Blessed Virgin."[22]

The gospel stories speak of the *betrothal* of Mary and Joseph, but Emmerich spoke unequivocally of a *wedding*. By then, she said, Mary's father Joachim was deceased, and Hannah "had by God's command married again."[23] Clearly the family was well-to-do, and the wedding festivities "on Mount Zion in Jerusalem" lasted "seven or eight days." Relatives of Joachim and Hannah were there, along with friends Mary had made in the temple. The festivities seem to have included ritual as well as feasting; we are also told: "Many lambs were slaughtered and sacrificed."[24] Emmerich did not explain why the wedding was held in Jerusalem rather than the home town of Nazareth, but perhaps the latter did not offer a venue of sufficient size.

Mary must have been a strikingly beautiful young woman:

> The Blessed Virgin had very abundant hair, reddish-gold in color. Her high, delicately traced eyebrows were black; she had a very high forehead, large downcast eyes with long black lashes, a rather long straight nose, delicately shaped, a noble and lovely mouth, and a pointed chin. She was of middle height.[25]

Emmerich's description of Mary's wedding attire and hair arrangement fill more than three pages and go into minute detail. Her hair was fixed by temple maidens:

> The adornment of her hair was indescribably beautiful. It was parted in the middle of her head and divided into a number of little plaits. These, interwoven with white silk and pearls, formed a great net falling over her shoulders and circling in a point half-way down her neck. The ends of the plaits were curled inwards, and the whole net of hair was edged with a decorated border of fringes and pearls, whose weight held it down and kept it in place.[26]

Mary wore a wreath on her head and a jewel-encrusted crown. And reportedly she wore four or five layers of clothing, all of which must have been heavy and hot! Yet we are told that she moved about in her rich dress very gently and with great modesty and seriousness.[27]

Chapter 2. Mary According to Anne Catherine Emmerich

After the wedding, Mary, Hannah, Hannah's second husband, and a number of others journeyed to Nazareth. Joseph, however, "went to Bethlehem after the wedding in order to settle some family affairs there. He did not come to Nazareth until later." Emmerich noted that Hannah procured a small house for the young couple, and Mary and Joseph moved in when the latter joined her from Bethlehem.

The Nativity

The Annunciation

Whereas the *Infancy Gospel of James* places the Annunciation at a well, Anne Catherine Emmerich placed it firmly in Mary's bedchamber, in the house procured by her mother in Nazareth. Joseph, who was already living with Mary, had gone away on a relatively short trip and "seemed ... to be on his way home."[28]

Mary, then "a little over fourteen years old," had retired for the night and knelt down to pray. The Angel Gabriel appeared, enveloped in a shaft of light, as "a shining white youth, with flowing yellow hair." Mary was "shy" but showed none of the hesitancy recorded in *Luke*. She immediately answered Gabriel's request with: "Be it done to me according to thy word."[29] Emmerich continued:

> As soon as the Blessed Virgin had spoken the words ... I saw the Holy Ghost in the appearance of a winged figure.... The head was like the face of a man, and light was spread like wings beside the figure, from whose breast and hands I saw three streams of light pouring down towards the right side of the Blessed Virgin and meeting as they reached her.[30]

The angel—and presumably the Holy Ghost—then disappeared, whereupon Emmerich declared: "I saw the Blessed Virgin wrapped in the deepest ecstasy. I saw that she recognized the Incarnation of the promised Redeemer within herself in the form of a tiny human figure of light, perfectly formed in all its parts down to its tiny fingers."[31] Emmerich may have been influenced by the preformationist theory, popular in the seventeenth and eighteenth centuries, that a tiny human figure was curled up in the head of every male sperm. Gestation consisted of the progressive growth of this preformed human body until it emerged into the world at birth.[32]

Emmerich noted that women were not permitted beyond the outer court of the temple in Jerusalem. Yet "Here in Nazareth ... a virgin is herself the Temple, and the Most Holy is within her, and the high priest is within her, and she alone is with Him."[33] Emmerich posed the question why the Redeemer did not come sooner; the reason was that

> she alone, and no creature before or after her, was the pure Vessel of Grace, promised by God to mankind as the Mother of the Incarnate Word, by the merits of whose Passion mankind was to be redeemed from its guilt. The Blessed Virgin was the one and only pure blossom of the human race, flowering in the fullness of time.... She was preordained in eternity and passed through time as the Mother of the Eternal.[34]

The notion that Mary may have been preordained to be the mother of Christ has far-reaching implications. It will be discussed further in Chapter 4.

Mary did not share her Annunciation experience with anyone, even with Joseph who remained unaware of her pregnancy.

The Visitation

In Anne Catherine Emmerich's account of the Visitation, Mary did not travel to see Elizabeth in Joseph's absence. Rather, she accompanied him on a trip to Jerusalem for the feast of Passover. Joseph was even with her when she went to the home of Elizabeth and Zachariah, though the two men waited at a distance while the two women greeted each other.

Emmerich's story gives the impression that the two women did not know each other, except by hearsay. But Elizabeth was alerted in a dream that Mary was on her way. Elizabeth "was a tall aged women with a small delicate face. Her head was wrapped in a veil. Mary saw her from far off and recognized her at once. She ran to meet her, while Joseph discreetly remained behind."[35]

As soon as the two women met, Emmerich related: "I saw a shining brightness in the Blessed Virgin and as it were a ray of light passing from her to Elizabeth."[36] Once in the house, the women embraced, Elizabeth exclaimed: "Blessed art thou among women...," and Mary responded with the *Magnificat*.

Chapter 2. Mary According to Anne Catherine Emmerich

Joseph left first, leaving Mary with Elizabeth and Zachariah. Mary and Elizabeth prayed together often. Mary also helped around the house and helped make clothes for her cousin and the latter's future child. Eventually:

> The Blessed Virgin retuned home to Nazareth after John's birth and before his circumcision. Joseph came to meet her halfway. When Joseph traveled back with the Blessed Virgin during the second half of her journey from [Judaea] he noticed from her figure that she was with child, and was sore beset by trouble and doubt, for he knew nothing of the Annunciation.[37]

Clearly they did not communicate. "Mary in shy humility had kept God's secret to herself," while "Joseph said nothing, but struggled in silence with his doubts. The Blessed Virgin, who had foreseen this trouble became thoughtful and serious, which only increased St Joseph's uneasiness."[38] Upon their arrival in Nazareth, Mary stayed for a few days with Hannah and other relatives. Meanwhile, "Joseph's uneasiness increased ... to such an extent that, now that Mary was preparing to return to him in his house, he made up his mind to leave her and to disappear in secret."[39]

"While he was harboring this thought," however, "an Angel appeared to him in a dream and reassured him." Nevertheless, Mary continued to live with Hannah and seems to have had little contact with her husband. She busied herself "with preparations for the Birth of Jesus. She is sewing and knitting coverlets and swaddling bands."[40] Meanwhile, Joseph lived alone; Hannah assigned her maidservant to look after him and supported him economically.[41]

The Birth of Jesus

Mary intended to have her child in her mother's house, and Hannah provided her "with plenty of everything that ... was customary for a person in her rank of life."[42] During that time Joseph traveled to Jerusalem to take "beasts for sacrifice," presumably to the temple. While there he developed a long-term plan to build a house in Bethlehem and take Mary there with him, because he disliked living in Nazareth.[43]

On the way back to Nazareth, however, an angel appeared to him and gave instructions that he should take Mary immediately to Bethlehem, where she would give birth. They should take with them only a "few and simple things." And "besides the ass upon which Mary was to sit, he was to take with him a she-ass one year old that had not yet had a foal. He was to let [the she-ass] run free and always to follow whatever path she took."[44] The ass made an appearance several times in Emmerich's Nativity story.

Needless to say, the story related in the *Infancy Gospel of James* that Joseph's two grown sons accompanied them on the journey to Bethlehem does not appear in Emmerich's account. Emmerich did not seem to believe that Joseph had been married before.

After many adventures, in which Joseph and Mary repeatedly were turned away from prospective lodgings, the couple finally arrived in Bethlehem. Joseph registered with the tax authorities and then looked for accommodation. But the city was filled with people there for the census, and all available space was taken.

So Joseph led them to a cave on the "road to the Shepherds' Valley," where he had sheltered as a boy to escape his brothers' torments. This statement lends support to the assertion that Joseph grew up in the vicinity of Bethlehem. We also learn that the "cave had been a place of devotion since Abraham's time, particularly for mothers and their babies. This was prophetic."[45]

Emmerich described the cave thus:

> From the west one came through a light wickerwork door into a moderately broad passage which was partly angular and partly semicircular. Towards the south it broadened out considerably, so the ground-plan of the whole can be compared to a head resting on its neck.... The walls of the cave as nature had made them were, though not quite smooth, clean and pleasant and had something attractive about them.... From the north side of the passage an entrance led into a smaller side-cave. Passing this entrance you came upon the place where Joseph lit his fire.[46]

Though a far cry from the luxury of Hannah's home in Nazareth, the cave provided at least primitive accommodation for the Holy Family and their animals. Joseph made it as comfortable as possible, with rushes and a rug for Mary to sleep on.

Emmerich placed the birth of Jesus in November rather than December. The celebration of Christmas was slow to take root. By the third and fourth centuries Christian communities were observing the Nativity on a variety of different dates. Eventually the institutional church

Chapter 2. Mary According to Anne Catherine Emmerich

chose December 25 to be the official date of the Nativity. It was the winter solstice in the Roman calendar, a day with a long tradition of symbolism in the ancient world. Conveniently the date was already a holiday; it was the Roman festival of Saturnalia and the festival of *Sol Invictus* ("Unconquered Sun"), sun god of the later Roman Empire.

Mary reportedly rested in the cave for at least one full day, the Sabbath, while Joseph went into Bethlehem to buy provisions. He offered to bring "some pious women he knew" to help with the birth. But Mary declined, "saying that she needed no human help."[47] Emmerich's story did not include the midwives mentioned in the *Infancy Gospel of James*.

Late in the evening, Joseph briefly left the cave. When he returned,

> he saw her [Mary] with her face turned toward the east, kneeling on the bed facing away from him. He saw her as it were surrounded by flames, the whole cave was as if filled with supernatural light. He gazed at her like Moses when he saw the burning bush; then he went into his own little cell in holy awe and threw himself on his face in prayer.[48]

Emmerich insisted that she saw the birth of Jesus "as an historical event and not as a Feast of the Church."[49] But in her description of the birth, she seemed to move back and forth between what she saw clairvoyantly and her own devotional response. For example:

> At midnight she [Mary] was wrapt in the ecstasy of prayer. I saw her lifted from the earth, so that I saw the ground beneath her.... The radiance about her increased, everything, even things without life, were in a joyful inner motion, the stones of the roof, of the walls, and of the floor of the cave became as it were alive.... [T]he Blessed Virgin, borne up in ecstasy, was now gazing downwards, adoring her God, whose Mother she had become.... I saw angels round her in human forms, lying on their faces and adoring the Child.[50]

Emmerich continued,

> [Mary] remained for some time rapt in ecstasy. I saw her laying a cloth over the Child, but at first she did not touch Him or take Him up. After some time I saw the Child Jesus move and heard Him cry. Then Mary seemed to come to herself, and she took the Child

up from the carpet, wrapping Him in the cloth which covered Him, and held Him in her arms to her breast.[51]

Mary wrapped the newborn child in swaddling clothes, and with Joseph now by her side, laid Jesus in the manger "which was filled with rushes and delicate plants and covered with a cloth hanging over the sides."[52] The miracles did not cease: "In the night of the Savior's Birth, an abundant spring welled up" in a nearby cave to provide fresh water for the Holy Family.[53]

The shepherds "who kept watch over their flocks by night," according to Emmerich, were stationed in a watchtower from which they could alert fellow shepherds in the fields of any impending danger. During the night of the Nativity they saw a glow of light over the cave and then heard the angels singing. After consultations, a group of shepherds brought gifts to the child the following morning.[54] The "presents were little animals not unlike roe-deer.... They had long necks, very clear beautiful eyes, and were very swift and graceful." The shepherds also brought "strings of dead birds hanging over their shoulders and carried some bigger live birds under their arms."[55] Over the next several days many others came, including women who helped care for Mary and her child.

Whereas Emmerich's description of the birth of Jesus was mystical and devotional, she described the circumcision in graphic detail. Three priests and a woman came to the cave to perform the ritual. The procedure involved use of a nine-inch knife—and also the priest's fingernails. We are told that the "Infant Jesus wept loudly after the sacred ceremony" and later that night was still "restless with pain and crying a great deal."[56] He remained bandaged for a couple of days.

On the day of the circumcision, Mary's cousin Elizabeth came, "riding on a donkey." Joseph "received her very warmly, and she and Mary embraced each other with great joy"[57] Evidently Elizabeth stayed with them for some time. The Holy Family seems to have lived in the cave for about six weeks. One wonders why better accommodation could not have been found by then.

Emmerich's story of the Magi occupies fully one-fifth of all the material she dictated relating to Mary. She gave their names as Mensor, Sair and Theokeno. The more familiar names described their characteristics: Kaspar meant "He goes with love"; Melchior: "He wanders about, he approaches gently and with ingratiating manners"; and

Chapter 2. Mary According to Anne Catherine Emmerich

Balthazar: "He makes rapid decisions, he quickly directs his will to the will of God."[58]

The Magi came from a long astrological tradition. For centuries, Emmerich explained, their ancestors had studied the stars and calculated that a great king would arise about that time. On the very night of the Nativity, at the end of November, Mensor and Sair were standing "on a pyramid-shaped tower looking though long tubes at the Star of Jacob, which had a tail." The star "split asunder before their eyes, and I [Emmerich] saw a great shining virgin appear therein, before whom a radiant child hovered."[59] Perhaps that was the constellation Virgo. Theokeno/Balthazar saw something similar from his own country, "a few days' journey to the east."

All three recognized what they saw in the night sky as of great significance and set off at once to "follow the star." Theokeno soon caught up with his fellow Magi, and the three and their attendants rode on camels toward the West.[60] Emmerich described the many places they passed through and the people who lived there.

The Magi reached Jerusalem in about four weeks. Herod had already heard rumors of the birth of a child, whom Jews suggested might be the Messiah, and he "was in a state of ill-humor and vexation."[61] The Magi's tidings of the birth of a great king only increased Herod's concern, and Emmerich noted his charge to the Magi, recorded in *Matthew*, that they should return to him with more information about the child.

By that time—shortly before December 25 in Emmerich's reckoning—the star had grown in size and "shone like a ball of fire" and "looked like the moon in daylight." Soon it shone "bright and clear above the hill" and finally looked to Emmerich "as big as a sheet."[62]

The Magi donned their royal robes and approached the cave, which was "filled with heavenly light." Mensor went in alone and saw, in the back of the cave, "the Virgin sitting with the Child, just as he had seem them in their visions." He rejoined Sair and Theokeno outside, and the three prepared a ritual to honor the "Newborn King of the Jews." The Magi then all went in together and knelt before the child. They presented their gifts and "Besought the newborn King to accept their hearts and souls and all their thoughts and deeds, begging Him to enlighten them and to grant them every virtue and, while they were on earth, happiness, peace, and love."[63]

The Magi were duly warned by an angel of Herod's wrath and warned Mary and Joseph of the threat to Jesus' life. But instead of fleeing immediately to Egypt, the Holy Family went to Jerusalem for Mary's purification and Jesus' presentation in the temple. There, as also recorded in *Luke*, they had the encounter with Simeon and Anna, but Emmerich provided the additional detail that Simeon passed away shortly after uttering the *Nunc Dimittis*.[64] After their visit to Jerusalem the Holy Family journeyed on to Nazareth, about two weeks after the Magi's visit.[65]

Emmerich reported that, many years later, the adult Jesus visited the Magi in their own country. In their temple they "showed him a representation of the Crib which, after their return from Bethlehem, they had caused to be made." It was made entirely of gold. The child "was sitting in a crib like that of Bethlehem, on a red cover.... Even the straw of the manger was represented."[66]

The Flight into Egypt

In Anne Catherine Emmerich's account the flight into Egypt began after the Holy Family had returned to Nazareth and when Jesus was six-to-nine months old. Herod's anger at the Magi's departure, and the continuing threat of a new king of the Jews, had not abated. But he had been in Rome and gave orders for the Massacre of the Innocents upon his return. Mary and Joseph set off with the child Jesus, traveling mostly through remote desert regions to avoid contact with Herod's troops. They had many adventures and suffered much hardship on the way.

At one point the Holy Family passed near the cave where Elizabeth and her son, John the Baptist, were hiding from Herod. Realizing that his relatives were thirsty, John—no more than two years old—"threw himself on his knees and cried to God with outstretched arms, then jumped up, ran, driven by the Spirit, to the high edge of the rocks and thrust with his staff into the ground, from which an abundant spring burst forth."[67] Joseph and Mary refreshed themselves but resumed their journey without even conversing with Elizabeth or greeting John.

On another occasion, the Holy Family fell among robbers. But "at the sight of the Infant Jesus a ray, like an arrow, struck the heart of the leader, who ordered his comrades to do no harm to these people."[68]

The robbers then took the family to their encampment and cared for them.

Emmerich also repeated the story in the *Infancy Gospel of Matthew* of the palm tree that "bowed down its head to them, as if it were kneeling." Mary refreshed herself and her family, and also "distributed the fruit from the tree among the many naked children who were running after her."[69] Also, perhaps echoing the dragons in *Pseudo-Matthew*, wild beasts showed them the way "just like a dog does when he wants you to follow him."[70]

The Holy Family finally arrived in Egypt and settled in Heliopolis. To support the family, Joseph did carpentry work and Mary wove carpets and knitted.[71] We recall that Mary had learned weaving and knitting as a temple virgin. The family joined the local Jewish community and participated in worship services, but Emmerich commented that religious practices were more lax there than in Palestine.

The Holy Family remained in Egypt for some time after Herod's death, "for there was still danger."[72] But when the danger had subsided an angel came to Joseph in a dream and instructed him to make preparations for their return to Nazareth. This time they traveled closer to the Mediterranean coast, passing through Gaza. Hannah was still alive when they arrived, and by then Jesus "was nearly eight years old."[73]

Mary Before and After the Crucifixion

Mary During Jesus' Ministry

Anne Catherine Emmerich stated that Joseph died when Jesus was approaching his thirtieth birthday and shortly before he began his public ministry. The Holy Family was then in Capernaum. "Mary sat at the head of his bed, holding him in her arms. Jesus stood just below her, near Joseph's breast. The whole room was brilliant with light and full of angels." Emmerich commented: "Joseph had of necessity to die before the Lord, for he could not have endured His Crucifixion; he was too gentle, too loving."[74]

Emmerich said little about Mary's activities during her son's three-year ministry. But she did offer additional information about the exchange at the Marriage Feast of Cana. For example, we learn that Jesus agreed to attend the wedding, at least in part to rebut criticism that he was spending too much time away from his family.

We also learn that Jesus had agreed to provide the second course of the banquet, including the wine. When the wine ran out, Mary reminded him, whereupon he replied: "Be not solicitous! Trouble not thyself and Me! My hour is not yet come." Emmerich suggested that "my hour" could refer to something as mundane as the banquet schedule and his responsibilities thereto. On the other hand, she defended Jesus' use of "Woman," to address his mother:

> These words were not uttered in harshness to the Blessed Virgin. Jesus addressed her as 'Woman' because, at this moment as the Messiah, as the Son of God, He was present in divine power and about to perform in presence of all His disciples and relatives an action full of mystery.[75]

Emmerich noted that in the marriage feast "we see Mary beginning the role of *mediatrix* that she had ever since continued."[76] We shall see in Chapter 4 that a campaign eventually developed in the Church of Rome to define Mary's role as Mediatrix of all Graces as infallible dogma; it has not yet succeeded.

From Palm Sunday to Pentecost

Emmerich mentioned that Mary was present with Jesus and his followers the day before the first Palm Sunday. She did not seem to accompany him on his triumphal entrance into Jerusalem. Later in the week, however, she attended a large gathering. There, in Emmerich words: "At last He [Jesus] spoke to His Holy Mother. He said through compassion she would suffer with Him all the cruel torture of His death, that with Him, she would die His bitter death, and still would have to survive Him fifteen years."[77] Mary's participation in the Sacrifice of the Cross is a theme that will be explored later in this book.

According to Emmerich, Mary attended the Last Supper but sat with the other women at a separate table. Mary stayed close to the places where Jesus was brought for trial, the scourging at the pillar, and his condemnation to be crucified. She confronted Peter, after the latter had denied Christ three times. Emmerich also mentioned the incident—not recorded in scripture but immortalized in the Stations of the Cross—when Jesus met his mother on the way to Calvary. Mary was jeered by the crowd for being the mother of a criminal.

Chapter 2. Mary According to Anne Catherine Emmerich

Emmerich saw Mary, along with "John and the holy women," at the foot of the cross. As Cassius, the Roman centurion, thrust the spear into Jesus' side, Mary felt "as if the thrust had transfixed her own heart, felt the sharp point piercing her through and through."[78]

After Joseph of Arimathea and Nicodemus had secured permission from Pontius Pilate, Jesus' body was taken down from the cross. "As soon as the Sacred Body was taken down, the men wrapped it in linen from the knees to the waist, and laid it on a sheet in His Mother's arms, which, in anguish of heart and ardent longing, were stretched out to receive it."[79]

Emmerich witnessed Mary removing the crown of thorns, cutting it so as to reduce further tissue damage. She washed, anointed and embalmed the wounds on Jesus' head and torso. She then bound the head but did not immediately cover the face.[80] After Jesus' body was transported to the tomb, Mary went in and Emmerich saw her "bending low over the corpse of her Son and weeping."[81]

"At the close of the Sabbath"—presumably after sundown on the Saturday evening— an angel appeared to Mary: "He announced to her that the Lord was near, and bode to go out to the little gate belonging to Nicodemus. A these words, Mary's heart was filled with joy." And at about nine o'clock:

> Floating down toward her in the midst of a great multitude of souls of the ancient Patriarchs, I saw the most holy soul of Jesus, resplendent with light and without a trace of wound. Turning to the Patriarchs and pointing to the Blessed Virgin, He uttered the words "Mary, My Mother."[82]

Mary then went alone to retread the path Jesus had taken as he carried the cross to Calvary. There she had an apparition which assured her Jesus "was about to come forth from the tomb alive, in a glorified body. Emmerich saw Jesus rise up from the tomb, and "saw the risen Lord appear to His Blessed Mother on Mount Calvary."[83] The following morning, Mary Magdalene and the other women found the empty tomb.

Sometime prior to the Ascension, Mary, Jesus' disciples, Joseph of Arimathea, the "holy women," and others were assembled for prayer. Emmerich commented:

Mary: Adept, Queen, Mother, Priestess

> They spoke in words full of mystery of their relationship to the Mother of the Lord and what she should be to them.... I saw the Blessed Virgin hovering over the assembly in a shining and outspread mantle whose folds embraced them all, and on her head descended a crown from the Most Holy Trinity.... I had the conviction that Mary was the legitimate head of them all, the temple that enclosed them all.[84]

Early Christian texts attesting to the disciples' reverence for Mary and her emergence as the group's spiritual leader will be examined in the next chapter.

As recorded in *Acts*, Emmerich stated that Mary was present with the disciples at Pentecost. There was the sound of rushing wind, and a "luminous cloud descended low over the house.... Afterwards there shot from the rushing cloud streams of white light.... The streams intersected one another in seven rays." Tongues of fire descended on each person, and an "effusion of heavenly light, a joyous courage pervaded the assembly." Emmerich noted that "they gathered around the Blessed Virgin who was ... the only one perfectly calm"![85] The reference to seven rays is interesting from an esoteric standpoint.

Mary's Last Days

Whereas scripture is silent on Mary's latter days, Anne Catherine Emmerich described them in some detail: "After Our Lord's Ascension Mary lived for three years on Mount Zion, for three years in Bethany, and for nine years in Ephesus, whither St John took her."[86] It will be recalled that Jesus spoke from the cross to entrust his mother to the Beloved Disciple.

John built Mary a house in a rural area outside the city of Ephesus, and she lived there alone, save for a young maidservant. The house had several rooms separated by wicker partitions. On a wall in Mary's oratory, "was a receptacle like a tabernacle.... In it stood a cross about the length of a man's arm in which were inserted two arms rising outwards and upwards in the form of the letter Y.... This cross was set in a little mound of earth or stone, like Christ's Cross on Mount Calvary."[87]

Behind the house, "the Blessed Virgin had created a kind of Way of the Cross. When she was living in Jerusalem, she had never failed, ever since Our Lord's death, to follow His path to Calvary with tears

Chapter 2. Mary According to Anne Catherine Emmerich

of compassion." She had paced out the distances between the "Stations of the Cross" and replicated them at her home.[88]

"An Apostle or disciple" sometimes visited her, but her most frequent visitor was the one whom Emmerich took to be John. "He was very slim and active, his face was long, narrow, and delicate, and on his bare head his long fair hair was parted and brushed back behind the ears." Emmerich noted that "this gave him a womanish, almost girlish, appearance." On a later date, though, she "saw John come into the house looking much older... and very thin and haggard."[89]

After she had been in Ephesus for three years Mary made a trip to Jerusalem.[90] In addition to visiting the sacred sites, she met with several of the Apostles and "assisted them with her advice." Mary made another trip to Jerusalem, eighteen months before her death, and while there she selected a burial site for herself on the Mount of Olives. Emmerich noted that "the Apostles caused a beautiful sepulcher to be prepared by the hands of Christian stonemasons."[91] This description of a grave site in Jerusalem does not settle controversy over where Mary died and was buried, because, as we shall see, her body may never have been brought there.

As Mary's days drew to a close, the Apostles were summoned to her bedside. Most came, though Emmerich noted that Thomas, who was in India, could not come because of the distance. She also noted that "Paul was not summoned." Mary's older sister Maria Heli was there and "other holy women." Mary sat up in bed and blessed each of the Apostles. She received the Eucharist and Peter administered Extreme Unction (the last rites).

Emmerich described Mary's passing thus:

> Mary's face was radiant with smiles as in her youth. Her eyes were raised towards Heaven in holy joy.... Two radiant clouds of light poured down, out of which appeared the faces of many angels. Between these clouds a path of light poured down upon Mary.... She stretched out her arms towards it in infinite longing, and I saw her body ... rise up so high above the couch that one could see right under it. I saw her soul leave her body like a little figure of infinitely pure light, soaring with outstretched arms up the shining mountain to Heaven.[92]

Mary's body settled back on the couch and was prepared for burial. But instead of making plans to transport her remains to the sepulcher

69

Mary: Adept, Queen, Mother, Priestess

in Jerusalem, the apostles carried the body to "Christ's tomb," on the nearby Way of the Cross, which they had enlarged for the purpose. Later a strange radiance" appeared over the tomb. Emmerich saw

> the soul of the Blessed Virgin, which had been following the appearance of Our Lord, pass in front of Him and float down into the tomb. Soon afterwards I saw her soul, united to her transfigured body, rising out of the tomb ... and ascending into the heavenly Jerusalem with Our Lord and with the whole glory.[93]

But then Emmerich commented: "I did not see the Blessed Virgin die in the usual manner, nor did I see her go up to Heaven, but I saw that first her soul and then her body were taken from the earth."[94]

Whether Mary died a "natural death," and whether her body and soul were reunited, are among the issues that distinguish the western doctrine of the Assumption from the Eastern Orthodox Dormition of Mary. The doctrine of the Assumption asserts that Mary was taken up, body and soul, into heaven, possibly even before her death. The doctrine of the Dormition ("Falling Asleep") affirms that Mary died a natural death, whereupon her soul was taken up to heaven; if her body was taken up, that occurred after her death. Some early writers questioned whether her body and soul were reunited, though modern Orthodoxy generally accepts that they were.

Notwithstanding Emmerich's account, the sepulcher in Jerusalem continues to be venerated as the site from which the Dormition took place. Moreover, a number of texts examined in the next chapter challenge the assertion that Mary spent her last years in Ephesus; indeed they suggest that she never went there.

---

[1] Clemens W. Brentano (ed.), *The Life of the Blessed Virgin Mary: From the Visions of Ven. Anne Catherine Emmerich* (transl.: M. Palairet), Tan Books, 1954/1970.
[2] *Ibid.*, 15-16.
[3] *Ibid.*, 4-20, and especially 397.
[4] *Ibid.*, 397.
[5] John 19:25.
[6] Brentano (ed.), *The Life of the Blessed Virgin Mary*, 40.
[7] *Ibid.*, 62.
[8] *Ibid.*, 72-73.
[9] *Ibid.*, 76.

Chapter 2. Mary According to Anne Catherine Emmerich

[10] Carl E. Schmöger (ed.),, *The Life of Jesus Christ and Biblical Revelations: From the Visions of Ven. Anne Catherine Emmerich*, vol. I (transl.: "an American nun"), Charlotte, NC: Tan Books, 1914/2011, 154-155. Little is known about the naming ceremony in biblical times, except that a sacrifice might be offered 80 days after the birth of a girl. In Sephardic Judaism the ceremony took more definite shape as the *zeved ha-bat* ("gift of a daughter").
[11] Brentano (ed.), *The Life of the Blessed Virgin Mary*, 94.
[12] *Ibid.*, 90. This was just part of Emmerich's description of Mary's outfit.
[13] *Ibid.*, 110.
[14] *Ibid.*, 115.
[15] *Ibid.*
[16] *Ibid.*, 117, 129.
[17] *Ibid.*, 117-118.
[18] The *Infancy Gospel of James* gave her age as 12. But 14 was more likely since Mary allegedly gave birth when she was 15, and conception seem to have taken place shortly after leaving the temple.
[19] Brentano (ed.), *The Life of the Blessed Virgin Mary*, 131.
[20] *Ibid.*, 132.
[21] *Ibid.*, 124. Unless Joseph's attitude changed after his marriage, perhaps we can see here justification for the claim of Mary's perpetual virginity.
[22] *Ibid.*, 132-133.
[23] *Ibid.*, 130. Following Jewish custom, Hannah may have married a brother of Joachim.
[24] *Ibid.*, 133. Sir Michael Palairet's translation refers to "Mount Sion." This is changed to "Mount Zion," throughout the chapter, to conform to standard spelling.
[25] *Ibid.*, 136.
[26] *Ibid.*, 135.
[27] *Ibid.*, 136.
[28] *Ibid.*, 141.
[29] *Ibid.*, 143.
[30] *Ibid.*, 144.
[31] *Ibid.*, 145.
[32] The theory had important implications for gender dynamics. It gave the mother no credit for the developing embryo, beyond providing a moist, fertile environment. The theory lost credibility when microscopy failed to detect a curled-up figure in the sperm, and when advances in obstetrics and gynecology revealed that the embryo developed not from the sperm but from the fertilized ovum.
[33] Brentano (ed.), *The Life of the Blessed Virgin Mary*, 145.
[34] *Ibid.*, 146-147.
[35] *Ibid.*, 151.

36 *Ibid.*, 152.
37 *Ibid.*, 166.
38 *Ibid.*
39 *Ibid.*, 167.
40 *Ibid.*, 168.
41 *Ibid.*, 167-168.
42 *Ibid.*, 169.
43 He may simply have disliked the location, or perhaps there was real tension with his in-laws.
44 Brentano (ed.), *The Life of the Blessed Virgin Mary*, 170-171.
45 *Ibid.*, 192.
46 *Ibid.*, 188-189.
47 *Ibid.*, 196.
48 *Ibid.*, 196-197.
49 *Ibid.*, 200.
50 *Ibid.*, 198-199.
51 *Ibid.*, 199.
52 *Ibid.* There is some confusion about where Jesus was laid. Earlier Emmerich suggested that it was a stone drinking trough adjacent to the manger.
53 *Ibid.*, 200.
54 *Ibid.*, 201-202.
55 *Ibid.*, 212.
56 *Ibid.*, 220-221.
57 *Ibid.*, 221.
58 *Ibid.*, 234.
59 *Ibid.*, 224-225. The Star of Jacob may have been a comet, and the "virgin" may have been the constellation Virgo.
60 Emmerich confidently identified *three* Magi riding *camels*, even though neither fact is recorded in the canonical scriptures. She also gave the Magi royal status.
61 Brentano (ed.), *The Life of the Blessed Virgin Mary*, 260.
62 *Ibid.*, 203, 265.
63 *Ibid.*, 265-268.
64 *Ibid.*, 296-299.
65 *Ibid.*, 262-263, 282-283.
66 Carl E. Schmöger (ed.), *The Life of Jesus Christ and Biblical Revelations: From the Visions of Ven. Anne Catherine Emmerich*, vol. III (transl.: an American nun), Charlotte, NC: Tan Books, 1914/2011, 541.
67 Brentano (ed.), *The Life of the Blessed Virgin Mary*, 317.
68 *Ibid.*, 320.
69 *Ibid.*, 323-324.
70 *Ibid.*, 319.

Chapter 2. Mary According to Anne Catherine Emmerich

[71] *Ibid.*, 327.
[72] *Ibid.*, 353.
[73] *Ibid.*, 356.
[74] Schmöger (ed.), *The Life Jesus Christ and Biblical Revelations*, 330.
[75] Carl E. Schmöger (ed.), *The Life Jesus Christ and Biblical Revelations: From the Visions of Ven. Anne Catherine Emmerich*, vol. II (transl.: "an American nun"), Tan Books, 1914/2011, 54-55.
[76] *Ibid.*, 55. Italics in original.
[77] Carl E. Schmöger (ed.), *The Life Jesus Christ and Biblical Revelations: From the Visions of Ven. Anne Catherine Emmerich*, vol. IV (transl.: "an American nun"), Tan Books, 1914/2011, 42.
[78] *Ibid.*, 314.
[79] *Ibid.*, 326.
[80] *Ibid.*, 326-331.
[81] *Ibid.*, 338.
[82] *Ibid.*, 357.
[83] *Ibid.*, 364.
[84] *Ibid.*, 412.
[85] *Ibid.*, 430.
[86] Brentano (ed.), *The Life of the Blessed Virgin Mary*, 357. The editor comments that elsewhere Emmerich gave Mary's life after the Ascension as either thirteen or fourteen years "and two months."
[87] *Ibid.*, 360. Others too have suggested that the cross was in the shape of a "Y."
[88] *Ibid.*, 363. We are told later that her Way of the Cross had twelve stations, rather than the now-customary fourteen (p. 373).
[89] *Ibid.*, 362.
[90] The journey would have been long and hazardous for the aging Mary. The land route from Ephesus to Jerusalem is more than 1,100 miles (1,800 km). The sea route is somewhat shorter, but neither Ephesus nor Jerusalem is on the coast, so some overland travel was inevitable.
[91] Brentano (ed.), *The Life of the Blessed Virgin Mary*, 364-365.
[92] *Ibid.*, 383.
[93] *Ibid.*, 388-389.
[94] *Ibid.*, 390.

Mary: Adept, Queen, Mother, Priestess

Chapter 3
Mary in Early Christian Writings

Chapter 3 studies how Mary was remembered or envisioned by Christians in the early centuries of the Common Era. It sheds light on phases of her life that are not covered by the scriptural record. Virtually no contemporary records of Mary's life after Pentecost survive. But, as the centuries went by, a trickle and then a flood of literature focused on her life and ministry.

The texts paint a picture of Mary playing an active, leadership role in the Judaic Christian community of Jerusalem. Early Christian writers took considerable interest in the circumstances of Mary's death. The apostles were summoned to her bedside; finally, Christ himself came to take up her soul to heaven. Mary's body was buried, but several sources report that her tomb was subsequently found empty.

Not long after Mary's death Jerusalem was destroyed by the Roman army, and the local Christian community collapsed.

Introduction

The canonical gospels were written in the latter part of the first century CE, and most of the extracanonical scriptures cited in Chapter 1 shortly thereafter. The *Infancy Gospel of James*, which provided much of our information about the historical Mary, is believed to date from about 145 CE. The *Infancy Gospel of Thomas* was written no later than the second century. The *Gospel* (or *Questions*) *of Bartholomew* may date from the third or fourth century. The *Infancy Gospel of Matthew* contains earlier material, but it may not have taken final form until the seventh century. The *Qur'an* reportedly was revealed to Muhammad over a period of some two decades, ending with his death in 632, but it may not have been compiled into book form until about 650.

At least one independent historian commented on the new Christian movement as early as the first century CE, and others did so in the second. The second century also saw the beginning of theological speculation about Mary and the awakening of Marian devotion. The oldest surviving prayer addressed to Mary dates from the third century.

From the end of the fourth century, and continuing through the end of the first Christian millennium, a veritable flood of literature focused on Mary's life and death. Manuscripts have been found over a vast swath of the Christian world, in languages from Irish to Greek, to Ethiopic, to Old Georgian. A remarkable degree of coherence among the texts indicates that Christian communities at great distances from one another were familiar with, and interacted with, a well-developed biographical narrative.

Clearly that narrative built upon scripture, especially the *Infancy Gospel of James*. But the content relating to Mary's later years went far beyond what is recorded in canonical or extracanonical scripture. Source material—oral traditions or possibly lost manuscripts—supporting that expanded narrative must already have been in place.

Some of the texts provide accounts of Mary's childhood and early adulthood, even a detailed description of her person. Some record ecstatic experiences at the Crucifixion and the Resurrection. A whole body of literature addresses the events and circumstances leading up to and following Mary's death. While details may vary from text to text, we learn of miracles that occurred during her last days, including the arrival of Jesus' disciples from their missionary outposts around the Christian world. Finally we learn of the arrival of Christ himself, Mary's death and burial, and the discovery of her empty tomb. Spared decay, her body was transported to Paradise.

Much of this literature has come to light only in recent times, through the discovery of ancient manuscripts and the diligent work of textual scholars. Support for the textual evidence has also come from artwork, some dating back to the second century. Finally, archeological excavations in present-day Israel and the Palestinian territories are revealing valuable information about the first-century Christian community in which Mary lived and worked. New archeological discoveries are continually being reported, and significant findings soon color historical opinion.

Chapter 3. Mary in Early Christian Writings

The texts, and perhaps even more importantly the artwork, show that early Christians saw Mary in a very different light than people did later. They saw Mary carrying on Christ's ministry, including a sacramental ministry, after Pentecost and exercising a leadership role in the early church and helping to craft an emerging Christian liturgy.

Over the centuries, texts were redacted or altered, as manuscripts were copied or translated. The intent seems to have been to bring the records into line with the changing beliefs and expectations of writers, their religious superiors, and their communities. Instead of a strong religious leader, prominently involved in the liturgy, an increasingly patriarchal church wanted a model of passive, self-sacrificial devotion. Memories of Mary's priestly ministry were particularly "inconvenient." In the Church of Rome, efforts to eradicate such memories continued into the twentieth century.

Fortunately, the wide distribution of the ancient texts ensured their survival. Artwork supporting the narrative of Mary's ministry—much of it in media like mosaics—was even more durable. With the rediscovery and examination of these materials, an understanding of the original Mary has won broad support in academic circles, though not yet in the popular consciousness. Even in academia, debate continues on just how strong and influential Mary may have been. And not surprisingly scholars argue over the translation of ancient texts—or different versions of a single text.

This chapter identifies the main sources of information. It then offers a narrative of Mary's life and death that may be compared with the scriptural record in Chapter 1 and Anne Catherine Emmerich's visionary biography in Chapter 2.

The Sources

The Early Centuries

The Jewish historian Titus Flavius Josephus (37–c.100), generally known simply as Josephus, kept detailed records of events in first-century Palestine. His *Antiquities of the Jews* (c.94 CE) contains one reference to the imprisonment and death of John the Baptist and at least one authentic but oblique reference to Jesus. The latter states that the Jewish Sanhedrim summoned "before them the brother of Jesus, who was called Christ, whose name was James."[1] This James, who features in our story, was known as "James the Just," possibly distinguished from "James the Less," son of Alphaeus, and almost certainly distinguished from "James the Great(er)," son of Zebedee.

A second reference to Jesus in *Antiquities of the Jews* is thought to be authentic at its core but to have been embellished by later Christian interpolation. It reads:

> Now there was about this time Jesus, a wise man, if it be lawful to call him a man; for he was a doer of wonderful works, a teacher of such men as receive the truth with pleasure. He drew over to him both many of the Jews and many of the Gentiles. He was [the] Christ. And when Pilate, at the suggestion of the principal men amongst us, had condemned him to the cross, those that loved him at the first did not forsake him; for he appeared to them alive again the third day; as the divine prophets had foretold these and ten thousand other wonderful things concerning him. And the tribe of Christians, so named from him, are not extinct at this day.[2]

Other writers mentioned Christianity as it spread beyond Palestine. For example the Roman historian Tacitus (c.56–c.120) spoke of Christians in Rome during the 60s CE and even related them to the historical Jesus. The Great Fire of Rome occurred in 64 CE, and the Emperor Nero is widely believed to have started the fire himself. But according to Tacitus, who made no secret of his own views on Christianity, Nero blamed Christians for the fire and unleashed a reign of terror: "Nero fastened the guilt and inflicted the most exquisite tortures on a class hated for their abominations, called Christians by the populace. Christus, from whom the name had its origin."[3] Tacitus noted that Pontius Pilate put Jesus to death, but the execution had failed to stop the "most mischievous superstition," and it had spread to Rome. He went on to describe the gruesome ways in which Christians were put to death during Nero's purge.

Writing a few years earlier than Tacitus, another Roman writer, Pliny the Younger (61–c.113), mentioned the Christians of the early second century. In his capacity as provincial governor and magistrate of Bithynia-Pontus, in Asia Minor, Pliny wrote to the Emperor Trajan seeking guidance on how to deal with Christians brought before his court for refusing to worship the state gods. He conceded that their practices seemed innocuous: they met in groups, sang hymns to Christ, and shared ritual meals. But he spoke of the Christians as a cult, called their beliefs "superstitious," and was concerned that they might be seditious.[4] In his reply Trajan offered advice for dealing

Chapter 3. Mary in Early Christian Writings

with the cases but did not encourage any widespread persecution of Christians—as Nero had done, and as other emperors would do later.

A significant source relating to the early church is the *Ecclesiastical History* by Eusebius, bishop of Caesarea (c.262–c.340). Naturally his work contained none of the anti-Christian rhetoric of Tacitus. Eusebius wrote from a Greek Christian perspective. On the other hand, like many of his contemporaries and later Christian writers, he had an anti-Semitic bias.

The first textual references to Mary, outside scripture, comes from two theologians. In about 155 CE, Church father Justin Martyr portrayed Mary as the Second Eve.[5] Soon thereafter Irenaeus, bishop of Lyon, in Roman Gaul, contrasted Eve's disobedience with Mary's willingness to become the mother of Christ.[6] These comments will be examined in more detail in Chapter 4.

An early third-century theological work refers to Christ's "advent by the spotless and God-bearing Mary."[7] The comment is significant because "God-bearer" translates the Greek *Theotokos*, rendered in the West as "Mother of God." It represented a major development in Mariology that would play out over the next several centuries. Again, it will be discussed further in Chapter 4. Mary was also addressed as *Theotokos* in a mid-third century intercessory prayer, discovered in Egypt.[8]

This was a time when the idea of praying to Mary was first gaining momentum. A hymn by Ephrem the Syrian (306–373) hints at her intercessory role: "Hear the benedictions given to Him in the Church by the Cherubim, and the blandishments of the Virgin Mother. In the chariot appears his vehement Majesty, in Mary His love. The Cherubim bless Him with trembling. The Maiden, because she is His Mother, love."[9] We almost sense tension, explored later in the Middle Ages, between a judgmental God and a merciful Mary.

Archeology has provided little definitive information about Mary. As noted in Chapter 1, excavations demonstrated that Nazareth was a small, relative unimportant village in the first century CE. But the interpretation of archeological evidence is often controversial. For instance, claims that the Talpiot Tomb in Jerusalem was the burial chamber of Jesus, Mary, and several family members[10] currently are rejected by a majority of archeologists, historians, and biblical scholars. Discovery of a house in Ephesus, where Anne Catherine Emmerich claimed that Mary lived, has to be balanced against the consensus view of the ancient texts that Mary died in or near Jerusalem.

More definitive information comes from artwork. Styles of dress, gestures by the principal figure, the identity and placement of supporting figures, and the depiction of symbolic objects all provide insights into how Mary was perceived by artists and their sponsors.

Life of the Virgin

The first complete biography of Mary was *Life of the Virgin*, which scholars attribute, with various degrees of confidence, to Maximus the Confessor (c.580–662). Here, for convenience, we shall assume his authorship, without intruding on their debate.

Maximus, also known as Maximus of Constantinople, served as a senior aide to the Byzantine Emperor Heraclius but eventually left public service to become a monk. Maximus is remembered as a scholar and theologian of the Eastern Church. He promoted the doctrine of *theosis*, or "deification," which eventually gained a place in Eastern Orthodox teachings.[11] Sadly, Maximus was falsely charged with heresy on another matter, was tortured and mutilated at the hands of the Byzantine emperor, and died in exile in present-day Georgia.

Life of the Virgin was originally written in Greek, but it survives only in eleven manuscripts in Old Georgian, some mere fragments. Translation into Old Georgian most likely occurred after his death. The work is now available in English translation, and all citations are taken therefrom.[12]

Life of the Virgin is a compilation of older accounts of Mary, including passages from the canonical and extracanonical scriptures; it draws heavily on the *Infancy Gospel of James*, for information concerning her birth and childhood, and upon texts in the Dormition tradition to be discussed shortly. Some of his sources are known, others not.

In addition to describing events in Mary's life and death in a more-or-less factual way, Maximus reflected at length on the more poignant incidents. Some sections of the text resemble prayers or meditations. For example, Maximus began with an appeal to people of all nations and stations in life to join him in a hymn of praise and glory to "the

Chapter 3. Mary in Early Christian Writings

all-holy immaculate, and most blessed Theotokos and ever-virgin Mary."[13]

Maximus bestowed on Mary a litany of accolades that included "the throne of the kind, more exalted than the cherubim and seraphim," "the Paradise of the tree of life," and "the urn of gold that received the manna of immortality."[14] The phrase "More honorable than the Cherubim, and beyond compare more glorious than the Seraphim" is also found in the "Hymn to the Theotokos" from the Liturgy of St John Chrysostom,[15] which dates from the fifth century, and in a prayer attributed to Peter of Damascus in the eleventh.

Maximus assured readers that his biography was guided by a number of principles:

> Now then everything that we will relate and make known is trustworthy and reliable, true testimonies taken from the assembly of the pious: first of all, from the holy evangelists and apostles; then from the holy and deeply devout Fathers, whose words are full of all wisdom and were written by the grace of the Holy Spirit.... And if we say some things from the apocryphal writings, this is true and without error, and it is what has been accepted and confirmed by the above-mentioned Fathers.[16]

That was an accurate description of what he wrote. His objective was to produce a biography that would accord with scripture and with the teachings of the "pious" and the "deeply devout fathers." In some cases words from a much later time were put into Mary's mouth, so she would support church teachings at the time *Life* was written.

Maximus ended *Life of the Virgin* with a multi-page litany of praise addressed to Mary, explaining what he had tried to accomplish. Part of it reads:

> Such are, O all-holy queen Theotokos, the mysteries of your glorious life. These are the story of your going forth, the hymn of your Dormition, the glory before your Dormition, the praise of your burial, and the wonders of your glorious translation. And now, O all-praised and glorified queen Theotokos, receive these humble words of your praise and glory given to you by your incapable and unworthy servant, which I have spoken according to my ability with faith and desire for your grace.[17]

Legends of Our Lady Mary

Another important source is E. A. Wallis Budge's *Legends of Our Lady Mary the Perpetual Virgin and her Mother Hanna* (1922).[18] It contains Ethiopian texts that found their way to the British Museum during times of colonial expansion. They were edited and compiled by Budge (1857–1934), a celebrated Egyptologist with numerous publications of his own.

Included in the collection are texts attributed to early Christian writers, such as "John the Son of Zebedee," "Bartholomew the Apostle," and Epiphanius (c.315–403), bishop of Salamis, Cyprus. Most of them are probably pseudepigraphical. Pseudepigraphy, in which a text is falsely attributed to a famous figure of the past, was a common literary device in ancient times. The intent might have been to honor the earlier figure, to ensure wide readership, or to provide cover for the real author.

Scholars believe that some of the texts may have been written as late at the sixteenth century. Yet all clearly came from an earlier tradition. We should note that the Ethiopian church is one of the oldest in Christendom, and it flourished free from much of the turmoil that rocked other parts of the Christian world. Moreover, some of the content is not found elsewhere, including descriptions of Mary's person and an ecstatic experience at the foot of the cross. "Legends" was a conservative term chosen by the editor to promote the book in the scholarly culture of his time and does not necessarily imply that the texts are any less believable than other sources.

The Dormition Literature

The Dormition literature consists of manuscripts that describe the end of Mary's life. Manuscripts of this genre have been discovered in many parts of the Christian world and in a variety of languages. Many of them are copies, translations or revisions of a smaller number of earlier texts. In one case, more than 100 manuscripts are derivatives of a single text.

One theory—tantalizing in its implications—is that a single proto-text existed from which *all* the Dormition manuscripts were derived; some scholars have suggested that such a text might date back to the second century. An alternative theory is that an oral tradition developed at an even earlier date, perhaps in apostolic times, and the texts and manuscripts we know of were based thereon. In any event, the narrative that emerges from the texts and manuscripts is sufficiently coherent that we can gain a good understanding of the events surrounding the end of Mary's life.

The most complete Dormition manuscript is a palimpsest in Old Syriac, dated reliably to the late fifth century.[19] A *palimpsest* is a manuscript overwritten by a later text, in this particular case overwritten in the ninth century. Scottish Semitic scholar Agnes Smith Lewis acquired the manuscript in Egypt in 1895 and published her translation of the undertext seven years later. The portion of interest to us is titled *Transitus Mariae* ("The Death of Mary").

The *Transitus* includes a statement attributed to James, bishop of Jerusalem and "called the brother of Jesus." James allegedly stated that the apostles "still living and those who were buried" assembled at the Dormition and agreed to write about Mary and her experiences: "[S]ix books were written about her (two of the apostles wrote each book) and all the signs and wonders and glories from heaven and from the earth which happened before her."[20]

The earliest Greek Dormition text is attributed to "John the Theologian and Evangelist." Textual clues reveal Gnostic influence, suggesting an early date for the text—or more probably the sources from which it was compiled—because the Gnostics were almost totally suppressed by the fourth century. It is of considerable importance to our story.

Interest in the Dormition literature increased substantially in the eighteenth century, when the Church of Rome sought support for the doctrine of Mary's Assumption, though the dogmatic decree was not actually issued until 1950. Study of the Dormition literature continues today because of its historical and theological significance.

Other Sources and Modern Scholarship

In addition to the major works mentioned above, several other texts are cited herein. We cannot assume that all the surviving texts have now been catalogued and analyzed. Previously unknown ones are continually being discovered, and existing ones are being reexamined, retranslated or reinterpreted. Some scholars are interested simply because this is a traditionally neglected area of Christian history. But much of the interest comes from feminist theologians and others looking for evidence of women's leadership roles in the early church, including Mary's own role.

Notable for its work is the Wijngaards Institute for Catholic Research, an international network of academics, most of them Roman Catholics.[21] An important product was Ally Kateusz's book *Mary and Early Christian Women* (2019. Kateusz, a cultural historian, has also written a number of journal articles, one of which is cited herein.

Mary from Childhood to Adulthood

Maximus the Confessor waxed eloquently on Mary's demeanor as a young person, commenting in *Life of the Virgin* that she was an excellent student, "an expert in every good subject and filled with understanding of the divine scriptures and with all wisdom, because she was to become the mother of the Word and Wisdom of God."[22] The title "Wisdom of God" merits some attention; it suggests an association with Sophia of the Wisdom Literature of Hellenic Judaism. The possible relationship between Mary and Sophia will be explored later in the book.

Legends of Our Lady Mary provides one of the few accounts of the death of Mary's mother Hannah. According to *Legends*, Hannah died while Mary was still in the temple:

> Now all these things concerning the death of Hannah took place whilst our Lady Mary was in the sanctuary. And they told her that Hannah her mother had died, and when our Lady Mary heard it, she wept and said, "Woe is me! Woe is me! My mother hath left me a sorrowful woman. Woe is me! Woe is me! O mother, who will be unto me like thee? Unto whom hast thou left me? Woe is me, O my mother! O daughters of Israel, come ye and weep for me and cast ye me not away; for I am an only daughter, and I have none (to take her place). Come, O Jeremiah, and make a lamentation for my mother Hannah, for she hath forsaken me, and I am alone in the house of brass. Who will pour water upon my hands? And the tears start in my eyes."[23]

The timing of Hannah's death seems to be controversial. A modern source, cited in Chapter 6, supports the claim of Hannah's early death. By contrast, Anne Catherine Emmerich testified that Hannah and her second husband hosted the wedding of Mary and Joseph.

Chapter 3. Mary in Early Christian Writings

Emmerich also testified that Mary was not an only child but had an older sister, Maria Heli.

Life of the Virgin asserts that Mary completed her term in the temple when she was twelve. Joseph was chosen to be her husband, and Maximus commented that the latter "was then more than seventy years old, so that no one could raise any suspicions whatsoever of marriage."[24] We may draw whatever conclusions we wish from that comment, but it may support the belief that Mary remained a virgin after Jesus' birth

According to *Legends of Our Lady Mary* the Annunciation took place "twelve years after she [Mary] had left her mother's house"—that is, when Mary was fifteen years old. After the Archangel Gabriel departed, Mary pondered: "Can it be true what my mother Hannah spake unto me? For she said unto me, 'The Son of God shall be born of thee.'"[25] Before she passed away, Hannah evidently had alerted Mary to what lay ahead. We recall that Anne Catherine Emmerich spoke of a sign borne by successive members of the female bloodline, indicating that one of them would bear the Messiah.

Maximus' account of the Annunciation, Visitation and Nativity follows the pattern described in scripture. Mary gave birth to Jesus in a cave in Bethlehem. Maximus placed Elizabeth at the birth, and it was she and not midwives who attested to Mary's continued virginity.[26] The shepherds came, and then the Magi. A remarkable interpretation of the visit of the Magi is found in a mosaic in the Basilica of Sant'Apollinare Nuovo in Ravenna, Italy. The Byzantine-style mosaic, believed to date from the period 560–620, shows the Madonna and Child, enthroned and flanked by four angels. Approaching from the left are the three Magi followed by a procession of twenty-two virgins bearing offerings.[27]

Jesus was circumcised eight days after his birth. After forty days, Mary and Joseph presented Jesus in the temple, where Simeon and Anna offered their prophecies. Maximus stated—supporting what Anne Catherine Emmerich would testify a millennium later—that the flight into Egypt occurred "just before the second year or a little later." He commented revealingly: "For this is the custom of the Scripture; events that took place much later are joined with things that took place earlier."[28]

Maximus dismissed the account of the young Jesus' miracles—and mischief—recorded in the *Infancy Gospel of Thomas* as "alien to the Church ... and an adversary of truth that was composed by some foolish men and storytellers."[29] *Life of the Virgin* describes the trip to Jerusalem, when Jesus was twelve years old, and then moves to the Baptism and the Wedding Feast in Cana.

Maximus explained Mary's remark to Jesus: "They have no wine," thus: "the desire of her heart revealed that she wanted to see his working of miracles, because she knew that he was the creator of all things." Maximus defended Jesus' response: "Woman, what is that to me," suggesting that "he honored her as a mother and yielded to the desire of her heart."[30] We also learn that during Jesus' ministry, "the holy mother went with him as much as was possible, seeing the miracles and hearing the teachings."[31]

Legends of Our Lady Mary credits Epiphanius, Bishop of Salamis, with a very detailed description of the adult Mary:

> She was grave and dignified in all her actions. She spoke little and only when it was necessary to do so. She listened readily and could be addressed easily. She paid honor and respect (i.e. she saluted) everyone. She was of middle stature, but some say that she was of more than middle height. She was wont to speak to every one fearlessly and clearly, without laughter, and without agitation, and she was specially slow to anger.
>
> Her complexion was of the color of ripe wheat, and her hair was auburn (or reddish). Her eyes were bright and keen, and light brown in color, and the pupils thereof were of an olive-green tint. Her eyebrows were arched (or semicircular) and deep black. Her nose was long, her lips were red and full, and overflowing with the sweetness of her words. Her face was not round, but somewhat oblong (i.e. oval). Her hand was long and her fingers were long. She was wholly free from all ostentatious pride, and she was simple, unpretentious, and inclined to excessive humility. She wore garments of natural colors (i.e. undyed homespun), and was content with them, a fact which is even now proved by her holy headcloth. And to sum up, she was filled with divine grace in all her ways.[32]

A text in the same collection, by a different author, offers forty-two "salutations" to the parts of Mary's body. The author must have medi-

Chapter 3. Mary in Early Christian Writings

tated and fantasized for a considerable time to encompass her from head to toe. Number 22 is as follows:

> Salutation to thine arms, and to thy forearms, and to thy bosom wherewith thou hast embraced Christ, the Pearl of the Godhead, the Hidden One. O Mary, thou chosen one, our Mother of angels and men, if the sinner celebrates the commemoration of thee in firm faith let him reign with thee in the kingdom of heaven.[33]

A Coptic text of unknown authorship paints a fanciful picture of Mary, from her temple years into adulthood. It claims that her clothes miraculously expanded to fit her as she grew up, never needed to be washed, and never wore out "until the day of her death." Presumably fashions did not change over time, or even from childhood to adulthood. The same text then assures us:

> Mary did not ever adorn herself, nor did she seek after outward shows as women do. She never painted her eyes, nor put saffron on her cheeks, nor ever plaited her hair. She never washed in a bath. She did not put choice perfume upon her, nor did she anoint her body with ointment. She did not wash with water.[34]

In *Life of the Virgin* Maximus the Confessor offered a description of a different kind, perhaps foreseeing the heights to which Mary would be elevated in future centuries:

> She is dressed in beauty and clothed with power ... for as the queen of all, she holds authority over all things, and from one end of the earth to the other end, all things submit to her and glorify her, for she reigns with her son and king and will reign especially in the last days when the end and conclusion of this fleeting world will take place.[35]

From everything we know Mary was highly exalted in consciousness. We can only join those commentators in speculating to what extent her consciousness shone through the physical form of the daughter of Hannah and Joachim.

Mary and the Passion and Death of Jesus

Maximus the Confessor' account of the events of Holy Week included a reflection on Mary's leadership role among Jesus' female disciples:

[Mary] was always inseparable from her Lord and king and son. And she held authority: as the Lord did over the twelve disciples then the seventy, so did the holy mother over the other women who accompanied him. As the holy gospel says: "There were many women who followed Jesus from Galilee and provided for him" (Matt 27:05). The holy Theotokos was the leader and director of them all.[36]

The very next sentence in *Life of the Virgin* refers to the Last Supper: specifically to a ritual sacrifice offered immediately prior to institution of the Eucharist. The passage has potentially far-reaching implications, but its translation is contested. The translation by Stephen Shoemaker, on whose work we have generally relied, indicates that Jesus made the offering. An earlier French translation by the Jesuit scholar Michel van Esbroeck, finally translated into English by Ally Kateusz, indicates that Mary did. The two translations are shown here side by side:

Shoemaker	Van Esbroeck/Kateusz
For this reason, when the mysterious and glorious supper took place, *and he sacrificed himself as a priest and was sacrificed, he offered and was offered*, at that time the Lord Jesus took care of the twelve disciples and whomever else he wished, and he gave them the exalted mysteries, the signs of the divine Passover. By the bread and the cup he gave his precious body and blood.[37]	For this reason, when the great mystery, the supper, took place, *she sacrificed herself as the priest and was sacrificed; she offered and was offered*. Then, the Lord Jesus presided over the twelve apostles and those he wanted, and he delivered the sublime mysteries and signs of God's Passover, he gave them some of his precious body and blood as the bread and the drink.[38]

Mary's performance of a sacrificial ritual at the Last Supper would be enormously important; it might imply that she played a role in the institution of the Eucharist and perhaps an even greater role in the Redemption than previously thought. Unfortunately, the scholarly debate is unlikely to be resolved any time soon. We understand that Old Georgian does not always distinguish between masculine and feminine pronouns. The translators used different manuscripts of *The*

Life of the Virgin, responded to different contextual clues, and interpreted the sentence structure differently.[39] Commendably they disclosed their biases, but they also stoutly defended their respective positions.

Kateusz argued her case in more detail in an article whose title mirrored the contested text: "She Sacrificed Herself as the Priest."[40] Citing "a Second Temple Jewish community where the impulse toward gender parity was strong"[41] Kateusz asserted that the joint participation of Mary and Jesus in the ritual of the Last Supper would not have been surprising at that time. She also pointed to later artwork depicting men and women concelebrating the Eucharist. For example, parallel mosaics in the Basilica of St Vitale at Ravenna, Italy, show the Emperor Justinian I holding the paten and the Empress Theodora holding the chalice.[42]

Life of the Virgin continues with an account of Jesus' betrayal, trial, and Crucifixion. As Jesus' life drew to a close, Mary, the *Mater Dolorosa*, stood at the foot of the cross. Maximus pondered her sorrow (in Shoemaker's translation):

> [I]t is neither in our power nor anyone else's power to describe the holy Virgin's sufferings and tears and groanings of her heart at each moment, for they are beyond nature, and as her birthing was beyond nature, so also her sorrow.... But she who suffers alone knows, and she alone completely understands the Lord who was born from her.... How did the immaculate mother endure the pain? How did she not give up her spirit as well?[43]

The "Homily of John the Son of Zebedee," one of the texts in *Legends of Our Lady Mary*, relates that Mary had an ecstatic experience at the cross. Later she shared her experience with John, who had stood with her:

> Hearken and I will tell thee an astounding and hidden mystery, which cannot be known by the heart (or mind) and cannot be comprehended by the understanding, which my Lord and my Son, Jesus Christ my beloved one and my Redeemer, revealed unto me at Golgotha, at the time of the sixth hour, which is noon, on the day of the Eve of the Sabbath. A shining cloud came and bore me along and took me up into the third heaven, and it set me down at the boundary of the earth, and my Son appeared unto me. And He said unto me, "Peace be unto thee, O Mary, My mother, thou

dwelling-place of God. Peace be unto thee, O virgin, who gavest birth to Me. From thy womb hath gone forth the river of peace. I will reveal unto thee an astounding wonder."

And I made answer to Him and said unto Him, "My Lord and my God! O my Son and my King, let it be as Thou wishest." And He answered and said unto me, "Look down on the earth below." And I looked and saw, and the whole world was like a thing of nothing, and the children of men were as naught.... And then I saw fourteen shining angels with the wood of the Cross in their hands, and on their breasts was the sign of the Cross of the Son of God, and in their hands were golden censers. And they came down to meet the soul of a righteous man, and angels of light came and angels of darkness" .... And they went out and surrounded it, and the angels crowned it with light, and they shook that soul thrice that they might carry it away from its body. And they said unto it, " Come, come forth, thou soul, in peace. Rejoice thou, O pure and bright soul, and be glad."[44]

Mary continued at length, describing, among much else, visiting Paradise, where she was greeted by Moses and the prophets as well as by Eve and the holy women Sara, Rebecca and Rachel.

Maximus took up his story in *Life of the Virgin* after Jesus "gave up the ghost." When the body of Jesus was taken down from the cross, Mary "washed away the blood with her tears." Then she broke into a kind of canticle capturing the enormity of what had happened. It began: "Oh, completion of the tremendous mystery! Oh revelation of counsels hidden for centuries. Oh death more wonderful than the wonderful Incarnation! The creator of all souls lies inanimate, the one who gives life to all lies dead. The Word of the Father is speechless."[45]

According to Maximus, Mary kept watch at the sepulcher: "[T]he Immaculate Mother was inseparable from the tomb, and she was watching and listening to everything that was happening and being said."[46] If true, it explains who Mary Magdalene's companion was in the passage in *Matthew*: "[T]here was Mary Magdalene, and the other Mary, sitting over against the sepulcher."[47] *Matthew*'s author—who omitted to mention that the mother of Jesus was present at the cross—could go no farther than acknowledge that "the other Mary" kept vigil at the tomb of her crucified son who had just redeemed the world.

Chapter 3. Mary in Early Christian Writings

That issue aside, Maximus went on to state that Mary was "a witness to everything until she saw even his glorious Resurrection." The other women did not understand what they were seeing. "Only the immaculate mother of the Lord standing there knew everything. And because of this, she received the good news of the Resurrection before anyone else, and before anyone else she became worthy of the ... divinely beautiful vision of her Lord and son."[48]

Legends of Our Lady Mary contains an ecstatic account of the Resurrection attributed to "Bartholomew the Apostle":

> Christ Himself, when He rose from the dead and appeared to her and the other women at the tomb mounted on the chariot of the Father of the Universe, cried out, saying ... "All Paradise rejoiceth in thee. I say unto thee, O My Mother, He who loveth thee loveth Life. Hail, thou who didst sustain the Life of the Universe in thy womb! .... I will give My peace, which I have received from My Holy Father, to My disciples, and to every one who shall believe in My Name and in Mary."
>
> And round and about Him there were standing hundreds of thousands of Archangels, and hundreds of thousands of the Cherubim, and millions of the Seraphim, and millions of the Powers, and their heads were bowed, and they made answer to the blessing, saying, "Amen, Hallelujah," to that which the Son did speak with His mouth to Mary. Then our Savior stretched out His right hand, which was full of blessing, and He blessed the womb of Mary, His Mother. And I [Bartholomew] saw the heavens open, and the Seven Firmaments were opened together. I saw a man of light shining brightly, like unto a pearl upon which it was impossible for any man to look. And (I saw) also a hand of fire which was of the color of snow, and it rested upon the belly of Mary and (her) breast. Now this hand was the right hand of the Father, and the right hand of the Son, and the right hand of the Holy Ghost.[49]

Mary's Post-Pentecostal Ministry

Mary in the Christian Community of Jerusalem

Between the Resurrection and the Ascension, "the Lord appeared to his holy mother many times"—more, Maximus the Confessor noted, than he did to his disciples. *Life of the Virgin* relates that Mary took up residence with John the Beloved in his house on Mount Zion in

Jerusalem. That would be consistent with the comment in *John*: "from that hour that disciple took her unto his own home."[50] Interestingly, from then on Maximus referred to John, not simply by name or as "the beloved disciple," but as "John the Evangelist" or "John the Theologian."[51] Evidently he was drawing upon a different set of source documents.

The New Testament records that Mary, other women, and Jesus' disciples gathered in the upper room at Pentecost.[52] Pentecost was a traditional Jewish feast, also known as the Festival of Weeks,[53] and the people who gathered that day were observant Jews. They observed Mosaic Law and took the words of Jesus seriously: "Think not that I am come to destroy the law, or the prophets: I am not come to destroy, but to fulfill."[54] On other days they worshipped in the temple and synagogues.

We may describe Jesus' followers as "Christians" and speak of the "church" of Jerusalem. But *church* (Greek: *ekklesia*) was a later projection back onto was a community of Jews distinguished from the larger Jewish population by their belief that Jesus was the Messiah, "the Anointed One," "the Christ." They formed a new Jewish sect, referring to themselves as followers of "The Way," probably a reference to *Isaiah*: "Prepare ye the way of the Lord."[55] The term *Christian* was not used until about 41 CE, and then in Antioch.[56] *Christianity* was coined by Ignatius of Antioch at the beginning of the second century.

After Pentecost, the New Testament tells us, the disciples were filled with the Holy Spirit and set out to bring the good news to people in the Roman Empire and beyond. But not everyone left Jerusalem. Mary and others remained in the city. Maximus the Confessor declared "[W]hen the apostles were dispersed to the entire world, the holy mother of Christ, as the queen of all, was dwelling at the center of the whole world."[57]

Mary pursued her post-Pentecostal ministry in what must have been a vibrant community of Judaic Christians in Jerusalem. She was in every way a Jewish woman. Mary was born into a Jewish family, raised in the temple, and probably followed traditional observances throughout her life; doubtless she "kept kosher." Her training in the temple, her unique experience of giving birth to Jesus, and perhaps the authority that came from higher consciousness gave her a position

Chapter 3. Mary in Early Christian Writings

of prominence, recognized by the disciples and others, and placed her in a leadership role in the community.

Life of the Virgin explains that Mary "was not only an inspiration and a teacher of endurance and ministry to the blessed apostles and the other believers, she was also a co-minister with the disciples of the Lord. She helped with the preaching, and she shared mentally in their struggles and torments and imprisonments."[58] Evidently Jesus' disciples sought Mary's counsel on return visits to the city. Texts and artwork testify that Mary was afforded special reverence by the disciples—and followers of her own—who prostrated themselves before her to receive her blessing.

In addition to preaching and offering pastoral care, Mary performed priestly roles that spanned Judaic tradition and the newly emerging Christian liturgy. An early third-century fresco in the Priscilla Catacombs of Rome shows a woman, most likely Mary, vested in liturgical robes (Figure 3.1). Even though the image was created far from Palestine, the figure is wearing a *Tallit*, or Judaic prayer shawl. Her hands are raised in blessing, a gesture used by Jewish temple priests, inspired by the psalmist's words: "Let my prayer be set forth in your sight as incense, the lifting up of my hands as the evening sacrifice."[59]

Figure 3.1

Centerpiece of an early third-century fresco in the Priscilla Catacombs, Rome. It shows a woman—most likely Mary—vested in ceremonial robes, including a *Tallit*, or Jewish prayer shawl. Her hands are raised in the "Evening Sacrifice" blessing.

Incidents will be discussed shortly in which Mary offered incense, another traditional priestly role. Mary, who grew up in the temple, no doubt continued to use familiar liturgical practices, which would have resonated with members of the Jerusalem community. Yet new practices were emerging too. We shall also see that Mary performed baptisms, healed the sick, and cast out demons.

Mary would not have been referred to as an "elder" in the Judaic Christian community of Jerusalem. That term (Greek: *presbyteros*, *presbytera*, masculine and feminine) became popular only later in the first century, as Christianity moved away from Palestine into a Greco-Roman environment.[60] Mary would have been called a "priestess" (Hebrew: *koheneth*;[61] Greek: *hiereia*), even the "high priestess." She would have been recognized as following in a long line of priestesses and prophetesses of Judaic tradition.[62]

According to the *Acts of the Apostles*, the Jerusalem community functioned as a kind of spiritual commune in which everything was shared:

> And all that believed were together, and had all things common; And sold their possessions and goods, and parted them to all men, as every man had need. And they, continuing daily with one accord in the temple, and breaking bread from house to house, did eat their meat with gladness and singleness of heart, Praising God, and having favor with all the people. And the Lord added to the church daily such as should be saved.[63]

We recall that Mary spoke out against social, economic and political inequalities in the *Magnificat*. The sharing that took place within the Jerusalem community was consistent with, and perhaps was even inspired by, Mary's own ideals.

Life of the Virgin mentions John's "departure," presumably to Ephesus. Thereafter, care of Mary fell to "the blessed James the son of Joseph, who was called the brother of the Lord on account of his great virtue" and who "became the first bishop of Jerusalem."[64] This seems to have been James the Just: the James who spoke at the Council of Jerusalem and who was mentioned by Josephus, though Maximus was more cautious than Josephus in depicting his relationship to Jesus. The identification of James as a "bishop" (Greek: *episkopos*) was clearly retroactive; that terminology arose in the second century—in Greco-Roman Christianity.

Few contemporary records of the Judaic Christianity of James survive. The days of the Jerusalem community were numbered, and Christianity would soon take a new direction, with little concern for either the liturgical traditions or social principles the community embraced.

Mary's Last Years

The various sources disagreed on how long Mary lived after the death of her son. The seventh- or eighth-century writer Hippolytus of Thebes claimed that Mary lived for eleven years after the death of Jesus.[65] Anne Catherine Emmerich gave her a total of fifteen years.[66] Other texts gave her as many as thirty years. According to *The Life of the Virgin*, Mary remained "in the world many years, so that the believers would be greatly strengthened by her grace .... [T]he queen of all creatures was approaching the eightieth year of this fleeting life." Even in her old age, however, "she did not cease in her devotions or her good works."[67]

Among those good works, Mary made daily visits to the sepulcher where Jesus had been laid after the Crucifixion. Both the *Transitus Mariae* and a related text known as *The Ethiopic Six Books*, claim that those visits were made at some danger to herself, since the Jews wanted to keep her away or even wanted to kill her. In the latter text, the Jews threatened Mary, complaining: "[B]ecause of the one who was born from her, the temple was destroyed."[68] The threat may have been real, or the story may simply be an example of anti-Semitic rhetoric typical of Christian writings of the period.

The *Transitus Mariae* reports that on one of her visits to the sepulcher:

> [S]he was carrying sweet spices and fire. And while she was praying and had lifted up her eyes and gazed to heaven, suddenly the doors of heaven were opened and a scent of myrrh went up, which the Lady Mary had thrown on the censer, and its odor went about all the regions of heaven. And in that hour came Gabriel the angel to her from heaven, and knelt to worship her; and he said to her: "Hail to thee, mother of God! thy prayer has been accepted to heaven before thy Son, our Lord Jesus Christ. And therefore thou shalt depart from this world unto life everlasting."[69]

The visit of the Archangel Gabriel and his prophecy of Mary's impending death will be discussed in due course. Meanwhile, the reference to incense—just one of several in the texts—calls for immediate comment. Incense played a prominent role in Jewish temple rituals, and Malachi had correctly prophesied its continued use beyond Judaism: "For from the rising of the sun even unto the going down of the same my name shall be great among the Gentiles; and in every place incense shall be offered unto my name, and a pure offering."[70] Perhaps the writers wanted to emphasize Mary's priestly status in a church where, by the fifth and later centuries, women were rarely seen in clerical roles.

On another occasion the *Transitus* palimpsest relates that Mary asked her attendants: 'Bring nigh unto me the censers of incense, for I wish to pray to my Master the Christ whom I have in heaven.'"[71] *The Ethiopic Six Books* mentions yet another occasion, possibly filling a gap in the palimpsest record. It reads thus: "The Blessed Mary summoned the virgin women and said to them: 'Bring incense and clothing so that I may make an offering to God.'"[72] "Clothing" probably meant ritual vestments.

The Ethiopic Six Books records that Mary asked Christ's blessing on the virgins: "[M]ay he bless these virgins who have come with me in order to minister to me, because of all the people of Israel, there is no one who had followed me except for them."[73] It adds, however, that other people came to Mary, seeking a blessing:

> [M]any men and women came to Mary, and they prostrated themselves before her, saying, "Have mercy on us and forgive us, and do not cast us away, O master." And the Blessed One, having extended her arms, blessed them and said, "May the Lord receive your prayer and your petition before the Lord Jesus Christ."[74]

Mary in Bethlehem

Several early texts attest that Mary moved from Jerusalem to Bethlehem, a distance of about six miles, or nine kilometers. They explain that she felt pressure to move because the authorities in Jerusalem were becoming concerned about the attention she was receiving in the capital. Other early texts do not mention that concern and keep Mary in Jerusalem throughout the period.

A separate tradition developed in the ninth century that she spent her final days in Ephesus, a city in Asia Minor, nearly 1,000 miles or 1,700 km, away.[75] Anne Catherine Emmerich also placed Mary in Ephesus. Based at least in part on Emmerich's visions, the ruins of a

Chapter 3. Mary in Early Christian Writings

house in Ephesus were identified, and the restored building has become a pilgrimage destination. Yet none of the early texts supports that tradition.

The Ethiopic Six Books states that the Archangel Gabriel appeared to Mary and said: "O Theotokos! Arise and go to Bethlehem, and remain there until you see armies of angels, the apostles, and every creature coming to you to pray to you and proclaim you blessed."[76] Mary's departure for Bethlehem, with several "virgins" who ministered to her, is also recorded in the *Transitus Mariae*.

The length of time Mary spent in Bethlehem varies substantially from one text to another. Some suggest that she took to her bed immediately upon arrival and passed away within a few days. Others suggest that she lived and worked there for months or even years, performing many remarkable deeds.

The *Transitus* palimpsest is one of the latter. It relates that, while in Bethlehem, Mary taught, healed the sick, baptized, and cast out demons. High-ranking women came, "year by year," from Rome, Athens, Alexandria, and other "distant regions" seeking counsel and healing.

One group of women asked her: 'Tell us, O Lady, mistress of the world, how our Lord Jesus the Christ was born of thee without intercourse with man' And the Lady Mary told them everything that they sought from her."[77] Evidently Mary felt comfortable speaking to the women about the Nativity, whereas, according to the *Gospel of Bartholomew*, her response to a similar question from Jesus' disciples was: "If I should begin to tell you, fire will issue forth out of my mouth and consume all the world."[78] The passage in the *Gospel of Bartholomew* was discussed in Chapter 1.

The comment that Mary shared intimate details of her life with those women should be read in the context of references to other groups of women who followed Mary.[79] Over the course of her life Mary may have had many disciples, as Jesus had his. Some of the stories they collected of Mary's life—including events like the Nativity—no doubt found their way into the canonical and extracanonical scriptures and eventually into the texts discussed in this chapter. Others, sadly, may never have been recorded.

The *Transitus Mariae* lists incidents in which Mary healed visitors of their ailments. She healed a woman "who had a demon that was ...

strangling her" and another woman stricken with leprosy: "[S]he straightway took water, and sealed them, in the name of the Father, and of the Son, and of the Holy Spirit. And she sprinkled (it) upon their bodies; and straightway they were healed."[80] The term *seal* was often used for baptism, and the words used suggest that Mary had indeed baptized the two women. Mary cast out two demons who were tormenting a third woman:

> [I]mmediately, when she had prayed over her, and had placed her hand upon her, and had spoken thus: "In the name of my Master Who is in heaven, I adjure thee at this time concerning this soul, that she may be healed." And straightway these demons came out of her, and they wailed, and cried out, saying: "What is there between us and thee, O Mother of God."[81]

Mary healed a boy from Egypt who had elephantiasis—and also his traveling companions, "who were very sick": "[I]n the hour that they went to her, and took refuge with the pure and holy Lady Mary in that hour they were healed from their afflictions." During a religious festival, "those that were cured were two thousand eight hundred souls, men, and women, and children."[82]

If the Roman and Jewish authorities had been concerned that Mary was attracting too much attention in Jerusalem, they must have been even more concerned about the miracles and wonders Mary was performing in neighboring Bethlehem—and learned of the flow of visitors from all parts of the empire.

Eventually Mary's ministry came to an end. According to the *Transitus*, on a Friday "the Blessed one was distressed" and asked for incense to be brought to her, "for I wish to pray to my Master the Christ whom I have in heaven.'" The virgins brought the censers; and Mary prayed thus: "My Master, the Christ, listen to the voice of Thy mother. And send me Mar John, that I may see him. And I thank Thee for Thy goodness. I know that Thou hearest me in what I ask from Thee.'"[83] *Mar*, meaning "my lord," is an honorific used in the Syriac and other eastern churches for bishops and saints.

Dormition and Assumption

Gabriel, the Great Angel, and the Palm Staff

The texts agree that Mary was alerted to her impending death, but the details of the announcement vary considerably. In one account, as

Chapter 3. Mary in Early Christian Writings

noted earlier, the Archangel Gabriel came to her at the sepulcher in Jerusalem and said: "Hail to thee, mother of God! thy prayer has been accepted to heaven before thy Son, our Lord Jesus Christ. And therefore thou shalt depart from this world unto life everlasting."[84] But then Mary went to Bethlehem, possibly for an extended period of time.

In the earliest Greek Dormition text, attributed to "John the Theologian and Evangelist," Mary was visited by a "Great Angel" shortly before her death. The Angel announced:

> Rise, Mary, and take this palm-staff, which was given to me by the one who planted Paradise, and deliver it to the apostles, so that while holding it they may sing before you, because in three days you will lay aside the body. For behold, I will send all the apostles to you, and they will bury you and will not leave you until they have carried you to the place where you will soon be in glory.[85]

The palm-staff evidently was cut from the Tree of Life. A short conversation ensued between Mary and the Angel, after which the latter warned:

> [D]o not hold on to the palm-staff, because many miracles will come to pass through it, and it will be a test for all the people of Jerusalem.... Go to the mountain then, and there you will learn my name, because I will not speak it inside Jerusalem, lest it be completely devastated. But you will hear it on the Mount of Olives.[86]

Essentially the same story appears in *The Life of the Virgin*. The Great Angel, now identified as Gabriel, delivered a message from Christ:

> It is time for my mother to come to me ... O blessed among women. Just as you have filled the inhabitants of the earth with joy, O blessed one, so now you will cause the host of heaven to rejoice by your ascension and make the souls of the saints to shine even more. Rejoice, as you cried out before, for you have the title "favored one" as an honor forever.[87]

In the text by "John the Theologian and Evangelist," Mary carried the palm-staff to the Mount of Olives, "with the Angel's light shining ahead of her." Upon her arrival, the "trees bowed their heads and venerated the palm-staff that was in her hand."[88] In the ensuring conversation it emerged that Christ was speaking through the Angel; or perhaps the Angel *was* Christ. The latter possibility would point toward Gnostic influence, because many Gnostics believed that Christ only *seemed* to take human form.[89]

Upon returning to her house, according to the text by "John," Mary bathed and dressed—again perhaps in ceremonial robes—and then uttered a long ecstatic blessing that included the following:

> I bless you, sign that appeared from heaven on the earth, until you chose me and dwelt in me.... I bless you because you gave me a measure of virility for the parts of your body and [because] I have been found worthy of the kiss of your bridal chamber, as you promised me before. I bless you so that I will be found worthy to partake of the perfect eucharist and your sweet-smelling offering, which is an abundance for all the nations....
>
> For you are hidden among the hidden, observing those who are not seen. You are the hidden race, and you are also the Pleroma ... and I have painfully given birth first to you and them to all who hope in you. Hear the prayer of your mother Mary crying out to you.[90]

The *Pleroma* (literally "Fullness") was a typical Gnostic term for heaven. Mary's ecstatic utterance may be compared with the one in the *Gospel of Bartholomew* cited in Chapter 1.[91]

According to *The Life of the Virgin*, Mary "informed her friends and acquaintances about the mystery of her Dormition, and they gathered around her. And they wept and lamented her separation from them, for after God they had her as their hope and intercession." Mary comforted then and then said:

> May the will of my son and God be upon me. He is my God, and I will glorify and exalt him, the God of my father. He is my son, born from me according to the flesh, but the father is also God the creator of all things.... And when I stand before him, I will not cease to pray and intercede on behalf of you and all Christians and the entire world.[92]

Arrival of John, the Other Apostles, and Christ

The summons to John and his arrival are described at length in the *Transitus* palimpsest.

> John the Apostle was in the city of Ephesus.... And the Holy Spirit informed him, saying, "The time is near for the mother of thy God to go out of the world; arise, and go to her to Bethlehem.... And I

Chapter 3. Mary in Early Christian Writings

will inform the Apostles, thy brothers, that they may all assemble at Bethlehem ... those who are alive and those who are dead."[93]

No doubt John expected to travel to Bethlehem by land or sea, a journey that could take him weeks or months. He prayed before setting off; but before he finished his prayer, the Holy Spirit caught him up in a cloud of light and deposited him at "the door of the upper chamber in which the Blessed one was lying." John opened the door and greeted Mary: "Hail to thee, Mother of God, and hail to the Christ who was born of thee! Be not grieved, lady, for thou art departing from this world with great glory."[94] Then we are told:

> [T]he Mother of God rejoiced greatly that Mar John had come to her.... Then Mary said to John: "Set the censer of incense." And he set it; and he spoke thus: "Lord Jesus, the Christ, do a miracle before Thy mother, as she is going out of this world, that the infidels who have not believed that Thou art the Son of God may be ashamed. For heaven and earth bear witness that this is the holy virgin who gave Thee birth."[95]

Mary might possibly have referred to her son as "Lord Jesus, the Christ" and "Son of God;" even the latter term was not unknown in Judaic tradition. But John is unlikely to have used the term "Mother of God," since the concept of the *Theotokos* did not emerge until the third century.

The Ethiopic Six Books recalls that Mary asked John: "'Put incense in the censer and pray.' And he did as she commanded him. And he prayed, saying, 'My Lord, Jesus Christ, hear my prayer. Receive my petition and receive the petition of your mother. Grant that she see you while still living.'"[96]

The *Narrative of John the Theologian and Evangelist* tells the story is a slightly different way. Mary asked a maidservant to summon all her "relatives and acquaintances"—not to the upper chamber in Bethlehem but to her house in Jerusalem. Upon their arrival, Mary prayed with them. Then "As Mary was praying Amen, behold, suddenly the apostle John arrived on a cloud. And he knocked on Mary's door, opened it and went in. When Mary saw him, her spirit was disturbed."[97]

Instead of the warm welcome John received in the *Transitus*, Mary reproached him for leaving her after Jesus had entrusted her care to him at the cross: "Now then, father John, do not forget what has been commanded to you regarding me. Remember that he loved you more than the others. Remember that, while you were reclining on his breast, he spoke to you alone the mystery that no one else knows except you and I."[98]

John tried to defend himself, but nevertheless wept bitterly. In the end Mary urged him to be patient and took him to another part of the house. She gave John a book, which she had received from the five-year-old Jesus, revealing "all things of creation."[99] She also wanted to give John custody of the palm-staff, but he declined until his fellow apostles could arrive, lest it suggest favored status and provoke "murmurings" among the Twelve. That impediment was soon eased by the arrival of the other disciples.

Several texts describe the arrival of the other disciples at Mary's house. The *Narrative of John the Theologian and Evangelist* tells it thus:

> After these things, ... while they were coming out of the inner chamber, behold, suddenly there was thunder .... [and] the apostles descended on a cloud from the corners of the world to Mary's door. Being eleven in number ... first Peter, second Paul—he was also carried on a cloud and numbered among the apostles, for at that time he had the beginnings of the faith of God. After them the rest of the apostles also met one another in the clouds at Mary's door."[100]

The inclusion of Paul among the "eleven" raises eyebrows. We recall that Anne Catherine Emmerich insisted that "Paul was not summoned" to Mary's deathbed.

Life of the Virgin states simply: "Then came the "sound of great thunder" and the descent of Jesus' other disciples from a cloud. Maximus mentioned a few other notables, including Timothy. Significantly, he did not mention James, son of Joseph and "brother of the Lord," who had cared for Mary while she was in Jerusalem.[101] No family members seem to have been at Mary's bedside; or perhaps, for some reason, the authors of the Dormition literature failed to mention them.

The texts do not agree on whether Thomas was among those transported. *The Ethiopic Six Books* claims that Thomas arrived with the others, proclaiming to Mary: "While I was still in the land of India, the Holy Spirit came and snatched me up and brought me to you."[102] But *Life of the Virgin* insists that he arrived after Mary's death.

Chapter 3. Mary in Early Christian Writings

In *Life of the Virgin*, Mary "explained to the disciples the rites of anointing her with myrrh and for burial. Then she extended her hands and began to give thanks to the Lord." She broke into a canticle, each verse a blessing addressed to Christ. According to the text it began with "I bless you, O king and only-begotten Son of the beginningless Father, true God of true God, who consented to become incarnate from me, your handmaid, through the incalculable good will of the Father and the assistance of the Holy Spirit."[103] Mary could not possibly have said those things, because the Nicene terminology was not formulated until three centuries after her death!

Finally, Mary fell silent, and Christ himself arrived. "[B]ehold the glorious and wonderful arrival of Christ her God and son took place, and there were with him innumerable hosts of angels and archangels and other hosts of seraphim and cherubim and thrones." Mary exclaimed: "I believe that all the things that you have said to me will be fulfilled," and "her glorious face shone with brilliance and divine glory."[104]

Mary "made an offering for the entire world and for every soul that calls upon the Lord and calls upon the name of his mother." Eventually

> the Lord held forth his right hand, blessed his mother and said to her: "Let your heart rejoice and be glad, O Mary blessed among women, for every grace and gift has been given to you by my heavenly Father, and every soul that calls on your name with holiness will not be put to shame but will find mercy and comfort both in this life and in the age to come. You, however, come forth to the eternal dwelling places, to unending peace and joy, to the treasure houses of my Father, so that you will see my glory and rejoice by the grace of the Holy Spirit."[105]

Mary's soul was taken up, and those in attendance prepared her body for burial.

Mary's Burial

In the Greek text attributed to "St John the Theologian," we read:

> [T]he Savior said to Peter, "Guard Mary's body, my dwelling place, diligently. Go out from the left side of the city, and you will find a new tomb. Place the body in it, and remain there until I speak to you." When the Savior had said these things, Mary's

> body cried out: "Remember me, king of glory, remember that I am your creation; remember that I guarded the treasure that was entrusted to me." Then the Lord said to the body, "I will not abandon you, my pearl, the inviolate treasure."[106]

The Ethiopic Six Books explains why it was necessary to guard Mary's body. Earlier, she had warned: "Behold, the Jews have been plotting among themselves to burn my body when I die."[107] Indeed, soldiers allegedly were sent to intercept the funeral procession. However,

> the Holy Spirit descended to the apostles and said to them: "Now go forth from this place and do not fear. Behold, I will cause you to pass between heaven and earth, and no one will be able to see you, because the power of the Lord is with you." And then the apostles went forth, carrying Mary's bier. And the Holy Spirit came, and he snatched them up and brought them to Jerusalem.[108]

The Jews might have wanted to burn Mary's body, so her tomb would not become a Christian shrine. On the other hand, this story may have been another example of anti-Semitic polemic.

Most of the texts—even those that placed Mary for a while in Bethlehem—agree that she was buried in Jerusalem. In the fifth century a church was built at the foot of the Mount of Olives, where the tomb was believed to have been located. The Church of the Sepulcher of St Mary, on the same site, is still revered as the burial place of Mary.

Life of the Virgin is one of the texts in which Thomas "was not able to arrive with the other" disciples. He finally reached the grave site "on the third day." He pleaded with them to open the tomb, so he could pay homage. But when the disciples did so they found it empty:

> Through the guidance of the Holy Spirit, the blessed apostles heard their brother's plea and opened the holy tomb with fear. But when they opened it, they did not find the glorious body of the holy mother of Christ, for it had been translated wherever her son and God wished.... They found only the burial wrappings and the shroud in which they had laid her to rest ... the body of the immaculate Virgin was not there ... it had been raised up to her son and God.[109]

Maximus commented that it was "understood that the late arrival of one of the apostles had taken place providentially for the revelation of

Chapter 3. Mary in Early Christian Writings

the mystery" of Mary's Assumption.[110] Eastern church father John of Damascus (c.675–c.749) affirmed that the "pure and spotless body was not left in the earth, but the abode of the Queen, of God's true Mother, was fixed in the heavenly kingdom.... Nor did she leave the grave empty; her body imparted to it a divine fragrance, a source of healing, and of all good for those who approach it with faith."[111]

The *Narrative of John the Theologian and Evangelist* does not mention Thomas, but relates that Christ came, attended by the Archangels Gabriel and Michael:

> The Lord told Michael to take the body of Mary up unto the cloud and to set it down in Paradise. And when the body was taken up, the Lord told the apostles to come closer to it. And when they came onto the cloud, they were singing with the voice of angels, and the Lord commanded the clouds to depart for the East, to the regions of Paradise.[112]

Stephen Shoemaker identified three texts with essentially the same ending: "And when they arrived in Paradise, they placed the body of Mary beside the Tree of Life. And they brought her soul and made it enter her body."[113] The reunion of Mary's body and soul anticipated the reunion believed to await all the righteous at the Last Day. But it should be noted that Paradise, to "the East," was not necessarily understood as a heavenly world.

The *Transitus Mariae* describes Mary's Assumption definitively into "the heavenly Jerusalem." This time it was accomplished without the help of Gabriel and Michael; rather, she encountered the archangels much later. The celestial city had twelve gates, named for the twelve apostles, and attended by cherubim and seraphim.

> [A]t the outer gate there were verily standing spiritual beings without end; and they were singing praises beside the city of the great King. And all the prophets were standing and singing praises with their harps; Abraham and Isaac and Jacob, and David the Psalmist. And they worshipped before the King (and his Mother).[114]

Mary entered each gate in turn. When she entered the first gate the angels worshipped her. At the sixth gate the assembled beings "cried out before her, 'Holy, holy, holy.'" At the seventh gate "fire worshipped before her." And when she entered succeeding gates, Mary was worshipped in turn by "rain and dew," the Archangels Gabriel

105

and Michael, "all the shining beings," and the apostles. At the twelfth gate "the Child who was born of her, praised and blessed her."[115]

It was not only archangels and other "shining beings" who worshipped Mary. By the time the *Transitus Mariae* was written—around 500 CE—Marian devotion had become a conspicuous part of the Christian religious experience, raising Mary to near-divine status. Mary allayed the hunger for a goddess, left by Christianity's official embrace of a masculine Deity—as the goddess Asherah had done in pre-Exilic Judaism, to the dismay of the prophets.[116]

Attitudes toward Mary and associated devotional practices probably varied widely in the fifth and sixth centuries, as they did during the Reformation, and continue to do today. But the notion that exalted beings worshipped Mary should give critics pause before they denounce Marian devotion as "Mariolatry."

Postscript

Mary probably died around 50 CE. Sometime in the 60s CE, James the "brother of Jesus," spiritual leader of the Jerusalem Christian community and Mary's caregiver after John's departure, was assassinated by an anti-Christian Jewish faction.[117] In 66 CE Jews throughout Judaea rebelled against Roman rule.[118] Four years later the Roman Army overran Jewish forces defending Jerusalem, sacked the city, and demolished the temple.

According to Eusebius the Judaic Christian community, in which Mary conducted her ministry, was warned "by a revelation" of the impending attack on Jerusalem. Members of the community took refuge in Pella, across the Jordan River,[119] but the community itself was never restored. Few Christians returned to Jerusalem until the fourth century.

The community's liturgical and social traditions were soon forgotten, and Christianity took on a new Greco-Roman persona as it spread beyond the homeland. It should be noted that *Mark*, the earliest gospel, is believed to have been written shortly after 70 CE, and the other gospels between then and the end of the first century.

---

[1] Josephus, *Antiquities of the Jews*, book 20, ch. 9, §1.

2. *Ibid*, book 18, ch. 3, §3.
3. Tacitus, *Annals*, book 15, ch. 44. Tacitus' full name was Publius (or Gaius) Cornelius Tacitus.
4. Pliny the Younger, *Epistulae*, book X, §96. Pliny's full name was Gaius Plinius Caecilius Secundus.
5. Justin Martyr, *Dialogue With Trypho*, (transl.: A. L. Williams), London Society for Promoting Christian Knowledge, 1930, §100:5, 210. Italicization in translation.
6. Irenaeus, *Against Heresies*, book III, ch. 22, §4 (transl: W. Rambaut), Christian Classics Library.
7. "A discourse by the most blessed Hippolytus, bishop and martyr, on the end of the world, and on Antichrist, and on the second coming of our lord Jesus Christ," Appendix to the Works of Hippolytus. Online: https://www.ccel.org/ccel/schaff/anf05.iii.v.i.i.html. Last accessed Dec. 4, 2020. The author of the statement is usually referred to as the "Pseudo-Hippolytus."
8. "Under thy compassion," *Rylands Papyrus* P 470, c.250 CE. John Rylands University Library, Manchester, UK.
9. Ephrem the Syrian, Hymn 18, "In Commemoration of the Mother of God," §44. Thomas Livias, *The Blessed Virgin in the Fathers of the First Six Centuries*, Burns & Oates, 1893, 430.]
10. Simcha Jacobovici & Charles R. Pellegrino, *The Jesus Family Tomb: The Discovery, the Investigation, and the Evidence That Could Change History*, Harper, 2007.
11. For further information on theosis See also John F. Nash, "Theosis: a Christian Perspective on Human Destiny," *The Esoteric Quarterly*, Spring 2011, 15-33.
12. *Life of the Virgin* (transl.: S. J. Shoemaker), Yale Univ. Press, 2012.
13. *Ibid.* §1, 36.
14. *Life of the Virgin* §1, 36-37.
15. The text of the hymn is reproduced in Chapter 5.
16. *Life of the Virgin* § 2, 38. "Apocryphal writings" refers to extracanonical gospels and other texts.
17. *Ibid.* §134, 158-159.
18. E. A. Wallis Budge, *Legends of Our Lady Mary the Perpetual Virgin and her Mother Hanna*, Medici Press, 1922. The work is headed: "Translated from the Ethiopic manuscripts collected by King Theodore at Makdala now in the British Museum, by Sir E. A. Wallis Budge ... sometime scholar of Christ's College, Cambridge, and Tyrwhitt Hebrew Scholar. Keeper of the Department of Egyptian & Assyrian Antiquities in the British Museum." A facsimile copy is available online at: https://archive.org/details/LegendsOfOurLadyMary/page/n11, and a digitized version at:

[19] https://archive.org/stream/LegendsOfOurLadyMary/LegendsOfOurLadyMary_djvu.txt.

[19] *Transitus Mariae.* Reproduced in Agnes Smith Lewis (ed.), *Apocrypha Syriaca*, Clay and Sons, 1909. Reprint: Cambridge University Press, 2012. Facsimile of original online: https://archive.org/stream/apocryphasyriaca00lewiuoft#page/32/mode/2up/search/Book+I. Techniques like multispectral imaging and x-ray fluorescence can reveal the underscript with minimal damage to the later text. In multispectral imaging, the manuscript is photographed in different light spectra, often revealing an underscript invisible to the naked eye. X-ray fluorescence speaks for itself.

[20] *Transitus Mariae*, 17. Parenthesis in original.

[21] The Wijngaards Institute's website is http://www.womenpriests.org/.

[22] *Life of the Virgin* §10, 43.

[23] "The History of Hanna," *Legends of Our Lady Mary the Perpetual Virgin and her Mother Hanna*, 31-32. Parenthesis in translation.

[24] *Life of the Virgin* §17, 48.

[25] "The History of Hanna," *Legends of Our Lady Mary*, 32.

[26] *Life of the Virgin* §31, 64-65.

[27] Basilica of Sant'Apollinare Nuovo, Ravenna, left lateral wall mosaic: https://en.wikipedia.org/wiki/Basilica_of_Sant%27Apollinare_Nuovo#/media/File:Sant_Apollinare_Nuovo_North_Wall_Panorama_01.jpg. Last accessed Sept. 17, 2021. Why 22 virgins? There are 22 letters in the Hebrew alphabet, which might suggest a link with the Virgin of Israel (*Jeremiah* 31:4, *Amos* 5:2).

[28] *Life of the Virgin* §41, 70. It is unlikely that Emmerich knew of Maximus' writings, since translations into western languages were not then available. But it is conceivable that she was aware of related traditions.

[29] *Ibid.* §62, 89.

[30] *Ibid.* §68, 96.

[31] *Ibid.* §72, 100.

[32] "Epiphanius of Salamis," *Legends of Our Lady Mary the Perpetual Virgin and her Mother Hanna*, xxiii. Parenthetical inserts presumably by the translator. Other writers attribute this statement to another Epiphanius, Epiphanius the Monk, who lived in the eighth or ninth century. See for example Geoffrey Ashe, *The Virgin: Mary's Cult and the Re-Emergence of the Goddess*, Arkana, 1976/1988, 79.

[33] "Salutations to the Members of the Body of The Blessed Virgin Mary," *Legends of Our Lady Mary the Perpetual Virgin and her Mother Hanna*, 236-244. Some of the salutations describe Mary's body at a level of detail invisible even in an apparition, where she would almost certainly be robed.

34 "Sahidic Fragments of the Life of the Virgin," vol. I. 15, fragment II A, vv. 13-17. J. Armitage Robinson (ed.), *Texts and Studies: Contributions to Biblical and Patristic Literature*, Cambridge Univ. Press, 1896. A closely similar text, possibly another version of the same original manuscript, found its way into the archives of the Council of Nicaea. This might suggest that both texts date from the fourth century or earlier.
35 *Life of the Virgin* §10, 43.
36 *Ibid.* §74, 102. Italicization removed. Scriptural reference included in translation.
37 *Life of the Virgin* §10, 43. Emphasis added.
38 Ally Kateusz, *Mary and Early Christian Women: Hidden Leadership*, Palgrave, 2019, 132-133. Emphasis added.
39 In Kateusz' translation, "and" is omitted, and a period is placed after "offered." "[S]he" is the subject of the first sentence, and "*she sacrificed herself as the priest and was sacrificed*" is an independent clause. In Shoemaker's translation, "the Lord Jesus" is the subject of a much longer sentence, and the sacrifice language—with masculine pronouns—is one of several dependent clauses. Shoemaker seems to have struggled to translate this passage from the Old Georgian. Kateusz had the advantage of working from Van Esbroeck's French translation, which already interpreted the passage and decided upon the feminine pronouns.
40 Ally Kateusz, "She Sacrificed Herself as the Priest," *Journal of Feminist Studies in Religion* (Spring 2017), 45-67.
41 *Ibid.*
42 *Ibid.* See also Kateusz, *Mary and Early Christian Women*, 175-177.
43 *Life of the Virgin* §84, 111.
44 "John the Son of Zebedee," *Legends of Our Lady Mary the Perpetual Virgin and Her Mother Hanna*, 245ff.
45 *Life of the Virgin* §89, 115.
46 *Ibid.* §92, 119.
47 *Matthew* 27:61.
48 *Life of the Virgin* §92, 119.
49 "Bartholomew the Apostle," *Legends of Our Lady Mary the Perpetual Virgin and her Mother Hanna*, xxxvii-xxxix. Parentheses by editor or translator, presumably to fill in missing portions of the manuscript.
50 *John* 19:25-27.
51 More recently, biblical scholars have suggested that John the Beloved and John the Evangelist may have been different men. Also there is considerable doubt that the fourth gospel and *Revelation* were written by the same author. Most radical is the suggestion that "the Beloved Disciple" was Mary Magdalene.
52 *Acts* 1:12-14.
53 The notion of Pentecost as "fifty days" came from *Leviticus* 23:16.

[54] *Matthew* 5:17.
[55] *Isaiah* 40:3. Multiple Jewish sects already existed, including the Pharisees, the Sadducees, the Zealots, and the Essenes.
[56] *Acts* 11:26.
[57] *Life of the Virgin* §§93-96, 120-123.
[58] *Ibid.* §97, 124.
[59] *Psalm* 141:2.
[60] Male clergy in Asia Minor, Rome, North Africa, and elsewhere adopted the term "elder" (*prebyteros*) intentionally to distance themselves from the priests of Judaic and pre-Christian Greco-Roman religion. Eventually "priest" became accepted in Christianity; ironically, however, many female clergy today reject the term "priestess," arguing that it has pagan associations!
[61] *Koheneth* is also spelled *kohenet* or *kohanoth.*
[62] See for example Jill Hammer, *Sisters at Sinai: New Tales of Biblical Women*, Jewish Publication Society, 2004.
[63] *Acts* 2:44-47.
[64] *Life of the Virgin* §97, 124-125.
[65] Rainer Riesner, *Paul's Early Period: Chronology, Mission Strategy, Theology*. Eerdmans Publishing, 1998, 120.
[66] "After Our Lord's Ascension Mary lived for three years on Mount Zion, for three years in Bethlehem, and for nine years close to Ephesus." Clemens W. Brentano (ed.), *The Life of the Blessed Virgin Mary: From the Visions of Ven. Anne Catherine Emmerich* (transl.: M. Palairet), Tan Books, 1954/1970, 357.
[67] *Life of the Virgin* §102, 128.
[68] *The Ethiopic Six Books*. Appendix D of Stephen J. Shoemaker, *Ancient Traditions of the Virgin Mary's Dormition and Assumption*, Oxford Univ. Press, 2002, 377.
[69] *Transitus Mariae*, 20.
[70] *Malachi* 1:11.
[71] *Transitus Mariae*, 25.
[72] *The Ethiopic Six Books*, 379. Kateusz suggested that the two texts had a common ancestor and the passage may have been redacted from the *Transitus*. See Kateusz, *Mary and Early Christian Women*, 30.
[73] *The Ethiopic Six Books*, 378. "Master" sounds odd, but the translator obviously was unable to suggest a gender-appropriate term of reverence. More often Mary was referred to as "Lady Mary" in the early Christian texts.
[74] *Ibid.*
[75] Shoemaker, *Ancient Traditions of the Virgin Mary's Dormition and Assumption*, 74-76.
[76] *The Ethiopic Six Books.*, 378-379.

Chapter 3. Mary in Early Christian Writings

[77] *Transitus Mariae*, 34.
[78] *Gospel of Bartholomew* II:5 (transl.: M. R. James), Gnostic Society Library. See Chapter 1 of the present book.
[79] For example the statement in *Life of the Virgin*: "[S]he held authority ... over the other women who accompanied [Jesus].... The holy Theotokos was the leader and director of them all"; §74, 102.
[80] *Transitus Mariae*, 34. Parenthesis in translation. The Trinitarian formula used in the baptisms would have been incomprehensible to Mary, but the post-Nicene readers of the text would have understood it perfectly.
[81] *Ibid.*, 34-35. Note that the term "Mother of God" was not used until the middle of the third century.
[82] *Ibid.*, 35.
[83] *Ibid.*, 25.
[84] *Ibid.*, 20.
[85] *Narrative of John the Theologian and Evangelist, concerning the Dormition of the Most Holy Theotokos and how the Undefiled Mother of Our Lord was Translated.* Appendix B of S. J. Shoemaker, *Ancient Traditions of the Virgin Mary's Dormition and Assumption*, 351-352.
[86] *Ibid.*, 353.
[87] *Life of the Virgin* §103, 130.
[88] *Narrative of John the Theologian and Evangelist*, 354.
[89] Institutional Christianity termed such belief the heresy of *docetism*, from the Greek *dokein*, "to seem."
[90] *Narrative of John the Theologian and Evangelist*, 356-357.
[91] *Gospel of Bartholomew* II:13.
[92] *Life of the Virgin* §§105-106, 130-132.
[93] *Transitus Mariae*, 26.
[94] *Ibid.*
[95] *Ibid.*
[96] *The Ethiopic Six Books*, 380.
[97] *Narrative of John the Theologian and Evangelist*, 358.
[98] *Ibid.*, 359.
[99] We are not told what form the book took or how it came into the hands of the child Jesus. Perhaps "book" is to be taken metaphorically.
[100] *Narrative of John the Theologian and Evangelist*, 360.
[101] The earliest date given for James' death is 62 CE, so he presumably outlived Mary.
[102] *The Ethiopic Six Books*, 382.
[103] *Life of the Virgin* §107, 134-135.
[104] *Ibid.* §109, 135.
[105] *Ibid.* §111, 136.
[106] *Narrative of John the Theologian and Evangelist*, 366.
[107] *The Ethiopic Six Books*, 380.

[108] *Ibid.*, 386.
[109] *Life of the Virgin* §117, 141.
[110] *Ibid.* §118, 142.
[111] John of Damascus, First Sermon on the Assumption. Online: https://sourcebooks.fordham.edu/basis/johndamascus-komesis.asp. Last accessed July 13, 2021.
[112] *Narrative of John the Theologian and Evangelist*, 369.
[113] Shoemaker, *Ancient Traditions of the Virgin Mary's Dormition and Assumption*, 163-164.
[114] *Transitus Mariae*, 65. Shoemaker's translation adds "and his Mother." See: "Fifth-Century Syriac Palimpsest Fragments of the Six Books," Appendix C of *Ancient Traditions of the Virgin Mary's Dormition and Assumption*, 374.
[115] *Transitus Mariae*, 65-66. It is worth noting that "shining being" is a direct translation of the Sanskrit *deva*. We shall speak of devas in later chapters.
[116] Asherah's influence in biblical Judaism will be discussed in a later chapter.
[117] Historians are unsure whether that occurred in 62 or 68 CE: i.e., before or after the rebellion began.
[118] The rebellion and Roman response are often referred to as the "First Jewish–Roman War."
[119] Eusebius of Caesarea, *Church History*, book III, ch. 5:3.

Chapter 4
Marian Doctrine and Beyond

The branch of theology known as *Mariology* began even before the fourth-century Councils of Nicaea and Constantinople affirmed Mary's virginity, and the fifth-century Council of Ephesus declared her to be the mother of God. It continues in the modern age, sometimes resulting in new formal pronouncements; during the last 200 years the Church of Rome raised Mary's Immaculate Conception and her Assumption into heaven to the level of dogma.

Less formal discussions have focused on Mary's role in the Redemption, as a priestly participant in the Sacrifice of the Cross, and as the Mediatrix of all Graces. An issue debated through the centuries is whether the Archangel Gabriel's announcement of Mary's pregnancy was entirely unexpected, or whether she was preordained "from the beginning" to be the mother of the incarnate Word.

This chapter focuses on Roman and Eastern Orthodox doctrine, but a few comments are made about a developing Anglican Mariology.

Introduction

In his first *Epistle to the Corinthians* Paul famously contrasted Christ with Adam: "For as in Adam all die, even so in Christ shall all be made alive."[1] Church father Justin Martyr may have been inspired by that passage when he contrasted Mary with Eve. Writing in about 155 CE he declared:

> For Eve, being a virgin and uncorrupt, conceived the word spoken of the serpent, and brought forth disobedience and death. But Mary the Virgin receiving faith and grace, when the angel Gabriel brought her the good news that the Spirit of the Lord should come upon her, and the power of the Highest should overshadow her, wherefore also that Holy Thing that is born of him is Son of God, answered, Be it unto me according to Thy word.[2]

Soon thereafter Irenaeus (c.130–c.202), bishop of Lyon, in present-day France, drew a sharp contrast between Eve's disobedience and Mary's willingness to become the mother of Christ.[3] Several other church fathers added comments on the same general theme. Thus was born *Mariology*: the branch of theology concerned with Mary, though the term itself was not coined until the nineteenth century.

By the time Mariology was born, Christianity had moved away from its Judaic origins to become a Greco-Roman religion. Along with other biblical characters "Mary" had to adapt to the new culture. She was no longer the Palestinian woman steeped in Jewish tradition. As early as the second and third centuries, we see the beginnings of the "European Mary" of institutional Christian tradition.

While Mariology continued to reference events in the life of the historical Mary, it also began to view her as a personage transcending those events and transcending her physical nature. She was transformed from a provincial woman—admittedly one who received an education and may have risen to the level of high priestess in the nascent Christian church—into a celestial entity overshadowing the whole world and playing a role in the divine economy. Whether she really *was* a celestial entity all along is something we shall explore later in the book.

This chapter examines the two Marian dogmas of the early church councils: Mary's virginity and her status as *Theotokos* ("Mother of God"). It also examines the two dogmas decreed more recently by the Church of Rome: her Immaculate Conception and Assumption into heaven.

The chapter then examines the expanding scope of Mariology to include topics like the queenship and priesthood of Mary, and her participation in the Sacrifice of the Cross and the Redemption. An important issue pertains to whether Mary was preordained, or predestined, to play her role in the Incarnation. If, as a number of influential Christian commentators have suggested, she was so preordained, that realization would invest Mary with a status different from the rest of humanity; it would also recast traditional understanding of the Annunciation.

Mary has largely been ignored in Anglicanism, except for her role in the Incarnation. Some hints of an expanding Anglican Mariology can be detected in the liturgies of churches in the Anglican Communion.

But the best prospects for a more formal Mariology may be coming from ecumenical dialogue with other branches of Christianity.

Mary's Virginity

The authors of scripture went to considerable lengths to portray Mary as a virgin—indeed as *virgo intacta*—at least until she gave birth to Jesus. In the second century Justin Martyr and Irenaeus referred to her as "the Virgin Mary" or "Mary the Virgin."

The Nicene Creed, drafted by the Council of Nicaea (325) and completed by the First Council of Constantinople (381), included the language: "[We believe] in one Lord Jesus Christ ... who for us men, and for our salvation, came down from heaven, and was incarnate by the Holy Ghost and of the Virgin Mary, and was made man."[4]

The Nicene Creed left open the question of whether Mary remained a virgin for the rest of her life. Many people in the early church assumed that Mary and Joseph had a normal conjugal life after the Nativity. *Matthew* 1:25 asserts that Joseph "knew her not till she had brought forth her firstborn son,"[5] suggesting the possibility that he "knew her" afterward. A number of early writers cited *Mark* 6:3 and *Matthew* 13:55-56 to argue that Mary bore as many as six more children. In Jewish society married couples were expected to have several children. Reflecting the new Greco-Roman perspective, however, Epiphanius of Salamis (c.315–403) labeled them *Antidicomarians*,[6] a polemical term suggesting that they were "adversaries of Mary."

One of the so-called Antidicomarians was the fourth-century writer Helvidius. Unfortunately Helvidius' writings are lost (or were destroyed), and we know nothing about him except for a rebuttal of his position by church father Jerome (342–420). Jerome insisted that the alleged brothers and sisters were either first cousins or were Joseph's children from a previous marriage. Moreover, citing Paul as an authority, Jerome argued that the virginal state was superior to consummated marriage.[7] Several other church fathers weighed in, requesting that Mary's perpetual virginity be made an article of faith.

The only formal declaration on Mary's perpetual virginity came from the Lateran Council of 649, a regional synod called by Pope Theodore I. It decreed:

> If anyone does not properly and truly confess in accord with the holy Fathers, that the holy Mother of God and ever Virgin and immaculate Mary in the earliest of the ages conceived of the Holy Spirit without seed, namely, God the Word Himself specifically and truly, who was born of God the Father before all ages, and that she incorruptibly bore (Him), her virginity remaining indestructible even after His birth, let him be condemned.[8]

The Eastern Orthodox churches did not participate in the Lateran Council on an official level, but two representatives attended as observers.[9] One of them, Maximus the Confessor, whose *Life of the Virgin* was cited in Chapter 3, declared:

> For just as [Christ] Himself became man without changing His nature or altering His power, so He makes her who bore Him a Mother while keeping her a Virgin. In this way He reveals one miracle through another miracle, at the same time concealing the one with the other. This is because in Himself, according to His essence. God always remains a mystery.... [T]he bonds of her virginity became even more indissoluble.[10]

The decree of the Lateran Council is binding only on Roman Catholics. For members of the eastern churches, and the churches that emerged from the Reformation, Mary's perpetual virginity is not an article of faith but is generally taken for granted.

Mary may have chosen a life of celibacy, or Joseph's age may have precluded marital intimacy. Those are not matters for us to comment on. Mary has sometimes been included in the pantheon of Virgin Mothers of ancient mythology, or associated with the astrological sign of Virgo. But mythology and astrology probably were not foremost on the minds of the church fathers.

Rather, Christianity's focus on Mary's virginity reflected surprising emphasis—contrary to the larger trend—on her physical form, rather than on her spiritual gifts and the contribution she made to Christ's mission. Not incidentally, the focus on her biological virginity coincided with deterioration in the status of women and in attitudes toward the human body that took place during the first several centuries of the Christian era. The impulse to decree Mary's perpetual virginity may have come at least in part from a desire to present her as a suitable object of devotion and model of "purity" in a patriarchal church.

Chapter 4. Marian Doctrine and Beyond

Mary *Theotokos*

The oldest known prayer addressed to Mary was found in a Greek papyrus dated to the late third century.[11] The prayer will be discussed in more detail in the next chapter, but it is important to the present discussion because it referred to Mary as *Theotokos*, a Greek word that literally meant "God-bearer," or "Birthgiver to God." In the West it would be translated as "Mother of God."

Whether Mary was simply the mother of Jesus, or could be considered the mother of God, may already have been a matter of controversy when the prayer was composed, and it became increasingly controversial in the fourth century. Eastern church father Basil of Caesarea (330–379) promoted the term *Theotokos* within the theological community.[12] But Theodore of Antioch (c.350–428) questioned its propriety. Theological debate centered on the relationship between the human and divine natures in Jesus Christ. Attracting less attention, but critically important for our story, were the implications for Mary.

The issue came to a head in an exchange of letters between two of the most powerful men in the church: Cyril (c.378–444), Patriarch of Alexandria, and his political rival Nestorius (c.386–450), Theodore's protégé and Archbishop of Constantinople.[13] Nestorius emphasized the distinction between the human and divine natures. He argued that Mary gave birth to the incarnate Christ, not to the divine Logos who existed before her and indeed before time itself. Mary should be therefore called *Christotokos* ("Christ-bearer"):

> It is clear that God the Word was not the son of David.... "Now the birth of Jesus Christ took place in this way. When his mother Mary had been betrothed to Joseph, she was found to be with child of the holy Spirit." But who would ever consider that the godhead of the only begotten was a creature of the Spirit?[14]

Cyril emphasized the unity of Jesus Christ's human and divine natures. Accordingly, he affirmed that Mary was *Theotokos*, arguing thus: "The Word is said to have been begotten according to the flesh, because for us and for our salvation he united what was human to himself hypostatically and came forth from a woman. For ... from the very womb of his mother he was so united."[15] "Hypostatically" referred to the unity of the two natures in one *hypostasis*, or "person."

The Council of Ephesus (431 CE) was convened to resolve the matter—and other issues which do not concern us here. Perhaps the revered Theodore could have swayed the bishops to his viewpoint, but he was now deceased. Instead, Cyril won the day, and the council decreed: "If anyone does not confess that ... the holy virgin is the Theotokos, for she bore in a fleshly way the Word of God become flesh, let him be anathema."[16]

Nestorius was condemned, deposed from his patriarchate, and sent into exile. But a substantial number of bishops and laity supported him and seceded from the Rome–Constantinople axis to form the Assyrian Church of the East.[17] Initially located primarily in the former Persian Empire the Assyrian Church eventually expanded to India and China.

The Council of Ephesus' main purpose may have been to affirm the hypostatic union of the two natures of Jesus Christ. But it posed another question, which mainstream theologians have carefully sidestepped: If Mary gave birth to God, why is she not considered divine herself? Ironically, it was that very issue that led Theodore and Nestorius to question the *Theotokos* title; they were concerned that the title implied that Mary was a goddess. The council chamber at Ephesus was built over the ruins of a temple of Artemis–Diana. According to legend a crowd gathered outside the building, during the proceedings, chanting "give us back our goddess!" Cyril and the mainstream church did just that! Despite repeated official denials, from that time onward Mary increasingly came to be seen as the feminine face of the Christian God.

Not surprisingly, the *Qur'an* warned that neither Jesus nor his mother should be regarded as divine: "Remember when God said to Jesus son of Mary: 'Did you really say to people 'Take me and my mother as two gods, instead of Allah?' [Jesus] said 'Glory be to You! What right have I to assert what does not in truth belong to me?... Worship Allah, my Lord and your Lord.'"[18]

Cyril of Alexandria preached a homily to the Council of Ephesus, which has become one of the most influential statements on Mary in the early church:

> Hail Mary Theotokos, venerable treasure of the whole world ... indestructible Mother and Virgin, for the sake of the one who is called "blessed" in the holy Gospels, the one who "comes in the

name of the Lord." We hail you, who held in your virginal womb him whom the heavens cannot contain; it is you through whom the Holy Trinity is glorified and adored throughout the earth; through whom the heavens exult; through whom the angels and archangels rejoice; through whom the demons are put to flight; through whom ... the fallen creature is raised up to heaven; through whom that all creation, once imprisoned by idolatry, has reached knowledge of the truth; through whom holy baptism has come to believers.[19]

In addition to bestowing many honors on Mary, the homily raised a number of Mariological issues that would be debated in the centuries to come. In particular, Cyril's statement: "[I]t is you through whom the Holy Trinity is glorified and adored," would be cited to support the possible designation of Mary as Co-Redemtrix with Christ and Mediatrix of All Graces.

The Immaculate Conception

Two other Marian dogmas: the Immaculate Conception and the Assumption, were defined by the Church of Rome in the nineteenth and twentieth centuries, respectively. But the beliefs on which they rest go back far in Christian history.

The *Infancy Gospel of James*, which dates from the second century, asserts that Mary's conception was the result of divine intervention, and in recognition of their blessing her parents presented her to the temple. Certainly Mary's origins were exceptional, but she was still a member of the human race—and, as a woman, a descendent of Eve.

Questions arose in the early church on whether Mary had ever been tempted to sin, or perhaps had even succumbed to temptation; that is whether—like Jesus' disciples—she shared normal human weaknesses. John Chrysostom (c.347–407) suggested that Jesus rebuked his mother at the Wedding Feast of Cana for displaying "some human feelings, like His brethren."[20]

Cyril of Alexandria—writing sometime before he championed the *Theotokos* doctrine. and before declaring that through her "the Holy Trinity is glorified and adored"—questioned her faith. He spoke in patronizing and misogynistic terms of Mary weeping at the foot of the cross (*John* 19:25), commenting that "women are ever prone to tears, and very much inclined to lament, especially when they have abundant occasion for shedding tears."[21] Cyril went on to suggest:

> The woman [Mary], as is likely, not exactly understanding the mystery, wandered astray into some such train of thought; for we shall do well to remember, that the character of these events was such as to awe and subdue the most sober mind. And no marvel if a woman fell into such an error.... What wonder, then, if a woman's frail mind was also plunged into thoughts which betrayed weakness?[22]

Most other writers from the period, however, insisted that Mary never sinned; that is, she never succumbed to what eventually came to be called *actual* sin. An actual sin is a thought, word or deed committed in conscious disobedience to God. Toward the end of his life Augustine of Hippo (354–430) singled out Mary as the one created being untouched by sin:

> We must except the holy Virgin Mary, concerning whom I wish to raise no question when it touches the subject of sins, out of honor to the Lord; for from Him we know what abundance of grace for overcoming sin in every particular was conferred upon her who had the merit to conceive and bear Him who undoubtedly had no sin.[23]

Emergence of the Doctrine—and Controversy

The notion that humanity inherited the sin of Adam and Eve, became a topic of discussion from the second century onward. *Original sin* was part of the "genetic code," passed on from generation to generation through the male sperm at the very moment of conception.[24] The question inevitably arose: Was Mary, who would bear the Savior, so tainted? Or perhaps she was spared through the grace of her son.[25]

As early as the fifth century, the Syrian Church observed December 8 as the feast of "the Conception of the Most Holy and All Pure Mother of God." But not until the ninth century did the Carolingian theologian Paschasius Radbertus openly suggest that Mary was conceived without original sin. And the first explicit statement of the Immaculate Conception came in a work by Anselm of Canterbury (c.1033–1109): "[I]t would be neither reasonable nor right for the ... evils of Adam to be transmitted to the man conceived from the Virgin."[26] By the thirteenth century December 8 was observed as the feast of the Immaculate Conception of Mary.

The concept of the Immaculate Conception did not enjoy universal support. Theologians lined up on both sides of the issue. John Duns

Chapter 4. Marian Doctrine and Beyond

Scotus (c.1266–1308) supported it. But Thomas Aquinas (1225–1274), whom the sixteenth-century Pope Pius V named Doctor of the Church and equated in importance with the greatest of the church fathers, was opposed: "If the soul of the Blessed Virgin," Aquinas wrote, "had never incurred the stain of the original sin, this would be derogatory to the dignity of Christ, by reason of His being the universal Savior of all." "All" must include Mary.[27]

Thomas Aquinas conceded that, in anticipation of the Redemption, Mary was made free from sin by the time she was born: "[T]he Blessed Virgin did indeed contract original sin, but was cleansed therefrom before her birth from the womb."[28] Some might suggest that Aquinas was splitting hairs, but it should be noted that he believed that the human soul entered the body sometime during pregnancy, not at the instant of conception.

Mary herself reportedly told mystic Bridget of Sweden (c.1303–1373): "[I]t is a truth that I was conceived without original sin.... A golden hour was my conception, for then began the principle of the salvation of all, and darkness hastened to light."[29] On the other hand, Catherine of Siena (1347–1380), one of only thirty-six named Doctors of the Church, claimed to have received a communication to the contrary. Although the church eventually favored Bridget's testimony, both women were canonized.

The two most powerful religious orders took opposite sides; the Franciscans supported belief in the Immaculate Conception, while the Dominicans—who numbered Aquinas and Catherine of Siena in their ranks—were opposed.

Two of the early Protestant reformers affirmed belief in the Immaculate Conception. Martin Luther (1483–1546) declared: "It is a sweet and pious belief that the infusion of Mary's soul was effected without original sin; so that in the very infusion of her soul she was also purified from original sin and adorned with God's gifts, receiving a pure soul infused by God; thus from the first moment she began to live she was free from all sin."[30] Swiss reformer Ulrich Zwingli (1484–1531) wrote: "I esteem immensely the Mother of God, the ever chaste, immaculate Virgin Mary."[31] Later generations of Protestants, including John Calvin, continued to place great emphasis on original sin but distanced themselves from any Marian doctrines other than the virgin birth of Jesus.

Mary: Adept, Queen, Mother, Priestess

A New Dogma—Decreed in a New Way

Belief in the Immaculate Conception grew stronger in Roman Catholicism after the Reformation. In 1662 Pope Alexander VII referred to an existing "doctrine asserting that the soul of the Blessed Virgin, in its creation and infusion into the body, was endowed with the grace of the Holy Spirit and preserved from original sin."[32] Alexander's purpose was to affirm belief in the Immaculate Conception for liturgical purposes; the notion that popes could issue dogmatic decrees lay two centuries in the future.

By the nineteenth century the doctrine was widely accepted, and in 1854 Pope Pius IX declared the doctrine to be infallible dogma. In his apostolic constitution *Ineffabilis Deus* ("Ineffable God") he wrote:

> We declare, pronounce, and define that the doctrine which holds that the most Blessed Virgin Mary, in the first instance of her conception, by a singular grace and privilege granted by Almighty God, in view of the merits of Jesus Christ, the Savior of the human race, was preserved free from all stain of original sin, is a doctrine revealed by God and therefore to be believed firmly and constantly by all the faithful.[33]

The decree drew upon language used centuries earlier by John Duns Scotus, that Mary's Immaculate Conception was secured "by a singular grace and privilege granted by Almighty God, in view of the merits of Jesus Christ."

The declaration by Pius IX was the first instance of a pronouncement of dogma *ex cathedra* (literally "from the chair [of Peter]"); hitherto, all dogmatic decrees had been issued by councils of bishops. Indeed, the pope's authority to define dogma was not officially recognized until the First Vatican Council in 1870. The council endorsed the concept of papal infallibility and retroactively confirmed the 1854 declaration.[34]

The 1854 decree was controversial, but—alone among all dogmas proclaimed by the church—it seemed to receive endorsement from above. During one of the apparitions at Lourdes, France, in 1858—just four years after Pius' decree—Mary reportedly told Bernadette Soubirous: "I am the Immaculate Conception." Yet, as noted, endorsement has not been consistent; Bridget of Sweden and Catherine of Siena seem to have received conflicting data.

The Eastern Orthodox churches reject the doctrine of Mary's Immaculate Conception since they attach a different interpretation to original, or "ancestral," sin—or even dismiss it outright. Humanity, in their view, has inherited collective weakness, but that is a condition to be healed rather than a cause for shame or guilt. Eastern theologians are fond of pointing out that *soteria*, the Greek word customarily translated as "salvation" can also mean "healing"; even in English "salvation" and "salve" come from the same root. Citing a work by Maximus the Confessor, twentieth-century Russian theologian Vladimir Lossky declared: "Christ healed all that belonged to man."[35]

As with so many Marian doctrines, the full implications of the Immaculate Conception were not recognized. The assertion that Mary was conceived without original sin, in anticipation of her giving birth to the Redeemer, raises the question of whether she had exercise of free will at the time of the Annunciation. If Mary had said "no," would she still have been conceived without sin?[36] Or had Mary, in some sense, already made the decision to bear Jesus before she was conceived, in which case her consent at the Annunciation was just a formality? A possible answer to those questions lay in the doctrine of Mary's "preordination," or "predestination," to be discussed later in the chapter.

Finally, the doctrine of the Immaculate Conception raises another troublesome thought. Mary was spared the inherited effects of Eve's—and Adam's—sin. But whereas the First Eve's sin was communicated to the whole human race, the Second Eve's relief from that sin was hers alone; it was not communicated to her "children." Baptism is required to remove the stain of original sin. For many centuries, the Church of Rome taught that baptism was so essential that the souls of unbaptized infants were forever denied entrance to heaven.[37]

The Assumption

Whereas the doctrine of the Immaculate Conception developed through a long process of theological discourse, belief in Mary's Assumption into heaven came primarily from popular devotion. There was a desire to spare her the ignominy of death; Mary's life, which had a miraculous, spotless beginning, ought to have a fittingly miraculous ending.

A feast day celebrating the "Memory of Mary" may have been observed even in apostolic times among Jewish Christians in the Jerusalem area, where she is believed to have passed away. Yet neither the canonical nor the extracanonical scriptures discuss the circumstances surrounding the end of Mary's life. To quote textual historian Stephen Shoemaker:

> [T]he early centuries of Christianity, as they are preserved for us today, maintain a profound silence regarding the end of Mary's life. The pre-Nicene Fathers show complete disregard for this event, not even mentioning her death, and only at the end of the fourth century does this gap in the early Christian tradition first generate any visible concern.[38]

From Dormition to Assumption

The Dormition literature, discussed in Chapter 3, eventually filled that gap. In parallel with emergence of the literature, the "Memory of Mary" evolved into a commemoration of Mary's Dormition, or "Falling Asleep." The feast of the Dormition may have been celebrated first in the Syrian Church. Under a decree by the Emperor Mauricius Flavius (r.582–602) it spread throughout the Byzantine Empire, and August 15 was chosen as the date of the feast.[39]

Eastern church father John of Damascus (c.675–c.749) preached three sermons on the Assumption, one of which was cited in Chapter 3. Notions of Mary's Assumption gained little traction in the Greek church. But when the August 15 feast spread to the West in the eighth century, the focus shifted from her Dormition to her Assumption into heaven. Along with a rapid expansion in Marian devotion in general, the Assumption quickly caught the imagination of people throughout the western church. Over the centuries great works of art captured the motif, including Titian's *The Assumption of the Virgin* (c.1517) and *The Assumption of Mary* by Peter Paul Rubens (c.1626).

By the eighteenth century, a campaign developed within the Church of Rome to declare the Assumption an official dogma, perhaps even to affirm that Mary never died. The campaign led to a great expansion in study of the Dormition literature, though the results were not precisely what the western theologians wanted. While the texts vary in detail, they are in almost complete agreement that Mary died a natural death. A smaller number of texts testify that Mary's body was assumed into heaven, or taken to an earthly Paradise, and even they insist that it was taken from the grave.

Stories of the Assumption from the early church mirror gospel accounts of the Resurrection: Mary's body was buried, but when the tomb was opened three days later it was found to be empty. The Assumption also anticipates what is believed to be the destiny of all faithful Christians: the general resurrection on the Last Day, in which the bodies of the faithful will be raised from the dead and reunited with their souls.[40]

Indirect support for the Assumption came from the absence of any alleged relics of Mary's body—prizes that would have been valued beyond measure in the medieval antiquities market. When the Council of Chalcedon convened in 451, the Emperor Marcian and the powerful Empress Pulcheria allegedly ordered Juvenal, Patriarch of Jerusalem, to bring the body of Mary to Constantinople. Juvenal had to explain that Mary left no physical remains.[41] But he was able to supply Mary's burial robe, reportedly left in the tomb after the Assumption.

The Dormition literature, notably the sermons of John of Damascus, and associated legends allowed proponents to claim that a dogma of the Assumption could be based on "tradition," as well as its centuries-old place in the liturgy. Issues of Mary's death and burial were swept aside, and the proposed dogma focused solely on the belief that she was taken up, body and soul, into heaven. Discussion continued through much of the nineteenth century and the early twentieth century. Finally, a majority of bishops indicated that they favored a new Marian dogma.

The Decree

Pope Pius XII proclaimed the dogma in 1950 in his apostolic constitution *Munificentissimus Deus* ("Most bountiful God"):

> [B]y the authority of our Lord Jesus Christ, of the Blessed Apostles Peter and Paul, and by our own authority, we pronounce, declare, and define it to be a divinely revealed dogma: that the Immaculate Mother of God, the ever Virgin Mary, having completed the course of her earthly life, was assumed body and soul into heavenly glory.[42]

The decree was greeted with great joy from the great majority of Roman Catholic clergy and laity, and brought new hope to people reeling from the devastation of World War II and the privations of the post-war period.

Theologians, scholars, and those in the church seeking ecumenical contacts with other denominations reacted with more reservation. They were concerned about the lack of scriptural support, or even support from the writings of the western church fathers. Moreover, they feared negative reaction from other branches of Christianity where tradition is not valued so highly in the formulation of doctrine.

Notwithstanding those reservations, the Second Vatican Council (1962–1965) confirmed the 1950 decree in its *Dogmatic Constitution on the Church* (*Lumen Gentium*).[43] The bishops declined to take a position on the issue of whether Mary died before the Assumption, allowing Roman Catholics to believe that she never suffered the "ignominy" of death.

In 1997, however, Pope John Paul II expressed his personal opinion that Mary did in fact die before she was taken up to heaven: "The Mother is not superior to the Son who underwent death.... To share in Christ's Resurrection, Mary had first to share in his death." He added: "Whatever ... the organic, biological cause of the end of her bodily life, it can be said that for Mary the passage from this life to the next was the full development of grace in glory, so that no death can ever be so fittingly described as a 'dormition' as hers."[44]

John Paul's statement was not an official one on behalf of the church, but it demonstrated a willingness to heed the message of the Dormition literature. It also eased tensions with the Eastern Orthodox Churches. Throughout the ages, the latter have consistently taught and revered the Dormition of Mary. The prevailing belief among Orthodox Christians is that Mary was taken up by Christ into heaven after the Dormition. Numerous works of art show her being lifted up from her funeral bier or from the tomb.

The 1854 and 1950 decrees bring to four the number of Marian dogmas recognized by the Church of Rome. The two dogmas of recent times are binding only on Roman Catholics, though many Christians of other denominations also affirm the underlying beliefs.

Further Marian Dogmas?

Two Marian dogmas were defined by the early church and two more by the Church of Rome. The breakaway Palmarian Catholic Church, which has its own popes, defined several others, including one in 1983 that offered an expanded understanding of the Real Presence in the Eucharist:

> We teach as infallible doctrine that [Mary] is able to be present in the Sacred Eucharist, since, at no moment has Mary ever been, or will be, removed from her Son.... Her presence kneeling in the Eucharist shows her adoration of God and her Omnipotence, which is omnipotence of supplication.[45]

Needless to say, Rome did not recognize the dogma, and it had already excommunicated the Palmarian Church's leaders. Nevertheless the concept of an association between Mary and the Eucharist is an interesting one, and we shall see that Roman Catholic leaders discussed a possible association at some length.

Other Marian dogmas have been proposed over the last 200 years by theologians or groups of theologians within the Roman Church. Reigning popes responded according to their own interest in Mariology, or their level of devotion to Mary. Also, popes were sensitive to the currents of opinion around them. Before we consider the proposals in detail it will be worthwhile to examine the changing environment in which they emerged and were addressed.

Background

Four popes known for their devotion to Mary were Pius IX, Leo XIII, Pius X, and Benedict XV. Their contiguous pontificates spanned the years 1846–1922. That period of nearly eight decades arguably represented the high-water mark of Roman Catholic devotion to Mary—and a corresponding willingness to consider new dogmas. Pius IX promulgated the dogma of the Immaculate Conception, the first in modern times. Both he and Pius X weighed in on the question of Mary's priestly role, to be discussed shortly. Three of the four popes discussed the concept of Mary as Co-Redemptrix with Christ. Leo XIII wrote eleven encyclical letters on the Rosary.

All four popes expressed great admiration for the French priest Louis-Marie Grignion de Montfort (1673–1716), whose writings promoted Marian devotion, but who also made many statements of doctrinal significance. For example, one of his themes was that the Devil is more afraid of Mary than of Christ. Later popes were not all so enthusiastic about de Montfort's teachings.

After Benedict XV's pontificate fewer popes gave Marian doctrine a high priority. More importantly, Roman Catholicism became increasingly self-conscious about the impact Marian devotion was having on its members and on its relationship with other branches of Christianity. An internal concern, which had arisen at times since the very earliest days of the church, was that devotion to a priestly Mary might encourage women's ambitions for ordination to the clergy.

The Second Vatican Council endorsed Pope Pius XII's dogma of the Assumption, affirmed Mary as Queen, spoke of her with "affection and piety as a most beloved mother," and approved of "the liturgical cult of the Blessed Virgin."[46] But it also took steps to slow the advance of Marian devotion and associated doctrine. The *Dogmatic Constitution on the Church*, issued during the council, warned darkly of "Marian excess" that might impede ecumenical outreach to other western denominations.[47] Perhaps it was a reaction against de Montfort's work, which by that time was being criticized for alleged hyperbole.

The *Dogmatic Constitution* exhorted "theologians and preachers of the divine word to abstain zealously both from all gross exaggerations as well as from petty narrow-mindedness in considering the singular dignity of the Mother of God." "Let them," it continued,

> assiduously keep away from whatever, either by word or deed, could lead separated brethren or any other into error regarding the true doctrine of the Church. Let the faithful remember moreover that true devotion consists neither in sterile or transitory affection, nor in a certain vain credulity, but proceeds from true faith, by which we are led to know the excellence of the Mother of God.[48]

Neither the council nor Paul VI cited examples of what might lead their separated brethren into error, or what might constitute gross exaggerations, sterile affection, or vain credulity.[49] Ironically, the new policy came at the very time when many Anglicans, Lutherans, and others were paying renewed attention to Mary and incorporating Marian devotions into their own religious practices. Paul initiated major ecumenical campaigns and noted the renewed attention in a 1974 encyclical letter.[50] But in the same letter he repeated the warning:

Chapter 4. Marian Doctrine and Beyond

"[E]very care should be taken to avoid any exaggeration which could mislead other Christian brethren about the true doctrine of the Catholic Church. Similarly, the Church desires that any manifestation of cult which is opposed to correct Catholic practice should be eliminated."[51]

John Paul II's election to the papacy in 1978 helped offset the shift in Rome's official policy toward Mary. His great personal devotion to her found support in the church and elsewhere. He even confided that reading de Montfort's *True Devotion to Mary* was "a decisive turning point in my life."[52] But John Paul still resisted pressure to declare new Marian dogmas. Pope Francis has been concerned with other issues in the church. The long-term effects of Vatican II's action are still playing out.

Proposed Dogmas

The nineteenth and twentieth centuries saw proposals to enshrine several of Mary's titles—and the roles they implied—in dogma. The titles included Mediatrix of Graces, Co-Redemptrix, Queen of Heaven, and Mother of the Church (or World). Some of the underlying concepts had roots in the Middle Ages; others were new.

Writing in the early eighteenth century Louis-Marie de Montfort affirmed:

> To Mary, His faithful spouse, God the Holy Spirit has communicated His unspeakable gifts and He has chosen her to be the dispenser of all He possesses, in such wise that she distributes to whom she wills, as much as she wills, as she wills, and when she wills, all His gifts and graces. The Holy Ghost gives no heavenly gift to men which He does not have pass through her virginal hands.[53]

Powerful words indeed; no other prominent churchman has suggested that Mary dispenses grace "to whom she wills, as much as she wills, as she wills, and when she wills"! Elsewhere de Montfort declared that Mary "was acclaimed 'Hail, full of Grace' by an angel sent from the throne of God. She is the Mediatrix of all Graces.... She is the Mother of Grace."[54]

Pope Leo XIII, who beatified de Montfort in 1888, seemed to echo his words when he wrote: "The recourse we have to Mary in prayer follows upon the office she continuously fills by the side of the throne of God as Mediatrix of Divine grace; being by worthiness and by merit most acceptable to Him, and, therefore, surpassing in power all the angels and saints in Heaven."[55] Leo went on to call Mary "our co-Redemptress." Pope Benedict XV wrote in 1918: "She suffers with her suffering and dying son, almost as if she would have died herself.... [O]ne can say, she redeemed with Christ the human race."[56]

Building on those statements, a campaign developed during the pontificate of Pope John Paul II, pressing for Mary to be designated "Co-Redemptrix with Christ, Mediatrix of all Graces, and Advocate of Humanity." Few people objected to such language in a devotional context, but formal definition as dogma might have had far-reaching theological and ecumenical implications. Advice from inside and outside the Church urged caution, and no action was taken before John Paul's death. Pope Francis has indicated in multiple statements that he does not consider Mary to be the Co-Redemptrix.[57]

De Montfort also commented on Mary's queenship. Mary, he wrote, was given "dominion over the elect," adding boldly: "Mary is the Queen of Heaven and earth by grace, as Jesus is King ... by nature and by conquest."[58] De Montfort was canonized by Pope Pius XII in 1947.

Four years after issuing the decree on Mary's Assumption, Pius XII wrote an encyclical letter *Ad Caeli Reginam* ("On the Queen of Heaven"), which began thus:

> From the earliest ages of the catholic church a Christian people... has addressed prayers of petition and hymns of praise and veneration to the Queen of Heaven. And never has that hope wavered which they placed in the Mother of the Divine King, Jesus Christ; nor has that faith ever failed by which we are taught that Mary, the Virgin Mother of God, reigns with a mother's solicitude over the entire world, just as she is crowned in heavenly blessedness with the glory of a Queen.[59]

Pius designated May 31 as the feast of the "Queenship of Mary." He insisted: "We do not wish to propose a new truth to be believed by Christians, since the title and the arguments on which Mary's queenly dignity ... are to be found in ancient documents of the Church and in the books of the sacred liturgy."[60] He did not claim scriptural support.

Chapter 4. Marian Doctrine and Beyond

In its confirmation of the dogma of the Assumption, the Second Vatican Council described Mary as: "exalted by the Lord as Queen over all things,"[61] suggesting that consideration was still being given to a formal declaration that she is Queen of Heaven.

The Eastern Orthodox churches have long considered Mary to be Mother of the World—a title also bestowed on divine personages in the religions of South Asia. The twentieth century saw signs that a similar title was being considered in the West. The logic was clear; Mary was the mother of Christ, and Christ was our brother. Humanity, or at least the faithful, comprised the Mystical Body of Christ and shared in his sacramental body in the Eucharist.

Pope John XXIII rejected a suggestion that Mary's Spiritual Motherhood, or "Spiritual Maternity," be raised to the level of dogma. Yet Vatican II promoted the notion that Mary should be honored as Mother of the Church:

> She is "the mother of the members of Christ ... having cooperated by charity that faithful might be born in the Church, who are members of that Head." Wherefore she is hailed as a pre-eminent and singular member of the Church, and as its type and excellent exemplar in faith and charity. The Catholic Church, taught by the Holy Spirit, honors her with filial affection and piety as a most beloved mother.[62]

On the Feast of the Immaculate Conception in 1990, Pope John Paul II came even closer to embracing the World Mother concept. Praying before a Marian icon in Rome he declared: "You who serve as Mother of the whole family of the children of God, obtain for the Church that, enriched by the Holy Spirit with the fullness of hierarchical and charismatic gifts, she [the Church] may continue with constancy towards the future."[63]

In 2018 "Celebration of the Blessed Virgin Mary Mother of the Church" was officially added to the Roman liturgical calendar, to be observed on the Monday following Pentecost Sunday.[64] This was not a dogmatic decree but authorization to use the term "Mother of the Church" in a liturgical context.

Preordination of Mary

For more than 1,000 years certain Christian commentators have suggested that Mary was not just a young Jewish woman, "highly favored" and "blessed ... among women," who consented to bear the Savior. Rather, she was preordained, or predestined, to be the mother of Christ. Some even said that Mary was created "in the beginning," before the rest of the human family, for that very purpose. The Annunciation may have been the moment when Jesus was conceived, but the conversation with the angel simply reaffirmed her long-standing commitment to the incarnational mission.

The doctrine of Mary's predestination was closely linked to another doctrine: the absolute primacy of Christ. This latter held that Christ was preordained, or predestined, to take human form before humanity was created—and, importantly, before the Fall of Adam. The Incarnation was not a hastily fashioned plan to redeem fallen humanity but was intended, from the very beginning, to serve a larger purpose.

Neither the predestination of Mary nor the absolute primacy of Christ was raised to the level of dogma. The two doctrines took definite form early in Christianity's second millennium and remained "minority" positions among theologians. Yet they are still discussed and seem to have gained increasing favor over the last two centuries. It should be stressed that the doctrines in no way imply support for Calvinist notions of the predestination of the elect—and by extension predestination of the damned. The Calvinist doctrine is an entirely separate issue, one that many people feel is antithetical to any reasonable understanding of divine justice.

Primacy of Christ

Early support for the absolute primacy of Christ came from the Benedictine theologian Rupert of Deutz (c.1078–c.1129) and from Robert Grosseteste (c.1168–1253), bishop of Lincoln and first chancellor of the University of Oxford. But its chief spokesperson was the Scottish philosopher and theologian John Duns Scotus (c.1266–1308). Duns Scotus was a Franciscan friar who taught, in turn, at the universities of Oxford, Paris and Cologne. He is considered one of the three most important philosopher–theologians of Western Europe in the High Middle Ages.[65]

Duns Scotus rejected the notion that the Incarnation was a "repair mission," made necessary by the sin of Adam and Eve. While he acknowledged that the Incarnation included a redemptive component, he boldly asserted: "I declare that even if no man or angel had fallen, nor any man but Christ were to be created, Christ would still have been predestined this way."[66] He went on to argue: "God willed this glory for Christ. Therefore, before any merit or demerit, He foresaw that Christ would be united with Him in the oneness of Person."[67] The real purpose of the Incarnation was the glory of God and his creation. It was both morally wrong and absurd to rejoice at man's sin—*O Felix Culpa*[68]—as the primary reason for the Incarnation.

Thus emerged what came to be known as the "Scotist"—after Scotus—or "Franciscan" position on the Incarnation. It was opposed by the "Thomist" or "Dominican" position, named for the Franciscans' rivals in theology and other areas, the Dominican Friars and their powerful spokesman Thomas Aquinas. For political as much as other reasons the Thomist position dominated western Christian thought in the centuries that followed.

Theologians in the Eastern churches rejected the notion of a "repair mission" on different grounds. They argued that Redemption was primarily a process of healing humanity's weakness, and the Incarnation was intended to unlock our potential for *theosis*, or "deification."[69]

Scriptural support for the doctrine of *theosis* comes from *2 Peter*: "Whereby are given unto us exceeding great and precious promises: that by these ye might be partakers of the divine nature."[70] Separately, Athanasius, patriarch of Alexandria, built upon *John* 1:14 to declare that Christ "was made man that we might be made god."[71] Gregory of Nyssa (c.335–c.395) stressed that theosis was the very purpose of humanity's creation. Our destiny, in the words of a modern writer, is to become "priests of the cosmos, rendering by [our] dynamic engagement with the world's order, a degree of divine life, a sacred blessing as it were, to all the fabric of God's created existence."[72]

The possibility of attaining theosis remained latent until Christ united the human and divine natures in himself. Even now, only the greatest saints attain theosis, and according to some commentators they can only do so in the hereafter. Russian Orthodox theologian Sergei Bulgakov (1871–1944) affirmed that Mary, "[r]aised up by her son ... has achieved perfect theosis."[73] But he did not specify when she was so blessed.

Predestination of Mary

If Christ was predestined to take human form he needed a mother; so the predestination of Mary followed almost as a corollary of the absolute primacy of Christ. As early as the fifth century Augustine of Hippo (354 –430) suggested that Christ had always known Mary: "Even before he was born of her, he had known his mother in predestination; and also before he, as God, had created her of whom he, as man, would be created, he had known his mother."[74] But again, several centuries elapsed before the doctrine took definite shape.

Meanwhile, from late antiquity onward, Mary was accorded increasingly high honors and raised to near-divine status. As already noted the Council of Ephesus (431) declared her to be the *Theotokos*, interpreted in the West as "Mother of God." The Synod of Hieria (754) affirmed that Mary was "higher than every creature whether visible or invisible."[75] The Second Council of Nicaea (787) recognized that she deserved a special level of reverence, later termed *hyperdulia* (literally, "above the level shown by slaves to their masters"). Hyperdulia was distinguished from *dulia*, owed to ordinary saints, and from *latria* ("service" or "worship"), owed to Christ and God.

In the eleventh century Peter of Damascus affirmed: "All generations proclaim you [Mary] blessed as the only Mother of God, more honored than the cherubim and incomparably more glorious than the seraphim."[76] A century later, Hildegard of Bingen (1098–1179) affirmed: "Mary, you are the bright matter through which the Word breathed all the virtues forth, as once he led forth, in the primal matter of the world, the whole of creation."[77] An antiphon by Francis of Assisi (c.1181–1226) associates Mary with each person of the Trinity:

> Holy Virgin Mary, among the women born into the world, there is no one like you. Daughter and servant of the most high and supreme King and of the Father in heaven, Mother of our most holy Lord Jesus Christ, Spouse of the Holy Spirit, pray for us ... at the side of your most holy beloved Son, our Lord and Teacher.[78]

These various Marian accolades laid the groundwork for Bernard of Clairvaux (1090–1153) to revive Augustine's affirmation of Mary's predestination to be the mother of Christ. In one of his seventeen published sermons on Mary, Bernard explained: "Now, when the Creator of men willed to become man and to be born in the human way, it was necessary for Him to select, or rather to create for Himself, out of all possible women, such a Mother as He foreknew would be worthy of Him and deserving of His esteem."[79] Bernard went on to identify Mary as "a virgin not newly discovered, nor discovered by chance, but chosen from eternity, foreknown and prepared for Himself by the

Chapter 4. Marian Doctrine and Beyond

Most High, guarded by angels, exhibited by the patriarchs under types and figures, announced from afar by the prophets."[80]

Bernard alluded to those "types and figures" in another sermon when he addressed Mary thus: "[T]ou art the true Rebecca chosen and predestined for the Son of the Most High."[81] Bernard was drawing a parallel between Isaac/Rebecca and Christ/Mary. Rebecca (Rebekah) was chosen to be the wife of Isaac, who had narrowly avoided sacrificial death at the hands of his father Abraham.[82] According to a rabbinic midrash, Rebecca received special blessings from God: "the well water rose up to her, the dough she kneaded was blessed, the cloud was visible over her tent, and the Sabbath candles burned from one Sabbath eve to the next."[83]

The Spanish abbess María de Ágreda (1602–1665) offered one of the clearest expositions of Mary's predestination. In her *Mystical City of God*, published posthumously, she identified six "instants" in the manifestation of God. The first three were concerned with the manifestation of the Trinity. The fourth instant brought forth "the Mother of the Divine Word incarnate":

> Thus, before all other creatures, was She conceived in the divine mind, in such manner and such state as befitted and became the dignity, excellence and gifts of the humanity of her most holy Son. To Her flowed over, at once and immediately, the river of the Divinity and its attributes with all its impetuosity, in as far as a mere creature is capable and as is due to the dignity of the Mother of God.[84]

The fifth instant brought forth the angels, and the sixth, humanity. Abbess Maria emphasized that "this most holy and pure Creature," Mary, was "formed and conceived in the divine mind from the beginning and before all the ages."[85] In Maria's account Mary, like Christ, was preordained to play her incarnational role before the Fall of man.

As noted in Chapter 2, nineteenth-century stigmatic Anne Catherine Emmerich boldly testified: "The Blessed Virgin was the one and only pure blossom of the human race, flowering in the fullness of time.... She was preordained in eternity and passed through time as the Mother of the Eternal."[86]

Also in the nineteenth century, Roman Catholic writer James Spencer Northcote linked the predestination of Mary directly to the absolute primacy of Christ:

> [The primacy] of Jesus Christ contains within itself, necessarily involves and supposes as a part of itself, the predestination of Mary also, because it was only in and through her that He was to receive His sacred Humanity.... Jesus Christ could only be the subject of a decree of predestination, inasmuch as He was the Son of Man and He was the Son or Man only inasmuch as He was the son of Mary. Mary, then, must needs have been included, virtually at least, if not expressly, in that decree which predestined Jesus to be the first-born of the elect.[87]

Northcote added that the Jews who awaited the Redeemer should also have been aware of the coming of Mary:

> [I]t is certain that she [Mary] was present in an especial manner to the mind of God, and was set before the minds of men in prophecy, from the beginning of the world, so that a devout student of the Old Law, "looking for the redemption of Israel," must needs have looked also for the coming of some very remarkable woman to be the Mother of the Redeemer.[88]

At the end of the Second Vatican Council Pope Paul VI reiterated: "Predestined from eternity by that decree of divine providence which determined the incarnation of the Word to be the Mother of God, the Blessed Virgin was on this earth the virgin Mother of the Redeemer."[89]

The preordination of Mary was never declared an article of faith in the Church of Rome, but it supported, and received support from, the dogma of the Immaculate Conception. In his preamble to the dogmatic declaration of the Immaculate Conception Pope Pius IX asserted that "God, by one and the same decree, had established the origin of Mary and the Incarnation of [Christ]."[90]

Pius IX pointed to the prophecy in *Genesis* in which God said to the serpent: "I will put enmities between you and the woman, between your seed and her seed."[91] He added, significantly: "so the most holy Virgin, united with him [Christ] by a most intimate and indissoluble bond, was, with him and through him, eternally at enmity with the evil serpent, and most completely triumphed over him."[92]

Pius IX seemed content to trace the predestination of Mary back to the Garden of Eden. In 1987, however, Pope John Paul II echoed the words of María de Ágreda: "In the mystery of Christ she [Mary] is present even 'before the creation of the world,' as the one whom the Father 'has chosen' as Mother of his Son."[93]

Such statements and similar ones about Mary's origins may be compared with a passage in *Proverbs*: "The Lord possessed me in the beginning of his way, before his works of old. I was set up from everlasting, from the beginning, or ever the earth was."[94] There the speaker was "Wisdom" (Hebrew: *Chokmah*, Greek: *Sophia*, Latin: *Sapientia*). She had a decidedly feminine persona, and her name was grammatically feminine in all three languages.

Whether the passage in *Proverbs* has any relevance to Mary, whether Sophia—to use her Greek name—was a personage in her own right, and whether Mary and Sophia might be related in some way are questions addressed later in the book.

Priesthood of Mary

A recurring theme in the narrative of ancient Christian texts and images was Mary's priestly role: she preached, baptized, and most importantly led public worship. No formal doctrine concerning that role has emerged or is anticipated in the foreseeable future. Indeed, from late antiquity through the twentieth century, Rome discouraged any focus on Mary's priesthood, lest it encouraged women's quest for ordination.

Yet, throughout the ages, high-ranking churchmen have made significant comments concerning Mary's sacerdotal role. Today, when Rome seems to be edging closer to ordaining women, and other sacramental denominations already welcome female clergy at all levels, the concept of Mary's priesthood has the potential to find a positive response across a broad spectrum of Christianity.

Mary and the Eucharist

A passage from the *Gospel of Bartholomew*, cited in Chapter 1, relates Mary's ecstatic experience in the temple when an angelic figure prophesied celebration of the Eucharist:

> And he [the angel] smote his garment upon the right hand and there came a very great loaf, and he set it upon the altar of the temple and did eat of it first himself, and gave unto me also. And again he smote his garment upon the left hand and there came a very great cup full of wine: and he set it upon the altar of the tem-

ple and did drink of it first himself, and gave also unto me. And I beheld and saw the bread and the cup whole as they were.[95]

German Benedictine abbess Elisabeth of Schönau (c.1129–1164) had a number of visions of Jesus, Mary, and other celestial beings. On one occasion, at Mass, she received a blessing from the "image of a regal woman, standing on high, clothed in the whitest vestments and wrapped in a purple mantle." Then, after receiving Communion Elisabeth had another vision: "I saw my Lady standing beside the altar, in a garment like a priestly chasuble ... and she had on her head a glorious crown."[96]

Elisabeth's vision may have inspired an early fifteenth-century painting of Mary vested in a chasuble: *Le sacerdoce de la Vierge* ("Priesthood of the Virgin"), from the School of Amiens, France.[97] The crown in the vision no doubt identified Mary as Queen of Heaven. Another painting relevant to this discussion is *The Virgin Adoring the Host* (1852), by Jean Auguste Dominique Ingres.[98] A detail is shown in Figure 4.1.

Figure 4.1

The Virgin Adoring the Host (1852) by Jean Auguste Dominique Ingres (detail).

Ingres painted several variations of this theme, each including images of the patron or persons the patron wished to favor.

Chapter 4. Marian Doctrine and Beyond

Charles de Condren (1588–1641), French mystic and doctor of the Sorbonne, Paris, affirmed Mary's continued mystical participation in the Mass:

> A Mass ... will be celebrated every day in the church of ... to the intention of the very blessed Mother of God ... I place her Son, Jesus Christ, into the hands (of Mary) by this foundation in as much as I can, and I beg her with my whole heart to offer it herself to God in this daily sacrifice as she does offer it and has offered it, in time and in eternity, on earth as in heaven.[99]

Condren's contemporary, Spanish Jesuit priest Ferdinand Chirino de Salazar (1575–1646) gave Mary both priestly and royal status:

> Christ the Lord has passed on to Mary much better and much more abundantly than in any other soul or even in the entire Church, the signification of his name. He who is called "Christ" ... poured out the abundance of his ointment on Mary, and so made her a saint, a queen, a priest, and a governess for ever.[100]

Nobody would expect the Church of Rome to follow the Palmarian Catholic Church's lead and include Mary in the Real Presence. Yet Pope John Paul II made some interesting comments about Mary and the Eucharist. He recognized that the gospels did not place Mary at the Last supper but suggested that her words at the Marriage Feast of Cana: "Whatsoever he saith unto you, do it,"[101] were prophetic of the institution of the Eucharist. And "the role she assumed at Cana in some way accompanies Christ throughout his ministry."[102] In consequence she "has a profound relationship" with the Eucharist.[103]

Mary and the Sacrifice of the Cross

The discussion of Mary's priestly role has often focused on her presence at the cross, reframing traditional notions of the *Mater Dolorosa*, or "Mother of Sorrows." Mary was not simply a devastated mother, watching her son die in agony on the cross. Because of the intimate spiritual relationship she had with Jesus, she was participating in the sacrifice unfolding before her—and doing so as the representative of humanity.

An early suggestion that Mary's sacrifice was of a sacramental nature was attributed to Albertus Magnus (c.1200–1280) but probably came from an unknown author.[104] In due course her role came to be compared more and more with that of the priest.

Mary: Adept, Queen, Mother, Priestess

Jan Mombaer (1460–1501), a monk and hymn writer who was drawn to the *devotio moderna* movement, suggested that Mary was the first Christian priest, "ordained" at the cross: "Mary, the true first priest, is clothed with the most bitter, motherly mourning ... and entered the sacristy of the mountain of Calvary and stands at the high altar of the cross like her Son, and offers the living fruit of her womb to the death ... so that he may life and suffer within us."[105]

One of the *Mystical Sermons*, compiled in the sixteenth century by the canonesses of St Agnes Convent, Arnhem, includes the insight: "She [Mary] offers with the chalice of her blessed hands, offers the most blessed body and blood, with which the High Godhead had clothed himself through her. She offers with her most holy and most blessed gift ... which is Christ."[106] French priest Julien Loriot (1633–1715) explored a similar theme:

> Mary is a divine priestess, she is a great sacrificer who takes the place of all people and offers to God in their name the greatest and most worthy sacrifice that has ever been offered, presenting to him his unique Son, so holy, so pure, so innocent, which makes St Epiphanius call her the priestess of our religion .... Oh blessed virgin, you truly are the priestess of our religion; you have put together in one sacrifice, the most perfect sacrifice which the earth has ever offered.[107]

Significantly, Epiphanius (c.315–403), bishop of Salamis, Cyprus, considered the possibility that Mary might have been martyred, in which case she would have offered herself in sacrifice in an overt, physical manner.[108]

In 1866 Cardinal Nicholas Wiseman, first Archbishop of Westminster and first Roman Catholic primate of England and Wales since the reign on Mary I, returned to the issue of Mary's participation in the sacrifice of the cross. Building on Mombaer's theme, he declared:

> Therefore does she [Mary] stand at the foot of the cross, that for lost man she may make a public and willing sacrifice of all that is dear to her on earth. Only she, His Mother, can thus put herself into strict uniformity with His Almighty Father .... [S]he became the priestess on the part of all mankind, who was allowed to accomplish the holocaust, which was considered too difficult and painful for Father Abraham, the sacrifice of a beloved child.[109]

Chapter 4. Marian Doctrine and Beyond

One of the most striking statements was made by Bishop Jean Nazlian, speaking at a Eucharistic congress at Lourdes in 1914:

> Mary is also something greater than temples or tabernacles ... she is priest .... A priest has the power to mystically produce the body of the Lord giving that body its sacramental form .... I allow myself to say that Mary is the first to say Mass, by agreeing to the Incarnation and so preparing the victim ... Mary fulfils in advance the sacrifice of the cross by preparing what is required for it .... More than any priest she can point at her crucified Son and say: "This is my body!" Mary is therefore not a priest who does not share in the sacrifice, but a priest who puts herself into the victim who is the heavenly bread.[110]

Michelangelo Buonarroti's sculpture, the *Pietà* (1498–1499), housed in St Peter's Basilica, Rome, famously depicts Mary holding the body of Jesus, taken down from the cross. In the light of Nazlian's comment, it may be considered as valid a symbol of the Eucharist as are depictions of the Last Supper.

Writing in 1943 Pope Pius XII linked Mary's role as the priestess for all humankind with notions of the immaculate second Eve; he also noted her offering of love as an element in the sacrifice of the cross: "It was she, the second Eve, who, free from all sin, original or personal, and always more intimately united with her Son, offered Him on Golgotha to the Eternal Father for all the children of Adam ... and her mother's rights and her mother's love were included in the holocaust."[111]

Theologian William Most (1914–2016) synthesized several of these comments thus:

> She [Mary] did all this not merely as a private person, but as a sacred person, designated by the Eternal Father to share in the offering, so that what the Father accepted as He looked down upon Calvary was *a joint work* of Mother and Son, the New Adam and the New Eve. Of course His offering alone would have abundantly sufficed without her, but it was part of the generous design of God that she should be associated in the work of the Redemption, in the atonement and earning of all graces.[112]

Virgo Sacerdos

Marist Brother John M. Samaha noted that the latter part of the nineteenth century saw an increase both in interest in Mary's sacerdotal role and in the desire by nuns and other women to emulate her:

> Around 1870, the idea of living as a victim began to gain popularity among a number of generous souls, especially women religious, who proposed to assist the priests through their prayers and sacrifices. They thought naturally of Mary praying and offering herself for and with her son, and they loved to consider her as their sacerdotal virgin or the virgin Priest. This devotion aroused great enthusiasm, and was at times expressed in formulas scarcely theological.[113]

Response from the level of the papacy has been mixed. Pope Pius IX endorsed a book by Monsignor O. van den Berghe (1873) in which he said: "Mary united herself so closely to the sacrifice of her divine Son that she has been called the 'Virgin Priest' (*Virgo Sacerdos*) by the Fathers of the Church." Whether the title *Virgo Sacerdos* was actually used by the church fathers is unclear. But the painting from the School of Amiens suggests that it was known in the fifteenth century. In 1906 Pope Pius X attached an indulgence to a prayer containing the language: "Mary, Virgin Priest, pray for us," explaining that, although Mary had never received the sacrament of Holy Orders, she nevertheless possesses as much dignity and grace as are found in the priesthood.[114]

Subsequent popes and their administrations have tried to downplay any suggestion that Mary was actually a priest, or priestess, "in the ordinary sense of the word."[115] In 1916 the Holy Office forbade the "the misuse of Marian statues and pictures" portraying her as a priest.[116] And in 1927 it forbade altogether devotion to Mary in her priestly role. Acknowledgement of her priestly status would embolden women pressing for ordination.[117]

Rome's efforts to suppress thoughts of *Virgo Sacerdos* have been unsuccessful. Feminist theologians, historians, and others inside and outside the church have become deeply interested in Mary's priesthood, its implications for our understanding of her earthly life, and its implications for women's role in ministry. The work of the Wijngaards Institute for Catholic Research and Ally Kateusz's influential book *Mary and Early Christian Women* (2019) were mentioned in Chapter 3. The Wijngaards Institute's primary thrust is the ordination of women, but it has accumulated an extensive catalog of testimonies to Mary's priestly ministry.

Where notions of Mary's priestly role can find an immediate response is in sacramental churches that already admit women to the priesthood. The first woman priest in the Anglican Communion was ordained in 1944, and the first female bishop in 1989. Katharine Jefferts Schori served as Presiding Bishop of the Episcopal Church (2006–2015), the first female primate in the Anglican Communion.

The first woman priest in the Lutheran World Federation was ordained in 1948. Not all Lutheran churches have bishops. But the first female bishop in the federation was ordained in 1992. Elizabeth Amy Eaton was elected Presiding Bishop and primate of the Evangelical Lutheran Church in America in 2013. The same year, Antje Zöllner Jackelén was elected Archbishop of Uppsala and primate of the Church of Sweden.

Anglican Mariology

Like their counterparts on the continent of Europe, the English reformers scrutinized Marian doctrine to determine what they could accept. The principal spokesmen on this topic in the newly independent Church of England were Thomas Cranmer (1489–1556), Archbishop of Canterbury; John Jewel (1522–1571), Bishop of Salisbury; and Hugh Latimer (1487–1555), Bishop of Worcester. We shall see in the next chapter that Latimer was the driving force behind the destruction of Marian shrines in England.

The English reformers insisted that the principal focus must be on Christ, but they recognized that Mary played a key role in the Incarnation. They accepted the decrees of the first four ecumenical councils, including the Council of Ephesus' declaration that Mary was the Mother of God. The reformers declined to take a position on whether Mary was preserved from original sin, but they acknowledged her perpetual virginity.

When Queen Mary I placed England once more under Roman obedience, Cranmer and Latimer were burned at the stake; Nicholas Ridley, Bishop of London, and many others met the same fate. After her brief reign, Queen Elizabeth I came to the throne. She and her chief theologian, Richard Hooker (1554–1600), promoted the notion of the *via media* ("middle way"), in which the Church of England sought a balance between Roman Catholicism and the more radical Protestantism of Scotland and continental Europe.[118]

Attitudes toward Mary, from then on, were divided between the "high-church" faction that wanted to preserve much of pre-Reformation English Christianity, including elements of Marian devotion, and the "low-church" faction, which promoted the more radical ideals of the Reformation.

Keeping the Flame Burning

Notable members of the high-church faction were the seventeenth-century Caroline Divines, so-called because their collective tenure spanned the execution of King Charles I and the restoration of the monarchy under Charles II. An early spokesman of the Divines was Bishop Lancelot Andrewes (1555–1626), best remembered for overseeing the translation of the King James Bible. Andrewes also wrote and preached on Mary, and shared some interesting insights.

Andrewes referred to Mary in a prayer as "allholy, immaculate, more than blessed mother of God and ever-virgin."[119] In one of his sermons Andrewes came close to proclaiming Mary to be Mother of all people.[120] In another he compared Mary's womb with the "womb of the Church" and noted the filial relationship between Christ and ourselves. Mary was the agent for "His participation of our human [nature], our participation of His Divine nature."[121] Andrewes' reference to participation in the divine nature affirmed the Eastern Orthodox doctrine of *theosis*.

Jeremy Taylor (1613–1667), Bishop of Down and Connor and vice-chancellor of the University of Dublin, defended the title "Mother of God." Of her perpetual virginity, he wrote:

> The scripture nowhere says that the blessed Virgin was a virgin perpetually to the day of her death: but as therefore it cannot be obtruded as an article of faith, yet there are a great many decencies and probabilities of the thing, besides the great consent of almost all the church of God, which makes it very fit to be entertained.[122]

Closer to our own time Oxford scholar and clergyman John Henry Newman (1801–1890) asked the rhetorical question: "Who can estimate the holiness and perfection of her who was chosen to be the mother of Christ?" Newman also noted that "Christ derived His manhood from her, and so had an especial unity of nature with her." But he warned that to dwell upon that unity of nature was impossible "without some perversion of feeling." "For, truly," he added, Mary "is raised above the condition of sinful beings, though by nature a sinner; she is brought near to God, yet is but a creature; and seems to lack her fitting place in our limited understandings, neither too high nor too low."[123] Like most Anglicans Newman was reluctant to display too much enthusiasm in his devotion to Mary.

Newman went on to become an early leader of the Tractarian Movement[124] and eventually converted to Roman Catholicism—where he wrote more extensively on Mariology. Meanwhile, Edward Bouverie Pusey (1800–1882), English clergyman and for many years spokesperson for the Tractarian Movement, wrote a major work addressing issues of Mariology.[125] In most cases he was critical of Roman doctrinal formulations, notably the recently defined dogma of the Immaculate Conception, but his work revealed great personal devotion to and respect for Mary.

Lex Orandi, Lex Credendi

Andrewes, Taylor, and the Tractarians were sharing personal insights; they did not speak for the Church of England or for Anglicanism as a whole. Indeed, Anglicanism is a liturgical, rather than a confessional, denomination; beliefs tend to emerge from the liturgy rather than from authoritative pronouncements.[126] Thus we may be obliged to look for cues about Marian beliefs in the liturgies of the Church of England and its daughter churches. Today, Anglicanism is represented by some forty-five autonomous churches that comprise the worldwide Anglican Communion, as well as by independent denominations like the Anglican Church of North America.

Mary is mentioned in the Nicene Creed in all liturgies. And in most Anglican liturgies the *Magnificat* holds its worthy place in Evening Prayer, with the memorable words: "[B]ehold, from henceforth all generations shall call me blessed."[127] Liturgies for August 15—the single feast dedicated to Mary—provide additional hints.

Scotland went through a long period of Calvinist dominance, and the official Church of Scotland was and remains Presbyterian. In that environment Mary played no larger a role than serving as "host mother" for the incarnating Jesus. But by the end of the seventeenth century, however, a viable Anglican alternative, the Scottish Episcopal

Church, was emerging. And in a reaction to the majority Calvinist sentiment, it became the highest of high churches.[128]

The *Scottish Liturgy* for August 15 declares: "O God, you have taken to yourself the blessed Virgin Mary, mother of your incarnate Son. May we who have been redeemed by his blood share with her the glory of your eternal kingdom."[129] Essentially the same language appears in the 1979 *Book of Common Prayer* of the Episcopal Church in the United States.

The liturgical manual *For All the Saints*, of the Anglican Church of Canada offers narratives for the various feast days, including this one for August 15, which appropriately hints at the Dormition and Assumption:

> Mary is honored because she was the Mother of Jesus Christ, the Son of God—and because the Gospels testify that she was a virgin when she conceived and gave him birth.... But it is not the only reason, for the evangelists also portray her as the archetype of all the people of God and the person who leads their praises of the Almighty.... An ancient tradition testifies that Mary was taken up in glory as soon as she died, and Christian devotion has never begrudged her the place of highest honor in the presence of God. It has delighted in the conviction that she who responded to God's perplexing call with praise must already enjoy the reward of faith—and that she who gave the Son of God his human life has received all the fullness of the eternal life which he was born to give.[130]

A few clues can also be found in other parts of the Anglican liturgy. The *Scottish Liturgy* includes Mary in the fellowship to be expected after baptism:

> Help us, who are baptized into the fellowship of Christ's Body to live and work to your praise and glory; may we grow together in unity and love until at last, in your new creation, we enter into our heritage in the company of the Virgin Mary, the apostles and prophets, and of all our brothers and sisters living and departed.[131]

It also offers this short insert which can be incorporated into the Eucharistic Prayer:

> As children of your redeeming purpose ... who honor Mary, chosen mother of your Son, and with all generations call her blessed, we offer you our praise.[132]

Eucharistic Prayer 6 in the *Book of Alternative Services* of the Anglican Church of Canada includes the following words: "[G]rant that we may find our inheritance with the Blessed Virgin Mary, with patriarchs, prophets, apostles, and martyrs ... and with all the saints."[133]

Many Anglicans reacted negatively to Rome's dogmatic decrees on the Immaculate Conception and the Assumption, insisting that the two doctrines lacked scriptural backing. Nevertheless, by the mid-twentieth century Anglican and Roman Catholic attitudes toward Mary, in both beliefs and devotion, were converging. Among the charges to the Anglican/Roman Catholic International Commission (ARCIC), an ecumenical initiative dating from 1966, was to explore mutual interest in Mary.[134]

In 2004 the ARCIC issued a landmark report: "Mary: Grace and Hope in Christ," commonly known as the "Seattle Statement." It noted that "[M]any Anglicans were drawn into a more active devotion to Mary, and Roman Catholics discovered afresh the scriptural roots of such devotion."[135] The commission also noted: "This study has led us to the conclusion that it is impossible to be faithful to Scripture without giving due attention to the person of Mary."[136] Commenting on the two recent dogmas, the ARCIC noted: "[W]e can affirm together that God has taken the Blessed Virgin Mary in the fullness of her person into his glory [and that] Mary, as *Theotokos*, holds the pre-eminent place within the communion of saints and embodies the destiny of the Church."[137]

The Seattle Statement was not binding either on Roman Catholicism or on member churches of the Anglican Communion. It was discussed by national conventions of some of the member churches, and, as expected, the response was mixed.

Individual beliefs continue to evolve. Rowan Williams, Archbishop of Canterbury from 2002 to 2012, described Mary as one "who stands on the frontier between promise and fulfillment, between earth and heaven, between the two Testaments." He went on to comment on "how deeply she speaks to us about the hope for the world's transfiguration through Jesus, how she stands for the making strange of what is familiar and the homeliness of what is strange." These contrasts underlie how "she can be represented in so many ways, thought about and imagined in so many forms."[138] Indeed they do.

On the other hand, efforts to develop a comprehensive Anglican Mariology are unlikely to be made at a time when other issues are viewed as more pressing.[139]

---

[1] *1 Corinthians* 15:22.

[2] Justin Martyr, *Dialogue With Trypho*, (transl.: A. L. Williams), London Society for Promoting Christian Knowledge, 1930, §100:5, 210. Italicization in translation removed.

[3] Irenaeus, *Against Heresies*, book III, ch. 22, §4 (transl: W. Rambaut), Christian Classics Library.

[4] The original version of the Creed, formulated by the Council of Nicaea in 325, stated only: "... who for us men, and for our salvation, came down and was incarnate and was made man."

[5] *Matthew* 1:25.

[6] "Against Antidicomarians," *The Panarion of Epiphanius of Salamis* (transl.: F. Williams) 2/e, Nag Hammadi and Manichaean Studies. Online: https://web.archive.org/web/20170916133936/http://www.masseiana.org/panarion_bk1.htm. Last accessed May 16, 2020.

[7] Jerome, *The Perpetual Virginity of Blessed Mary: Against Helvidius*, c.383. See for example https://www.conservapedia.com/Helvidius. Last accessed May 11, 2020.

[8] Canon 3, Lateran Council, 649. Online: https://classicalchristianity.com/2012/03/25/canons-of-the-lateran-council-of-649/. Last accessed Aug. 22, 2019. Parenthesis in translation. Skeptics have seized upon the statement that Jesus was conceived "without seed" to raise the issue of whether he had a Y chromosome, and if so where it came from.

[9] Pope Theodore died before the council met, and his place was taken by Pope Martin 1. Neither the council nor Martin's election were approved by the Byzantine emperor, and after the council, Martin and Eastern participant Maximus the Confessor were abducted and brought to trial in Constantinople.

[10] Maximus the Confessor, "Various Texts on Theology, the Divine Economy, and Virtue and Vice," *Philokalia*, (transl.: G. Palmer *et al.*), Eling Trust, 1977, vol. 2, 166.

[11] "Sub Tuum Praesidium Prayer," Univ. of Dayton. Online: https://udayton.edu/imri/mary/s/sub-tuum-praesidium-prayer.php. Last accessed Oct. 4, 2019. See also

Chapter 4. Marian Doctrine and Beyond

http://www.preces-latinae.org/thesaurus/BVM/SubTuum.html. Last accessed Dec. 15, 2019.

[12] See the extensive discussion in Antoine Nachef, *Mary:Virgin Mother in the Thought of the Cappadocian Fathers*, doctoral dissertation, Univ. of Dayton, 1997, especially 32ff.

[13] Rivalry between Alexandria and Constantinople had been going on for a long time. Cyril's uncle Theophilus, Patriarch of Alexandria, (not to be confused with Theophilus of Antioch) had succeeded in having John Chrysostom deposed as Archbishop of Constantinople—though Chrysostom was later hailed as one of the greatest of the eastern church fathers. To what extent politics entered into the Ephesus decision is a matter of debate.

[14] Nestorius of Constantinople, Second Letter to Cyril (transl.: unknown). Papal Encyclicals Online.

[15] Cyril of Alexandria, Second Letter to Nestorius (transl.: unknown). Papal Encyclicals Online:
https://www.papalencyclicals.net/councils/ecum03.htm. Last accessed Sept. 17. 2019.

[16] First anathema, Council of Ephesus. Papal Encyclicals Online. An *anathema* is a curse. Nestorius may not have taught that Jesus Christ was two "persons"; but the charge of "Nestorian heresy" is leveled against them and the Assyrian Church of the East.

[17] The Council of Chalcedon (451) decreed that the human and divine natures were indeed distinct, even though united in a single hypostasis. Although the two main protagonists of the Council of Ephesus were deceased by then, many people interpreted the outcome as a vindication of Nestorius and condemnation of Cyril. In any event the Council of Chalcedon produced its own schism and formation of the Coptic Church, which looked to Cyril as its "founding father."

[18] *Qur'an* 5:116-117.

[19] Cyril of Alexandria, "In Defense of the Theotokos," homily, Council of Ephesus, June 22, 431.

[20] John Chrysostom, Homily 21. Philip Schaff (ed.), *A Select Library of the Nicene and Post-Nicene Fathers of the Christian Church*, vol. 14, "Works of St Chrysostom," Scribner, 1906, 74.

[21] Cyril of Alexandria, *Commentary on John* (transl.: T. Randell), book 12, vol. 2, 1874/1885, commentary on verse 19:25. This passage and the next are included in all current compilations of Cyril's *Commentary*, but some scholars question the attribution to Cyril.

[22] *Ibid.*

[23] Augustine of Hippo, "On Nature and Grace," *Retractions*, ch. 42 (36).
[24] Paul hinted at original sin in *Romans* 5:12, and the concept was developed by Irenaeus, Augustine, and others. The belief that original sin was transmitted through the male semen was first suggested by Augustine.
[25] Jesus was obviously spared because he was conceived by the Holy Spirit rather than a human father. The doctrine of the Immaculate Conception refers to Mary's conception.
[26] Anselm of Canterbury, *Concerning Virginal Conception and Original Sin* (transl.: J. Hopkins & H. Richardson), 1099, ch. 12. Online: https://jasper-hopkins.info/DeConceptu.pdf. Last accessed Aug. 24, 2019.
[27] Thomas Aquinas, *Summa Theologiae* (complete & unabridged version), (transl.: Fathers of the English Province), Coyote Canon Press, 1850-1851. Interestingly, in 1879—just 25 years after dogmatic definition of the Immaculate Conception, and nine years after Vatican I—Pope Leo XIII directed clergy to take the teachings of Thomas as the basis of their theological positions and decreed that all Roman Catholic seminaries and universities teach Thomas' doctrines.
[28] *Ibid*.
[29] *Revelations of St Bridget: On the Life and Passion of Our Lord and the Life of His Blessed Mother* (transl,: 1611), Tan Books, 1965/2015, 14-15.
[30] Martin Luther, Sermon: "On the Day of the Conception of the Mother of God," December 1527. Hartmann Grisar, *Luther* (transl: E. Lamond), Kegan Paul *et al.*, 1915, vol. IV, 238.
[31] Quoted in E. Stakemeier, *De Mariologia et Oecumenismo*, Rome, 1962, 456.
[32] Alexander VII, Apostolic Constitution, *Sollicitudo omnium ecclesiarum*, December 8, 1661. Alexander attributed the doctrine "especially" to three earlier popes: Sixtus IV, Paul V, and Gregory XV.
[33] Pius IX, Apostolic Constitution *Ineffabilis Deus*, Rome, December 8, 1854. An apostolic constitution is the most solemn form of legislation issued by the Pope. It may supersede the importance of a papal bull.
[34] The decision on papal infallibility led to the secession of dissenting bishops and formation of the Old Catholic Church, which survives today.
[35] Vladimir Lossky, *The Mystical Theology of the Eastern Church* (transl.: anon.), St Vladimir's Seminary Press, 1944/1976, 153-155. Lossky went on to say "The work accomplished by Christ is related to our nature.... It is a new nature, a restored creature which appears in the world. It is a new body, pure from all taints of sin, free from external necessity, separated from our iniquity and from every alien will."
[36] Another possibility is that the Immaculate Conception was somehow retroactive.

Chapter 4. Marian Doctrine and Beyond

[37] Medieval western theologians invented *Limbo* [literally, "on the fringes (of hell)"] to house infants who died before they could be baptized. In 2007 the Roman church downgraded limbo from a doctrine to "a possible theological opinion."

[38] Stephen J. Shoemaker, *Ancient Traditions of the Virgin Mary's Dormition and Assumption*, Oxford Univ. Press, 2002, 10.

[39] *Ibid.*, 19-20, 115-116.

[40] The doctrine of the general resurrection is based primarily on *1 Corinthians* 15:12-23.

[41] Shoemaker, *Ancient Traditions of the Virgin Mary's Dormition and Assumption*, 68-69.

[42] Pius XII, Apostolic Constitution *Munificentissimus Deus*, 1950, §44.

[43] Paul VI, *Dogmatic Constitution on the Church* (*Lumen Gentium*), Vatican City, November 21, 1964, ch. VIII, §59. This document was one of the principal statements to come from the council. It was issued in the pope's name, but its provisions had been approved by the assembled bishops by a vote of 2,151 to 5.

[44] John Paul II, General Audience, Wednesday, June 25, 1997, §§ 3, 4.

[45] Clemente Domínguez y Gómez, Papal Document 45, Palmarian Catholic Church, 1983. See Magnus Lundberg, "A Pope of their Own: El Palmar de Troya and the Palmarian Church," *Uppsala Studies in Church History*, Uppsala University Sweden, 2017, 195-196. The conservative Palmarian Catholic Church, headquartered in El Palmar de Troya, Spain, was founded in 1978 by Clemente Domínguez, who took the name Pope Gregory XVII. Three other popes have served since his death in 2005.

[46] Paul VI, *Dogmatic Constitution on the Church*, 1964, ch. VIII, especially §§53, 66, 67.

[47] Critics complained that the council "threw Mary under the bus."

[48] Paul VI, *Dogmatic Constitution on the Church*, ch. VIII, 1964, §67.

[49] The Vatican II warning called to mind the 1916 warning against "the misuse of Marian statues and pictures, dressed in priestly robes."

[50] Paul VI, Encyclical Letter *Marialis Cultus*, 1974, §32.

[51] *Ibid.*

[52] Louis-Marie de Montfort, *True Devotion to Mary* (transl.: F. W. Faber), Tan Books, 1712/2010, viii. The book was written in 1712 but was first published in 1843

[53] *Ibid.*, 11.

[54] Louis-Marie de Montfort, *The Secret of Mary* (transl.: E. Doherty), Montfort Publications, c.1708/2001, 12.

[55] Leo XIII, Encyclical on the Rosary *Lucunda Semper Expectatione*, Vatican City, 1894, §2.

[56] Benedict XV, "Inter Soldalica," *Acta Apostolicae Sedis* ("Acts of the Apostolic See"), March 22, 1918. Italicization removed.

[57] His most recent statement was on May 24, 2021. See: https://www.romereports.com/en/2021/03/24/pope-francis-explains-why-he-does-not-consider-our-lady-co-redemptrix/. Last accessed June 24, 2021. In 2019 Francis dismissed the concept as "foolishness."
[58] Louis-Marie de Montfort, *True Devotion to Mary*, 2.
[59] Pius XII, Encyclical letter *Ad Caeli Reginam*, October 11, 1954, §1.
[60] *Ibid.*, §6.
[61] Paul VI, *Dogmatic Constitution on the Church*, ch. VIII, §59.
[62] *Ibid.*, §53.
[63] John Paul II, prayer before the Roman Icon of Our Lady, "Salus Populi Romani," December 8, 1990.
[64] Congregation for Divine Worship and the Discipline of the Sacraments, "Decree on the Celebration of the Blessed Virgin Mary Mother of the Church in the General Roman Calendar," Vatican City, Feb. 11, 2018.
[65] The others are Thomas Aquinas and William of Ockham.
[66] *Dico tamen quod lapsus non fuit causa praedestinationis Christi. Immo etsi nec homo nec angelus fuisset lapsus, nec plures homines creandi quam solus Christus, adhuc fuisset Christus praedestinatus sic.* John Duns Scotus, *Opus Parisiense*. Quoted in Maximilian Mary Dean, *A Primer on the Absolute Primacy of Christ: Blessed John Duns Scotus and the Franciscan Thesis*, New Bedford, MA: Academy of the Immaculate, 2006, 37, 128.
[67] *Ibid.*, 37.
[68] *O felix culpa quae talem et tantum meruit habere redemptorem* ("O happy sin that earned for us so great, so glorious a Redeemer." The *Exultet*, attributed to Ambrose of Milan (c.340–397), traditionally chanted during the lighting of the paschal candle in the Easter Vigil service
[69] For further information on *theosis* see John F. Nash, "Theosis: a Christian Perspective on Human Destiny," *The Esoteric Quarterly* (Spring 2011), 15-33.
[70] *2 Peter* 1:4.
[71] Athanasius of Alexandria, "Incarnation of the Word," 54, *Nicene and Post-Nicene Fathers*, vol. 4, Christian Literature, 1892, 65.
[72] J. A. McGuckin, "The Strategic Adaptation of Deification," Michael J. Christensen & Jeffery A. Wittung (eds.), *Partakers of the Divine Nature*, Baker Academic, 2008, 107.
[73] Boris Jakim, "Sergius Bulgakov: Russian *Theosis*," *Partakers of the Divine Nature*, 253.
[74] Saint Augustine, *Homilies on the Gospel of John* (transl.: E. Hill), Hyde Park, NY: New City Press, 1990, Homily 8, 178.
[75] Synod of Hieria, Canon 15. Online: https://sourcebooks.fordham.edu/source/icono-cncl754.asp. The iconoclastic canons of the synod were overturned by the Second Council of

Nicaea (787), but this canon was allowed to stand. In the nineteenth century Pope Pius IX used similar language in his *ex cathedra* pronouncement *Ineffabilis Deus*.

76 Peter of Damascus, "A Treasury of Divine Knowledge," *Philokalia* (transl: G. Palmer *et al*.), Thatcham, UK: Eling Trust, 1977, vol. 3, 130.

77 Hildegard of Bingen, Antiphon "O Splendidissima Gemma," *Symphonia*, (transl: M. Atherton), *Hildegard Selected Readings* (New York: Penguin Books, 2001), 117.

78 Marian Antiphon, "Office of the Passion of the Lord," *The Prayers of St Francis*, 9. Online: http:www.ofm.org. Last accessed Oct. 17, 2020.

79 Bernard of Clairvaux, Second Sermon on the Glories of the Virgin Mother" (transl.: "a priest"), *St Bernard's Sermons on the Blessed Virgin Mary*, Tiverton, UK: Mount Melleray Abbey, 1987, 15.

80 *Ibid*., 18.

81 Bernard of Clairvaux, "Sermon for the Sunday within the Octave of the Assumption of Mary," *St Bernard's Sermons on the Blessed Virgin Mary*, 228.

82 *Genesis* 24:3-67. Rebecca bore Isaac two sons, Jacob and Esau.

83 Tamar Kadari, "Rebekah: Midrash and Aggadah," citing *Genesis Rabbah* 60:16. Online: https://jwa.org/encyclopedia/article/rebekah-midrash-and-aggadah.

84 María de Ágreda, *Mystical City of God*, vol. 1, §42 (transl.: F. Marison), (Hammond, IN: Conkey, 1722/1902), 56.

85 *Ibid*. The English translation of the *Mystical City of God* received an *Imprimatur* from the Roman Catholic bishop of Fort Wayne, IN.

86 Clemens W. Brentano (ed.), *The Life of the Blessed Virgin Mary: From the Visions of Ven. Anne Catherine Emmerich* (transl.: M. Palairet), Tan Books, 1954/1970, 146-147.

87 J. Spencer Northcote, *Mary in the Gospels: Or Lectures on the History of Our Blessed Lady as Recorded by the Evangelists*, London: Burns, Lambert & Oats, 1867, 32.

88 *Ibid*., 41.

89 Paul VI, Dogmatic Constitution *Lumen Gentium*, Vatican, November 21, 1964, §61.

90 Pius IX, Apostolic Constitution *Ineffabilis Deus*, Rome, December 8, 1854, "Liturgical Argument."

91 Genesis 3:15.

92 Pius IX, "*Ineffabilis Deus*, "Interpreters of the Sacred Scripture."

93 John Paul II, Encyclical letter *Redemptoris Mater*: "On the Blessed Virgin Mary in the life of the Pilgrim Church," Vatican, March 25, 1987.

94 *Proverbs* 8:22-23

95 *Gospel of Bartholomew* II:18-21 (transl.: M. R. James), Gnostic Society Library.

[96] Elisabeth of Schönau, *First Book of Visions*, ch. 5. Cited in Anne L. Clark, "The Priesthood of the Virgin Mary: Gender Trouble in the Twelfth Century," *Journal of Feminist Studies in Religion* (Spring 2002), 5-24.

[97] A detail from the painting is shown in Chapter 10.

[98] Ingres painted several variations of the same theme; this is the one at the Metropolitan Museum of Art. All show Mary as the central figure, but the other figures are chosen to suit patrons' taste.

[99] Charles de Condren, *Lettres du P. de Condren publiées par P. Auvray et A. Jouffrey*, Paris 1943, appendix 1, § 6. Parenthesis in translation. Cited in http://www.womenpriests.org/charles-de-condren-died-in-1637/. Last accessed Aug. 29, 2019.

[100] Ferdinand C. de Salazar, *Canticum*, vol. 2, 92, 94-95. Cited in https://www.google.com/search?client=firefox-b-1-d&q=Ferdinand+Chirino+de+Salazar. Last accessed Aug. 29, 2019.

[101] *John* 2:5.

[102] John Paul II, *Rosarium Virginis Mariae*, Apostolic Letter, Vatican, October 16, 2002, §21.

[103] John Paul II, *Ecclesia de Eucharistia*, Encyclical Letter, Vatican, April 17, 2003, ch.6, §53.

[104] John M. Samaha, "Priestly Dimension of Mary," Univsity of Dayton. Online: https://udayton.edu/imri/mary/p/priestly-dimension-of-mary.php. Last accessed June 9, 2021.

[105] Quoted in Ineke Cornet, *The Arnhem Mystical Sermons: Preaching Liturgical Mysticism in the Context of Catholic Reform*, Brill, 2018, 212. The *devotio moderna* movement, which began in the 14th century with the work of Gerard Groote, called for spiritual renewal through humility, obedience, and simplicity of life.

[106] Sermon 138. Quoted in Cornet, *The Arnhem Mystical Sermons*, 211.

[107] Julien Loriot, Sermon 10 on the Purification, ib. 316. Cited in http://www.womenpriests.org/mrpriest/loriot.asp. Last accessed Nov. 22, 2018.

[108] See for example Stephen J. Shoemaker, *Ancient Traditions of the Virgin Mary's Dormition and Assumption*, Oxford Univ. Press, 2002, 15fn.

[109] Nicholas Wiseman, *Sermons on our Lord Jesus Christ and his Blessed Mother*, 2/e, Duffy, 1866, 342-343.

[110] Jean Nazlian (or Naslian), Proceedings of the 25th Congrès Eucharistique International, Lourdes, Secretariat General, 1914. Online: https://archive.org/details/xxvecongreseucha00inte/page/36/mode/2up. Last accessed Jan. 14, 2020. Nazlian was the Armenian Catholic bishop of Trabzon, Turkey, later elevated to archbishop.

[111] Pius XII, Encyclical letter *Mystici Corporis Christi*, ("The Mystical Body of Christ"), Vatican, June 29, 1943, §110. It should be noted that in 1943

Chapter 4. Marian Doctrine and Beyond

information about the atrocities in the Nazi death camps was quite limited, and "holocaust" was understood in a more general sense.

[112] William G. Most, *Mary in Our Life*, ch. 16. Emphasis in original. Online: https://www.catholicculture.org/culture/library/most/getchap.cfm?WorkNum=213&ChapNum=18. Last accessed Aug. 29, 2019.

[113] Samaha, "Priestly Dimension of Mary."

[114] Pius X, *Acta Sanctae Sedis* ("Acts of the Holy See"), May 9, 1906. Pius proclaimed: "Three hundred days of indulgence acquires whoever piously and devoutly has recited this prayer." See also the discussion in Samaha, "Priestly Dimension of Mary."

[115] Raniero Cantalamessa, "Mary, Mother and Model of the Priest," Third Advent Sermon, 2009. Online: http://www.piercedhearts.org/scriptures/commentaries_sunday/cantalamessa/advent_sermons/3_advent_sermon_2009.htm. Last accessed Nov. 22, 2018.

[116] The "Holy Office," originally titled the Supreme Sacred Congregation of the Roman and Universal Inquisition, was founded in 1542 with the charge of combating heresy. From 1908 to 1965 it was known as the Supreme Sacred Congregation of the Holy Office. Today it is known as the Congregation for the Doctrine of the Faith.

[117] Factors considered to disqualify women from ordination included menstruation and childbirth. Natal and menstrual blood were believed to defile the Sacrament. Uta Ranke Heinimann, *Eunuchs for the Kingdom of Heaven: Women, Sexuality and the Catholic Church*, Penguin Books, 1990, 2-5.

[118] John F. Nash, *The Sacramental Church*, Wipf & Stock, 2011, chs. 3, 5.

[119] Lancelot Andrewes, *The Preces Privatae of Lancelot Andrewes*, Bishop of Winchester (transl.: F. E. Brightman), Methuen, 1903, 85. The original was written in Latin.

[120] Lancelot Andrewes, sermon Dec. 25, 1609. See Marianne Dorman, "Andrewes and the Caroline Divines' Teaching on the Blessed Virgin Mary," Ecumenical Society of the Blessed Virgin Mary. November, 2000. Online: http://anglicanhistory.org/essays/dorman3.pdf. Last accessed Sept. 16, 2019.

[121] Lancelot Andrewes, sermon Dec. 25, 1614. Online: http://anglicanhistory.org/lact/andrewes/v1/sermon9.html. Last accessed Sept. 16, 2019.

[122] Jeremy Taylor, *Ductor Dubitantium*, 1660. Quoted in Colin Podmore, "Blessed Virgin: Mary and the Anglican Tradition," Assumptiontide Lecture, Walsingham, 2014

[123] John Henry Newman, sermon "The Reverence Due to the Blessed Virgin," Feast of St Mary the Virgin, Oxford, 1832. For more on Newman's

thoughts on Mary see Philip Boyce, *Mary: The Virgin Mary in the Writings of John Henry Newman*, Gracewing, 2001.

[124] The Tractarian (or "Oxford") Movement was a major component of the Catholic Revival Movement within Anglicanism, which sought to reaffirm the traditions of the pre-Reformation English Church. See for example Nash, *The Sacramental Church*, especially chs. 6-7.

[125] Edward B. Pusey, *An Eirenicon*, D. Appleton & Co.,1866. Online: http://anglicanhistory.org/pusey/eirenicon1.pdf. Last accessed December 15, 2019.

[126] Anglicans are fond of the motto *Lex orandi, lex credendi*, literally: "the law of what is prayed [is] the law of what is believed," but more generally conveying the notion that doctrine emerges from common worship.

[127] *Luke* 1:46–55.

[128] Nash, *The Sacramental Church*, 70-89.

[129] Scottish Episcopal Church, *Scottish Liturgy* 1982 with Propers and Revised Common Lectionary, 1982, §21.

[130] Anglican Church of Canada, *For All the Saints*, 246.

[131] Scottish Episcopal Church, *Scottish Liturgy*, 1982, 11.

[132] *Ibid.*, 28.

[133] Anglican Church of Canada, *Book of Alternative Services*, 1985, 208, 210.

[134] The ARCIC was an initiative of Michael Ramsey, 100th Archbishop of Canterbury, and Pope Paul VI.

[135] Anglican/Roman Catholic International Commission, "Mary: Grace and Hope in Christ," Seattle Statement, 2004, §65. Online: https://iarccum.org/doc/?d=16. Last accessed Aug. 24, 2019.

[136] *Ibid.*, §77.

[137] *Ibid.*, §58.

[138] Rowan Williams, *Ponder these Things: Praying with Icons of the Virgin*," Sheed and Ward, 2002, xv.

[139] At the time of writing, the very survival of the Anglican Communion is threatened by disagreements over gender inclusiveness as it applies to marriage and ordination to the clergy. Anglican churches in Britain, North America, Australia, and New Zealand are also concerned about declining membership.

Chapter 5
Marian Devotion and Intercession

Chapter 5 studies the ways Christians have expressed devotion to Mary and asked her favors. Marian devotion and intercession began in antiquity and flourished, in parallel with the doctrinal developments discussed in Chapter 4, throughout the Middle Ages and beyond. Mary's feast days graced the liturgical calendar; church buildings, abbeys, and shrines were dedicated to her; prayers and hymns were composed and devotional practices created in her honor; religious orders and sodalities sprang up to serve her.

Mary served two distinct needs in the spiritual lives of the masses. People needed a goddess, and some forms of Marian devotion rose to the level of adoration or worship. They also wanted a sympathetic mother. Mary was thought to be sensitive to people's needs and responsive to their pleas—perhaps more understanding of human failings than the Christ who courageously trod the road to Calvary. Despite rejection by major segments of Christianity after the Reformation, Marian devotion and intercession continued to expand in Roman Catholicism and Eastern Orthodoxy.

The repertory of Marian devotion and intercession extends beyond the spoken word to include art, music, ritual and dance.

Introduction

Marian doctrine attempts to define Mary, devotion expresses love for her, and intercession seeks her help. But whereas dogma comes with the claim that, once formulated, it is universally and eternally valid, devotion and intercession are organic; their modes of expression evolve over time and may vary from place to place.

By the end of the second century Mary had been transformed from a provincial, Middle Eastern, Jewish woman into an upper-class, European, "Christian" woman appropriate to the culture of a Greco-Roman church. By the fifth century she had become a celestial being with only tenuous connections to her physical form or her life in Palestine. Marian devotion evolved with a focus on this "new Mary."

Devotion to Mary met a deeply felt human need. Yet that need was always ambiguous. On the one hand, people needed a *queen*, a *goddess*. In the ancient world queens and goddesses might be perceived as serene highnesses, exuding beauty and reigning in peace. But they could also be seen as warriors, fiercely protecting their children, their people, or causes they had embraced. Archetypal warrior figures included the Canaanite Anath, the Hebrew Esther and Judith, the Greek Antigone, and the Hindu Durga. In *Proverbs* we read of the personified Wisdom (Chokmah/Sophia): "Strength and honor are her clothing."[1]

The need to worship a divine feminine figure ran deep. As Christianity spread throughout the pagan world, Mary—and occasionally other female saints—took the place of traditional feminine deities. Striking examples were the cult of the Collyridians, to be discussed shortly; the Marian cult in Ireland; and the tradition of Black Madonnas of continental Europe. "Conversion to Christianity" meant that a country's ruling elite embraced the new religion. The masses might know little about Christianity or might just pay lip service to it; Christianization was often quite superficial, and the old religions lurked close to the surface.

People also needed an intimate, compassionate Mother. Life for the average person in antiquity and the Middle Ages, to quote English philosopher Thomas Hobbes, was "nasty, brutish and short." Work was hard and hours long, hunger and sickness were rife, men died in battle, women died in childbirth, children died in infancy. Church sermons stirred anxiety about what lay beyond the grave. People weighed down by guilt or shame trembled before the One "who shall judge the quick and the dead."[2] But they were less fearful approaching Mary. The Mother of Sorrows felt their pain, and the Mother of Mercy held them in her arms. Perhaps she could use her influence to secure forgiveness for their sins or secure a more favorable response to their petitions.

Concerns about the propriety of Marian devotion, or the heights to which it should go, were raised throughout Christian history. The Second Council of Nicaea (787) distinguished reverence for Mary, termed *hyperdulia* (literally, "above the level shown by slaves to their masters"), from *latria* ("service" or "worship"), reserved for Christ and the Father. In the other direction, hyperdulia was distinguished from *dulia*, owed to the saints. Whether those canonical distinctions helped, or help today, is open to question.

The Protestant reformers sought to rid Christianity of anything resembling a goddess. Marian devotion, in their view, was idolatrous, and intercession was either pointless or distracted from a relationship with Christ. But the resurgence of Marian devotion in high-church Anglicanism, Lutheranism, and elsewhere shows that the need for a female figure of high spiritual stature is not easily suppressed.

Marian devotion and intercession can be expressed in multiple ways. Spoken prayer may be the most direct way to articulate praise or petitions. But it cannot always capture our deepest aspirations; indeed, words can sometimes become a hindrance. Spoken prayer may give way to ritual gestures, postures or movements; to acts of sacrifice or asceticism; or to silence. Or it may give way to song and more complex musical forms, and to the visual and performing arts. The chapter ends with comments on Marian devotion and intercession in the arts.

Marian Devotion in the Early Church

The Beginnings of Devotion

Some scholars believe that a feast day celebrating the "Memory of Mary" was observed among Jewish Christians in the Jerusalem area, where the mother of Jesus is believed to have passed away. But the Jerusalem community collapsed when the Roman army destroyed the city in 70 CE, and familiar liturgical practices likely were lost. No direct evidence has been discovered connecting the "Memory of Mary" to the feast of the Dormition of Mary, observed in the Byzantine Empire from the sixth century onward.

Devotion to a real or imagined *living* Mary may have developed as early as the second century. A fresco in the Priscilla Catacombs of Rome, dated to the "first half of the second century," depicts the Madonna and Child and a prophet, possibly Isaiah. We do not know the story behind the image or whether a text was associated with it. But the investment of resources and the commissioning of the fresco

Mary: Adept, Queen, Mother, Priestess

show a significant level of reverence. A detail from a neighboring fresco was shown in Figure 3.1.

The oldest known prayer addressed to Mary, an intercessory prayer, is dated to the late third century. Briefly mentioned in Chapter 4, it is significant not only for the early usage but also because it refers to Mary as *Theotokos* ("God-bearer" or "Mother of God"), a term with important doctrinal implications. The prayer was originally written in Greek, but it is better known by its Latin title *Sub tuum Praesidium* ("Under thy protection"). An English translation is as follows:

> We turn to you for protection, Holy Mother of God.
> Listen to our prayers and help us in our needs.
> Save us from every danger, glorious and blessed Virgin.[3]

The Collyridians

Devotion to Mary occasionally rose to the level of outright worship. Indeed, Marian worship may have begun even before the Council of Ephesus declared her to be the mother of God. Unfortunately for historians of religious practices, the earliest example is known only through the writings of a detractor.

Epiphanius of Salamis (c.315–403) condemned a sect, "brought to Arabia from Thrace and upper Scythia." On certain days of the year, he alleged, priestesses of the sect performed a kind of eucharistic ritual in which small loaves or cakes (Greek: *kollyris*) were sacrificed to Mary. Appropriately, he called them the *Collyridians*.[4] Their practice represented one of the few instances in the whole of Christian history in which sacramental ritual has been created with a Marian focus.

Epiphanius prayed to God that he could stamp out that "idolatrous sect." But he seemed more upset that the Collyridian sect was led by women! Not only were women unfit to serve in such roles, they "are unstable, prone to error, and mean-spirited."[5]

No other writer mentioned the Collyridians, and some scholars are unsure whether they really existed. In any event they could probably be relegated to a footnote in history were it not that their customs closely mirrored those of a Judaic cult in the century or so preceding the Babylonian Exile. Jeremiah the prophet condemned ritual sacrifices to deities—one of whom bore an interesting title:

> Seest thou not what they do in the cities of Judah and in the streets of Jerusalem? The children gather wood, and the fathers kindle the

fire, and the women knead their dough, to make cakes to the queen of heaven, and to pour out drink offerings unto other gods, that they may provoke me to anger."[6]

Jeremiah did not identify the "queen of heaven," but probably she was Asherah, consort of Abraham's god El Shaddai.[7]

The parallels are striking. Both cults allegedly were comprised of, or at least led by, women—to the horror of their respective detractors. And in both cases cakes were sacrificed to a female personage. Interestingly, though, it was not the Collyridians who would name Mary "Queen of Heaven" but institutional Christianity!

Epiphanius wrote in the late fourth century and if, as he claimed, the Collyridians migrated all the way to Arabia, the sect may have been active in their original homelands a century or more earlier. Nobody would suggest that the Collyridians were part of an unbroken lineage dating back to the time of Jeremiah. But the two groups may have been linked by ongoing patterns of ritual sacrifice of cakes to a goddess. We know that cakes were offered to the Greek goddesses Demeter and Persephone.[8] It is entirely possible that, with the spread of Christianity, goddess cults preserved their liturgical customs and simply allowed Mary to take the place of former patrons. Thrace and upper Scythia were Celtic lands with a rich history of goddesses.[9] As we shall see, other Celtic people offered cakes to Mary.

Marian Devotion in the Middle Ages

Mary, "Great Beyond Measure"

The Middle Ages offers many examples in which Mary was accorded great reverence. Perhaps it did not reach the sacramental level exhibited by the Collyridians, but certainly we find instances of Marian adoration. In the eleventh century, or thereabouts, Peter of Damascus offered this hymn of praise:

> Thus I, too, unworthy believer that I am, entreat you, holy Queen, that I may be allowed to perceive the gifts of grace bestowed on you and on the other saints, and to understand how you display so many virtues.... Rightly do we, who have been saved through you, pure Virgin, confess that you are the Mother of God, extolling you with the angelic choirs. For God, whom men cannot see, on

whom the ranks of angels do not dare to look, has through you become visible to men as the Logos made flesh.... For with the true faith we confess that you are the Mother of God and we bless you, the ever-blessed. All generations proclaim you blessed as the only Mother of God, more honored than the cherubim and incomparably more glorious than the seraphim.[10]

In the West, Anselm of Canterbury (c.1033–1109) wrote three poems dedicated to Mary, the third of which began:

Mary, great Mary,
most blessed of all Marys,
greatest among all women,
great Lady, great beyond measure,
I long to love you with all my heart.[11]

The month of May was named for the Greek goddess Maia, mother of Hermes. But in medieval Europe only a small step was needed to rededicate it to Mary, mother of Jesus. Although Mary had many feasts throughout the year, May 1, May (Mary's) Day, was a special day on the liturgical calendar. As Christianity spread across Europe, May Day absorbed traditions of the Roman festival of Flora, goddess of flowers, as well as Celtic traditions of Beltane. The highlight of May Day celebrations was crowning of the May Queen with a wreath of flowers. The Queen of the May was a conflation of Maia, Flora, other pre-Christian goddesses, and Mary. In later centuries, and especially where Marian devotion was more focused, the wreath was placed on a statue of Mary. Whether May Day, and similar, celebrations could be considered liturgical or sacramental in nature is a matter of debate.

Hildegard of Bingen (1098–1179) affirmed: "Mary, you are the bright matter through which the Word breathed all the virtues forth, as once he led forth, in the primal matter of the world, the whole of creation."[12] In identifying Mary with "bright matter," Hildegard was drawing upon the etymological connection between the words "mother" (Latin: *mater*) and "matter" (*materia*).[13] Some modern esotericists continue to exploit that connection.

The Rhineland, where Hildegard lived and worked, had a rich Celtic tradition, with an emphasis on the sacredness of nature. One of her Marian hymns combined age-old Celtic imagery with hints of the modern active woman:

Chapter 5. Marian Devotion and Intercession

> Hail to you, O greenest fertile branch! You budded forth amidst breezes and winds in search of the knowledge of all that is holy. When the time was ripe your own branch brought forth blossoms.... The heat of the sun exudes sweat from you like the balsam's perfume.... [I]n you O gentle Virgin, is every fullness of joy, everything that Eve rejected. Now let endless praise resound to the Most High![14]

No medieval apologist paid Mary more attention than Hildegard's contemporary, Bernard of Clairvaux (1090–1153). He explored Mary's relationship with the "woman clothed with the sun,"[15] in *Revelation*, and made much of the image's symbolism. The moon under her feet symbolized the folly of man, but also the church militant "that shines with borrowed splendor."[16] The serpent crushed beneath her heel was the embodiment of error: "It is through Mary alone that every impious heresy has been vanquished."[17] The twelve stars in her diadem could be divided into three constellations of four, each constellation corresponding to a "prerogative" of grace: that of the heavens, the flesh, and the heart.[18]

The devotion expressed by Bernard and Hildegard was not without context. Not far from where they wrote, the Kabbalists of southern France and Spain were writing of the Shekinah's betrothal to the Holy One. The *Sepher ha-Zohar*, or "Book of Splendor," asserted: "we should make a beautiful canopy with beautiful decorations to invite the Supernal Bride, who is the Shekinah."[19] In a reference to the *Song of Solomon*, Bernard wrote: "Mary's womb is the Bridegroom's marriage-bed."[20] Mary, in the emerging devotional imagination, was both the mother and the bride of Christ.

During the same period the troubadours of southern France and Spain were bringing the feminine to the forefront of poetic attention and extolling the sweetness and softness of their *domnae*. Comparisons with Mary often lay near the surface of their work. In one case a thirteenth-century troubadour composed a canticle to Mary herself, based on the theme of the Second Eve; following is an excerpt:

> The good which Eve lost through her temerity,
> Holy Mary regained through her great humility....
> The good which Eve lost when she lost Paradise,
> Holy Mary recovered through her great wisdom....
> All the good Eve lost through committing great folly
> was regained by the glorious Holy Virgin Mary.[21]

The troubadours' idealization of women helped offset traditionally negative attitudes toward the female sex among celibate churchmen, attitudes based on the notion that Eve had brought sin into the world and that women in general were the root cause of male concupiscence. Rather than seeing women as the cause of men's woes, the troubadours praised women—at least noblewomen—for their beauty, grace and virtue. Mary, blessed among all women, was obviously worthy of the greatest praise.

Titles like Queen of Heaven seemed perfectly appropriate. And devotional practices emerged that later generations, even in the Roman or Eastern Orthodox churches, might regard as exaggerated. Medieval mystic Thomas à Kempis, author of the famous devotional text, *The Imitation of Christ* (c.1418–1427), urged people to bow at the name of Mary, as well as the name of Jesus.[22]

Development of Marian Devotion and Intercession

Bernard of Clairvaux confessed that he approached devotion to Mary with a mixture of joy and trepidation:

> It is true, there is nothing gives me greater delight than to preach on the glories of the Virgin Mother, yet neither is there anything that causes me greater fear. For without speaking of the unutterable treasures of her merits ... whatever can be said on that ineffable subject ... does not fully satisfy, does not fully please, is not quite acceptable.[23]

Bernard overcame his fear, however, and wrote seventeen sermons on Mary, most of them linked to her principal feast days. For her role in Christ's Incarnation Bernard accorded Mary the very highest place in creation, above the level of the angels. Certainly Christ was higher still, but that created a gulf which Mary could help bridge: "So great a Mediator is Christ that we need another to mediate between Him and us."[24]

The tall spires and soaring, vaulted roofs of Gothic cathedrals provided an apt metaphor for the increasingly transcendent God of scholastic theology.[25] The rood screen—or in Eastern churches the iconostasis—hid Jesus from the faithful. He no longer walked among his flocks; he was hidden in the tabernacle or on an altar the people could not see. Perhaps, in his transcendence, Christ had forgotten us, or perhaps our sins had driven him away.

Chapter 5. Marian Devotion and Intercession

As Christ receded into the distance, Mary took his place in the mass consciousness. Small intimate churches, as well as great cathedrals like Notre Dame de Paris, were dedicated to Mary and lavishly decorated. Lady Chapels became the norm in large churches and cathedrals.

Mary was accessible, compassionate, and sympathetic to human weakness. Christ had died for our sins and would return to "sit upon the throne of his glory,"[26] but Mary was our Mother now. She was "on the people's side" and could protect them from an angry God—as well as from other hostile powers. To quote a modern writer:

> For the people of the Middle Ages, devotion to the Blessed Virgin offered an experience of a female figure intrinsically related to God, along with an experience of the power of love to blot away sin and the power of mercy to ameliorate deserved justice, experiences that were not otherwise readily available in the situation of the times.[27]

Identification of Mary as mediator reminds us that devotion did not always flow solely from an urge to express love or adoration. To be sure, we have the exuberant expressions of pure devotion that we saw in Anselm and Hildegard; but we also have prayers, like the *Sub tuum Praesidium*, with intercessory intent. Intercessory prayers often began with expressions of devotion or praise.[28] A good example is the ancient hymn *Tota pulchra es, Maria*, which begins with complimentary language drawn from the *Song of Solomon* 4:7 and *Judith* 15:10:

> You are beautiful in every way, Mary,
> and the original stain is not in you.
> You are the glory of Jerusalem,
> you are the joy of Israel,
> you give honor to our people.

It continues with "You are an advocate of sinners.... Mother most merciful," and ends with "Pray for us, plead for us, to the Lord Jesus Christ."[29] Implicit in such combinations of devotion and intercession, was the unspoken belief that flattery would persuade Mary to plead more fervently on behalf of petitioners. In the secular world, one had to "soften up" a civil ruler with praise before submitting a petition.

People addressed their petitions to Mary in the hope that she would intercede on their behalf with Christ, and that her son could not refuse her. She was viewed as the special protectress of women and children—anticipating by nearly a millennium Mary's own statements concerning the focus of her ministry. People also prayed to Mary, as well as to Christ and the saints, on behalf of the dead. The intent was to reduce the time a soul had to spend in purgatory, perhaps even to tip the balance between heaven and hell.

An interesting correlation can be seen between Marian devotion—and more particularly intercession—and the way Mary was depicted in religious art. As intercession became an increasingly common religious practice, so did the tendency to portray Mary in a devout, intercessory pose. An example is shown in Figure 5.1.

The transformation of Mary's persona from an assertive religious leader to a demure, prayerful figure may have been motivated primarily by misogyny. But a positive side effect was to make Mary seem accessible to larger numbers of people. Cynics suggest that we create God in our own image; perhaps Christians adapted Mary to meet their own religious needs.

Figure 5.1

Madonna della Pace ("Madonna of Peace") detail, by Bernardino di Pinturicchio (c.1452).

The Mary of devotion was demure, submissive, and "European." But artists portrayed her as the most beautiful of women.

Chapter 5. Marian Devotion and Intercession

How Devotion and Intercession were Expressed

In the Middle Ages, feast days like the Nativity of Mary, the Annunciation (Lady Day), May (Mary's) Day, and the Visitation graced the liturgical calendar and were celebrated with fairs and pageants, as well as with festive church services. Marian devotion extended throughout the Christian world, but England became known as "Mary's Dowry" because of the intensity of its devotion.

Pilgrimages to Mary's shrines became a major element of the religious experience. One popular pilgrimage destination was Walsingham, near Norfolk, England, where a devout Saxon noblewoman reportedly experienced a Marian apparition in 1061.

Pilgrims often chanted litanies offering praise and invoking Mary's bounty or mercy. In the *Litany of Loreto*, for example, the liturgist called on: "Mother of Christ... Mother of the Church.... Mother of divine grace.... Mother most pure.... Mother most chaste...." and later ".... Mystical rose.... Tower of David.... House of gold.... Ark of the covenant.... Gate of heaven.... Morning star...."[30] Each invocation was followed by the response "Pray for us." Long litanies whiled away the long days of traveling.

Mary acquired a number of titles in late antiquity and the Middle Ages. Eusebius Sophronius Hieronymus (c.347–420), better known as the "St Jerome" of Latin Vulgate fame, is credited with the title "Star of the Sea," though the etymology connecting Mary and *Maris* (the Latin for "sea") is questionable, and "Star" may have been a later transcription error.[31] Be that as it may, a plainchant setting of the hymn *Ave Maris Stella* ("Hail, Star of the Sea") was in use by the eighth century. Its first verse is as follows:

Ave, maris stella,	Hail, star of the sea,
Dei mater alma,	Nurturing Mother of God,
atque semper virgo,	And ever Virgin
felix cæli porta.	Happy gate of Heaven

Four medieval Marian anthems were prescribed to be chanted or sung during the evening office of Compline, one for each liturgical season. An English translation of the *Alma Redemptoris Mater*, for use during Advent, is as follows:

> Loving Mother of the Redeemer, who remains the accessible Gateway of Heaven, and Star of the Sea,

Mary: Adept, Queen, Mother, Priestess

> Give aid to a falling people that strives to rise;
> O Thou who begot thy holy Creator, while all nature marveled,
> Virgin before and after receiving that "Ave" from the mouth of
> Gabriel, have mercy on us sinners.

The other three antiphons all refer to Mary as Queen (Latin: *Regina*): the *Ave Regina Coelorum*, *Regina Coeli*, and *Salve Regina*. Here is an English translation of the *Ave Regina Coelorum*, used during Lent:

> Hail, Queen of Heaven.
> Hail, by angels mistress owned.
> Root of Jesse, Gate of Morn
> Whence the world's true light was born:
> Glorious Virgin, Joy to thee,
> Loveliest whom in heaven they see;
> Fairest thou, where all are fair,
> Plead with Christ our souls to spare.
>
> Hail, Queen of Heaven.
> Hail, Lady of Angels
> Hail! thou root, hail! thou gate
> From whom unto the world a light has arisen:
> Rejoice, glorious Virgin,
> Lovely beyond all others,
> Farewell, most beautiful maiden,
> And pray for us to Christ.

The joyful *Regina Coeli*, used during Eastertide, consists of three couplets (versicle and response) which may be recited or chanted antiphonally. In Latin and English it reads as follows:

V.	*Regina caeli, laetare, alleluia.*	Queen of Heaven, rejoice, alleluia.
R.	*Quia quem meruisti portare, alleluia.*	For He whom you did merit to bear, alleluia.
V.	*Resurrexit, sicut dixit, alleluia.*	Has risen, as he said, alleluia.
R.	*Ora pro nobis Deum, alleluia.*	Pray for us to God, alleluia.
V	*Gaude et laetare, Virgo Maria, alleluia.*	Rejoice and be glad, O Virgin Mary, alleluia.
R.	*Quia surrexit Dominus vere, alleluia.*	For the Lord has truly risen, alleluia.

Chapter 5. Marian Devotion and Intercession

The antiphon *Salve, Regina*, prescribed for the long season of Pentecost, is heavy in intercessory language. An English translation, still in use today, is the following:

> Hail, holy Queen, Mother of Mercy,
> Hail our life, our sweetness and our hope.
> To thee do we cry,
> Poor banished children of Eve;
> To thee do we send up our sighs,
> Mourning and weeping in this valley of tears.
> Turn then, most gracious advocate,
> Thine eyes of mercy toward us;
> And after this our exile,
> Show unto us the blessed fruit of thy womb, Jesus.
> O clement, O loving, O sweet Virgin Mary.

The title "Queen of the Angels" also has a long history. The chapel of Our Lady of the Angels at Porzioncula, Italy, was built in the fourth century to house relics brought by hermits from the Holy Land; later it achieved fame through connections with Francis of Assisi (1182–1226). On the other side of the world, the mission of Nuestra Señora la Reina de los Ángeles ("Our Lady, Queen of the Angels") would be founded in 1784, subsequently developing into the city of Los Angeles, California.

On a different note, the title of *Mater Dolorosa* ("Mother of Sorrows") paid special reverence to Mary as the mother who watched her son die and held his body when it was taken down from the cross. The synod of Cologne created the feast of the Our Lady of Sorrows in 1413. The popular meditation on Mary's "seven sorrows" also developed. The seven sorrows were Simeon's prophecy, the flight to Egypt, loss of the child Jesus, the encounter with Jesus on the way to Calvary, the crucifixion, the descent from the cross, and Jesus' burial.

Marymas

The term *Marymas* may have been applied to more than one Marian feast in the Middle Ages, depending on location. In Celtic Scotland it was applied to the feast of the Dormition/Assumption on August 15.[32] Echoing the rite of the Collyridians, centuries earlier, people baked barley cakes, or *bannocks* and offered them to Mary. The custom survived in the Scottish Highlands until recent times.[33] Studies by folklorists in the nineteenth century probably captured the essence of its traditional form.

According to one account the man of the house handed out portions of the bannock to family and neighbors, while all sang the hymn *Iolach Mhoire Mháthair* (Gaelic: "The Paean of Mary Mother"):

> On the feast day of Mary the fragrant,
> Mother of the Shepherd of the flocks,
> I cut me a handful of new corn, I dried it gently in the sun....
> I toasted it to a fire of rowan,
> And I shared it round my people....
> In the name of Mary Mother, Who promised to preserve me....
> In peace, in flocks, In righteousness of heart.[34]

The tradition of the bannocks may have developed from Celtic "Beltane cakes,"[35] and we note that the pagan festival of Beltane evolved into May Day, or "Mary's Day." Jeremiah, who condemned a cake ritual in his own time, would immediately have recognized the maypole as Asherah's cult symbol.[36] It is also worth noting that the Collyridians may have been ethnic Celts.[37]

The rowan was considered a sacred tree in Scotland, and its wood was burned only for ritual purposes. Also we read:

> The fifteenth day of August was an auspicious day to collect herbs for winter preservation; medicinal herbs were brought to the church to be laid on the altar and blessed. Their association with Mary and her complete translation to heaven ensured such herbs became powerful medicine and thus many healing herbs and flowers became associated with the Virgin. Marjoram was Mother of God's Flower, bee balm and lemon balm were both called Sweet Mary, catnip was Mary's Nettle, sage was Mary's Shawl, dandelion was known as Mary's Bitter Sorrow. Most of all it was lavender, representing cleanliness and purity that was Mary's favorite.[38]

Other folk customs involved the offering of cakes to Mary. One tradition sought an end to prolonged rain. It prescribed the Northumberland rhyme "Rain, rain, go away...." Then, "If, in a little while, it rains still, you must bake a little oaten cake and leave it on your doorstep for the rain-spirit, for that will please our Lady who rules him. Bless the cake and give it good reverence."[39]

Chapter 5. Marian Devotion and Intercession

Impact of the Reformation

We saw in Chapter 4 that Martin Luther and Ulrich Zwingli both expressed belief in the Immaculate Conception. Luther expressed great devotion to Mary, declaring that she is "the highest woman and the noblest gem in Christianity after Christ.... She is nobility, wisdom, and holiness personified. We can never honor her enough."[40]

In 1521 Luther addressed a commentary on the *Magnificat* to Prince John Frederick, Duke of Saxony. Reflecting on the words "My soul doth magnify the Lord," he wrote:

> These words express the strong ardor and exuberant joy whereby all her mind and life are inwardly exalted in the Spirit. Wherefore she does not say, "I exalt the Lord," but, "My soul doth exalt Him." It is as though she said, "My life and all my senses float in the love and praise of God and in lofty pleasures, so that I am no longer mistress of myself; I am exalted, more than I exalt myself, to praise the Lord." That is the experience of all those through whom the divine sweetness and Spirit are poured; they cannot find words to utter what they feel.[41]

By contrast, the prominent humanist Desiderius Erasmus (c.1466–1536) was scathing in his criticism of "the Marian cult." In his view it was offensive to project onto Mary titles from biblical Judaism and pagan religion. Moreover, he urged that Mary should be described as "gracious" rather than "full of grace."[42] Erasmus' attack on Mary influenced generations of Protestants, motivated as much by hostility toward Rome as by concerns about Mary herself. Marian devotion, to quote one modern commentary, became "a casualty of both the new form of evangelical spirituality introduced by the reformers and continuing polemic with Rome."[43] Some Protestant writers rejected the *Theotokos* doctrine.

The reformers were unanimous in rejecting any suggestion that Mary or the saints could intercede with God on behalf of a person, alive or dead; thus it was pointless, even blasphemous, to pray to them.[44] Most of Mary's feast days, and those of the saints, were abolished; pilgrimages, many of which had Marian themes, were banned; statues and shrines were desecrated or destroyed.

Folk tales and customs sometimes betrayed ongoing devotion to Mary in the most Protestant of countries, just as goddess worship had survived in biblical Judaism despite the prophets' best efforts to suppress it. And individuals within Anglicanism and Lutheranism kept the flame of Marian devotion alive, laying the groundwork for a more general reinstatement of Mary in their respective traditions.

Lutherans generally look to their founder for guidance on which Marian topics should take precedence. In 1933 German Lutheran pastor Dietrich Bonhoeffer preached a sermon on the *Magnificat*, which he described as "the oldest Advent hymn" and "the most passionate, most vehement, one might almost say, most revolutionary Advent hymn ever sung." He rejected the traditional, submissive image of Mary presented by the church, to capture something of the assertive woman who ministered to the people of Jerusalem. The Mary who uttered the *Magnificat*

> is not the gentle, sweet, dreamy Mary that we so often see portrayed in pictures, but the passionate, powerful, proud, enthusiastic Mary, who speaks here. None of the sweet, sugary, or childish tones that we find so often in our Christmas hymns, but a hard, strong, uncompromising song of bringing down rulers from their thrones and humbling the lords of this world, of God's power and of the powerlessness of men. These are the tones of the prophetic women of the Old Testament: Deborah, Judith, Miriam, coming alive in the mouth of Mary.[45]

Bonhoeffer's statement may represent the strongest affirmation of the "real" historical Mary ever made by a prominent mainstream churchman.

Marian devotion in Anglicanism will be discussed in its own section later in this chapter.

Marian Devotion in Eastern Orthodoxy

Mary continued to receive great attention in the Eastern Orthodox churches and in the post-Reformation Church of Rome.

In the eastern churches Mary has traditionally been known as "Mary Theotokos." The technical term decreed by the Council of Ephesus is left untranslated and uninterpreted, to serve as a basis for individual and collective contemplation. Another Marian title is *Panagia*, meaning "The Most Holy One." Numerous Orthodox churches are dedicated to Mary, and she is the subject of countless icons. Icons will be discussed later in the chapter.

The most famous and most extensive Marian devotion in the Orthodox churches is the *Akathist to the Most Holy Mary Theotokos*, said to have been written by the Syrio-Greek hymnographer Romanos the Melodist (c.490–c.556). An *akathist* (Greek: *akathistos*, "not sitting") is a devotion during which participants are expected to stand in an expression of reverence. The *Akathist to the Theotokos* is comprised of twenty-four stanzas, one for each letter of the Greek alphabet. Stanzas are in pairs. A short stanza in prose and ending with the people's response "Alleluia," is followed by a longer stanza combining prose and poetry, and ending with "Rejoice, O Bride Unwedded."[46]

The *Akathist to the Theotokos* follows the story of Mary through the several stages of the Incarnation, beginning with the Annunciation and continuing through the Nativity and Simeon's prophecy, to the Magi's visit to Bethlehem. This last stage is commemorated thus:

> *Priest* (or *Cantor*): Beholding the star leading to God, the Magi followed its brightness; and holding it as a lantern, they searched for the powerful King, and reaching the Unreachable, they rejoiced and cried to him: Alleluia.
>
> *People*: Alleluia.
>
> *Priest*: The Chaldean children in the hands of the Virgin saw him who fashioned humankind. And perceiving him to be the Lord, even though he had taken the form of a slave, they hastened to pay tribute with gifts and to greet the blessed Lady:
>
> Rejoice, mother of an unsetting star;
> Rejoice, dawn of the mystic day.
> Rejoice, who extinguished the furnace of error;
> Rejoice, who enlighten initiates of the Trinity.
> Rejoice, deposer of the inhuman tyrant from his rule;
> Rejoice, discloser of the Lord Christ who loves humankind.
> Rejoice, redeemer from pagan religions;
> Rejoice, deliverer from the mire of sin.
> Rejoice, for you have caused the worship of fire to cease;
> Rejoice, releaser from the flames of passions.
> Rejoice, guide of the faithful to chastity;
> Rejoice, gladness of all generations. Rejoice, O Bride unwedded.
>
> *People*: Rejoice, O Bride unwedded.[47]

The *Akathist* concludes with a lyrical section devoted to praise of Mary "whom the poet adorns with the most beautiful of adjectives asking her to accept his poetical offering and to intercede for the salvation of human race from the earthly sin."[48] An extract is as follows:

> *Priest*: Unsuccessful is every hymn that attempts to pay homage to the multitude of Your mercies. For even if we offer You odes in number equal to the sands, O holy King, yet we do nothing worthy of what You have given us who cry to You: Alleluia.
>
> *People*: Alleluia.
>
> *Priest*: We see the holy Virgin, as a light-bearing torch who brings light to those in darkness. For she lit the spiritual light, and thus leads everyone to divine knowledge, enlightening the mind with the light of dawn and is honored by such praises:
>
> Rejoice, ray of the spiritual Sun;
> Rejoice, beam of the unsetting luster.
> Rejoice, lightning completely illuminating souls;
> Rejoice, thunder that stuns the enemies.
> Rejoice, for the glowing light you make rise upon the earth;
> Rejoice, for you spring forth the flowing river.
> Rejoice, you who illustrate the image of the font;
> Rejoice, you who wash away the stain of sin.
> Rejoice, water washing consciences clean;
> Rejoice, cup that mixes great joy.
> Rejoice, sweet smelling fragrance of Christ;
> Rejoice, life of the mystical feasting.
> Rejoice, O Bride unwedded.
>
> *People*: Rejoice, O Bride unwedded.[49]

The Eastern Orthodox churches were unfazed by the Reformation. Devotion to Mary continued as it had in the Middle Ages. Part of the prayer that became the "Hail Mary" in western Christianity was already familiar in Eastern Orthodoxy, sung three times at the end of Vespers during the All-Night Vigil. It is also used many times in the course of daily prayer: "Theotokos, Virgin, rejoice, grace-filled Mary, the Lord with thee. Praised thou among women, and praised the fruit of thy womb, because it was the Savior of our souls that thou didst bear."

Chapter 5. Marian Devotion and Intercession

An Orthodox hymn quotes from Peter of Damascus in affirming Mary's place in the angelic hierarchy: "Mother of our God. More honorable than the Cherubim ... more glorious than the Seraphim":

> It is truly meet and right to bless you, O Theotokos,
> Ever-blessed and most-pure mother of our God.
> More honorable than the Cherubim,
> And beyond compare more glorious than the Seraphim,
> Who without corruption gave birth to God the Word,
> True Theotokos: we magnify you.[50]

Russian Orthodox priest Sergei Bulgakov (1871–1944) cited the hymn when he wrote:

> The Orthodox Church venerates the Virgin Mary as "more honorable than the Cherubim, and beyond compare more glorious than the Seraphim," as superior to all other created beings. The Church sees in her the Mother of God, who, without being a substitute for the One Mediator, intercedes before her Son for all humanity. We ceaselessly pray to her to intercede for us. Love for the Virgin is the soul of Orthodox piety, its heart, that which warms and animates its entire body.[51]

Mary is accorded the highest honor in the Russian Orthodox Church. Nikolai Berdyaev (1874–1948) was able to say, without great exaggeration: "The Mother of God takes precedence of the Trinity and is almost identified with the Trinity. The people have felt the nearness of the interceding Mother of God more vividly than that of Christ."[52] Mary Theotokos is considered to be the holy protectress of Russia and is described as "Mother of the World"[53]—a title that found resonance in the West with the pronouncements of recent popes. "Mother of the World" also took on great significance in modern esotericism.

Marian Devotion in Roman Catholicism

Exuberant Devotion to Mary

While Mary lost favor in the Protestant world, devotion to her increased within Roman Catholicism. Indeed, Marian devotion in the West came to be understood, with some justification, as a purely Roman Catholic phenomenon. Louis-Marie de Montfort (1673–1716),

French preacher and Mariologist canonized in 1947, offered an important reason for venerating Mary:

> Jesus gave more glory to God his Father by submitting to his Mother for thirty years than he would have given him had he converted the whole world by working the greatest miracles. How highly then do we glorify God when to please him we submit ourselves to Mary, taking Jesus as our sole model.[54]

In a warning to any Christian who might feel that Marian devotion was superfluous, he declared: "He who has not Mary for his Mother has not God for his Father."[55]

A popular intercessory prayer is the *Memorare* ("Remember"). Originally forming part of a longer fifteenth-century prayer, it took its present form after the Reformation; a modern English translation is as follows:

> Remember, O most gracious Virgin Mary, that never was it known that anyone who fled to your protection, implored your help, or sought your intercession, was left unaided.
> Inspired by this confidence, I fly unto you, O Virgin of virgins, my Mother.
> To you do I come, before you I stand, sinful and sorrowful.
> O Mother of the Word Incarnate, despise not my petitions, but in your mercy, hear and answer me. Amen.[56]

The most famous Marian prayer is the *Ave Maria*, or "Hail Mary":

Ave Maria, gratia plena, Dominus tecum.	Hail Mary, Full of Grace, the Lord is with thee.
Benedicta tu in mulieribus, et benedictus fructus ventris tui, Iesus.	Blessed art thou among women, and blessed is the fruit of thy womb, Jesus.
Sancta Maria, Mater Dei, ora pro nobis peccatoribus, nunc et in hora mortis nostrae. Amen.	Holy Mary, Mother of God, pray for us sinners now, and at the hour of our death. Amen.

Traces of the prayer, which draws upon *Luke* 1:28, 42, can be found as early as the sixth century. And a partial form, used in the Eastern Orthodox churches, has already been mentioned. The sentence "Holy Mary, Mother of God...." reportedly was added by Dutch Jesuit priest

Peter Canisius (1521–1597), with the intention of repairing the damage done to the church by the Reformation. The present form of the Ave Maria dates from 1568, when Pope Pius V included the Latin text in his revision of the Roman Breviary.

One year after he published the full text of the Hail Mary, Pius V gave official approval to the devotion of the Rosary (Latin: *rosarium*, "garland of roses"). According to tradition, Dominic de Guzmán (1170–1221), founder of the Order of Preachers (Dominicans), received a set of prayer beads during a Marian apparition in 1214.[57] The associated devotional practice was promoted by Alain de la Roche, (c.1428–1475), a theologian of uncertain nationality.

The Rosary devotion—counted off, bead by bead—consists of five "decades," each of which includes the Lord's Prayer, ten Hail Marys, and the "Glory be to the Father...." Recitation of the Rosary traditionally is devoted to one of the three sets of "Mysteries of the Rosary": the Joyful Mysteries, the Sorrowful Mysteries, and the Glorious Mysteries, according to the day of the week. For example, Thursday is dedicated to the Joyful Mysteries: The Annunciation, the Visitation, the Nativity, the Presentation in the Temple, and the Finding of Jesus in the Temple. Each decade of the Rosary is dedicated to one of five Mysteries prescribed for the day.

The Rosary steadily grew in popularity, and several popes have encouraged its use. In 1974 Pope Paul VI issued the Apostolic Letter *Marialis Cultus* which devoted fourteen sections to use of the Rosary in the Church of Rome. A fourth set of mysteries, the Luminous Mysteries, was added by Pope John Paul II in 2002.

Another devotion involving the *Ave Maria*, or Hail Mary, is the *Angelus*. Short versicles and responses bracket three recitations of the Hail Mary. Its modern English form is the following:

V. The Angel of the Lord declared unto Mary,
R. And she conceived of the Holy Spirit. Hail Mary....
V. Behold the handmaid of the Lord.
R. Be it done unto me according to thy word. Hail Mary....
V. And the Word was made flesh.
R. And dwelt among us. Hail Mary....
V. Pray for us, O Holy Mother of God.
R. That we may be made worthy of the promises of Christ.

A short concluding prayer may be added.

The name *Angelus* comes from the opening Latin words: *Angelus Domini* ("The Angel of the Lord"). The Angelus may have originated in medieval monastic practices in which three Hail Mary's were recited at the Compline bell. In many Roman Catholic churches, convents, and monasteries today, the Angelus bell is tolled three times daily: at 6:00 a.m., 12:00 noon, and 6:00 p.m. People interrupt whatever they are doing to recite the prayer.

Cardinal Nicholas Wiseman (1802-1865), first archbishop of Westminster, was a strong devotee of Mary. In the 1860s he wrote the famous *Prayer for England*. It begins with praise for Mary as "Queen and Mother" but quickly changes to intercessory language aimed at the "conversion of England," a popular theme in British Roman Catholicism through the middle of the twentieth century:

> O Blessed Virgin Mary, Mother of God and our most gentle Queen and Mother, look down in mercy upon England thy "Dowry" and upon us all who greatly hope and trust in thee.
> By thee it was that Jesus our Savior and our hope was given unto the world; and He has given thee to us that we might hope still more.
> Plead for us thy children, whom thou didst receive and accept at the foot of the Cross, O sorrowful Mother.
> Intercede for our separated brethren, that with us in the one true fold they may be united to the supreme Shepherd, the Vicar of thy Son.
> Pray for us all, dear Mother, that by faith fruitful in good works we may all deserve to see and praise God, together with thee, in our heavenly home. Amen.[58]

May Day and the month of May continued to inspire poets to sing Mary's praises. Here is part of a whimsical poem by Gay Lowry that awakens memories from pre-Christian times:

> Lanterns were strung from the moonbeams,
> A rose bush surrounded the throne
> Of the loveliest fairy princess,
> A dreamland ever owned.
>
> Her eyes were filled with star dust,
> Her hair was the gold of the sun,

And she danced with the grace of a bluebird,
Till the night of her fairies was done.

Perhaps you have heard of these splendors,
Perhaps you have seen them as I,
Dance in the mist of twilight,
Under the evening sky.

But if you've not dreamed in the May time,
Of fairies, and moonlight, and love,
You've missed the gift of springtime,
Granted by Mary above.

So tonight as the shadows start falling,
Say a prayer to the Queen of the May,
That you may dream of fairies and moonlight
Till the rose-colored dawn of day.[59]

A Change in Attitude?

Rome's attitude toward Mary has been ambiguous since the mid-twentieth century. Pope Pius XII continued the tradition, established in the nineteenth century, of strong support for Marian devotion and the development of associated doctrine. He proclaimed the dogma of the Assumption in 1950 and encouraged the notion of Mary as Queen of Heaven. He declared 1954 to be an international "Marian Year" of special celebration and reverence to Mary.

Then, as noted in Chapter 4, the Second Vatican Council (1962–1965) signaled a major shift in attitude. It warned against "Marian excess" and "gross exaggerations [that] could lead separated brethren or any other into error regarding the true doctrine of the Church."[60] Pope Paul VI issued a similar warning in 1974.[61] In response to those warnings, numerous images of Mary were removed from Roman Catholic churches, moved to less conspicuous locations, or covered over.[62] Marian devotional practices were curtailed.

The pontificate of Pope John Paul II saw a partial reversal. The Polish-born pope was among the most pro-Mary popes in recent times. Elected in 1978, he allowed himself to be seen participating actively in Marian devotions and made several bold statements, including promoting Mary as Mother of the World. He also erected a large statue of Mary, the *Madonna della Colonna*, outside St Peter's basilica.

John Paul proclaimed another Marian Year to span the calendar years 1987–1988, and intended to lay groundwork for the new millennium. His encyclical letter *Redemptoris Mater* ("Mother of the Redeemer"), announcing the event, is the longest Marian encyclical in the church's history. Part of it reflects on the angel's greeting at the Annunciation, assigning Mary multiple high honors derived from her association with Christ:

> When we read that the messenger addresses Mary as "full of grace," the Gospel context, which mingles revelations and ancient promises, enables us to understand that among all the "spiritual blessings in Christ" this is a special "blessing." In the mystery of Christ she is present even "before the creation of the world," as the one whom the Father "has chosen" as Mother of his Son in the Incarnation. And, what is more, together with the Father, the Son has chosen her, entrusting her eternally to the Spirit of holiness. In an entirely special and exceptional way Mary is united to Christ."[63]

Yet John Paul was careful to place his comments in the context of Vatican II:

> [T]he Marian Year is meant to promote a new and more careful reading of what the Council said about the Blessed Virgin Mary, Mother of God, in the mystery of Christ and of the Church, the topic to which the contents of this Encyclical are devoted. Here we speak not only of the doctrine of faith but also of the life of faith, and thus of authentic "Marian spirituality," seen in the light of Tradition, and especially the spirituality to which the Council exhorts us.[64]

Whether or not Pope Paul VI or the bishops who attended the council would have concurred, he cited as an example of "authentic "Marian spirituality" the writings of Louis-Marie de Montfort.

In 2011 Pope Benedict XVI affirmed that "the Angels encircle the august Queen of Victories, the Blessed Virgin Mary."[65] Seven years later, during the pontificate of Pope Francis, the feast of the "Blessed Virgin Mary Mother of the Church" was added to the liturgical calendar, to be observed on the day after Pentecost.[66]

Despite these signs of a retreat from the harsh rhetoric of Vatican II, Roman Catholics remain unsure about the permissible limits of Marian devotion. A return to the exuberant, unselfconscious devotion of earlier centuries may take decades, if it occurs at all.

Chapter 5. Marian Devotion and Intercession

Marian Devotion in Anglicanism

The English Reformation formally began in 1534 when the Convocation of Canterbury declared that it no longer recognized papal authority. Instead, it named the monarch—then King Henry VIII—"supreme head of this our Catholic Church in England."[67] Henceforth, the newly independent Church of England was to be "catholic and reformed"—institutionalizing an internal tension that has never been completely resolved. Another important date was 1549, when Thomas Cranmer, Archbishop of Canterbury, published the first Book of Common Prayer, the church's official liturgy.[68]

In some respects the Church of England distanced itself from the more extreme reformism of continental Europe. But its early leaders shared their neighbors' resistance to Marian devotion and intercession. They also inherited a special hostility to Mary from Erasmus, who had served as Lady Margaret Professor of Divinity at the University of Cambridge in the 1510s. Hugh Latimer (c.1487–1555), a Cambridge graduate and Bishop of Worcester, emerged as a leading iconoclast. In 1538, at his urging, Henry's chief minister Thomas Cromwell ordered the destruction of statues of Mary at the shrines of Walsingham, Ipswich and Worcester. Pilgrimages to the sites were prohibited.

Henry's death in 1547 ushered in period of turmoil in which the boy-king Edward VI reigned for six years, and then his half-sister Mary I for five years. The latter reestablished Roman Catholicism and placed England once again under papal authority. Cranmer, Latimer, and many others were burned at the stake. The persecution of reformers antagonized the English people and did nothing to promote a sense of continuity with the pre-Reformation church, with its strong tradition of Marian devotion.

The situation finally stabilized when the Elizabeth I acceded to the throne in 1558. Elizabeth restored the Church of England, as it had been structured under her father, Henry VIII, and sought to unify the traditionalist and reformist factions within it. Arguably, Elizabeth did more than anyone to set Anglicanism on the path it would follow over subsequent centuries.

The Church of England liturgical calendar, published in 1561—the third year of Elizabeth's reign—contained five Marian feasts: the Conception, Nativity of Mary, Annunciation (Lady Day), Visitation and Purification.[69] Collects for the five feasts were written and scriptural readings selected for the 1559 edition of the Book of Common Prayer. Cranmer had preserved Mary's *Magnificat* in the liturgy of Evening Prayer from 1549 onward. Notwithstanding those liturgical developments, devotion to Mary languished for more than a century after the Reformation.

Revival of Marian Devotion

Efforts to revive Marian devotion began in the seventeenth century with the work of the Caroline Divines: "high-church" Anglican clergy who valued traditions extending back to the pre-Reformation English church.

One of them was Lancelot Andrewes (1555–1626), who oversaw much of the work on the King James Bible. Andrewes selected *Psalm* 2:7 as the theme for his Christmas sermon in 1609. But he modified "Thou art My Son, this day have I begotten Thee" to create an affirmation for Mary: "Thou art my Son, this day I brought Thee into the world."[70]

John Donne (1572–1631), metaphysical poet, scholar, and dean of St Paul's Cathedral, London, devoted part of a poem to Mary:

> For that fair blessed mother-maid,
> Whose flesh redeem'd us, that she-cherubin,
> Which unlock'd paradise, and made
> One claim for innocence, and disseizèd sin,
> Whose womb was a strange heaven, for there
> God clothed Himself, and grew,
> Our zealous thanks we pour. As her deeds were
> Our helps, so are her prayers; nor can she sue
> In vain, who hath such titles unto you.[71]

Of all the Caroline Divines, Mark Frank (1612–1665) emerged as the leading exponent of Marian devotion. In a sermon preached on the feast of the Annunciation he said:

> Give we her in God's name the honor due to her. God hath styled her "blessed" by the Angel, by Elizabeth; commanded all generations to call her so, and they hitherto have done it, and let us do it too... [T]he first Christians... speak of her as the most blessed among women, one "highly favored," most "highly" too.[72]

Yet Frank felt compelled to caution his audience that Marian devotion should not be allowed to compete with the worship of Christ: "But all the while give Dominus tecum all the glory, the whole glory of all to him; give her the honor and blessedness of the chief of the saints."[73]

Frank's close contemporary, the Welsh metaphysical poet Henry Vaughan (1621–1695), was less cautious. Vaughan drew upon the long tradition of Marian devotion from medieval Wales when he wrote:

> Bright Queen of Heaven! God's Virgin Spouse.
> The glad world's blessèd maid!
> Whose beauty tied life to thy house.
> And brought us saving aid.
> Thou art the true Loves-knot; by thee
> God is made our ally.[74]

Catholic Revival Movement

The work of the Caroline Divines influenced the Tractarian Movement, spearheaded by a group of Oxford University clergy who perceived a spiritual decline in the Church of England. The movement began in 1833, when Fr John Keble delivered a provocative sermon at St Mary's Church, Oxford. It earned its name from a series of ninety essays, or "tracts," published over the next several years, addressing issues of theology, ecclesiology, and individual sanctity.[75] Among much else it led to the revival of monastic orders in Anglicanism.

The Tractarian Movement formed part of the larger Catholic Revival Movement in Anglicanism, which also included the revival of Gothic church architecture and the restoration of ceremonial ritual in Anglican worship. Clergy and others on both sides of the Atlantic participated in the larger movement.[76]

The Catholic Revival Movement gave Anglicans permission to express devotion to Mary, and many responded. High-church Anglicans have adopted traditionally Roman Catholic Marian devotions, like the Hail Mary, the Rosary, and the Angelus. The *St Augustine's Prayer Book*, first published in 1947 by the Order of the Holy Cross, an Anglican monastic community, offers a wealth of material, including Marian antiphons for Evensong or Compline and several Marian litanies. It also includes a prayer attributed to St Augustine:

> Thou, O Mary, hast perfectly fulfilled the will of the heavenly Father, thy greatest honor and blessedness is not to have been the mother only, but also to disciple of Christ. Blessed art thou to have heard the Word of God and to have kept it within thy heart. Thou didst harbor the truth of Christ in thine understanding, even more than his human flesh in thy womb. Thou art the beauty and the dignity of earth, O Blessed Virgin Mary. Amen.[77]

Pilgrimages to shrines like Walsingham have again became commonplace. The shrine of Our Lady of Walsingham, destroyed during the Reformation, has been restored and, since 1921, includes separate Anglican and Roman Catholic chapels.[78] "Mary's Dowry" has been recovered on a small scale.

Anglican devotion has focused on Mary's role in the Incarnation, and that focus has minimized residual fears of mariolatry. Through Mary, Christ came into the world; she provided the means by which the divine and human natures were united. Anglicans could agree with Hans von Balthasar: "In Mary heaven and earth finally converge, here the finite encounters the infinite. Heaven, being masculine, takes the initiative and bestows its infinity on the earth; the earth ... responds accordingly and brings forth her fruit."[79]

Questions are still raised concerning the propriety of Marian devotion and intercession. Yet Donald Coggan, Archbishop of Canterbury from 1974 to 1980, not usually considered high-church in sympathies, posed an interesting question concerning the relationship between Mary and Christ:

> Who knows the influence of a mother on her unborn child? Here is a world of mystery which is still not wholly understood. But is it not possible that something of the concept of dedicated servanthood which was at the heart of this young pregnant woman "got through" to the child as yet unborn, and became an integral part in the shaping of his manhood and his ministry?[80]

Coggan added, insightfully, "There may be more in this than has been generally recognized." Indeed there may! The argument that Mary retains special influence with her son is often cited in Roman Catholicism as a justification for Marian intercession.[81]

Frank Griswold, Presiding Bishop of the Episcopal Church from 1998 to 2006, who *was* known for his high-church sympathies, included an intercessory prayer in a book of devotions: "Mary, our sister, Mother of the Word Incarnate.... Pray for us that your courage and endurance may find a home in our hearts, and let your loving intercession embrace all those who grieve and bear the wound of loss."[82]

Notwithstanding Archbishop Coggan's insights, most Anglicans remain resistant to the concept of Marian intercession. Yet dialogue with Eastern Orthodox theologians has helped clarify the issue. In its Dublin Statement the Anglican–Orthodox Joint Doctrinal Discussions explained:

> All prayer is ultimately addressed to the Triune God. We pray to God the Father through our Lord Jesus Christ in the Holy Spirit. The Church is united in a single movement of worship with the Church in heaven, with the Blessed Virgin Mary, "with angels and archangels, and all the company of heaven." The Orthodox also pray to the Blessed Virgin Mary and Theotokos and the saints as friends and living images of Christ.... The Blessed Virgin Mary played a unique role in the economy of salvation by virtue of the fact that she was chosen to be Mother of Christ our God. Her intercession is not autonomous, but presupposes Christ's intercession and is based upon the saving work of the incarnate Word.[83]

Marian Religious Orders and Sodalities

The Carmelites, whose full name is the Order of Our Lady of Mount Carmel, date from medieval times. According to tradition, Berthold of Calabria established a hermit colony on Mount Carmel in 1185, drawn there by the belief that Elijah offered sacrifice on the mountain and confounded the prophets of Baal.[84]

The hermits built a chapel dedicated to Mary on Mount Carmel but were forced to abandon the site when crusaders retreated from the area. Undeterred, the hermits approached Albert of Jerusalem, the Latin Patriarch, and requested a monastic rule. Albert provided the rule, which enjoined obedience, fasting and silence, as well as attendance at Mass and the daily offices. The rule provided for both male and female orders. In due course the Carmelites migrated to western Europe, though they continued to revere their legendary ties with Mount Carmel.

In the thirteenth century the Carmelites' prior general, Simon Stock, had an ecstatic vision in which Mary gave him a brown scapular, promising salvation to those who died wearing it; the scapular duly became part of the Carmelite habit. Other famous Carmelites were the mystics Teresa of Ávila (1515–1582) and John of the Cross (1542–1591).

The Company of Mary was founded as a missionary religious congregation by Louis-Marie de Montfort in 1705. Its constitution emphasizes the role Marian devotion plays in the life of its members: "[D]evotion toward her [Mary] is an integral part of their spiritual life and apostolate. The 'total consecration' to Jesus through Mary is the most outstanding mark of the Marian character of our inspiration."[85] A companion order for women, the Daughters of Wisdom, was established in 1707, with the primary mission of caring for the sick.

The Society of Mary (Marists) was founded by Jean-Claude Colin and a group of other seminarians in Lyon, France, in 1816. The aftermath of the French Revolution was a stressful time for clergy and members of religious orders, but the Marists were sustained by the maxim: "I [Mary] was the mainstay of the new-born Church; I shall be again at the end of time."[86] Those words, to quote Colin, "were always before us." The maxim acknowledges Mary's leadership role in the early church and points to her ongoing—and future—ministry.

The Marist ideal spread to many other countries, offering opportunities for both men and women. The Society of Mary and the Marist Sisters, formally known as the Sisters of the Holy Name of Mary attempt to imitate Mary in their spirituality and daily work. In Colin's words, they must "think as Mary, judge as Mary, feel and act as Mary in all things."

A notable Marist, Peter Julian Eymard, left the society to found his own religious order: the Congregation of the Blessed Sacrament. His special mission was to promote the notion of an intimate link between Mary and the Eucharist. In May 1868 Eymard coined the title of Our Lady of the Most Blessed Sacrament. Later he described what a statue of Mary should look like: "The Blessed Virgin holds the Infant in her arms; and He holds a chalice in one hand and a Host in the other." He exhorted the members of his order and others to invoke Mary thus:

> Let us ... honor the Blessed Virgin by a daily sacrifice. Let us go to Our Lord through her; shelter ourselves behind her, take refuge

beneath her protecting mantle; clothe ourselves in her virtues. Let us be, in short, but Mary's shadow. Let us offer all her actions, all her merits, all her virtues to Our Lord. We have only to have recourse to Mary and to say to Jesus: "I offer thee the riches that my good Mother has acquired for me."[87]

Numerous lay sodalities, confraternities, and other groups have been established to promote devotion to Mary and encourage members to imitate her in their spiritual lives and daily work. The Sodality of Mary was founded in 1563 by the Belgian Jesuit priest Jean Leunis. Initially intended for boys in Jesuit schools, it soon expanded to provide opportunities for men and women in all walks of life. The sodality's goal is to foster "an ardent devotion, reverence, and filial love towards the Blessed Virgin Mary."

The Confraternity of the Holy Rosary was founded by the Dominican Order in the sixteenth century. Members strive to pray the entire Rosary weekly, while holding in their thoughts the collective needs of the confraternity.[88]

Marian devotion is now supported by Anglican religious orders and lay organizations, including the Society of Mary formed in 1931 as the combination of two earlier groups. Not to be confused with the Roman Catholic religious order of the same name, it now operates in many countries. These organizations seek to popularize devotions, like the Rosary, the *Angelus*, and the *Regina Coeli*, once popular only in Roman Catholic circles.

Marian Devotion and Intercession in the Arts

Art, which may combine color and physical form; and music, which combines sound and abstract form; have provided rich opportunities for humanity to express its devotion to God, to Christ, and to Mary. From time immemorial, song has been recognized as a way to enhance the power of words, and in turn musical instruments added power to song. Alternatively, instrumental music, including organ music, can sometimes express one's deepest aspirations without the need for—or the intrusion of—words.

Sacred dance played a significant role in Judaism, and continues to play conspicuous roles in many world religions. To quote Roman

Catholic priest, Thomas Kane: "Art, ritual and dance can elevate and expand our spiritual horizons. Symbols can express what the heart feels and the tongue cannot articulate."[89] Sadly, Marian devotion has rarely been permitted to include ritual, and dance has made few inroads into any kind of Christian worship.

Mary in Art

According to legend, Luke the Evangelist painted a portrait of Mary—and, incidentally, listened to her stories while she posed for him. Whether or not the legend is true, art may have been the first medium through which Marian devotion was expressed. The early second-century fresco of the Madonna and Child and a prophet, in a Roman catacomb, has already been mentioned; other Marian frescos are found in the same and neighboring catacombs. Sacred art graced the basilicas of late antiquity; medieval churches, cathedrals and abbeys; and the palaces of the Renaissance. Mary was a favorite subject.

Notwithstanding occasional doubts about the propriety of religious images,[90] the eastern churches are famous for their icons. Icons have long been regarded as visual prayers, "written" and copied, over and over, in ongoing acts of devotion. Copying an icon is compared to copying a scriptural manuscript. It is not considered plagiarism; reproduction preserves the original image and brings treatment of the depicted subject to a larger audience.

The oldest surviving icon, *Christ Pantocrator* ("Christ Ruler of the Universe"), at the St Catherine's Monastery, Mount Sinai, dates from the sixth century. A Byzantine-style icon of the Madonna and Child, now in the Basilica of St Mary Major in Rome, is one of several claimants to be the very portrait painted by Luke.[91] The thirteenth-century Byzantine icon, *Virgin Theotokos of the Passion*, also known as *Our Lady of Perpetual Help*, is considered a masterpiece; originally at the Keras Kardiotissas Monastery in Crete, it is now enshrined in the Church of St Alphonsus, Rome.

Among the best-known icons of the Russian Orthodox Church is the twelfth-century *Theotokos of Vladimir*, which shows an exuberant child Jesus clutching Mary's clothes and reaching up to her face.[92] *Panagia* ("Most Holy One") icons typically show the standing figure of Mary facing the viewer, with her hands extended in blessing and with the image of the child Jesus over her heart. A famous example,

Chapter 5. Marian Devotion and Intercession

shown in Figure 5.2, is the thirteenth-century "Great Panagia" in the Savior Minster at Yaroslavl, Russia.

Figure 5.2

Mary Theotokos of Yaroslavl, Russia (c.1114).

A *Panagia*-style icon, it shows Mary carrying the divine Jesus in her heart. Mary and Jesus have similar haloes, and both have their hands raised in blessing.

Marian icons from the Eastern Orthodox tradition have become of great interest in the West in recent years. Former Archbishop of Canterbury Rowan Williams (1950–) meditated on a copy of the *Theotokos of Vladimir*. Williams noted that Mary's gaze is toward us and suggested that she may be burdened by the intensity of his love, love that "we do not know how to respond to." Mary represents us, and we in turn may ask "[H]ow shall we bear this unqualified love focused upon us!"[93]

Another contemporary writer, Mirabai Starr, has written poems to accompany a series of Marian icons; here is part of one of them:

Mary is the quintessential Mother, the feminine face of the Holy One, fierce protector and gentle consoler.

189

She is inspiration, wisdom, vital essence of compassion and forgiveness.
She reaches into the heart of the wounded world with tangible healing.
She is Mother of the Divine, and Mother of us all.[94]

Sacred art was approached in a more conventional manner in the West, but artists' devotion still lay close to the surface. Among the timeless works of western Marian art is the *Lucca Madonna* by early Renaissance painter Jan van Eyck (<1390–1441), which shows Mary breastfeeding a naked baby Jesus. Other great masterpieces are *The Annunciation* and *Madonna of the Star* by Fra Angelico (c.1395–1455), the *Madonna of the Magnificat* and *Madonna of the Book* by Sandro Botticelli (c.1445–1510), the *Madonna of Loreto* by Caravaggio (1571–1610), and the *Coronation of the Virgin* by Diego Velázquez (1599–1660). The famous sculpture *La Pietà* by Michelangelo Buonarroti (1475–1564) shows Mary holding the crucified body of Jesus.

It was customary, particularly during the Renaissance, to portray Mary as the most beautiful of women and to adorn her in the finest of clothing and accessories. Clearly this reflected commendable devotion on the part of artists and patrons. Yet it did not please everybody. Dominican friar Girolamo Savonarola (1452–1498) famously complained: "You have made the Virgin appear dressed as a whore."[95] The holy but narrow-minded Savonarola campaigned against the glories—and admitted extravagances—of the Florentine Renaissance. Savonarola went to the stake in 1498. By then the Florentine Renaissance was in steep decline, and by the end of the century it was over.

From Florence the Renaissance spread throughout Europe followed by the Baroque and Romantic periods, each of which provided new opportunities to express Marian devotion through art. Interest continues to modern times.[96] Paul Gauguin (1848–1903), Pablo Picasso (1881–1973), and Salvador Dali (1904–1989) all painted important Marian works. British sculptor Barbara Hepworth (1903–1975) created a sensitive representation of the Madonna and Child.[97]

In addition to depicting Mary as beautiful, the custom has been to portray her in a submissive, prayerful posture. As Dietrich Bonhoeffer noted, this may contrast strongly with what we know of the real historical Mary. And such portrayal has led Christian feminists to look elsewhere for a role model to present to modern empowered women.[98] That said, for many centuries the prayerful image resonated with the church's expectations of women, and may have provided the masses—men as well as women—with a figure with whom they could identify, as they offered their own devotional and intercessional prayers.

Mary in Music

Chanting of the psalms, including antiphonal chanting, originated in the eastern church, where it may have been adapted from Jewish temple chants. Ambrose of Milan (c.340–397) expanded on those musical forms to create "Ambrosian Chant." The more familiar Gregorian Chant, named in honor of Pope Gregory I, followed some two centuries later. Local variations on Gregorian chant, like the Sarum chant in southern England, also became popular. A millennium or more later, the medieval chants are still renowned for their serene beauty and sensitive spirituality—and are still performed on a regular basis.

Beginning at the Renaissance composers created polyphonic settings of the Marian antiphons, often with instrumental accompaniments. For example, Peter Philips (c.1560–1628) set the *Alma Redemptoris Mater* to five-part harmony. His older contemporary Orlando di Lasso (1532–1594) composed a six- or eight-part setting of the same text, one version accompanied by brass instruments. The *Ave Regina Coelorum* inspired settings of the Mass by Guillaume du Fay (1397–1474), Jacques Arcadelt (c.1507–1568), Giovanni Pierluigi da Palestrina (c.1525–1594), and Tomás Luis de Victoria (c.1548–1611).

The Baroque era saw a wide range of polyphonic music dedicated to Mary. Some was intended for liturgical use, while works requiring larger choirs and multiple instruments were more suited to the concert hall. Claudio Monteverdi (1567–1643) composed the *Marian Vespers of 1610*; Marc-Antoine Charpentier (1643–1704) composed a setting of the *Litany of Loreto*; and Giovanni Pergolesi (1710–1736) wrote a twelve-movement setting of the *Stabat Mater*. The medieval texts were not forgotten. In the classical era Wolfgang Amadeus Mozart (1756–1791) and Johannes Brahms (1833–1897) wrote settings of the *Regina Coeli*.[99]

The *Ave Maria* is the most popular Marian text, and one of the most popular texts of any kind, in western sacred music. Franz Schubert (1797–1828) included his *Ave Maria*, frequently sung as a tenor solo, in a collection of seven songs published in 1825. In 1853, French composer, Charles Gounod (1818–1893) set the words to Johann Sebastian Bach's Piano Prelude No. 1 in C Major. The *Ave Maria* appears as a soprano aria in the opera *Otello* by Giuseppe Verdi (1813–1901). Pietro Mascagni (1863–1945) adapted the Intermezzo from his opera *Cavalleria Rusticana* to provide another setting. Many other composers have written their own melodies or arranged others' for the same purpose. Some of the works have found their way into motion picture scores and recordings by popular music artists.

Mary's ecstatic utterance at the Visitation, the *Magnificat*, has been a popular theme from medieval times to the present. Traditionally chanted or sung in Matins and Vespers, it also became a canticle in the Anglican service of Choral Evensong. In addition to at least eight settings for Gregorian chant, the *Magnificat* has been set to music by more than 100 composers, including Josquin des Prez (c.1452–1521), Dietrich Buxtehude (c.1638–1707), Johann Sebastian Bach (1685–1750), Felix Mendelssohn (1809–1847), John Villiers Stanford (1852–1924), and Herbert Howells (1892–1983).

Martin Luther reassured us that the Reformation did not signal the end of rich sacred music: "Next to the Word of God, the noble art of music is the greatest treasure in the world. It controls our thoughts, minds, hearts, and spirits."[100] Buxtehude, Bach, and many others heeded his words. But in some of the new denominations, emphasis shifted to congregational singing. A vast array of congregational hymns is available to us today. Sadly, except for Christmas carols, relatively few of those hymns mention Mary.

Mary in Dance

Sacred dance has been conspicuously absent in Christian tradition, even though the extracanonical *Acts of John* asserts that Jesus led his disciples in a dance at the Last Supper.[101] Mary's forebear, Miriam the Prophetess, led the Israelite women "with timbrels and with dances."[102] And Mary herself reportedly danced with the temple virgins:

> They stood opposite each other in pairs, and danced in various figures and crossings.... [I]t was like a minuet. Sometimes there was a swaying, circular motion of the body, like the movement of the Jews when they pray. Some of the young girls accompanied the dancing with flutes, triangles, and bells.[103]

Chapter 5. Marian Devotion and Intercession

Whereas most other religions included dance in their liturgies, institutional Christianity had inhibitions concerning the human form. With few exceptions, sacred movement—worship with the body—was either outlawed or distilled into highly stylized gestures like elevation of the consecrated host, genuflection, and the Sign of the Cross. Yet if dance was repressed in the liturgy it survived in religious festivals outside the churches, until Puritanism condemned all forms of dancing.

Pre-Christian dance traditions occasionally were adapted for Christian use. An early example was the medieval tradition of dancing around the maypole on May Day. Moorish styles may have influenced the liturgical dances of the *Los Seises* choirboys, performed for the last 500 years in the Cathedral of St Mary, Seville, Spain. The *Matachine* dance tradition of Latin America, now represented by multiple dance groups, celebrates Marian feasts, especially the feast of Our Lady of Guadalupe, December 12. With origins in Spanish sword dancing, the *Matachine* was brought by the *conquistadors* to the Americas, where it incorporated indigenous styles and symbolism.

The Shakers created dances, and both music and dance were important components of their worship services. The popular hymn *Lord of the Dance* was based on a Shaker song. Shakers practiced gender equality and believed that God was both male and female; but they did not venerate Mary.

With strong ecclesiastical backing, religious themes thrived in the visual arts and music; without it, ballet developed a largely secular ethos. In recent years a number of professional Christian ballet companies have been formed, including Ballet Magnificat! in Jackson, Mississippi, and Paradosi Ballet Company in Tacoma, Washington. Despite its promising name the former has yet to offer a production with a Marian theme, and the latter is entirely evangelical in its focus.

A very few ballets have been created with Marian themes. An example was *Primitive Mysteries*, a work choreographed by Martha Graham for her own dance company, with music by Louis Horst. The work premiered in 1931 with Graham playing Mary.[104] Notable also was *A Dancer's Christmas*, performed annually from 1980 to 2008 by the Boston Liturgical Dance Ensemble.[105]

Introducing sacred dance into the liturgy faces stiff challenges. But attitudes may be changing. In 1999 ballerina and choreographer Carla DeSola wrote:

> In the liturgy, when the body is treated as a sacrament, dance focuses people's attention on the now, and on the presence of God in space and time.... Movement is all around us, every day, and the sacred and profane are held together in the dimensions of space, time, rhythm, dynamic energy and beauty. From their spiritual depths, dancers can perceive such movement as expressions or manifestations of God's activity.[106]

One of DeSola's own dance performances was titled "My Soul Magnifies the Lord."[107]

The Church of Rome, which imposes clerical celibacy and rejects female ordination, might seem an unlikely place to expect change. Yet powerful voices inside the church are calling for greater emphasis on liturgical movement, including sacred dance.[108] Efforts also have been made to promote liturgical dance in other mainline Christian denominations. Acceptance, inside and outside Roman Catholicism, is highest where ethnic populations preserve indigenous dance traditions.

A pervasive problem is the layout of church buildings. The linear style, with its long center aisle and far-off chancel, may be ideal for processions; but it rarely provides a stage area where dance can be performed or seen. Chancels were not designed for dance performance, though sacred dance is performed before the high altars at San Fernando Cathedral, San Antonio, Texas;[109] Grace Cathedral, San Francisco, California;[110] St Ignatius Church, Boston College, Massachusetts;[111] and elsewhere.

Another major issue is the availability of professional dancers or instructors. Few churches have the resources to retain a dance director, comparable to a choir director, or to hire lead performers for special offerings. A third issue affects non-Roman sacramental churches and their liturgical repertories: few congregations are sufficiently progressive to consider incorporating dance into their services but also sufficiently "high church" to venerate Mary.[112]

The prospects for using dance as a medium for Marian devotion, and for telling Mary's story, should improve as more women fill the ranks of the clergy—and as women reimagine their clerical roles. Until now

Chapter 5. Marian Devotion and Intercession

the main goal of female clergy has been to demonstrate their ability to perform traditionally male sacerdotal roles. But we can foresee a time when women develop the confidence to see a larger potential of ordination—the potential to develop a uniquely feminine liturgy. For inspiration they can turn to their prototype, Mary, High Priestess of the Christian community of Jerusalem.

Beyond formal liturgy and professional ballet, endless opportunities exist for individuals and small groups to incorporate dance into their own Marian devotion and intercession. Guided by faith, love, and trust in the body as "sacrament," people can allow movement—hand movement or full body movement—to express their deepest aspirations.[113]

---

[1] *Proverbs* 31:25.
[2] *2 Timothy* 4:1. The same language appears in the Apostles' Creed.
[3] "Sub Tuum Praesidium Prayer," Univ. of Dayton. Online: https://udayton.edu/imri/mary/s/sub-tuum-praesidium-prayer.php. Last accessed Oct. 4, 2019. See also http://www.preces-latinae.org/thesaurus/BVM/SubTuum.html. Last accessed Dec. 15, 2019.
[4] Epiphanius, "Against Collyridians," *The Panarion of Epiphanius of Salamis* (transl.: F. Williams), 2/e, Nag Hammadi and Manichaean Studies.
[5] *Ibid.*
[6] *Jeremiah* 7:17-18. See also 44:15-18.
[7] John F. Nash, "The Feminine Face of God in Judaism and Christianity," *The Esoteric Quarterly*, Fall 2020, 65-102.
[8] Allaire Brumfield, "Cakes in the Liknon: Votives from the Sanctuary of Demeter and Kore on Acrocorinth," *Hesperia: Journal of the American School of Classical Studies at Athens* (Jan.-Mar. 1997), 147-172. Demeter and Persephone (Kore) were credited with revealing the secrets of cultivating grains, and in gratitude their devotees made appropriate offerings.
[9] According to the Greek historian Herodotus, the Scythians worshipped a *heptad*, a pantheon of seven gods, all paired with goddesses.
[10] Peter of Damascus, "A Treasury of Divine Knowledge," *Philokalia*, (transl: G. Palmer *et al.*), Eling Trust, 1977, vol. 3, 130.
[11] Anselm of Canterbury, "Third Great Prayer to Mary," (transl: J. Roten), Univ. of Dayton, online: https://udayton.edu/imri/mary/a/anselm-of-canterbury.php. Last accessed Sept 28, 2019. See also Anthony Jose-

maria, *The Blessed Virgin Mary in England*, vol. II, iUniverse, 2008, 225-226.
12. Hildegard of Bingen, Antiphon "O Splendidissima Gemma," *Symphonia*, (transl: M. Atherton), *Hildegard Selected Readings*, Penguin Books, 2001, 117.
13. The etymological similarity does not extend to Greek. "Mother" in Greek is *mitera*, but "matter" is *hyle*.
14. Hildegard of Bingen, Hymn "De Sancta Maria," *Book of Divine Works*, Bear & Co., 1987, 379.
15. *Revelation* 12:1.
16. Bernard of Clairvaux, "Sermon for the Sunday within the Octave of the Assumption," *Sermons on the Blessed Virgin Mary*, Augustine Publ., 1987, 209. The moon is also a powerful feminine symbol.
17. *Ibid.*, 210.
18. *Ibid.*, 214-215.
19. *Zohar*, 21, *Trumah*: 80, verse 789. See also John F. Nash, "The Shekinah in Esoteric Judaism," *The Esoteric Quarterly* (Summer 2005), 33-40.
20. Bernard, "Sermon for the Sunday within the Octave of the Assumption," 203.
21. King Alfonso X of Castile and unnamed assistants, *Cantigas de Santa Maria* ("Songs of Holy Mary"), 1257–1283. Online: https://earlymusicmuse.com/troubadours-cantigas/. Last accessed July 13, 2020.
22. Thomas à Kempis, *Founders of the New Devotion: Being the Lives of Gerard Groote, Florentius Radewin and Their Followers*, English translation, Kegan Paul, 1905, 64.
23. Bernard of Clairvaux, "Fourth Sermon on the Feast of the Assumption," *Sermons on the Blessed Virgin Mary*, 200.
24. Bernard of Clairvaux, "Sermon for the Sunday within the Octave of the Assumption," 207.
25. Some writers have suggested that they also demonstrated the power of the institutional church.
26. *Matthew* 25:31.
27. Jill Raitt *et al.*, *Christian Spirituality*, vol. 2, Crossroad, 1987, 412.
28. "Petition" is often associated with requests for oneself, while "intercession" is reserved for requests for others. Here, for convenience, "intercession" is used for both.
29. See for example https://www.ourcatholicprayers.com/tota-pulchra-es.html. Last accessed February 10, 2020. In addition to what may have been the original Gregorian chant, polyphonic settings of the hymn have been created by numerous composers.
30. See for example: http://prayers.viarosa.com/LitanyOfLoreto.html. Last accessed September 5, 2009.

Chapter 5. Marian Devotion and Intercession

[31] Reportedly, Jerome proposed the title "Drop of the Sea," whose Hebrew form resembled the Aramaic *Maryam*. "Drop" was changed to "Star" in later copies of his writings.

[32] Later, supporters of Mary Queen of Scots claimed the term and chose another date in August.

[33] Parts of the Scottish highlands and western islands were largely untouched by the Reformation, allowing traditional customs to be retained longer than was possible in other parts of the country.

[34] Alexander Carmichael, *Carmina Gadelica*, vol. 1, Oliver & Boyd, 1900, 195-197. See also Mara Freeman, *Kindling the Celtic Spirit*, HarperOne, 2000, 254-256.

[35] J. A. MacCulloch, *The Religion of the Ancient Celts* (Edinburgh: T. & T. Clark, 1911), 265-266.

[36] Nash, "The Feminine Face of God in Judaism and Christianity."

[37] Scotland may have another link with Scythia, allegedly the original home of the Collyridians. The *Declaration of Arbroath*, addressed to Pope John XXII by the Scottish barons in 1320, claimed that the Scots "journeyed from Greater Scythia by way of the Tyrrhenian Sea and the Pillars of Hercules, and dwelt for a long course of time in Spain... Thence they came, twelve hundred years after the people of Israel crossed the Red Sea, to their home in the west where they still live today." Text from https://www.historyfiles.co.uk/FeaturesBritain/Medieval_TextArbroath01.htm. Last accessed April 8, 2021.

[38] Source: http://feastsandfestivals.blogspot.com/2012/08/15th-august-assumption-of-blessed.html. Last accessed Feb. 9, 2021.

[39] Claire Nahman, *Earth Magic: A Wisewoman's Guide to Herbal, Astrological, & Other Folk Wisdom*, Destiny, 1994, 187.

[40] Martin Luther, Christmas sermon 1531. Quoted in Barry Spurr, *See the Virgin Blest*, Palgrave, 2007, 42.

[41] "Works of Martin Luther: The Magnificat Translated and Explained (1520-1)." Online: http://www.godrules.net/library/luther/NEW1luther_c5.htm. Last accessed Jan. 18, 2021.

[42] Diarmaid MacCulloch, *The Reformation*, Penguin Books, 2003, 100

[43] Jill Raitt *et al.*, *Christian spirituality: High Middle Ages and Reformation*, vol. 2, Routledge, 1987, 411.

[44] MacCulloch, *The Reformation*, 576.

[45] Dietrich Bonhoeffer, Sermon on the Third Sunday of Advent, 1933. Online: http://locusthoney.blogspot.com/2011/12/sermon-on-magnificat-by-dietrich.html. Bonhoeffer was executed by the Nazis on April 9, 1945, in the closing days on World War II.

[46] The Akathist is sometimes divided into 12 *kontakia* (Greek singular: *kontakion*, "thematic hymn"), each consisting of a short and long stanza.
[47] Greek Orthodox Archdiocese of America, "The Akathist Hymn and Small Compline." Online: https://www.goarch.org/-/the-akathist-hymn-and-small-compline. Last accessed May 22, 2020.
[48] Greek Orthodox Archdiocese of America, "The Akathist Hymn." Online: https://www.goarch.org/akathisthymn. Last accessed May 22, 2020.
[49] Greek Orthodox Archdiocese of America, "The Akathist Hymn and Small Compline.
[50] "Meet It Is." Hymn to the Theotokos from the Liturgy of St. John Chrysostom.
[51] Sergei Bulgakov, *The Orthodox Church*, St Vladimir's Seminary Press, 1935/1988, 116.
[52] Nikolai Berdyaev, *The Russian Idea* (transl.: R. M. French), Lindisfarne Press, 1946/1992, 24.
[53] Maria Skobtsova, *Veneration of the Mother of God* (transl: S. Janos), YMCA Press, Paris, 1992/2001, 109-126.
[54] Louis-Marie de Montfort, *True Devotion to Mary* (transl.: F. W. Faber), Tan Books, 1712/2010, 9.
[55] *Ibid.*, 13.
[56] Source: https://www.vaticannews.va/en/prayers/the-memorare.html. Last accessed April 21, 2021. It formed part of the 15th-century prayer: "Ad sanctitatis tuae pedes, dulcissima Virgo Maria," and portions may date to earlier times. But attribution to Bernard of Clairvaux lacks historical support.
[57] Prayer beads are also used in other religions, including Buddhism and Sufism.
[58] Nicholas Wiseman, "Prayer for England." See for example: https://vultuschristi.org/index.php/2010/09/prayer-for-the-conversion-of-e/. The "conversion of England" did not mean conversion to Christianity; it meant conversion to Roman Catholicism.
[59] Gay Lowry, "The Gift of the Springtime." Cyril Robert, *Our Lady's Praise in Poetry*, Marist Press, 1944. For a collection of May poems see https://udayton.edu/imri/mary/m/may-poetry.php. Last accessed May 11, 2020.
[60] Paul VI, *Dogmatic Constitution on the Church* (*Lumen Gentium*), Vatican City, November 21, 1964, ch. VIII, 67.
[61] Paul VI, Encyclical Letter *Marialis Cultus*, 1974, §32.
[62] Clarissa P. Estés, *Intie the Strong Woman*, Sounds True, 2011, 81-130. Ally Kateusz, *Mary and Early Christian Women: Hidden Leadership*, Palgrave, 2019, 14-16.
[63] John Paul II, Encyclical letter *Redemptoris Mater*, part I, §8, March 25, 1987.

Chapter 5. Marian Devotion and Intercession

64. *Ibid.*, part 3, §48.
65. Benedict XVI, Angelus address, St Peter's Square, Sunday, October 2, 2011.
66. Congregation for Divine Worship and the Discipline of the Sacraments, "Decree on the Celebration of the Blessed Virgin Mary Mother of the Church in the General Roman Calendar," Vatican City, Feb. 11, 2018.
67. John F. Nash, *The Sacramental Church*, Eugene, OR: Wipf & Stock, 2011, 44.
68. *Ibid.*, 53-54.
69. The feast of the Assumption, previously celebrated on August 15, was abolished on the grounds that it was ascriptural and possibly exalted Mary above Christ.
70. Quoted in Marianne Dorman, "Andrewes and the Caroline Divines: Teachings on the Blessed Virgin Mary," Ecumenical Society of the Blessed Virgin Mary, 2000.
71. John Donne, *A Litany*, c.1609, verse V. Four sources all have *cherubin* instead of *cherubim*, so we can assume that it is not a typographical error.
72. Marianne Dorman, "Andrewes and the Caroline Divines."
73. *Ibid.*
74. Henry Vaughan, *Silex Scintillans*, 1650.
75. Nash, *The Sacramental Church*, ch. 6.
76. *Ibid.*, chs. 6-7.
77. *St Augustine's Prayer Book*, revised edition, 2014. Online: https://www.forwardmovement.org/Content/Site170/FilesSamples/15127 7StAugusti_00000077574.pdf. Last accessed Aug. 31, 2019.
78. The Anglican shrine was created by Alfred Hope Patten (1885–1958), a Church of England clergyman. The Roman Catholic shrine was restored in 1897.
79. Hans U. von Balthasar, *Engagement with God* (transl.: J. Halliburton), Ignatius Press, 1975, 39
80. Quoted in Geoffrey Rowell *et al.*, *Love's Redeeming Work: The Anglican Quest for Holiness*. Oxford Univ. Press, 2001, 703.
81. Tract 71, "On the Controversy with the Romanists," *Tracts for the Times*. Project Canterbury. Online: http://anglicanhistory.org/tracts/tract71.html/. Last accessed Sept. 21, 2019. John Henry Newman identified suggestions that Mary retained a kind of maternal authority over Christ as an important issue dividing the Anglican and Roman Catholic positions. See Nash, *The Sacramental Church*, 171.
82. Frank T. Griswold, *Praying Our Days: A Guide and Companion*, Morehouse Publ., 2009, 135.
83. Anglican–Orthodox Joint Doctrinal Discussions. Dublin Agreed Statement: *The Mystery of the Church*. 1984, III, §§66, 75.

[84] *1 Kings* 8:28-46.
[85] Source: Montfort Missionaries, Company of Mary. Online: http://www.montfortian.info/smm/our-mission.html. Last accessed June 14, 2021.
[86] Source: Our Lady of Lourdes and St Peter Chanel. Online: http://ollspc.com/society-of-mary/. Last accessed Dec. 20, 2019. See also François Drouilly, *15 Days of Prayer with Jean-Claude Colin* (trans.: P. Gage), New City, 2002, 114.
[87] Source: Salve Maria Regina. Online: https://www.salvemariaregina.info/SalveMariaRegina/SMR-143.html. Last accessed Aug. 30, 2019.
[88] Source: New Advent. Online: http://www.newadvent.org/cathen/13188b.htm. Last accessed Aug. 30, 2019.
[89] Thomas Kane, "Shaping Liturgical Dance," Robert Gagne, *et al.*, *Introducing Dance in Christian Worship*, Pastoral Press, 1999, 120.
[90] Controversies erupted in the eighth and ninth centuries, known as the "icon wars." Opposition to icons ran parallel to opposition to religious images in Islam, and were based on some of the same concerns. The controversies were finally settled in 843 by a regional synod in Constantinople, which ruled that the veneration of icons did not imply idolatry.
[91] Several Renaissance artists sought to capture the scene of Luke painting Mary. One such work is Rogier van der Weyden's *Saint Luke Drawing the Virgin* (c.1435-1440).
[92] The original icon currently is displayed at the Church of St. Nicholas in Tolmachi, Moscow.
[93] Rowan Williams, *Ponder these Things: Praying with Icons of the Virgin*, Paraclete, 2006, 30. Archbishop Williams meditated on a sixteenth-century copy of the original icon.
[94] Mirabai Starr, *Mother of God: Similar to Fire*, Orbis, 2018, 13.
[95] Charles Dempsey, *Sandro Botticelli*: Grove Art Essentials, Oxford Univ. Press, 2016.
[96] See for example Terrence E. Dempsey, "The Image of Mary in Twentieth-Century Art." Online: https://ecommons.udayton.edu/cgi/viewcontent.cgi?article=1511&context=marian_studies.
[97] The work, now at St Ives Parish Church, Cornwall, was created in memory of her son who died in 1953 in military action in Thailand.
[98] Nash, "The Feminine Face of God in Judaism and Christianity."
[99] The young Mozart wrote three settings: K.108, 127 and 276. Brahms wrote one: Op. 37, no. 3.
[100] Martin Luther, Foreword to *Symphoniae Iucundae*, published in Wittenberg by Georg Rhau (1488–1548).

Chapter 5. Marian Devotion and Intercession

[101] *Acts of John* §94, Gnostic Society Library.

[102] *Exodus* 15:20. See also: "O virgin of Israel: thou shalt again be adorned with thy tabrets, and shalt go forth in the dances of them that make merry" (*Jeremiah* 31:4).

[103] Clemens W. Brentano (ed.), *The Life of the Blessed Virgin Mary: From the Visions of Ven. Anne Catherine Emmerich* (transl.: M. Palairet), Tan Books, 1954/1970, 115.

[104] The Martha Graham Dance Company was founded in 1926. Revived in 1999, the ballet has now been performed with three other ballerinas in the lead role.

[105] See http://www.blde.org/a-dancers-christmas.html. Last accessed Mar. 5, 2021. The ensemble was directed by Jesuit priest Robert VerEecke who is also referenced elsewhere in this book.

[106] Carla DeSola, Introduction to Gagne, *et al.*, *Introducing Dance in Christian Worship*, 3. Esotericists will also recognize the *Eurythmy* dance styles that emerged within the Antroposophical movement. See for example Rudolf Steiner, *The Early History of Eurythmy* (transl.: F. Amrine), Steiner Books, 2015.

[107] DeSola, Introduction to Gagne, *et al.*, *Introducing Dance in Christian Worship*, 9.

[108] Ronald Gagne, Thomas Kane, & Robert VerEecke, *Introducing Dance in Christian Worship*, (entire book).

[109] Kane, "Shaping Liturgical Dance," 114-115. See also the video: https://www.youtube.com/watch?v=Snjc-BA3TBU. Last accessed March 2, 2021.

[110] See for example: https://www.mothersylvia.com/dance.html. Last accessed Jan. 23, 2021.

[111] A stage was built, extending the chancel at St Ignatius Church, to accommodate liturgical dance and other activities.

[112] The accolade "God's frozen people," awarded to high-church Anglicans and Lutherans is not entirely undeserved.

[113] Yogic *mudras* may provide ideas for hand movements. *Tai chi*, stripped of its martial arts associations, may provide inspiration for full body movements.

201

Mary: Adept, Queen, Mother, Priestess

Chapter 6
Mary Reveals Herself to the World

This chapter examines Mary's apparitions, visitations and communications to people like ourselves. Marian apparitions have become more frequent and are witnessed by larger, more diverse groups of people than hitherto. Some apparitions are accompanied by messages to witnesses, the church, or humanity at large. The apparitions at Zeitoun, Egypt, lasted for three years and were seen by thousands of people, many of them Muslims; those at Medjugorje, Bosnia–Herzegovina, have continued for four decades.

Mary has also communicated by locution or telepathy with certain individuals at greater length and in greater detail, in the expectation that her words would be published. Communications with three such individuals are discussed here: a fourteenth-century nun and two people in our own time.

Mary seems to be revealing more of herself, seeking to be known in new ways and seeking new awareness of her work. In turn we listen to what she is saying, learn of her ongoing ministry, and decide what our response should be. The chapter ends with an attempt to summarize the broad dimensions of her message to the modern world.

Introduction

Mary allegedly appeared to the apostle James the Greater in 40 CE, in Zaragoza, Spain. The incident, known as Our Lady of the Pillar, was an example of *bilocation*,[1] since she was still alive at the time, probably living in Jerusalem. The term Marian *apparition* generally refers to a visitation from Mary after her Dormition or Assumption into heaven.

According to tradition St Nicholas (270–343), Bishop of Myra and precursor of Santa Claus, had two visions of Mary. In 948 Bishop

Mary: Adept, Queen, Mother, Priestess

Conrad of Constance (Konstanz) testified that he saw Mary consecrate bread and wine in the Chapel of Our Lady of the Hermits at Einsiedeln, Switzerland; she was accompanied by Christ and an entourage of angels and saints.[2] In 1061 Mary appeared to English noblewoman Richeldis de Faverches in the village of Walsingham, England. She appeared to Benedictine abbess Elisabeth of Schönau (c.1129–1164), reportedly wearing Eucharistic vestments and a crown. Mary appeared to Dominic de Guzmán, founder of the Order of Preachers (Dominicans), in 1214, and gave him the Rosary. Thirty-seven years later, she appeared to Simon Stock, prior general of the Carmelites (Order of Our Lady of Mount Carmel), to give him the brown scapular. Teresa of Ávila (1515–1582), Carmelite mystic and mentor of John of the Cross, is said to have experienced multiple apparitions of Mary. These are just a few of many reported visitations to people of exceptional piety throughout Christian history.[3]

Marian apparitions have continued into modern times, have increased in frequency, and in several cases have been seen by multiple witnesses. Apparitions have been reported on six continents, witnessed by men, women, and children from many walks of life. Locations graced by Marian apparitions include large cities, wilderness areas, fields, caves, churches, monasteries, and people's homes.[4] Recent Marian apparitions rarely have been one-time phenomena. More commonly they have been series of incidents extending over weeks, months or years, usually but not always involving the same group of witnesses.

Five notable series of apparitions will be discussed in this chapter. Four involved Roman Catholic witnesses, and the fifth involved a wide variety of witnesses including Coptic Christians and Muslims.

We do not presume to know Mary's intentions or the way her will interacts with that of Christ and others at levels above our own. But the increasing frequency and changing nature of the apparitions suggest that she wishes to reveal more herself and promote her ongoing ministry. Apparitions are powerful spiritual experiences for witnesses; they may raise the consciousness of onlookers or pilgrims who visit apparition sites later; and many of them attract media attention. Some apparitions have included messages addressed to the witnesses or larger audiences.

On the other hand, apparitions do not provide a medium for the communication of large volumes of material, such as new revelation or

Chapter 6. Mary Reveals Herself to the World

teachings. To overcome that limitation, and to ensure a wide dissemination of information, Mary also seems to have chosen another method to further her ministry. She has communicated with selected individuals who served as scribes, or amanuenses (singular: *amanuensis*), and who published her teachings. Material was "dictated," by telepathy or some similar method, and the amanuenses either wrote it down themselves or relayed it orally to stenographers.

This chapter discusses three individuals who received such communications: Bridget of Sweden in the fourteenth century; Geoffrey Hodson, who wrote during the twentieth century; and Anna Raimondi, alive today. Raimondi described the process of communication in some detail.

These latter communications belong to a larger category of phenomena in which individuals have received teachings on various subjects from higher sources. Hildegard of Bingen (1098–1179) claimed to have been so inspired, as also was María de Ágreda (1602–1665) cited in Chapter 4. Chapter 2 was devoted in its entirety to the work of Anne Catherine Emmerich.[5] The teachings of many of the great theologians may not have been "their own." The utterances of the prophets and the canonical scriptures may also fall into that category.

Whether revelation stopped upon closure of the scriptural canon, or has continued throughout history, is of course a matter of controversy. Most Christian teachers insist that the Bible contains all divine revelation needed until the end of the age. Yet the decrees of the ecumenical councils, even those without explicit scriptural backing, were deemed to be endorsed by the Holy Spirit. In the Eastern Orthodox churches mystical theology and *theoria*—direct knowledge of God—are valued more than theological speculation. Esotericists assert that important new knowledge has been revealed during the last two centuries and that the process can be expected to continue.

Credibility of Marian Apparitions

The Church of Rome reported 386 significant Marian apparitions during the twentieth century.[6] Its official investigative body, the Sacred Congregation for the Doctrine of the Faith (CDF), approaches each incident with great caution. It restricts investigations to incidents involving witnesses within its own communion, judged to be of good moral character, and not seeking to benefit financially or otherwise. It also requires that the form of the apparition and any reported message conform to church doctrine. This latter criterion could be criticized because it triggers the rejection of incidents that might provide a new understanding of Mary or new teachings, even when Mary herself may be speaking.

Of the 386 incidents, the CDF rejected seventy-nine apparitions as invalid. But it judged that eight "were of a character that could not be attributed to natural phenomena, delusion or fraud": Fátima, Portugal (1917); Beauraing, Belgium (1932–1933); Banneux, Belgium (1933); Zeitoun, Egypt (1968–1971); Akita, Japan (1973–1979); Syracuse, Italy (1953); Manila, Philippines (1986); and Betania, Venezuela (1976–1991).[7] No opinion was issued on the remaining incidents.

A further eleven incidents were deemed "worthy of faith" by local bishops. Most often bishops withhold judgment, preferring to remain above the inevitable controversy. Occasionally, bishops forbid witnesses or others from visiting an apparition site or from discussing their experiences; but warnings are not always heeded—and may simply draw attention to the incidents in question.

Separately, but employing similar criteria, the Coptic Orthodox Church approved the apparition at Zeitoun and four others, all in Egypt: Edfu (1982), Shoubra (1986), Assiut (2000–2001), and Warraq el-Hadar (2009).[8]

The Anglican Communion does not take a corporate position on apparitions, but individual bishops recognize the medieval apparition at Walsingham, the ones at Lourdes in 1858, and an apparition in 1994 at a 137-year-old Anglican church in Yankalilla, South Australia. Individual Lutheran clergy have come to accept the Marian apparition at Guadalupe, Mexico.[9] The Eastern Orthodox churches express great devotion to Mary but attach no importance to apparitions. They are suspicious of western interest in apparitions, in some cases even questioning whether witnesses were deceived by evil forces.[10] Most other religious bodies are either silent with respect to Marian apparitions or dismiss them out of hand.

The positive pronouncement by an investigative committee does not guarantee that an apparition is valid. Nor do negative pronouncements, or silence on the part of religious bodies, necessarily mean that all other incidents are hoaxes or the products of wishful thinking, misguided piety, mental illness, or mass hysteria. Religious bodies speak only for themselves; what they may or may not say has author-

Chapter 6. Mary Reveals Herself to the World

ity only for their own members. Religious bodies are concerned to protect their own credibility; they are cautious, and the number of endorsements is understandably small.

The small number of official endorsements does not necessarily imply that Marian apparitions are rare. Countless people may witness apparitions that are of great personal significance but go unreported. Individuals so blessed may not want publicity or may fear resistance or persecution by religious or civil authorities. Or the individuals may fall outside the boundaries of interest of the major religious denominations. Modern author Clarissa Pinkola Estés claims that Marian apparitions are actually quite common. Estés suggests that Mary "seems to pay no attention" to investigative committees or criteria of validity. "She keeps appearing without any authority's permission, without institutional sanction, to those in need."[11] Large numbers of people are also impacted through healings or transformative experiences at apparition sites.

That said, from the perspective of studies like the present one, the caution of investigative bodies plays a useful role in filtering information. An individual's experiences, however profound, are not always relevant to the collective picture of Mary built up over the centuries by other apparition witnesses, scripture writers, religious teachers, and scribes recording the teachings of higher beings.

The whole topic of Marian apparitions has low credibility in the public consciousness. Part of the blame can be laid on the news media. Tabloids and talk shows often sensationalize the least credible claims, while quality news media may be reluctant to report more credible claims for fear of negative reaction from the public, advertisers, or competitors within their own industry.

Credibility of Other Communications

As in the case of apparitions, the validity of communications to individuals can neither be confirmed with complete certainty, nor definitively be rejected. We must rely on subjective judgments, and all such judgments—along with the communications themselves—remain controversial.

Although Bridget of Sweden is one of the three individuals considered here, the last 150 years have seen an explosion in the number of people claiming to have received teachings from higher beings. They range from serious esotericists to popular New Age practitioners, to

outright charlatans. In response, criteria have emerged within the esoteric community to help identify claims that deserve attention. Factors supporting validity are:
- The communications offer new knowledge; they do not simply rehash existing knowledge or offer platitudes.
- They build in a credible way on existing knowledge and help create a more comprehensive and consistent picture of historical events or understanding of the larger reality.
- They honor the dignity of all humanity and inspire love, wisdom and service.

Red flags warning against acceptance are:
- The communications flatter the alleged recipient.
- They are exploited for monetary gain, notoriety or power.
- They threaten people who do not accept their message, or they promote separatism, hatred or violence.[12]

The Church of Rome has sectarian and doctrinal concerns, whereas the esoteric community is nonsectarian and concerned with the expansion of knowledge. Both face the common challenge of discerning between reliable and unreliable witnesses, and between credible and less credible information in situations where factual observation or science may be inapplicable. The Sacred Congregation for the Doctrine of the Faith rejects a majority of claims in its jurisdiction. The esoteric community is not homogeneous and has no central authority. But a consensus usually develops among groups of esotericists to accept or reject a particular claim of communication from a higher source; again a great majority of claims is rejected.[13]

Again, rejection does not necessarily mean that a claim is fraudulent or that the communication is invalid. The individual may be well-intentioned and of sound mind, and the experience may have great personal value; but the information received may not contribute meaningfully to the body of knowledge comprising "modern esotericism."

As individuals as well as collectively, our attitude toward supernatural or paranormal phenomena must find a balance between gullibility and closed-mindedness. We must make up our own minds which, if any, of the apparitions or other communications described here might

Chapter 6. Mary Reveals Herself to the World

be relevant to our understanding of Mary and our relationship with her.

Marian Apparitions

Five notable series of apparitions are discussed here. For literary convenience, cautionary prefixes like "reportedly," "allegedly," or "it is claimed that..." have mostly been omitted. Credibility should be judged according to the criteria already discussed. The outcome or status of investigations by religions authorities is noted in each case.

Guadalupe, Mexico

Juan Diego Cuauhtlatoatzin (1474–1548), known today simply as Juan Diego, was a Nahuan, or Chichimec, peasant and a convert to Christianity. A sizable fraction of the indigenous population had converted—often under coercion—in the early years of the Spanish conquest and occupation of Mexico.

On December 9, 1531 Juan Diego witnessed the apparition of a "young woman" on Tepeyac Hill, Guadalupe, now a suburb of Mexico City.[14] Speaking to him in his native Nahuatl language, she identified herself as Mary, "mother of the very true Deity," and asked that a shrine in her honor be built on the hill. The *conquistadors* had recently destroyed a temple on that site, dedicated to the Aztec mother goddess Tonantzin.

Diego approached his bishop, the Basque Franciscan Don Juan de Zumárraga, with the request; but the latter demanded a sign of authenticity. When Diego reported this to Mary, she agreed to furnish a sign when he came to Tepeyac Hill the following day. Diego missed the scheduled meeting with Mary because his uncle, Juan Bernardino, fell gravely ill. After a physician predicted imminent death, Diego fetched a priest to give Bernardino the last rites.[15] Bernardino was an elder in the Aztec religion but, like Diego, had converted to Christianity.

Having missed the meeting, Diego was too ashamed to go to Tepeyac Hill, but Mary found him and assured him that Bernardino had recovered. She instructed him to climb the hill—on December 12—and gather flowers. He found a variety of flowers, including Castilian roses, miraculously blooming on the barren hilltop in mid-winter. Mary arranged the blooms in Diego's cloak, saying: "My youngest son, these different kinds of flowers are the proof, the sign that you will take the bishop. You will tell him for me that in them he is to see my wish and that ... he is to carry out my wish.... [I]n you I place my absolute trust."[16] Flowers symbolize truth in the Aztec culture.

When Diego opened his cloak before the bishop, an image of Mary was imprinted on the fabric.[17] Early reproductions of the image shows her wearing a pink, patterned robe, covered by a deep-blue mantle emblazoned with stars.[18] Later versions show rays of light radiating from the periphery of the figure.[19] The image, known as Our Lady of Guadalupe, has become the subject of Marian devotion throughout Latin America and also a symbol of Mexican cultural identity.

Juan Diego witnessed a total of four apparitions of Mary, while his uncle had a vision of his own, as well as the healing. The authenticity of the apparitions at Guadalupe was controversial, even in the sixteenth century, and two major religious orders weighed in. The Franciscans—the order to which Bishop de Zumárraga belonged—dismissed the apparitions and claimed that the image on Diego's cloak was painted by a local artist.[20] The Dominicans supported Diego's testimony and eventually swayed the church authorities in Mexico to accept it. The feast of Our Lady of Guadalupe, December 12, is celebrated in many countries, and Guadalupe remains the most popular pilgrimage destination in the Western Hemisphere. Juan Diego was finally canonized by Pope John Paul II in 2002.

The imprinting of Mary's image on Juan Diego's cloak can be compared to the story of Veronica immortalized in the sixth Station of the Cross. According to that tradition, Veronica was moved by compassion to wipe Jesus' face with her veil, as he carried the cross to Calvary, only to find an imprint of his face on the veil.

Lourdes, France

The most famous apparitions of the nineteenth century were the eighteen visions experienced by Bernadette Soubirous at Lourdes, France. They began on February 11, 1858, when Bernadette, a fourteen-year-old peasant girl, reported seeing "a lady" at the entrance of a cave, or grotto, on the bank of the Gave River (Figure 6.1). Bernadette described the lady as "wearing a white dress, a blue girdle and a yellow rose on each foot, the same color as the chain of her rosary; the beads of the rosary were white."[21]

The lady first spoke to Bernadette on the third apparition, February 18, using the local Occitan language. Bernadette reported that the lady said "she could not promise to make me happy in this world, only in the next."²² At the seventh appearance, February 23, the lady entrusted a secret to Bernadette, which the latter never divulged. Secret messages would also be communicated in several apparitions elsewhere.

Figure 6.1

Our Lady of Lourdes. Representation of the Marian apparition in the grotto in 1858.

The sole witness, 14-year-old Bernadette Soubirous, described Mary as "a Lady." Later, Mary reportedly told Bernadette "I am the Immaculate Conception."

Lourdes is now the most-visited apparition site in Europe, and the scene of numerous authenticated healings.

On the ninth appearance, on February 25, the lady told Bernadette Soubirous to dig in the dirt around the grotto and to drink the muddy water. The following day, water flowed from that location; and on March 1, a woman reportedly was cured of paralysis after dipping her hand into the spring.

During most of the apparitions, the lady did not identify herself. Pressed by clergy and town authorities, Bernadette repeatedly asked her name. Finally, on the sixteenth appearance, March 25, the lady identified herself in Occitan as: *"Que soy era Immaculada Councepciou"* ("I am the Immaculate Conception"). Bernadette did not understand the term, but her local priest knew at once that it referred to the recently defined dogma.[23]

After the last apparition, on July 16, 1858, Bernadette commented: "I have never seen her [Mary] so beautiful before ... so lovely that, when you have seen her once, you would willingly die to see her again!"[24]

Bernadette Soubirous entered a convent and remained in quiet seclusion for the rest of her life. Thirty years after her death, Bernadette's body was exhumed and found to be intact. She was canonization by Pope Pius XI in 1933—not because of the apparitions but in recognition of her personal piety.

Lourdes became the most famous pilgrimage site in Europe. Roughly five million pilgrims visit the grotto each year. Laboratory tests have not detected any chemical or pharmaceutical agents in the spring water. But more than seventy medically significant, and otherwise-unexplainable, healings have been documented by the International Medical Committee, involving conditions ranging from nervous disorders to cancers to blindness.[25]

Fátima, Portugal

In 1917 Lúcia Santos and her cousins Jacinta and Francisco Marto, reported a series of six apparitions at Fátima, Portugal. On May 13, 1917 the three children "beheld a Lady all dressed in white. She was more brilliant than the sun, and radiated a light more clear and intense than a crystal glass filled with sparkling water, when the rays of the burning sun shine through it."[26] The lady asked them to devote themselves to the Holy Trinity and to pray "the Rosary every day, to bring peace to the world and an end to the war"—presumably World War I, which was then in its most deadly phase.

During the second apparition on June 13, the lady revealed that Francisco and Jacinta would be taken to Heaven soon, but Lúcia would live longer in order to spread her message and devotion to the Immaculate Heart of Mary. The prophecy relating to Francisco and Jacinta came true.

At the last apparition, on October 13, 1917, Mary told the children: "I want to tell you that a chapel is to be built here in my honor. I am the Lady of the Rosary. Continue always to pray the Rosary every day. The war is going to end, and the soldiers will soon return to their homes." The war did end thirteen months later.

Chapter 6. Mary Reveals Herself to the World

Mary had promised a sign or miracle during the October 13 apparition, and thousands of curious people came to witness it. Lucia suddenly cried, "Look at the sun!" Whereupon:

> The rain at that moment had stopped; the sun was clearly seen. There was no cloud to obscure it, yet it did not strain the eyes of any man to look on its unveiled light. The people could see that the sun was strangely spinning. It began to revolve more rapidly, more frighteningly. It began to cast off beams of many-colored lights in all directions. Shafts of brilliant red came from the rim of the revolving star and fell across the earth, the people and the trees; and green lights came and violet and blue in mixed array. [The sun] begins careening, trembling in the sky for seventy thousand witnesses to see. Now... it appears to plunge from its place in the Heavens and fall upon the earth. People are crying.[27]

Only the three children saw Mary and heard her words, but the large crowd of onlookers saw the "dancing sun." Many formally testified, providing an essentially consistent account of the incident. No evidence exists that the sun actually moved, or that the earth's orbit suffered any kind of perturbation. The incident seems to have been a case of mass hallucination, but not one that could have been orchestrated by human agency.

Francisco and Jacinta Marto died in the influenza pandemic of the postwar years. Francisco Marto died in 1919, at the age of ten; and Jacinta in 1920, at the age of nine. Lúcia survived and was sent to the school of the Sisters of St Dorothy in Porto, Portugal; in 1928 she entered the convent of the Sisters of St Dorothy in Tui, Spain.[28] Sr Lúcia eventually left the Dorothean order to become a Discalced Carmelite. She died in 2005 at the age of ninety-seven.

In her memoirs Lúcia Santos claimed that Mary had entrusted three secrets to her. Two were disclosed in 1941 and the third in 2000. Both the content and the process of disclosure have been controversial. The "secrets" included a graphic vision of hell, warnings of the threat of communism (but, interestingly, not of fascism), and prophecy of a pope's assassination. Meanwhile, Fátima too became a favored pilgrimage site.

Zeitoun, Egypt

A series of apparitions of a quite different nature occurred at El-Zeitoun, a suburb of Cairo, Egypt. On April 2, 1968 an ethereal female figure was seen moving on the roof of a Coptic Church dedicated to Mary. According to local tradition, the Holy Family stayed on that site during their flight into Egypt.

The first witnesses were Muslim workers at a bus garage across the street. Fearing that a woman might be contemplating suicide, they called the police. The police found no one there and suggested that the phenomenon might be a reflection from street lights. But a crowd gathered, and people declared that the figure was Mary, "a beautiful girl in a bright gown of light and had branches of olive tree in her hand, and around her flew white doves."[29]

One week later another sighting was reported. From then on the sightings became more frequent, sometimes two or three times a week. Apparitions varied from a few minutes to eight hours. Photographs of the phenomena soon appeared in the news media and are still available online. Fr Boutros Gayed, rector of the church described the apparitions thus:

1. The first was in full luminous stature. She was wearing a long robe extending to below Her feet. Sometimes She was surrounded by bright stars, and at other times She had a shawl about Her head, and Her hands were extended forward.
2. The Virgin used to walk over the church, especially over the middle dome, and to bow in front of the cross that shone, then, with a bright light.
3. She sometimes made Her apparition with a babe in Her arms.
4. She sometimes appeared like a luminous shape over the eastern dome. Her features were clear.
5. The apparition of the Virgin was accompanied with, or preceded by, the appearance of white pigeons that used to circle the church.
6. Sometimes a lightning-like light appeared. It shone for a while and then disappeared. Sometimes a luminous mist spread everywhere and it gave off the strong pleasant scent of incense that pervaded the whole place.
7. I have seen the Virgin myself reflected against the surface of the moon whose disk got bigger as the moon got nearer to the church. The Virgin made Her apparition carrying a babe in Her arms.[30]

Chapter 6. Mary Reveals Herself to the World

During the apparitions, a number of healings, confirmed by physicians, took place inside the church. A large cathedral has now been built adjacent to the church.

A high-level ecclesiastical commission was appointed to investigate the matter, and on May 4, 1968, Pope Kyrillos VI of the Coptic Orthodox Church of Alexandria issued a statement affirming the validity of the apparitions. Separately, a Vatican envoy dispatched to Cairo witnessed the apparitions and sent a report to Pope Paul VI, whereupon the Church of Rome issued an affirmative opinion. Intensive investigations by the police failed to detect any physical explanation for the sightings or evidence of fraud.

The Zeitoun apparitions were not accompanied by any verbal communication. But everybody present saw "something," and believers identified it as Mary. The apparitions were witnessed by large numbers of people, including Christians and non-Christians, and people of all ages and educational levels; they were even witnessed by Egyptian President Gamal Abdel Nasser. By contrast, many other apparitions were witnessed only by children, whose testimony could be questioned on the grounds of their immaturity.

The Zeitoun apparitions continued through 1971. They seem to have been targeted, at least in part, at the majority Muslim population, emphasizing the devotion to Mary in early Islam and the references to her in the *Qur'an*. More directly they were targeted at the Coptic Church, which was also blessed by four other apparitions in modern times. Perhaps, the Zeitoun apparitions will overcome the perception that Marian apparitions are a purely Roman Catholic phenomenon and will encourage the other "eastern churches" to take greater interest.[31]

Medjugorje, Bosnia–Herzegovina

The apparitions at Medjugorje, a small village in what is now Bosnia–Herzegovina, began on June 24, 1981. At that time the country was part of Yugoslavia, whose repressive communist regime regarded religion as hostile to the state.[32]

Four young people: Mirjana Dragićević, Ivanka Ivanković, Vicka Ivanković, and Ivan Dragićević reported seeing a vision of Mary on a hillside outside the village. The following day, they and two others: Marija Pavlović and Jakov Colo, had a similar vision and climbed the hill to approach Mary.[33] They called her the *Gospa*, an old Serbo-

Mary: Adept, Queen, Mother, Priestess

Croatian word for "Lady" or "Our Lady." The six witnesses, two boys and three girls, ranged in age from ten to sixteen.

Word of the apparitions soon spread, and people flocked to Medjugorje. The authorities became alarmed and tried to silence the six witnesses. But despite harassment, interrogation and threats, the six refused to recant their accounts. A local priest first dismissed the witnesses' stories but eventually defended them, whereupon he was sentenced to three years' hard labor.

In 1992 priest and writer Fr Janko Bubalo questioned the witnesses about the Mary's appearance. They testified that she appeared to be eighteen-to-twenty years old, of slender build, and about 5 feet 5 inches (165 cm) tall. Her face was long and oval. She had black hair. Her eyes were blue with delicate eyelashes and thin black eyebrows. She had a small nose and rosy cheeks. She had reddish lips and her smile was "like some indescribable gentleness." Her simple dress was bluish-grey and fell freely all the way down to the little "whitish cloud" on which she stood. Her pure-white veil covered her head and shoulders and also reached down to the cloud. She wore a crown of twelve golden stars on her head.[34]

Mirjana Dragićević-Soldo offered another description of Mary, as she appeared on the second day of the apparitions:

> A beautiful blueness encompassed the woman. Her skin was imbued with an olive-hued radiance, and her eyes reminded me of the translucent blue of the Adriatic. A white veil concealed most of her long, black hair, except for a curl visible near her forehead and locks hanging down below the veil. She wore a long dress that fell past her feet. Everything I saw seemed supernatural, from the unearthly blue-gray glow of her dress to the breathtaking intensity of her gaze.[35]

Writing later in life, Dragićević-Soldo revised her estimate of Mary's age to "20–25."[36]

These descriptions are generally similar to the ones at Lourdes in 1858. On Christmas Day, 1981, however, Dragićević-Soldo reported seeing Mary in a golden dress of unearthly brilliance. "Describing her dress as 'golden' hardly defines it," she commented, "The 'color' of her dress ... is almost like light—but an ethereal sort of light that

Chapter 6. Mary Reveals Herself to the World

bends, flows, and undulates according to Our Lady's movements and the feelings she wishes to convey."[37]

When Fr Bubalo asked whether Mary was beautiful, the witnesses' reply was: "Her beauty cannot be described. It is not our kind of beauty. It is something ethereal, something heavenly, something that we'll only see in Paradise—and then only to a certain degree."[38] In her autobiography Mirjana Dragićević-Soldo recalled asking Mary, "How is it possible that you are so beautiful?" Mary gently smiled and explained. "I am beautiful because I love. If you want to be beautiful, then love."[39]

Perhaps unique to the Medjugorje apparitions, the witnesses have not only seen Mary, they have *touched* her. Reportedly: "Our Lady has embraced them, held their hands, and Marija even received a kiss by Our Lady on her birthday."[40]

Although Mary frequently warned that prayer was needed to avert the evils of the world, including those stemming from the breakup of Yugoslavia, she avoided messages that might create fear. As one of the witnesses explained to pilgrims: "[N]ever trust anyone who spreads fear, because faith that comes from fear in not true faith, and Our Lady doesn't want people to love her out of fear."[41] Reportedly the children who witnessed the Fátima apparitions were traumatized by a graphic vision of hell.

Mary seems eager to send a message that transcends religious sectarianism. Vicka Ivanković (now Vicka Ivanković-Mijatović) reported that Mary once said: "God did not divide people into different religions. Those people divided themselves." Speaking for herself, Ivanković-Mijatović commented: "[E]ach one of us should worship God in our own way and pray to Him in our own way. There is only One God and we all believe in One God."[42]

Yet all of the witnesses are Roman Catholic, and much of what Mary taught them related to its traditions. Vicka Ivanković-Mijatović was asked whether she had discerned Mary's views on contraception and abortion, issues which feature prominently in Roman Catholic moral teachings. Her reply was: "Our Lady did say those committing abortions are committing a great sin.... People who have abortions will be held responsible for the grave sin they commit." But Mary refrained from commenting on contraception.[43]

The apparitions continue to the present, and the original witnesses, now in late-middle age, are still involved. As of January 2020, three of them continued to see Mary daily, and at least one—Marija Pavlović—was doing so a year later.[44] Whereas the witnesses of many earlier Marian apparitions took religious vows and withdrew into monastic seclusion, all six of the Medjugorje witnesses married and have children.

Setting the apparitions at Medjugorje in a category by themselves have been Mary's messages to the world—1,300, to the time of writing. They cannot be said to offer new knowledge. Rather, the messages inspire and console; they encourage faith and prayers for peace; they reinforce traditional practices, like the Rosary, and fasting. While they promote her own special mission of peace, the messages insist that the path of love leads through her son.

Three messages are reproduced here for purposes of illustration. The first, recorded August 2, 2015, emphasized that Mary sees herself as an emissary of her son:

> Dear children, I, as a mother who loves her children, see how difficult the time in which you live is. I see your suffering, but you need to know that you are not alone. My Son is with you. He is everywhere. He is invisible, but you can see Him if you live Him. He is the light which illuminates your soul and gives you peace. He is the Church which you need to love and to always pray and fight for—but not only with words, instead with acts of love. My children, bring it about for everyone to come to know my Son, bring it about that He may be loved, because the truth is in my Son born of God—the Son of God.... If you live His word, you will love with a merciful love; you will love each other. The more that you will love, the farther away you will be from death. For those who will live the word of my Son and who will love, death will be life. Thank you. Pray to be able to see my Son in your shepherds. Pray to be able to embrace Him in them.[45]

In a message recorded February 2, 2020, Mary spoke of her role as Mother of God and drew attention to the Eucharist and the Sacrifice of the Cross. It also invited "apostles of my love" to follow the path of discipleship:

> Dear children, by the act of the decision and love of God, I am chosen to be the Mother of God and your mother. But also by my

Chapter 6. Mary Reveals Herself to the World

will and my immeasurable love for the Heavenly Father and my complete trust in Him, my body was the chalice of the God-man. I was in the service of truth, love and salvation, as I am now among you to call you, my children, apostles of my love, to be carriers of truth; to call you to spread His words, the words of salvation, by your will and love for my Son: that with your actions you may show, to all those who have not come to know my Son, His love. You will find strength in the Eucharist—my Son who feeds you with His Body and strengthens you with His Blood. My children, fold your hands and look at the Cross in silence.... My children, apostles of my love, fold your hands, look at the Cross. Only in the Cross is salvation. Thank you.[46]

A message recorded January 25, 2021, was purely devotional in nature:

Dear children! I am calling you at this time to prayer, fasting and renunciation, that you may be stronger in faith. This is a time of awakening and of giving birth. As nature, which gives itself, you also, little children, ponder how much you have received. Be joyful bearers of peace and love that it may be good for you on earth. Yearn for Heaven; and in Heaven there is no sorrow or hatred. That is why, little children, decide anew for conversion and let holiness begin to reign in your life. Thank you for having responded to my call.[47]

Mary reportedly told Vicka Ivanković-Mijatović that the Medjugorje apparitions were "the last time She [Mary] would appear in this way and that She will not come in this form again." However, Mary promised to leave "a visible, permanent and indestructible" sign on the hill where the apparitions have taken place.[48]

The Church of Rome has yet to issue an official opinion on the Medjugorje apparitions. Informally, there is more confidence in the validity of the earlier apparitions than in later ones.

Pope John Paul II called the village "A great center of spirituality" and expressed his own desire to pay a visit. He met privately with Mirjana Dragićević-Soldo, as she was known by then, in July 1987 and told her: "Take good care of Medjugorje, Mirjana. Medjugorje is the hope for the entire world."[49] An investigation in 1993 recommended that the church "accept Medjugorje as a holy place, as a shrine." The most recent investigative commission submitted confidential findings in 2014, but no action has yet been taken.[50]

In an interview in 2017 Pope Francis expressed his personal reservations concerning the authenticity of the later apparitions and their messages. "I personally am more suspicious," he said, "I prefer the Madonna as Mother, our Mother, and not a woman who's the head of an office, who every day sends a message at a certain hour. This is not the Mother of Jesus. And these presumed apparitions don't have a lot of value."[51] Whether or not his suspicions are justified, his characterization of Mary could be criticized as unduly narrow. Indeed, we shall see in the next chapter that esoteric teachers have portrayed her very much as "head of an office."

Notwithstanding his reservations, Pope Frances approved Roman Catholic pilgrimages to Medjugorje in 2019. By then an estimated forty million visitors of all faiths had already visited Medjugorje from all over the world. None saw Mary; many shared experiences of healing and/or spiritual renewal; some came away disappointed or disillusioned.[52] Not unexpectedly, skeptics dismiss the apparitions as a hoax.

The frequency of apparitions at Medjugorje is declining, and it is likely that they will soon come to an end. Meanwhile, a huge library of messages and other material has been accumulated, much of it awaiting detailed study and analysis.

Communications with Bridget of Sweden

Who Was Bridget of Sweden?

Bridget of Sweden (c.1303–1373), birth name Birgitta Birgersdotter, was born into the Swedish aristocracy. She married a nobleman at age fourteen and went on to bear eight children. Upon her husband's death in 1344, Bridget resolved to devote the rest of her life to prayer and service. She founded a religious community that became the Order of the Most Holy Savior, now known simply as the Brigittines. Initially, the order's houses followed a familiar medieval pattern: they were double monasteries in which men and women slept in separate dormitories but worked and worshipped together. Over time the order was richly endowed by the Swedish royal family, but the monks and

Chapter 6. Mary Reveals Herself to the World

nuns lived in poverty and donated all resources not needed for their basic needs to the poor. Bridget was canonized eighteen years after her death.

From the age of ten onward Bridget experienced visions similar to those of Anne Catherine Emmerich. She also received communications from Jesus and Mary, and the latter are of particular interest here. Her visions and communications are recorded in the twelve-volume *Revelations of St Bridget*, originally penned in Swedish but soon translated into Latin. English translations are now available.[53]

Bridget's *Revelations* have always been controversial. Moreover, they are not free from devotional bias. Aside from that concern, Bridget's communications from Mary meet the criteria listed above. Tentatively we accept their validity, allowing Bridget's story to be compared and contrasted with other sources of knowledge about Mary, and absorbed into the larger picture that is emerging.

Mary's Revelations

Mary told Bridget of many incidents in her life and that of her son, describing both the scenes and the feelings she experienced. Following is a very small sample of the available material.

Mary shared her impressions of the time she was presented to the temple:

> As the time approached, when by rule, virgins were presented in the temple of the Lord, I went up among them in submission to my parents, thinking that nothing was impossible to God. And as He knew that I desired nothing, wished nothing but Himself, He could, if it pleased Him, preserve me in my virginity; if not, His will be done.[54]

Then, when her time came to leave the temple: "After hearing all the instructions in the Temple, I returned home, inflamed with still greater love of God, enkindled daily by new fervor and desire of love."[55] Soon thereafter, in Bridget's account, the Archangel Gabriel appeared to Mary and the familiar Annunciation scene unfolded.

In one conversation with Bridget Mary reflected on why she was chosen: "I had three virtues by which I pleased my Son. I had such humility that no creature, whether angel or men, was humbler than I. Second, I had obedience by which I strove to obey my Son in all things. Third, I had outstanding charity."[56] In return Mary received

Mary: Adept, Queen, Mother, Priestess

honors, the most important of which was to give birth to Jesus: "Once, I had the Son in my womb together with his divine nature. Now he is to be seen in me with both his human and divine natures as in a mirror."[57]

Bridget's devotional life was strongly focused on Christ's Passion, and Mary provided detailed descriptions of the trial, the scourging, the road to Calvary, and the Crucifixion. Mary also reflected on her thoughts and feelings after the Crucifixion:

> At the death of my Son, all things were disturbed. For the divinity, which was never separated from Him, not even in death, in that hour of His death seemed to partake of His suffering.... So the angels grieved, as it were, for his Passion, although they are impassible. But they rejoiced at His future glory and for the benefits to result from His Passion. The elements, too, were all troubled; the sun and moon lost their splendor—the earth quaked; the rocks were rent, the graves opened, at the death of my Son.[58]

Mary commented on her later life and ministry:

> I lived a long time in the world after the Ascension of my Son, and God so willed it that many souls, seeing my patience and life, might be converted to Him, and the Apostles of God and other elect confirmed. And even the natural constitution of my body required that I should live longer, that my crown might be increased.[59]

"That my crown might be increased" would seem to refer to Mary's continued spiritual development and expansion of consciousness. Esotericists would understand it as progress on the initiatory path.

Mary often referred to herself in royal terms: "I am the Queen of Angels,"[60] and "I am the Queen of Heaven."[61] Bridget described a vision of Mary as Queen, and explained its significance:

> [I, Bridget,] saw the Queen of Heaven, the Mother of God, wearing a priceless and inestimable crown on her head, with her wonderfully beautiful hair hanging down over her shoulders, a golden tunic gleaming indescribably bright, and a mantle of the color of azure on a calm day.... The crown signifies that she is the Queen and Lady and Mother of the King of Angels. Her hair hanging down signifies that she is a pure and immaculate virgin, the sky-colored mantle that she was dead to temporal things. The golden

tunic signifies that she was ardent and burning with the love of God both inwardly and outwardly.[62]

Bridget added that during the same vision: "Her Son placed seven lilies in the crown, and between the lilies he placed seven gems.... Her beauty completes the joy of the holy angels and of all holy souls."[63]

Mary declared that praise for her and for her son were the same: "Know for certain that all praise of my Son is praise of me. And those who dishonor him dishonor me, since my love for him and his for me was so ardent that the two of us were like one heart."[64] She insisted that the story of the Assumption was true, commenting:

> I was taken up to God's glory in body and soul. Hear how much my Son has honored my name! My name is Mary, and the Gospel says. When the angels hear this name, they rejoice in their understanding and give thanks to God because he worked so great a grace through me and with me and because they see the humanity of my Son glorified in his divinity.[65]

Elsewhere in her communications to Bridget, Mary affirmed the veracity of the Immaculate Conception.[66] Yet the Church of Rome did not elevate the Immaculate Conception to the level of dogma until the nineteenth century—nearly 500 years after Bridget's death—and the Assumption not until the twentieth century.

Communications with Geoffrey Hodson

Geoffrey Hodson and His Work

Geoffrey Hodson (1886–1983) was raised in the Church of England but questioned his faith at college age. In his early twenties he was drawn to the Theosophical Society and went on to serve therein for six decades as a writer and lecturer. Through the Theosophical Society he came into contact with the Liberal Catholic Church and was ordained a priest.[67] His pastoral and liturgical work included an active healing ministry.[68] Although Hodson was born in Britain, he traveled the world and eventually settled in New Zealand.

From a young age Hodson displayed clairvoyant ability, and he devoted much of his life to studying the vast hierarchy of ethereal beings known as *devas* (Sanskrit: "shining ones"). The several orders of nature spirits comprise the junior members of the deva evolution, the "choirs" of angels of Christian tradition the senior members.[69]

From 1921 until the month of his death Hodson kept a diary recording his insights as well as transcripts of contacts with devas and advanced members of the human kingdom.[70] Some of the entries concern Mary or were communicated by her. In a few instances Mary appeared to him, but in most cases she spoke to him—a phenomenon technically known as *locution*—or impressed messages on his mind by some form of telepathy.[71] Hodson originally intended to reserve his diary for personal reflection, but eventually he consented to posthumous publication and wrote an introduction for that purpose. A few references to Mary can also be found in Hodson's other writings.

To understand Hodson's messages from Mary and his discussion of her, we need to know something of the Theosophical teachings that informed his life and work. In addition to his belief in devas, and his work with them, two other beliefs were relevant.

The first was a belief in the cycle of rebirth: every human soul incarnates multiple times on its journey to perfection.[72] Mary explicitly referred to one of Hodson's previous lives, and his diary also records references to several other incarnations.[73]

Belief in reincarnation is commonly assumed to be antithetical to Christian teachings, but that assumption can be challenged. A few passages in the New Testament support belief in reincarnation,[74] and such belief may have continued into the early church. Later Christian teachers asserted that belief in reincarnation was condemned by the Second Council of Constantinople (553 CE); but that does not seem to be true.[75] In fact no evidence can be found that any ecumenical council canon, *ex-cathedra* papal decree, or authoritative pronouncement by an other representative body ever addressed the issue. An estimated twenty-five percent of Christians find the concept of reincarnation meaningful and see no conflict with their faith.[76]

The second belief was in the existence and work of *masters*, or *adepts*, who have completed the incarnational cycle and reached a stage of "relative perfection." In addition to entries recording contacts with Mary herself, Hodson's diary records a number of relevant communications from masters and archangels, some of whom are named.

Masters might be compared with saints, but a better comparison would be with those in Eastern Orthodox tradition deemed to have attained *theosis*, or "deification."[77] According to Theosophical teachings, masters may or may not retain physical bodies or create new ones.

Hodson faced skeptics, even within the Theosophical Society. But his work meets the applicable standards of acceptability, and a broad consensus has developed that the teachings he attributed to Mary and other evolved beings are probably authentic. This does not mean that the teachings represent infallible dogma. Rather, it means that they should be taken seriously and may be accepted, pending some new, more credible, revelation that contradicts or supersedes them.

Contacts with Mary

During a visitation in 1945 Mary told Hodson that he lived in Palestine, 2,000 years ago, and that they knew each other: "I was Miriam, the Mother of Jesus.... I knew you in that life and befriended you."[78] Thirty years later she referred to an encounter with Jesus, in that same lifetime, which was both tragic and transformative:

> I first knew you in Nazareth when you came with your servant to visit My Son, Jesus. I witnessed the tragedy, your outbreak of indignation, your response to My Son's advice, your flood of tears for your deceased servant who died to save your life (received a spear-thrust from a Roman centurion). I heard My Son's promise and saw you as a young boy, departing dutifully for your home and duties awaiting you there.[79]

Mary also commented on incidents in Hodson's current lifetime: "I first knew you as an infant baptized in the church dedicated to Me at Wainfleet-St Mary [Lincolnshire, England]; next, in that small church in the little square in Manchester, where you used to come to meditate and where I caused you to see My aura shining through and around My statue." The latter experience probably took place some time after 1912, when Hodson was in his late twenties.[80]

In the 1945 visitation, in which Mary explained "I was Miriam," she also told him: "I have given you messages in this life" and urged: "Could you not collect all your writings of Me and publish them as an aid to My cause amongst men?"[81] Hodson reflected on the visitation: "This experience seems like an answer to an unspoken wish, that I might again have contact with Her and receive direct assurance of the correctness of the teachings concerning Her. I now feel utterly sure and rededicate my life to Her service."[82]

It is unclear what messages and writings Mary was referring to; he had written little about her up to that time. And notwithstanding his profession of lifelong dedication, Hodson did not respond to her plea. Most of the information Hodson acquired from Mary, or that related to her, was recorded in his diary and not published until after his death. Perhaps he felt obliged to conceal his dedication to Mary from the Theosophists who formed his primary teaching audience. More puzzling, he even concealed his devotion from the Liberal Catholic Church in which he served as a priest.

Yet if Hodson had paid little overt attention to Mary before—or after—1945, we learn that she had paid attention to him. Mary revealed that she had assisted him in the research leading to two of his early books: "I assisted in your [clairvoyant] studies of prenatal life," which were published as *The Miracle of Birth* (1929). And "I also came to you in the remains of the beech forest in Gloucestershire." Hodson began serious study of nature spirits in a beech forest in Gloucestershire, England, leading to *The Brotherhood of Angels and of Men* (1927).[83]

In 1975 Hodson recorded another contact: "Today, while resting, I found myself thinking about the Blessed Lady Mary and then became aware of Her presence."[84]

When Hodson was eighty-nine years old, Mary expressed appreciation for his lecturing and healing work: "Now in your ninetieth bodily year we have communed, you have opened the mental lines of communication by your talk with its reverent references to Me. This has drawn Me much closer to you.... [W]e are a 'team,' My direct co-worker in the darkening world."[85]

Mary continued to encourage Hodson in his last years: "Please continue writing and draw upon Me when needed."[86] Mary was mindful of his declining strength, however. When Hodson was ninety-two, he wrote in his diary: "At this point, the Blessed Lady Mary becomes visible before me ... and, as it were, reaches out and touches my head as if to warn and protect me from brain-fatigue."[87]

Hodson typically referred to Mary as "Our Lady Mary" or "The Blessed Lady Mary." Interestingly, the honorific "The Lady Mary" appears in several of the texts in E. A. Wallis Budge's *Legends of Our Lady Mary the Perpetual Virgin and her Mother Hanna* (1922), cited in Chapter 3. Also, it is believed that priestesses in the ancient mystery schools were addressed as "the Lady ...."

Mary's Appearance and Demeanor

As early as 1929 Geoffrey Hodson reported a vision of a female figure. He was hesitant to identify the figure as Mary, though his description matches almost exactly those of Marian apparitions:

> She is radiant and beautiful beyond description, and shone forth as the incarnation of perfect womanhood, the apotheosis of beauty, love, tenderness. The glory of divinity is all about her. A glowing happiness, an ecstasy of spiritual joy, shines through Her wondrous eyes. In spite of the intensity of Her exaltation Her gaze is soft and tender, and in some way full of the happy laughter of children and the deep and calm contentment of maturity. Her splendid aura of soft yet brilliant hues forms a shining halo of glory all about Her, veiling and yet revealing Her immortal loveliness. Deep blue, silvery white, rose, golden yellow, and the soft green of young leaves in spring flow continually throughout Her lovely auric robes in wave on wave of color and of living light. And ever and anon Her rich deep blue pervades the whole, lit up by stars and bright gleams of silvery hue.[88]

By 1945, when Mary appeared to him again, he had no doubt who it was:

> Our Lady ... appeared as a highly spiritual, wonderfully refined young lady of perhaps twenty-eight years. She spoke in a voice of compelling sweetness and beauty and with the most engaging charm .... Her shining blue aura seemed to enfold me for a moment, and its light to fill the room. A still peace pervaded me from the highest levels down to the physical."[89]

On another occasion Hodson commented on Mary's appearance "in all Her wondrous blue."[90] Blue has been the favored color of Mary's robes in apparitions since Lourdes. Hodson's wife Sandra later inserted an editorial note in the diary: "Geoffrey sees Our Lady ... as a very beautiful feminine Being surrounded by forces outraying from Her to produce a specially shaped and formed aura, with colorings of white, gold, rose, and sky blue, shot through and shining beyond with white radiance."[91] That description might be compared with depictions of Our Lady of Guadalupe.

Hodson described Mary as "the highest possible imaginable spiritualized Queen."[92] He also described her as a priestess, as an adept in her own right, as Mother of the World, even as an expression of the feminine aspect of Deity. These titles and roles will be explored in the next two chapters.

Hodson never felt overawed or intimidated in her presence: "One of the most remarkable attributes of Our Lady Mary is Her complete humility. She did not, and does not, assume or appear in Her most exalted state as, for example, the Adept Queen of the Angels. I reverently responded to Her Presence as a visiting (if Adept) Friend."[93] Despite the attitude of humility, Hodson never questioned the great authority with which Mary spoke.

In the 1945 visitation Hodson, who was then around sixty years old, estimated Mary's age as "perhaps twenty-eight years." For comparison the Medjugorje witnesses initially judged her to be "eighteen-to-twenty years old," though one of them later revised that estimate to "20–25." Estimating ages, always difficult, is influenced by one's own age. In any event, the consensus is that Mary appears as a young woman. We recall that Mary is believed to have been about fifteen when she gave birth to Jesus.

Mary has transcended the personality level and is not constrained to appear in any particular form:

> Although the Lady Mary is no longer limited to expressions as a Person, having long ago won emancipation and liberation therefrom, for the sake of all mankind She does assume the restrictions of a highly spiritualized "Personality" in order to come as near as possible to those whom She helps.[94]

Mary appears in a way that will be recognized and accepted by targeted witnesses. She "responds to and permits Herself to be mentally molded by our religious conceptions, and Who permits Herself to be seen in forms acceptable and helpful to those who are accorded the appropriate vision."[95]

In contrast with the apparitions in which Mary spoke—all, that is, except Zeitoun—Mary never urged Geoffrey Hodson to engage in devotional practices, even to pray. Her sole concern seems to have been to provide information that he might incorporate into his lectures and writings. More of Mary's communications with Hodson will be presented in the next chapter, along with insightful statements about

Chapter 6. Mary Reveals Herself to the World

her by masters, archangels and others. Hodson provided some of the most important esoteric teachings yet revealed concerning Mary.

Communications with Anna Raimondi

Anna Raimondi and Her Work

Anna Raimondi describes herself as a "motivational speaker, teacher, intuitive and author," whose "mission is to give others the tools they need to live their lives in joy, while following their souls' mission."[96] She gives readings whose purpose is described thus:

> During a reading, Anna uses her intuitive spiritual gifts to connect to those on the other side of the veil—passed loved ones, spirit guides, power animals and angels.... Feel the love that continues from this life through eternity as Anna sees, hears, feels and allows those on the other side to communicate and heal those on the earth plane.[97]

Raimondi claims that her book *Conversations with Mary* (2017) was dictated by Mary. She explained: "I knew that the book would be Mary speaking.... Whether she was waking me up in the middle of the night, interrupting my thoughts, or speaking as I sat at my computer, I let whatever she had to say come through. I didn't write this book... Mary did. With utmost care I typed as she dictated.[98] When the author was taking dictation: "Mary's energy is soft yet strong, and overwhelms me. Often, my heart will begin to race and thoughts start flooding my mind."[99]

The book consists of a brief introduction followed by ten chapters in question-and-answer format, addressing topics like "What is a soul," "Why are we here," and "What happens when we die." Ostensibly the author asked the questions and Mary responded, but the actual process was more complicated. Raimondi explained: "Before sitting down to write, I pray and meditate. I feel the presence of Mary and begin to write. She sometimes gives me the answers and I have to go back and write the questions. Sometimes, she gives me both."[100] Each chapter is followed by a guided meditation to raise awareness of Mary and, where appropriate, to draw upon ideas from the preceding discussion.

Raimondi was raised Roman Catholic and demonstrated familiarity with traditional Marian devotions, as well as with reported apparitions

229

Mary: Adept, Queen, Mother, Priestess

at Guadalupe, Lourdes, Fátima and elsewhere. Raimondi also showed that she was familiar with references to Mary in the canonical and extracanonical Christian scriptures and the *Qur'an*.

Raimondi seemed generally familiar with the esoteric literature; but she did not refer to Hodson's or similar work, and we do not know whether she was aware of or influenced by it. The topic material does overlap to a degree, permitting useful comparisons. For example, in her introduction, Raimondi spoke—as did Hodson—of Mary as a personification of the Feminine Aspect of Deity, one of several such personifications that include the Buddhist Kuan Yin.[101] But Mary's communications to Raimondi are more voluminous than those reported by Hodson and are addressed to a different readership: the general public rather than an esoteric elite.

Raimondi's claims that the book was dictated by Mary can be held up against the standards listed earlier to help determine whether they are credible. *Conversations with Mary* passes most of the tests. The information provided in the book is either new or presented in a new way, and it and builds upon earlier knowledge. It honors human dignity and inspires love. It neither flatters the author; nor does it threaten people or encourage separatism.

Raimondi promoted her book and has been interviewed on talk shows. But the publicity has helped disseminate the communications from Mary. By contrast, Hodson was criticized for not disseminating the communications he received.

One red flag is that Raimondi now offers a line of jewelry with a Marian motif.[102] This raises a difficult issue; she could be accused of exploiting her contacts with Mary for commercial purposes. Yet we must remember that, unless an individual has private means, he or she needs to earn a living; Raimondi's ability to continue her work depends on the viability of her enterprise. For context, we should remember that church institutions, religious orders, and sodalities have long sold medals, statues, pictures, and other paraphernalia inspired by Marian apparitions—not infrequently implying that the products convey a blessing.[103] The industry is profitable, even if an apparition's witnesses do not benefit personally.

In the final analysis, we must each evaluate the material Anna Raimondi offered and decide what credibility it deserves. The present

Chapter 6. Mary Reveals Herself to the World

author is persuaded that her contacts with Mary were probably authentic and that the book merits attention.

Contacts with Mary

Anna Raimondi shares the following information on her website:

> Since I was a child, I have been blessed with the gift of clairvoyance and ability to hear the voice of Mother Mary. I have devotedly prayed with her and listened to her advice, as she offers me guidance, solace, love, and wisdom. Mary communicates with me so that I can share her messages with other people, and she wants everyone to know they have a refuge in her and God.[104]

Like Hodson, Raimondi received messages through locution or telepathy, though she witnessed at least one apparition. *Conversations with Mary* recalls an apparition when Raimondi was five years old: "She [Mary] said, 'Anna, I am here for you always. Always come to me.' A total unconditional love overtook me, there was a feeling that was and remains so extraordinary and so difficult to describe in words." Raimondi continued:

> I knew without a doubt that this was Mary, although she didn't look like the renderings I had seen of her in books or even in churches. She was dressed in a well-worn brown robe, the fabric appeared rough, but radiated warmth. There was a light brown dress underneath. She had olive skin, wide, soft mahogany-colored eyes and coffee-colored hair that hung to her waist where a hemp belt was tied and held her dress together. She wore a tan-colored covering adorning the top of her head, but no hood. Her face stood out in repose. Her penetrating eyes captured my attention.[105]

The apparition was atypical. More generally, as Hodson noted, Mary adjusts her appearance to conform to people's expectations. In fact, a few pages later in *Conversations with Mary*, Mary reiterated: "I look like what the beholder wants me to look like. If one wants me to be of fair skin and light eyes, so be it. If that brings comfort, so be it." Mary went on to say: "I am a being now of love and comfort. I have no skin color and all skin colors. I have no distinguishing features not and yet carry the beauty of all the world as I embrace your energies and raise your vibrations."[106]

In several of the recent apparitions Mary has worn a blue robe, and Mary told Raimondi: "I am the blue vibration of truth."[107] More than a century earlier, Theosophist and Hermeticist Anna Kingsford (1846–1888) declared that " in token of her Divine Motherhood and heavenly derivation and attributes, [Mary] is represented as clad in celestial azure.[108]

Mary's Life in Palestine

Raimondi questioned Mary about the account of her presentation in the temple found in the *Infancy Gospel of James* (discussed herein in Chapter 1). Mary confirmed the accuracy of the account, explaining: "With heavy hearts, yet ones filled with gratitude for their [her aged parents'] blessings, I was given to the temple at the age of three to be raised by the priests in the ways of my religion and my people." Mary continued: "It was with great sorrow that they [her mother and father] passed on when I was but a young girl. They passed prior to my betrothal to Joseph well before the birth of my son."[109]

The comment about Mary's parents' early death conflicts with the visions of Anne Catherine Emmerich who "saw" Hannah and her second husband at Mary's and Joseph's wedding (see Chapter 2).[110] But it is consistent with the account of Hannah's death in *Legends of Our Lady Mary*, discussed in Chapter 3.[111]

Mary shared her experience as a young person in Palestine: "When I was a girl, I played, laughed, and cried as girls do. My life as a child was not extraordinary although my faith and love for God was always foremost."[112] Later in life that carefree attitude changed as she saw Jesus grow up and undertake his redemptive mission: "Even as time moved on, and I began to recognize the purpose of my son's life and death, my pain was raw. I accepted his life's journey and my part in it.... It was as difficult as life on earth can ever be. I knew he lived for a bigger purpose and took my solace in that."[113]

Mary described her physical appearance in Palestine: "[A]s a Middle Eastern woman, my skin was dark, my eyes a deep brown, and I was small in stature.... My dark wavy hair came down to my waist."[114] That was essentially how Mary appeared to the five-year-old Raimondi.

This description of Mary may be compared with the one offered by Epiphanius of Salamis and discussed in Chapter 3.[115] Mary's height seems to be in doubt: "small in stature," versus Epiphanius' "of middle stature, but some say that she was of more than middle height."

Chapter 6. Mary Reveals Herself to the World

Otherwise there was substantial agreement on her physical characteristics and attire.

Raimondi pressed Mary on her sufferings during Jesus' passion and death, and Mary replied candidly and at some length:

> I endured great emotional pain during my son's last days and during his persecution. I witnessed the purity of his love as he spread it to all people even as he was rejected. As a mother and a person who loved him and his message, the way people treated him caused me great pain. I didn't understand fully the true reason for the circumstances of my son's suffering for it wasn't revealed to me until later. Yet, my faith in God never wavered. I was angry at those who tortured him and tormented him. I was angry and frustrated that people could not understand that Jesus came to show them how to save themselves. Instead they killed the one who lived for them. People say that Jesus died for the sins of mankind. That is not totally true. He lived for the sins of mankind; to help teach people how to live and not to sin and transgress against God; and yet they couldn't hear his message. They couldn't see that he only wanted to love them and bring them the peace they were looking for. God did not destroy my son's flesh; men did. As his mother, the one who brought him into the world and love him as only a mother could, the pain my son endured tore at me and left a piece of me frayed.[116]

Mary continued:

> I grieved for Jesus and longed for him the rest of my days on earth. I went on and lived my life, giving and receiving, smiling and crying, but never forgetting the pain. The pain was housed in my heart, but my life went on. I recognized that life is a gift and must be lived. I lived for my son and my other children and helped spread Jesus' message. At my death, God granted me the release of my feelings of anger and forgiveness. I so loved my son, grieved and missed him. Yet I recognized within days of his passing that his words and the goodness he spoke of would change my people and the entire world if they would only listen. And so it was and so it is.[117]

The reference to "my other children" warrants attention. It could refer to the alleged siblings of Jesus: James, Joses, Juda, Simon, Salome, and another sister.[118] Or Mary might be using the term "children" to mean her followers, even humanity as a whole. Raimondi did not press Mary for clarification.

Mary's Teachings

Throughout their conversations Mary stressed the importance of prayer. But she added: "prayers must be followed with action: compassion and love for all people must be demonstrated."[119]

Mary urged: "You should pray for the end of suffering" and for healing of humanity and the planet. Yet she cautioned against discouragement when efforts to heal a sick person seem to fail. "Remember," she added, people "pass through life and dwell in the kingdom.... Don't cry for those who pass on; rejoice for they are with God."[120]

Mary encouraged use of the Rosary: "The Rosary is a powerful weapon against evil. It is not only in the prayers said on the beads, but in the energy it creates in the repetition of the prayers. The prayers become a mantra and raise the vibration in and around all who say it."[121] Lest her comments on the Rosary might suggest a disproportionate focus on Roman Catholic prayer, she added: "I am the Queen of Peace for all people. I don't speak peace for only a select few but for the world."[122]

Mary warned against religious exclusivism: "Any religion that focuses on sharing love and peace is good but there is no 'one perfect religion.' ... The chosen people don't fill one church or temple and not another.... A religion should be welcoming of all people, for all people were created by God."[123] Importantly, she also reassured people who claim to be "spiritual rather than religious": "It is not necessary to join a group but proclaim God in your heart and share that Love with others!"[124] We recall the message of inclusiveness Mary gave to Vicka Ivanković-Mijatović at Medjugorje.

Mary discussed the afterlife, explaining: "Upon entering the Divine realm all must go through a life review.... All must see and feel the love and happiness that they gave and received as well as the hate, anger and pain given to others."[125]

Importantly, Mary seemed to support the notion of reincarnation: "Earth is indeed a classroom, a place to learn to be closer to and to unite with God. Those souls who have lived in opposition to the Truth must return to earth to learn what they didn't learn." They must "leave the realm of pure Love and return to human form." Similarly,

Chapter 6. Mary Reveals Herself to the World

people who strive for perfection but fall short of their goal "choose to come back to the earth to become 'better' and more loving. They also come back to teach others about love and to heal the planet and its people."[126] The reference to "good people" coming back refutes suggestions that reincarnation is a punishment for "bad people"—or at best an opportunity to correct mistakes, like children repeating a grade in school.

Mary asserted that, on its long journey to perfection, the soul passes through five "levels," comparable with infancy, childhood, adolescence, maturity, and old age—this last being the level of the "old soul."[127] These levels do not correlate with the five major initiations discussed in esoteric teachings; rather they seem to be stages on the Path of Aspiration and possibly the earliest stages of the Path of Discipleship. After reaching the fifth level, the seeker must still "surrender to God, recognize his great love and truly love and have compassion for yourself and others. You must give up the cravings of the ego, and sit in prayer and meditation to connect with God. You must live your life in accordance with the will of God."[128]

The Medjugorje apparitions showed that one of the advantages of continuing revelation, as compared with an original deposit of faith like scripture, is the opportunity to receive guidance on contemporary issues. Taking advantage of a similar opportunity, Raimondi asked Mary "whether or not it is moral for two women or two men to be married and have a family." Mary replied: "If there is love between two people and they are in line with what is good in the world, and follow God, then it is right. God does not oppose. They can be a family. If they bring children into the unit, that is also a family." She added, significantly: "God is not judging the sexual desires of people. If people love each other, so be it."[129]

As in the issue of reincarnation, Mary seemed willing to take a position contrasting with that of the major Christian denominations. On the issue of same-sex marriage she took a position challenging that of a prominent esoteric teacher.[130]

Mary Revealed

Clearly Mary wants to be known in new ways, and she commented in *Conversations with Mary*: "The people are ready."[131] From the various contacts discussed in this chapter we gain fresh insights into the life of the historical Mary and get a glimpse of her ministry in the modern world.

Mary was eager to confirm that she was raised in the temple. Her communications to Bridget of Sweden, Anna Raimondi—and Anne Catherine Emmerich—all supported, in general terms if not in detail, the account offered in the *Infancy Gospel of James*. Mary seemed to be raising the text to canonical status. In her communications with Raimondi Mary shared more intimate details of her life as a child and as an adult. The heart-wrenching recollection of her suffering during the passion and death of her son went beyond anything that scripture could capture.

Now Mary is a celestial being. Every witness to an apparition has commented on the light that emanates from her form. Mary's elevated consciousness is clearly evident. Lúcia Santos described her vision at Fátima as "more brilliant than the sun." In Hodson's 1929 vision Mary was "lit up by stars and bright gleams of silvery hue." We may compare her light-filled apparitions to the Transfiguration of Christ: "[H]is face did shine as the sun, and his raiment was white as the light."[132]

Mary's beauty transcends that of women still in physical embodiment. Bridget of Sweden remarked: "Her beauty completes the joy of the holy angels and of all holy souls." Bernadette Soubirous declared: "I have never seen her so beautiful before ... so lovely that, when you have seen her once, you would willingly die to see her again!" A Zeitoun witness testified that she appeared as "a beautiful girl in a bright gown of light." Mary told one of the Medjugorje witnesses: "If you want to be beautiful, then love." Hodson reported that she appeared as "the incarnation of perfect womanhood, the apotheosis of beauty, love, tenderness. The glory of divinity is all about her. A glowing happiness, an ecstasy of spiritual joy.... immortal loveliness."

Mary also appears eternally young, never more than late-twenties and sometimes as young as eighteen. Perhaps that youthfulness expresses a reinterpretation of "perpetual virginity," given that the Hebrew word *almah*, on which the assertion of Mary's virginity mainly rests, could mean a "young woman."[133]

Mary seems comfortable with her exalted status. She proclaimed to Bridget: "I am the Queen of Angels ... Queen of Heaven," and to Diego: "mother of the very true Deity." In one of her messages at

Chapter 6. Mary Reveals Herself to the World

Medjugorje Mary explained: "[B]y my will and my immeasurable love for the Heavenly Father and my complete trust in Him, my body was the chalice of the God-man."

Indeed Mary is so comfortable with her status that she can meet people on their own level. She commands authority without overwhelming those with whom she comes into contact. Children had no hesitation in asking her questions. Hodson commented: "I reverently responded to Her Presence as a visiting (if Adept) Friend." Mary is willing to present herself in whatever physical, ethnic or religious form may be acceptable to the people she seeks to reach.

When reaching out to people in the Church of Rome Mary promotes traditional forms of devotion, like the Rosary. At the same time she urges a global perspective that extends beyond sectarian boundaries. Mary was willing to distance herself from Rome on issues like same-sex marriage but not on abortion. She spoke, to both Hodson and Raimondi, about reincarnation as though it was never in question.

Mary urges us to pray for peace. Prayer is needed to avert the evils of the world. Mary urges us to pray for healing, and we shall see in the next chapter that she has special concern for women and children. In several cases, healings were associated with apparitions, and in one case, Lourdes, an ongoing healing ministry developed with numerous certified successes.

Apart from healings, Mary has been sparing in displaying "signs and wonders." Without the miracle of the flowers, the apparition at Guadalupe would likely never have been reported. Photographs of the Zeitoun apparitions, widely reported in the news media, helped convince a skeptical public. On the other hand, the "dancing sun" phenomenon at Fátima was controversial and may have excited tabloid curiosity rather than true faith. We do not know whether the promised "permanent sign" at Medjugorje has been put in place.

Mary never sought to compete with Christ. In a message delivered at Medjugorje she urged people "to come to know my Son, bring it about that He may be loved, because the truth is in my Son born of God—the Son of God." In another message she noted: " I was in the service of truth, love and salvation, as I am now among you to call you, my children, apostles of my love, to be carriers of truth; to call you to spread His words." One of the ways to find her son was in the Eucharist.

The apparitions at Zeitoun and Medjugorje were qualitatively different from previous ones and strikingly different from each other. Moreover, we learn that apparitions with a devotional focus may be coming to an end. We can only suppose that communications with selected individuals, like those with Bridget of Sweden, Geoffrey Hodson, and Anna Raimondi, will be among Mary's ongoing modes of self-revelation. Chapter 7 will show that Mary has revealed a great deal about herself and her ministry through esoteric teachings.

---

[1] Bilocation has been reported among individuals in many world religions. It is said to be relatively common among Christian stigmatics; both Therese Neumann and Padre Pio allegedly had that ability.

[2] Source: http://www.miraclehunter.com/marian_apparitions/approved_apparitions/apparitions_0040-0999.html#ensiedeln. Last accessed Jan. 30, 2021.

[3] For a comprehensive list see: http://www.miraclehunter.com/marian_apparitions/saints/index.html. Last accessed Jan. 30, 2021.

[4] "Apparitions Statistics, Modern." Univ. of Dayton. Online: https://udayton.edu/imri/mary/a/apparitions-statistics-modern.php. Last accessed Oct. 4, 2019.

[5] In Emmerich's case, Clemens Brentano served as her "stenographer."

[6] Hundreds more incidents reported each year are considered too trivial to warrant serious investigation.

[7] "Apparitions Statistics, Modern: Marian Apparitions of the Twentieth and Twenty-first Centuries." Online: https://udayton.edu/imri/mary/a/apparitions-statistics-modern.php. Last accessed Oct. 5, 2019.

[8] Source: http://www.miraclehunter.com/marian_apparitions/approved_apparitions/coptic.html. Last accessed March 26, 2020.

[9] Luisa Feline Freier, "How Our Lady of Guadalupe Became Lutheran: Latin American Migration and Religious Change," Dept. of Latin American, Caribbean and Iberian Studies, University of Wisconsin–Madison, 2009.

[10] Gregory Jensen, "Apparitions in the Tradition of the Orthodox Church: Eastern Orthodox Reflections in Honor of the 90th Anniversary of Fatima." Online: https://www.academia.edu/6130154/Apparitions_in_the_Tradition_of_the_Orthodox_Church_Eastern_Orthodox_Reflections_in_Honor_of_the_90th_Anniversary_of_Fatima. Last accessed Oct. 4, 2019.

Chapter 6. Mary Reveals Herself to the World

[11] Clarissa P. Estés, *Untie the Strong Woman*, Sounds True, 2011, 184.
[12] An interesting exercise is to test the six criteria on certain books of the Bible.
[13] In some cases competing groups of esotericists identify different claimants as authentic.
[14] The dates are based on the Julian calendar then in use. "December 9" was the 19th according to the Gregorian calendar now used, and "December 12" was the 22nd. Notwithstanding, the Feast of Our Lady of Guadalupe is sill celebrated December 12, probably to avoid conflict with Christmas.
[15] Carl Anderson & Eduardo Chavez, *Our Lady of Guadalupe: Mother of the Civilization of Love*, Doubleday, 2009, 13-15.
[16] *Ibid.*, 17.
[17] *Ibid.*, 19.
[18] See for example D. A. Brading, *Mexican Phoenix: Our Lady of Guadalupe. Image and Tradition over Five Centuries* (Cambridge: Cambridge Univ. Press, 2001).
[19] The name "Guadalupe" calls for comment. It could have originated from the Nahuatl *Tecuatlanopeuh* ("woman on the rocky hill"), which sounds similar. But Guadalupe is also a Spanish place name, and skeptics point out that the image of Our Lady of Guadalupe resembles a relief sculpture of the Madonna and Child, dated to 1499, in the chapel of the Monastery of Guadalupe, in Caceres, Spain.
[20] Bishop Juan de Zumárraga never expressed an opinion on the authenticity of the apparitions, or even mentioned them, in his writings. His silence and that of many contemporaries raised questions about the historicity of Juan Diego and the apparitions. By canonizing Diego, Rome laid those questions to rest.
[21] See for example "Biography of Bernadette Soubirous." Online: https://www.biographyonline.net/spiritual/bernadette-soubirous.html. Last accessed Sept. 29, 2019.
[22] *Ibid.*
[23] That message was interpreted as supportive of Pope Pius IX's somewhat-controversial decree *Ineffabilis Deus* (1854).
[24] "Biography of Bernadette Soubirous."
[25] For detailed records see Bernard François et al., "The Lourdes Medical Cures Revisited," *Journal of the History of Medicine and Allied Sciences* (Jan. 2014), 135–162.
[26] Louis Kondor (ed.), *Fatima in Lucia's Own Words: Sister Lucia's Memoirs* (transl.: Dominican Nuns of Perpetual Rosary, Fátima, Portugal: Secretariado Dos Pastorinhos, 2007), 174.
[27] John de Marchi, "Chapter 10 - 6th Apparition - October 13th," *The True Story Of Fatima*. Online:

https://ia800407.us.archive.org/33/items/TheTrueStoryOfFatima/TheTrueStoryOfFatima1952.html#ch10. Last accessed Oct. 29. 2019.

[28] The order's patron is the fourth-century virgin–martyr Dorothea of Caesarea.

[29] "Apparition of the Theotokos in Zeitoun." Online: http://www.orthodoxchristianity.net/forum/index.php?topic=8613.0. Last accessed Oct. 2, 2019.

[30] "The Apparitions of Virgin Mary at Zeitoun Church, Egypt." Online: http://www.zeitun-eg.org/stmary9.htm. Last accessed Oct. 2, 2019.

[31] The "eastern churches" consist of three main groups, each with its own history. The Coptic Orthodox Church's origins lay in opposition to the Council of Chalcedon (449 CE), which decreed that the human and divine natures of Jesus Christ are distinct. The Oriental Orthodox Churches opposed the Council of Ephesus' (431), which decreed that Jesus Christ is a single *hypostasis*, or "person." The much larger family of Eastern Orthodox Churches separated from Rome in 1054 over issues that included the *filioque* clause in the Nicene Creed. The Eastern Orthodox Churches retain the original form of the Creed which states that the Holy Spirit proceeds from the Father alone, whereas the Church of Rome adopted a revised version in which the Holy Spirit proceeds jointly from the Father and the Son.

[32] After the collapse of the communist regime, the country was wracked for three years by ethnic warfare, war crimes, and NATO bombing. The Federation of Bosnia and Herzegovina finally won its independence in 1995.

[33] Some disagreement exists as to precisely who witnessed the apparition on June 24. Some accounts say only two, while others say all six. The account cited here comes from Mirjana Soldo, *My Heart Will Triumph*, CatholicShop Publ., 2016, 28.

[34] "The Image of the Queen of Peace." Online: https://www.medjugorje.org/vint1.htm. Last accessed Oct. 4, 2019.

[35] Soldo, *My Heart Will Triumph*, 28.

[36] *Ibid.*, 309.

[37] *Ibid.*, 128.

[38] "The Image of the Queen of Peace."

[39] Soldo, *My Heart Will Triumph*, 83.

[40] Medjugorje Web: https://www.medjugorje.com/medjugorje/questions-and-answers.html#24a. Last accessed Feb. 6, 2021.

[41] Soldo, *My Heart Will Triumph*, 232.

[42] Finbar O'Leary (ed.), *Vicka: Her Story*, Dufour, 2013/2017, 48.

[43] *Ibid,*, 74, 77.

[44] Mary said she would entrust ten secrets to each of them, after which they would see her at intervals varying from once a month to once per year.

Chapter 6. Mary Reveals Herself to the World

Three of the witnesses: Vicka Ivanković-Mijatović, Ivan Dragićević, and Marija Pavlović-Lunetti, had yet to receive their last secret—as of January 2020—and continued to have daily visions. Most the visions have been at Medjugorje, though some occurred elsewhere.

[45] "Our Lady Of Medjugorje. English Messages from 2015": https://www.medjugorje.org/msg15.htm. Last accessed Jan. 31, 2021.

[46] "Our Lady's Latest Second-of-the-Month Message": https://www.medjugorje.com/medjugorje-messages/latest-2-message.html. Last accessed Feb. 13, 2020.

[47] Medjugorje Web: https://www.medjugorje.org/. Last accessed Jan. 31, 2021.

[48] O'Leary (ed.), *Vicka: Her Story*, 37.

[49] Soldo, *My Heart Will Triumph*, 198. John Paul also reportedly told Soldo: "If I were not the pope, I would have gone to Medjugorje a long time ago." With his ties to the Solidarity Movement in Poland, Pope John Paul II recognized the significance of the Medjugorje apparitions in another then-communist country.

[50] "The Church's Position on Medjugorje": https://www.medjugorje.org/church.htm. Last accessed Oct. 4, 2019.

[51] Interview, Vatican City, May 13, 2017. Catholic News Agency: https://www.catholicnewsagency.com/news/36030/pope-francis-i-am-suspicious-of-ongoing-medjugorje-apparitions. Last accessed July 8, 2021.

[52] Anna Raimondi, mentioned later in this chapter, declared that she "got nothing out of" a visit to Medjugorje. See https://spiritualbizmagazine.com/cover-story-anna-raimondi/. Last accessed July 9, 2021.

[53] Two sources cited here are the greatly abridged *Revelations of St Bridget*, Tan Books, 1862/2015; and the much longer *The Revelations of Saint Bridget of Sweden: Books 1-5,* edited by Darrell Wright, CreateSpace Indep. Publ. Platform, 2016.

[54] Bridget of Sweden, *Revelations of St Bridget*, 18-19.

[55] *Ibid.*, 19.

[56] Bridget of Sweden, *The Revelations of Saint Bridget of Sweden*, book 1, ch. 42. (Pages not numbered.)

[57] *Ibid.*

[58] Bridget of Sweden, *Revelations of St Bridget*, 57-58.

[59] *Ibid.*, 67.

[60] Bridget of Sweden, *The Revelations of Saint Bridget of Sweden*, book 1, ch. 7. (Pages not numbered.)

[61] *Ibid.*, chs. 8, 9, 10.

[62] *Ibid.*, ch. 31. See also book 5, revelation 4, in which Christ extolled the beauty of his mother..

[63] *Ibid.*
[64] *Ibid.*, ch. 8.
[65] *Ibid.*, ch. 9.
[66] Bridget of Sweden, *Revelations of St Bridget*, 14-15. As noted earlier, Bernadette Soubirous (1844–1879) received a similar confirmation of the Immaculate Conception, but Catherine of Siena (1347–1380) claimed to have received dissenting information.
[67] The Liberal Catholic Church claims the apostolic succession via its parent, the Old Catholic Church, which seceded from Rome after the First Vatican Council over the issue of papal infallibility.
[68] John F. Nash, "Great Esotericists: Geoffrey Hodson (1886–1983)," *The Esoteric Quarterly* (Spring 2018), 79-84.
[69] According to modern esoteric teachings the deva evolution exists in parallel with the human kingdom. For the most part we are unaware of devas, but clairvoyants and other intuitive people may come into contact with them—visually or otherwise—in nature, sacred spaces, and elsewhere. Or devas may contact us; the Archangel Gabriel's appearance to Mary at the Annunciation was a notable example. Christian angelology is based on the work of the Pseudo-Dionysius (fifth century), who identified nine choirs of angels: Seraphim, Cherubim, Thrones, Dominions, Virtues, Powers, Principalities, Archangels, and Angels.
[70] Sandra Hodson (ed.), *Light of the Sanctuary: The Occult Diary of Geoffrey Hodson*, Theosophical Publishers, 1988. The diary was edited by his second wife, Sandra, and published posthumously. The book currently is out of print, but a complete online version is available: http://www.minhtrietmoi.org/Theosophy/Hodson/Light%20of%20the%20sanctuary.htm. Last accessed Oct. 7, 2019. Page numbers cited herein are from the print version.
[71] Locution technically implies audible speech, but it may not be heard by anyone but the intended recipient. The distinction between it and telepathy may not be significant.
[72] Belief in the cycle of rebirth was promoted by Pythagoras, Plato, and other Greek philosophers, and is a central tenet of the religions of South Asia today. Contra to Pythagoras, however, Theosophy insists that souls incarnate only in human bodies; transmigration into animal bodies is not considered possible.
[73] In addition to incarnations in ancient Egypt, Hodson reportedly had a lifetime subsequent to the one in Palestine, in which he regressed spiritually. Yet he was told: "The excursion was not all loss, as it brought knowledge and experience and set your will for this incarnation [in the 19th and 20th centuries] towards the occult life." S. Hodson (ed.), *Light of the Sanctuary*, 115.

Chapter 6. Mary Reveals Herself to the World

[74] For example: "[H]is disciples asked him, saying, Why then say the scribes that Elias [Elijah] must first come? And Jesus answered and said unto them, Elias truly shall first come, and restore all things. But I say unto you, That Elias is come already, and they knew him not, but have done unto him whatsoever they listed. Likewise shall also the Son of man suffer of them. Then the disciples understood that he spake unto them of John the Baptist" (*Matthew* 17:10-13).

[75] The assertion rests on the alleged condemnation of church father Origen (c.184–c.253), who taught that the soul preexisted the body—an obvious prerequisite for reincarnation. But nowhere in the proceedings of the Second Council of Constantinople is Origen's condemnation mentioned, and it is doubtful whether the bishops ever voted on such a measure. The "anathemas" against Origen were discovered in the 17th century.

[76] Belief in reincarnation is reported to be more common among Roman Catholics (28 percent), but less common among Evangelicals.

[77] See the discussion of *theosis* in Chapter 4. See also John F. Nash, "Theosis: a Christian Perspective on Human Destiny," *The Esoteric Quarterly* (Spring 2011), 15-31.

[78] S. Hodson (ed.), *Light of the Sanctuary*, 116.

[79] *Ibid.*, 266. Parenthesis in original. The circumstances of the servant's death, and what followed, are found in a diary entry about a month earlier. The proto-Hodson, a boy of "about nine years old," and his "servant-guide," described as an Egyptian initiate-teacher, were in the crowd when Jesus and some disciples came through a town in Palestine. The excited crowd surged forward, pushing the boy into the back of a Roman soldier. The soldier turned around, preparing to stab the boy with his javelin, but the servant stepped forward to take the spear thrust. The proto-Hodson reacted angrily, whereupon Jesus stopped and spoke to him: "Do not abuse this man who was but doing his duty. Rather express gratitude for him who has done so much for you and now has given you his life, thereby saving yours." *Ibid.*, 263.

[80] The possible timing of that visit and identity of the church are discussed in John F. Nash, "Adept, Queen, Mother, Priestess: Mary in the Writings of Geoffrey Hodson," *The Esoteric Quarterly* (Winter 2019), 37-63.

[81] S. Hodson (ed.), *Light of the* Sanctuary, 116.

[82] *Ibid.*

[83] *Ibid.*, 266.

[84] *Ibid.*, 267.

[85] *Ibid.*, 266. No transcript of his "talk" has been located.

[86] *Ibid.*, 285.

[87] *Ibid.*, 418.

[88] Geoffrey Hodson, *The Miracle of Birth*, Theosophical Publ. House, 1929, 63.
[89] *Ibid.*, 115-116.
[90] *Ibid.*, 418.
[91] *Ibid.*, 415. The causal level is the upper part of the mental plane. Some writers narrow it down to the second mental subplane, counted from above.
[92] *Ibid.*, 267.
[93] *Ibid.* Parenthesis in original.
[94] *Ibid.*, 268.
[95] *Ibid.*, 284.
[96] See https://www.annaraimondi.com/. Last accessed Oct. 9, 2019.
[97] See https://www.annaraimondi.com/readings1. Last accessed Oct. 9, 2019.
[98] Anna Raimondi, *Conversations with Mary: Messages of Love, Healing, Hope, and Unity for Everyone*, Atria, 2017, 189.
[99] *Ibid.*, 190.
[100] *Ibid.*, 189.
[101] *Ibid.*, 11.
[102] See https://www.annaraimondi.com/store. Last accessed Oct. 9, 2019.
[103] At what point this practice crosses the line into Simony is debatable.
[104] See https://www.annaraimondi.com/. Last accessed Oct. 9, 2019.
[105] Raimondi, *Conversations with Mary*, 2.
[106] *Ibid.*, 17.
[107] *Ibid.*, 32.
[108] Anna Kingsford & Edward Maitland, *The Perfect Way, or the Finding of Christ*, Field & Tuer, 3/e, 1890, 54. The book is a transcript of lectures Kingsford delivered in 1881-1882.
[109] *Ibid.*, 22.
[110] Michael Palairet (ed.), *The Life of the Blessed Virgin Mary from the Visions of Ven. Anne Catherine Emmerich*, Tan Books, 1954/1970, 133.
[111] "The History of Hanna," *Legends of Our Lady Mary the Perpetual Virgin and her Mother Hanna*, 31-32.
[112] Raimondi, *Conversations with Mary*, 17.
[113] *Ibid.*, 16.
[114] *Ibid.*, 17.
[115] "Epiphanius of Salamis." Reproduced in E. A. Wallis Budge, *Legends of Our Lady Mary the Perpetual Virgin and her Mother Hanna*, Medici Press, 1922, xxiii.
[116] Raimondi, *Conversations with Mary*, 63-64.
[117] *Ibid.*, 64.
[118] *Mark* 6:3; 15:40.
[119] Raimondi, *Conversations with Mary*, 67.

[120] *Ibid.*, 172.
[121] *Ibid.*, 134.
[122] *Ibid.*, 67.
[123] *Ibid.*, 93-94.
[124] *Ibid.*, 105.
[125] *Ibid.*, 111.
[126] *Ibid.*, 113.
[127] *Ibid.*, 152-153.
[128] *Ibid.*, 153.
[129] *Ibid.*, 96.
[130] Alice A. Bailey stated: "Homosexuality is what you call a 'left-over' from the sexual excesses of Lemurian times.... Egos who individualized and incarnated in that vast period of time are the ones who today demonstrate homosexual tendencies. In those days, so urgent was the sexual appetite, the normal processes of human intercourse did not satisfy the insatiable desire of the advanced man of the period. Soul force, flowing in through the processes of individualization, served to stimulate the lowest centers. Hence, forbidden methods were practiced. Those who thus practiced them are today, in great numbers, in incarnation, and the ancient habits are too strong for them." *Esoteric Healing*, Lucis Trust, 1953, 62. It should be noted that a number of students of Alice Bailey's teachings have challenged her position on homosexuality.
[131] Raimondi, *Conversations with Mary*, 32.
[132] *Matthew* 17:2.
[133] It must be conceded, however, that *almah* probably did not extend to a 29-year-old woman!

Mary: Adept, Queen, Mother, Priestess

Chapter 7
Mary in Esoteric Teachings

Chapter 7 explores the way Mary is portrayed in modern esoteric teachings. The teachings provide important detail on Mary's roles as Adept, Queen and Mother, and touch on her role as Priestess.

The primary mission of Mary's Palestinian incarnation was to give birth to Jesus, but she went on to attain the fifth initiation—adeptship—in the same lifetime. After her passing Mary made the rare transition from the human to the deva evolution, literally to reign as Queen of the Angels. She now serves as Mother of the World, with special concern for the welfare of women and children.

Theosophical teachings on the World Mother built upon the religious traditions of South Asia. Contrasting views emerged. One is that the World Mother is a position or office in the Planetary Hierarchy, and Mary is the latest of a series of individuals to hold that office. The other is that the Mother is a being or entity, and the historical Mary was one of several *avataras* she sent to Earth on specific missions.

Esoteric Teachings

What is Esotericism?

Esotericism, in its most general sense, is simply the study of the inner, less obvious aspects of reality—contrasting with the literal, tangible, outer appearances of things. The Nicene Creed affirms belief in God, creator "of all that is, seen and unseen"; esotericism focuses on the unseen.

Aside from church buildings, pews, hymnals, and organizational structures, much of Christianity is esoteric. The Eucharist is the supreme example of an esoteric reality. Mysticism is an esoteric practice. Marian apparitions, along with the more extensive communications to individuals like Anne Catherine Emmerich, Bridget of Sweden, Geoffrey Hodson, and Anna Raimondi, are esoteric phenomena.

In its narrower sense esotericism pertains to fields of inquiry that overlap with mainstream religious teachings but, for historical and other reasons, developed outside the jurisdiction of institutional religion. Western esotericism grew out of the mystery traditions of ancient Egypt, Chaldea, and elsewhere and developed into a number of streams, including the Kabbalah, Hermeticism, Rosicrucianism, and early Freemasonry.[1] Eastern esotericism had its origins in the Vedas and Upanishads of India and developed through such movements as Advaita Vedanta, Kashmir Shaivism, esoteric Buddhism, and the various forms of yoga.[2]

Eastern esotericism developed in an environment of inclusiveness and tolerance and, accordingly, was more closely integrated into its companion religions. By contrast, western esotericism developed on the fringes of, or outside, mainstream Judaism and Christianity; it was viewed with suspicion, and frequent efforts were made to suppress it.

Eastern and western esotericism began to merge in the eighteenth and nineteenth centuries, following imperial excursions into Asia. The great contribution of the Theosophical Society, founded in 1875 by Helena Petrovna Blavatsky (1831–1891) and others, was to interpret elements of eastern esotericism to a western audience. What we know as "modern esotericism" is largely the work of the Theosophical Society and other individuals influenced by it. Helena Ivanovna Roerich (1879–1955) and Alice Ann Bailey (1880–1949) were two important esoteric teachers whose work followed in the Blavatskian tradition.

The Theosophical Society and traditional Christian institutions initially were suspicious of each other, but the suspicion lessened over time, allowing for cross-fertilization of ideas. An important development was the "Christianization" movement in the Theosophical Society, to which Anna Kingsford (1846–1888), Annie Wood Besant (1847–1933), Charles Webster Leadbeater (1854–1934), and Geoffrey Hodson (1886–1983) contributed. Today we find traditional Christians studying esotericism and lifelong esotericists active in mainstream Christian denominations.[3] Similar overlap may be occurring between esotericism and other western religions like Judaism and Islam.

Modern esotericism addresses many of the same issues as does traditional Christianity, including the nature, status and work of Mary. Some of the teachings referenced in this chapter allegedly were communicated by members of the angelic kingdom. Other teachings were

Chapter 7. Mary in Esoteric Teachings

communicated by *adepts* or *masters*.[4] Such individualities are members of the human family who, like Mary, completed their incarnational cycle and attained a level of relative perfection. On their path to perfection they attained five major *initiations*, or expansions of consciousness, which Christian esotericists compare with the Birth, Baptism, Transfiguration, Crucifixion and Resurrection/Ascension of Jesus Christ.

In eastern esotericism the masters are sometimes known as *mahatmas* ("great souls"). In western esotericism they are referred to as adepts, elder brothers, or inner chiefs. Collectively, they comprise the Hierarchy of Masters, part of the Planetary Hierarchy which is responsible for the inner governance of the planet and the long-term advancement of humanity.[5] As noted in Chapter 6, masters may or may not retain enduring physical bodies; but all have the ability to materialize a body for a particular purpose.

Several of the masters identified their base of operation as India or Tibet, and their teachings are referred to as the trans-Himalayan teachings. Others gave Egypt as their location, and their teachings are referred to as the Luxor teachings. No significant difference in concepts exists between the two.

Some of the authors whose work is cited in this chapter named the masters who revealed information to them. Those named most frequently were the Masters Morya, Kuthumi, and Djwhal Khul of the trans-Himalayan Brotherhood, and the Master Polidorus of the Luxor Brotherhood. Geoffrey Hodson also named the Archangel Bethelda as one of his teachers.

Adept, Queen, Mother, Priestess

Writing for the Archangel Bethelda in 1928, Geoffrey Hodson exclaimed: "She [the heavenly mother] is the High Priestess ... the Mother of the world."[6] Fifty years later the Master Polidorus gave him the enigmatic command: "Consider the three Offices—Queen, Priestess, and Mother of aspiring souls—the World Mother. Meditate upon the mystery of the deific Feminine Principle and its triple function of Queen, Priestess, and Mother of aspiring souls."[7] Repetition of "Queen, Priestess, and Mother" implies that the three titles have considerable importance. If Mary is the World Mother and an expression of the "deific Feminine Principle," and both Polidorus and Hodson affirmed that she is, then she shares those titles.

Neither Hodson nor his sources elaborated on Mary's role as Priestess. Fortunately, earlier chapters have already presented a substantial body of knowledge supporting Mary's priestly role. Very likely she served thus in the Christian community of Jerusalem. And prominent Roman Catholic commentators asserted that her participation in the Sacrifice of the Cross conveyed priestly status on her—status that she continues to hold.

Testimony to Mary's role as Priestess is found in the Tarot. The "High Priestess" card in the Tarot deck created by Arthur Waite and Pamela Colman Smith, and some other decks, draws upon traditional iconography of Mary as well as of the Egyptian goddess Isis.[8]

What Hodson and several other esoteric teachers, along with their respective sources, have provided is detailed evidence supporting Mary's titles of Adept, Queen and Mother. The title of this book, *Mary: Adept, Queen, Mother, Priestess*, seems amply justified. In the next chapter we shall examine the assertion that Mary also expresses or represents the Feminine Aspect of Deity.

Mary the Mother of Jesus

We saw in Chapter 6 that Mary commented on her lifetime in Palestine in her communications to Geoffrey Hodson and Anna Raimondi.

Helena Roerich offered an insightful glimpse into the life of Mary as mother of Jesus. Writing for the Master Morya she referred to Jesus as "the Great Pilgrim," perhaps a reference to travels during his "silent years" as well to his itinerant ministry. Roerich went on to comment that Mary "was as exceptional as Her Son" and that she communicated important values to him from an early age:

> The Mother came from a great family and was the embodiment of refinement and nobility of spirit. She was the One who laid the foundation for His first high ideals, and sang a lullaby to Him in which She foretold His miraculous future. She took great care to safeguard Her Child, and was a source of strength for His great achievements.[9]

In contrast to portrayals of Mary as a simple peasant woman, who did little more than take care of Jesus' physical needs, Roerich affirmed that she was gifted and had an instinctual grasp of her son's mission.

Chapter 7. Mary in Esoteric Teachings

Mary was able to support Jesus as he prepared for and embarked on his ministry:

> She knew several languages, and thus made the path easier for Him. Nor did She object to His long pilgrimages, and gathered all that was necessary to make the travels easier. She rightly valued the common people and knew that they would guard the treasures of His Teaching. She recognized the grandeur of the Culmination and thus could give heart to those of diverse character who were weakened by doubt and rejection. She was prepared to experience the same achievement as Her Son, and He entrusted to Her His decision, which was confirmed by the Teachers. It was the Mother who understood the mystery of His wanderings. For the fundamental truth about the Mother's life to be clear, one must understand the local conditions of those times. However, She was led by Her insight into the future and was able to rise above the customs of Her country.[10]

Roerich concluded her account of Mary with: "In truth, very little is known about Her, but when one speaks about the Great Pilgrim one has to say a word about the Mother who led Him to the Highest."[11]

Mary, Feminine Adept

In a work written sometime between 1920 and 1924, but published posthumously, Charles Leadbeater declared that Mary "became, indeed, an adept" during her Palestinian lifetime. He added, refuting an opinion that had taken root in the Theosophical Society: "Adeptship can be reached in a woman's body just as in a man's."[12] Doubts that individuals could attain the fifth initiation in a female body have mainly been confined to western esotericism; multiple female Buddhas and Bodhisattvas are revered in Buddhism. Among them is Kuan (or Kwan) Yin, often called the "Goddess of Compassion" and the patroness of many temples in East Asia.

Writing many years later Geoffrey Hodson reaffirmed that the historical Mary attained the fifth initiation, overcoming unusual challenges to do so:

> Having been ... the Mother of Jesus in the reality of His appearance amongst men and His attainment of Adeptship whilst using that body, She did Herself attain to Adeptship, took the Fifth Initiation in the Egyptian Mysteries, having also been trained in their

Chaldean form, as a woman, meaning in a female body. The tests were very severe in those days, especially for beginners, even for males, but She passed through them all successfully, almost overriding them as it were, instead of being subjected to them. She was then one of earth's Adepts.[13]

We were not given more specific information about Mary's initiation—for example, whether she traveled to Chaldea, Egypt or elsewhere for the initiatory training, or whether it was available closer to home. Perhaps she traveled there on the inner planes. But the fact that Hodson's principal teacher was the Master Polidorus of the Luxor Brotherhood gives his knowledge of the Egyptian Mysteries substantial credibility. We also note that Hodson had past lives in Egypt,[14] in addition to the lifetime in Palestine.

Nor were we told when Mary attained the fourth initiation. But it is likely that she did so also during her Palestinian incarnation; the attainment of two major initiations in a single lifetime is not uncommon.[15] The fourth initiation involves the complete renunciation of the personality. Because of the great suffering it entails, it is often referred to as the "crucifixion initiation." Most probably, and appropriately, Mary attained the initiation through her participation in the Sacrifice of the Cross. In a communication to Anna Raimondi, she shared the great suffering that only a mother could experience at seeing her son tortured and slain.[16] Reports that Mary experienced an ecstatic experience at the foot of the cross provide supporting evidence that she was in the process of a major initiation.

We can assume that Mary was already a third-degree initiate at the start of her Palestinian lifetime. She was recognized as a special child when she was born to Hannah and Joachim.[17] It would be tempting to speculate that Mary attained the third initiation as Miriam the Prophetess, sister of Moses; reincarnating souls sometimes choose a familiar name.[18]

Mary presents herself as female in her apparitions, but since she tailors her appearance to people's expectations, that persona does not necessarily imply femininity "at her own level." Whether Mary retains her feminine gender is part of the larger question of whether gender has meaning above the physical or personality level.

Hodson pondered the question in 1975, first asserting that "all Monads are sexless," but quickly adding that "certain predominances

Chapter 7. Mary in Esoteric Teachings

might remain, especially for a time."[19] He also made the statement: "Our Lady ... may be described as Monadically and inherently feminine wherever personality was concerned.[20] Juxtaposition of "Monadically and inherently" with "wherever personality was concerned" seems self-contradictory, leaving us unsure whether Hodson believed that Mary's femininity applies only to her persona or is intrinsic to her very being.

We should remember, however, that the distinction between sex and gender was less clear when Hodson was writing than it is today. The social sciences now define sex (male–female) as a physical characteristic, while gender (masculine–feminine) is a characteristic that extends beyond, and may not even include, the physical.[21] Esotericists of Hodson's generation, and earlier, either did not grasp the distinction, or they spoke of positive (active) and negative (passive, receptive) polarities in place of gender.[22]

Hodson rightly affirmed that "Difference of sex can in no remotest sense be conceivably applied to Deity and Monads."[23] But he cited "certain cosmogonies, especially the Hindu," which attach "universal attributes of positivity, negativity, and a generative interaction" to their deities.[24]

Hodson suggested that the alignment of monads with positivity or negativity—or what we would prefer to call masculinity or femininity—has deep roots and long-lasting consequences. And he ventured to say: "Our Blessed Lady is Monadically ... negative, or is inherently of a polarity that is more negative than positive."[25] Clearly, Hodson was struggling to find language to express the concepts he wished to present.

The conclusion seems to be that Mary does indeed have a feminine gender, above and beyond the female persona of her apparitions. As we shall see, her femininity accords with the ministry she has undertaken.

In a message to Hodson Mary provided her own perspective on the nature and consciousness of an adept, explaining how personality eventually gives way to a sense of all-pervading unity:

> Adepts are no longer Themselves at all from this point of view, especially that of Offices assigned and fulfilled, even though traces of the last human personality remain, especially as long as the body lasts in which Adeptship was reached. "All Oneness,"

alone, justly describes the consciousness and state of being of the Adept. Happy are those human beings who are beginning to experience foreshadowings of this surrender and mergence of selfness in the All Oneness which governs, rules utterly, the life and work of every Adept. Indeed, We are not "people" any longer but, to use "light" for a simile, are just as Rays emanating from within and radiating from without the Solar Logos, the Great Lord of Light.[26]

Queen of the Angels

We saw in Chapter 5 that the concept of Mary's Queenship has deep roots in Christian tradition and even has its own feast day. The title "Queen of the Angels" also goes back far in Christian history, though it rested on devotional rather than doctrinal grounds. Esotericists have discussed the title and suggest that it is factually true.

Writing in the early 1920s Theosophist Charles Leadbeater affirmed: "[B]ecause of the greatness which made Her [Mary] worthy" to give birth to Jesus, "it was possible for Her later to become the Queen of the Angels, high above the offspring of our small cycle of evolution."[27]

One of the tenets of the trans-Himalayan teachings is that, upon attainment of adeptship, an individual is presented with an array of opportunities for further spiritual growth and service. In 1928 Leadbeater explained that "finding the seven paths open before her, she [Mary] chose to enter the glorious Deva evolution and was received into it with great honor and distinction."[28]

It will be recalled that the angels are the senior members of the deva evolution. Leadbeater also explained: "She [Mary] is in truth a mighty Angel, having under Her a vast host of subordinate Angels, whom She keeps perpetually employed in the work which is especially committed to Her.[29] Transition to the Deva evolution is not a common occurrence. People do not ordinarily become "angels" when they die; they remain members of the human family, even though disembodied. But we shall see that adeptship provides more flexibility.

Also in the late 1920s, Geoffrey Hodson proclaimed that the angels who build human bodies in the mother's womb "have, as their Queen, a Holy One, who won freedom from the burden of the flesh and, as-

Chapter 7. Mary in Esoteric Teachings

cending, joined the Angel Hosts."[30] In the same work Hodson recorded a message from Mary, relayed by the Archangel Bethelda, who was then serving as his primary teacher. It recognized women's special place in Mary's heart and urged chivalry toward all people:

> Uplift the women of your race till all are seen as queens, and to such queens let every man be as a king; that each may honor each, seeing the other's royalty. Let every home, however small, become a court, every son a knight, every child a page. Let all treat all with chivalry, honoring in each their royal parents, their kingly birth, for there is royal blood in every man; all are the children of the King.[31]

The notion of Mary's transition from the human to the angelic kingdom resonated across multiple esoteric traditions. Corinne Heline, whose background lay in Rosicrucianism as well as Theosophy, commented: "Upon the completion of her earth mission, the holy Virgin was lifted out of the human stream and translated into the angelic evolution."[32] She now enjoys a relationship not only with devas but also with the higher ranks of the vegetable kingdom—flowers:

> The Blessed Lady is known as Queen of the Angels because of her intimate relationship with these bright beings. During each month of the yearly cycle the angels infuse the body of the earth with a particular emanation that manifests in certain rhythms of tone and color. In this pulsating color-music are formed the celestial patterns of the flower kingdom.[33]

Heline declared that Mary's "translation into the angelic realm is known in the Church as the Assumption.... Its full significance has, however, been lost since the early days of Christianity."[34]

In 1975 Hodson reiterated that, after her death, Mary "left the human kingdom altogether and entered the Angelic Hierarchy, being naturally moved to do so, knowing that with Her nature She could best help onward the evolution of human beings and animals as a Member of the Angelic Hosts."[35]

Hodson explained that the human and devic kingdoms have masculine ("positive") and feminine ("negative") polarities, respectively, noting that the "Orders of Beings are of equal evolutionary stature." [36] It seems clear that Mary's inherently monadic femininity facilitated her transition to the devic kingdom. Transition from one kingdom to the other becomes possible upon the attainment of adeptship, when

Mary: Adept, Queen, Mother, Priestess

their respective members "are able to transcend the restrictions of either [kingdom]."

In Anna Raimondi's book *Conversations with Mary*, Mary affirmed: "I am the Queen of Angels and heaven." Mary went on to speak of her mission: "I am here, as the other masters in spirit and the angels, to teach and enlighten my children and lead all to the kingdom. I pray that my messages will be heard and the world find love and peace."[37] Mary has done the same countless times at Medjugorje.

In part, at least, love and peace could come from closer contact with the deva evolution, to which Mary made her transition. In *The Angelic Hosts* (1928) Hodson wrote: "All angels are instinctively loving.... [T]hey pour forth toward the object of their affection an impersonal love combined with reverence and a certain spiritual recognition of identity of essence."[38]

Hodson noted that, in its early stages of development, a deva "rejoices in a life of entire freedom, an existence which, compared to the human lot, is one of continuous ecstasy." Later, as the deva undergoes the process of individualization, corresponding to evolution from an animal into a human being, "a change occurs within the soul of the angel; a sense of responsibility begins to make an insistent demand for expression in action."[39] Hodson continued:

> The days of his [the deva's] irresponsible freedom and superabundant joy are drawing to a close, for that which is growing within him will brook no denial; under its irresistible influence ... gradually he changes from an angel who plays to an angel who works. Even in his play he served, for that, too, was an expression of the divine play, a manifestation of the divine happiness, freedom and joy.[40]

Such are the orders of beings over which Mary is believed to preside. We need to become more aware of devic presence—particularly the presence of the angels—in the countryside, our homes, our churches, and our rituals. Joy and play may be important elements of that presence.

Hodson and Raimondi use the traditional titles of "Queen of Heaven" and "Queen of the Angels." But we may ask: Is "Queen" still an appropriate title in an age when monarchies may be considered anachronistic? Should we not refer to Mary as "President," "Prime Minister," or even "Chief Executive Officer"? No, "Queen" has timeless, archetypal meaning; it calls to mind serene majesty, supreme power combined with femininity. "Queen" captures a confident, poised self-concept unmatched by any modern executive title. In 1978, the Master Polidorus referred to Mary as "Her gracious Majesty."[41]

"Queen" invites, not just respect, but adoration. Lest we hesitate to express that level of devotion, we should recall that early Christian writings recorded numerous instances when the heavenly hosts adored Mary. The esoteric literature records few examples in which masters or archangels discouraged adoration of Mary.

Mother of the World

The term "Mother of the World" appears in the Kabbalistic text *Sefer ha-Bahir* ("Brilliance"), attributed to a first-century rabbinic sage Nehuniah ben HaKanah and published in Provence in the twelfth century. Interestingly, the Mother is associated with the sephirah *Binah* ("Understanding") in the Kabbalistic Tree of Life, the complement of the masculinized *Chokmah* ("Wisdom").[42] Suggestions of an association between Chokmah—however mutilated—and the Mother of the World are highly significant and will be commented on later in the book.

The World Mother also has a long tradition in Hinduism and Buddhism. And Chapters 4 and 5 showed that notions of Mary as World Mother have gained traction in Christian teachings over the last two centuries.

Some of the early Theosophists were influenced by Ramakrishna (1836–1886), famous devotee of the World Mother in her role as Kali, consort of Shiva. Others were influenced by Buddhist belief in the goddess Kuan Yin, Mother of Compassion. Christian esotericists in the Theosophical Society and elsewhere identified Mary as the World Mother.

The esoteric literature provides alternative depictions of the World Mother. One view is that the Mother is an *entity*, a *being*, or perhaps a *principle*. The other is that "World Mother" is a *position*, or *office*, analogous to the presidency of a nation, and held by a succession of entities. A *being* is a monad, in this case a highly exalted one.[43] A *position* is an opportunity for a succession of monads to perform a specified service.

The alternative depictions of the World Mother affect our understanding of Mary. If the World Mother is an office, Mary might be one of the office holders. If the Mother is an entity, then the historical Mary might have been a manifestation or incarnation of that entity; that is, she might have been an *avatara*, as the term in used on South Asian religions.[44] We shall return to these issues later in the book—and will also see that a broader definition allows a human Mary to be considered an avatara.

In what follows we trace the evolution of the concept of World Mother, as it took shape among Theosophists and other esoteric teachers, from the late nineteenth century onward.

Anna Kingsford

Anna Kingsford was a contemporary of Blavatsky's, with a brief association with the Theosophical Society. She is better known for her work as a Hermeticist and feminist. Significantly, Kingsford converted to Roman Catholicism in her twenties.[45]

Anna Kingsford did not discuss the World Mother directly, but she laid the groundwork in Christian esotericism for many of the ideas expressed decades later. In a lecture in 1880 she connected Eve, Mary, and the empowered woman of her feminist aspirations:

> The word which shall come to save the world, shall be uttered by a woman. A woman shall conceive, and shall bring forth the tidings of salvation. For the reign of Adam is at its last hour; and God shall crown all things by the creation of Eve. Hitherto the man hath been alone, and hath had dominion over the earth. But when the woman shall be created, God shall give unto her the kingdom; and she shall be first in rule and highest in dignity.... So that women shall no more lament for their womanhood: but men shall rather say, "O that we had been born women!"[46]

Kingsford continued with a strong reference to Mary's role in the new world order she foresaw:

> For the woman is the crown of man, and the final manifestation of humanity. She is the nearest to the throne of God, when she shall be revealed. But the creation of woman is not yet complete: but it shall be complete in the time which is at hand. All things are thine, O Mother of God: all things are thine, O Thou who risest from the sea; and Thou shalt have dominion over all the worlds.[47]

Chapter 7. Mary in Esoteric Teachings

Helena Roerich

Helena Roerich was a major contributor to esoteric writings on the World Mother. She was neither a Christian—by then she had embraced Buddhism—nor a member of the Theosophical Society, though she had translated Helena Blavatsky's *The Secret Doctrine* into Russian.

Roerich wrote extensively about the World Mother, whom she viewed as an entity. The Mother, according to Roerich, revealed herself directly to humanity in the remote past. But the destruction of Atlantis disrupted the pattern of manifestation, and the Mother was forced to withdraw: "After Atlantis the Mother of the World veiled Her Face and forbade the pronouncement of Her Name until the hour of the constellations should strike. She has manifested Herself only partly; never has She manifested Herself on a planetary scale."[48]

Writing in the 1920s, Roerich predicted that the veil would soon be lifted, and the Mother of the World would once again play a conspicuous role in human affairs. Evidently "the hour of the constellations" was about to strike. A star, which "has been the symbol of the Mother of the World," is approaching the Earth and will usher in "the Epoch of the Mother of the World.... The approach of this very great Epoch ... will substantially change the life of the Earth."[49] Although Roerich was writing forty years after Kingsford had made a similar prediction, she felt free to add: "Today is the beginning of the feminine awakening." In Roerich's eyes, the reemergence of the World Mother and the empowerment of women were intimately connected.

The World Mother's withdrawal from public view, upon the destruction of Atlantis, may have mirrored the withdrawal of the masters from overt participation in human affairs. Similarly, the reemergence of the Mother would seem to mirror the anticipated return of the masters and "externalization" of the Planetary Hierarchy, sometime after 2025. Writing for the Master Djwhal Khul, Alice Bailey declared that the culmination of that process will be the reappearance of the Christ,[50] a scenario similar in concept—though not in detail—to the Second Coming of Christ, described in traditional Christian teachings.

Helena Roerich described some of the World Mother's attributes, including comments on the Mother's *playfulness*: a concept not unknown in the East but foreign to western religion. In a passage that calls to mind Rogers and Hammerstein's Maria in *The Sound of Mu-*

259

sic, she wrote: "Rejoice in the Great Play of the Mother of the World!.... She beckons to Her children from far-distant fields: 'Hasten, children! I wish to teach you. I have keen eyes and alert ears ready for you. Sit ye down upon My garment. Let us learn to soar!'"[51]

Elsewhere Roerich stressed that progress at the human level is to be achieved through joy, reflecting the joy at divine levels: "The play of the Mother of the World is in joy. She enfolds the enlightened ones in Her veil of joy. Rejoice amidst flowers; and in the midst of snow—equally redolent—also rejoice!"[52] The World Mother's playfulness and joy are not totally out of context when we recall Hodson's comments on the consciousness of the deva evolution.

Roerich warned that "woman is the personification of self-sacrifice," and the same is true of the World Mother. However, joy can still come from right aspiration: "How beautiful is the Image of the Mother of the World! So much beauty, self-renunciation and tragedy is in this majestic Image! Aspire in your heart to the Highest, and joy and exultation will enter your soul."[53] Roerich did not identify Mary as Mother of the World, but others did.

The Early Theosophists

Annie Besant's landmark book *Esoteric Christianity or The Lesser Mysteries* (1901/1905) reaffirmed Anna Kingsford's work of twenty years earlier. It also launched the Christianization movement within the Theosophical Society that would play out over the next several decades. While the movement attracted powerful supporters, it also met with strong resistance from members—and nonmembers like Roerich—who continued to be drawn to Eastern religions.

Besant boldly placed "Mary, the World Mother" at the dawn of creation, anticipating by eighty years a similar statement by Pope John Paul II. "When the Logos comes forth from 'the bosom of the Father,'" Besant wrote, the Logos makes

> as it were a sphere enclosing the Divine Life, coming forth as a radiant orb of Deity, the Divine Substance, Spirit within and limitation, or Matter, without. This is the veil of matter which makes possible the birth of the Logos, Mary, the World-Mother, necessary for the manifestation in time of the Eternal, that Deity may manifest for the building of the worlds.[54]

Chapter 7. Mary in Esoteric Teachings

It is worth noting, however, that Besant placed Mary at the dawn of creation to birth the universe rather than to be the mother of Christ. The role she assigned to Mary comes closer to that claimed by the personified "Wisdom" (Hebrew: Chokmah, Greek: Sophia) in *Proverbs* and the Wisdom books of the Septuagint.[55] We shall return to Chokmah/Sophia and her possible relationship to Mary later in the book.

The Christianization movement shifted into high gear in 1927 when the Hindu writer Nibaran Chandra Basu published a two-part article on the Mother in *The Theosophist*.[56]

The following year Annie Besant preached a sermon at the Liberal Catholic Church in Adyar, India, declaring that the Mother of the World "is coming forward to take Her special place ... to be recognized publicly as She has ever been active spiritually." March 25—the traditional feast of the Annunciation, "Lady Day"— was to be observed as World Mother Day.[57] Mothers would fully be appreciated in the coming "Age of Motherhood." Besant lamented: "It is a constantly-repeated phrase that every great man had a great mother. But while the great man is admired and honored, she who gave him his physical body is often forgotten, treated with disregard and disrespect."[58] The same could be said of Mary.

Charles Leadbeater still viewed the World Mother as an entity who manifested in various forms. But he began to single out Mary as the latest, or most important, manifestation:

> Our Lady of Light is hailed as Virgin, though Mother of All. She is thus the essence of the great sea of matter, and so She is symbolized as Aphrodite, the Sea-Queen, and as Mary, the Star of the Sea, and in pictures She is always dressed in the blue of the sea and of the sky. Because it is only by means of our passage through matter that we evolve, She is also to us Isis the Initiator, the Virgin-Mother of whom the Christ in us is born.... [She] is represented as Eve, descending into matter ... and then when She rises clear of matter, once more as Mary the Queen of heaven.[59]

Like Hildegard of Bingen, esotericists often make the etymological connection between "mother" (Latin: *mater*) and "matter" (*materia*); they see matter as the feminine receptacle—the womb—into which masculine Spirit descends in the creative act. Here, Leadbeater envisioned the World Mother as the *essence* of matter, participating not only in creation but in the redemptive act of Christ. Collectively, that redemptive act raised the consciousness of the whole human race; individually, it urged Mary forward on the initiatory path and raised her to the Queenship of Heaven.

Leadbeater sought to locate the World Mother within the Planetary Hierarchy. Writing in 1928 he commented: "The World-Mother ... is a mighty Being who is at the head of a great department of the organization and government of the world."[60] Elsewhere he was more specific, but also offered the alternative perspective that the World Mother is an office rather than an entity:

> Just as there is an office of Bodhisattva or the World Teacher [the Christ], so there is an office of the World Mother. These offices are held by great adepts who have reached the utmost point of development within humanity first and then have taken a step beyond humanity and become superhuman. The office of World Mother is held by Our Lady Mary.[61]

Geoffrey Hodson

Geoffrey Hodson's understanding of the World Mother, like Leadbeater's, evolved over time. Writing for the Archangel Bethelda, in *The Angelic Hosts* (1928), Hodson boldly described the Mother as consort of the Solar Logos, who gave birth to and sustains the solar system. He also related her to Isis, Mary—and the element *Water*:

> [T]he divine Mother is for ever giving birth and, through Her, the life of the system is eternally renewed. The element of water is the eternal mother, the heavenly woman, the Virgin Mary, ever producing, yet ever immaculate, the Universal Isis, the goddess queen of the solar system, the spouse of the solar deity. Her life is outpoured freely for the sustenance and nutrition of the system. She is the eternal and unsolvable mystery, for, remaining virginal and immaculate, yet is She ever pregnant and ever giving birth. The solar system is Her child which She nourishes upon Her bosom.[62]

Hodson continued: "Men, throughout all the ages, have worshipped Her as the Mother of God." Then he added, presumably at the archangel's urging, a statement that merits close attention:

> She is represented on every plane by an advanced member of that race, who assumes the office of head of the water angels of that plane; each is a representative, at her level, of the Supreme Queen,

Chapter 7. Mary in Esoteric Teachings

the Eternal Mother, the Star of the Sea. They form a living chain of conscious life through which Her power and Her attributes may be made manifest throughout the system.[63]

First, the statement relates the World Mother again to the Water element; she is "head of the water angels." "Star of the Sea"; perhaps other devas, like the fire devas, report to the Logos. Second, it anticipated in surprising detail how Hodson would describe Mary many years later: as Adept, as Queen of the Angels, as World Mother—even as an expression of the Feminine Aspect of Deity. But Hodson may not have grasped the statement's significance at the time.

Over the next four decades Hodson explored a succession of depictions of the World Mother and her earthly manifestations. His first reference to the World Mother in *Light of the Sanctuary*, dated 1941, spoke of "the divine Office of World Mother"[64] but did not identify who held that office.

In 1945 Mary herself told Hodson: "I was Miriam, the Mother of Jesus, and now hold the Office of World Mother."[65] But fourteen years later Hodson had a vision of Kuan Yin, which suggested to him that there might be two World Mothers:

> It seems possible that there are two World Mothers, one for the Fourth Root Race and one for the Fifth Root Race. The former assumes the Kwan [sic] Yin individuality and the latter that of the Virgin Mary, whilst at the highest level the two are expressions of the one Divine Principle, like twin *Avataras* of the Feminine Aspect of Deity, in the main ministering to the East and the West.[66]

Along with his fellow Theosophists Hodson followed South-Asian religious custom in viewing avatars and avataras as divine manifestations, distinct from ordinary members of the human lifewave.

An entry in Hodson's diary, dated 1975, expanded the number of individualities associated with the World Mother:

> Our Lady entered the Angelic Kingdom on attaining Adeptship, and has chosen to minister to mankind under the Parviti [sic], true Kwan Yin, Ishtar, Hathor-Isis, Lady Mary Individualities.... All of these Divine Beings are—for none of Them have disappeared—incarnations of Divine Motherhood.[67]

Hodson never abandoned the view that the World Mother is a being who manifested through multiple avataras. But in his latter years he seemed to align himself more with the view that "World Mother" is an office, and Mary currently holds that office. In a message to Hodson in 1976 Mary again referred to "My Office of World Mother."[68]

We have to assume that Mary was appointed to the office of World Mother sometime during the last 2,000 years, based on her qualifications, and with her consent and desire to serve in that capacity. Mary's consent, like her transition to the deva evolution, may have been a natural choice based on her monadic femininity. "Each Adept," she explained to Hodson,

> pursues both a particular path of Self-expression that is decided largely by the nature of the Monad, and fulfils the associated duties sometimes but not always as an Adept Official.... I in My turn, continuing to express innate Monadic accentuations, serve as far as I am capable in the Department known as "World Mother."[69]

We recall Leadbeater's comment that "The World-Mother ... is a mighty Being who is at the head of a great department of the organization and government of the world."[70] A Department of World Mother would be a fourth, complementing the three, corresponding to the three Rays of Aspect, described in the esoteric literature.[71] The problem of fitting another major department into the threefold structure is not unlike the problem of fitting a feminine element into the Christian Trinity.

Hodson's clearest exposition of the view that World Mother is an office is found in *Illuminations of the Mystery Tradition*, another book compiled from his writings and published posthumously. In an undated passage he stated that tenure of that office is of finite duration. Mary is the current office holder for our Earth, and Isis was one of her predecessors:

> That Official is the World Mother for a planet and a period, and the basis of truth in the successive ideas of the civilizations and religions of the world. There is such a Being, there is such an official, and Mary the mother of Jesus now holds that Office, as Isis held it in earlier days.[72]

Hodson did not name Isis as Mary's immediate predecessor, or explain where other individualities, like Parvati or Ishtar, might fit into the succession.[73] Nor did he repeat the suggestion that the office might be shared by two (or more) individualities at the same time.

Chapter 7. Mary in Esoteric Teachings

When Hodson identified Mary, Isis, Kuan Yin, and others as "Divine Beings" and "incarnations of Divine Motherhood," he placed them in the category of *avataras*, as the term is used in South Asian religions: as personages who "descend from above." Yet Hodson also seemed convinced that Mary was a member of the human family who had attained the fifth initiation and was appointed World Mother "from below." Mary herself explained that, upon attaining adeptship, she made the choice among several options to "serve as far as I am capable in the Department known as 'World Mother.'"

Could Mary still be considered an avatara if she was appointed to the office of World Mother from the ranks of humanity? The answer appears to be "yes." Alice Bailey, amanuensis to the Master Djwhal Khul, defined an avatar as:

> a Being Who—having first developed His Own nature, human and divine, and then transcended it—is capable of reflecting some cosmic Principle or divine quality and energy which will produce the desired effect upon humanity, evoking a reaction, producing a needed stimulation and, as it is esoterically called, "leading to the rending of a veil and the permeation of light."[74]

Bailey added: "The response or reaction of humanity ... establishes in due time the recognition of something transcendent, something to be desired and striven for, something which indicates a vision which is first a possibility and later an achievement."[75]

Importantly, Bailey did not emphasize the need for a an avatar or avatara to be a *manifestation* of a higher being or principle, merely that he or she *reflect* "some cosmic Principle or divine quality." Mary, who developed and transcended her human nature in attaining adeptship, certainly demonstrated her ability to reflect the cosmic Principle of motherhood as a qualification for appointment as World Mother.

We are even justified in claiming that Mary incarnated in Palestine as an avatara. She was probably a third-degree initiate and had yet to transcend her lower nature, but her mission to serve as the mother of Jesus reflected "divine quality and energy." Few would question that her mission "produced the desired effect upon humanity," rent a veil and permeated light, and evoked "the recognition of something transcendent ... a possibility and later an achievement." Mary did not have to be a divine manifestation or incarnation in order to meet the criteria of *avatara*, according to modern esoteric teachings.

Bailey described avatars and avataras as "messengers." Mary might qualify as an avatar, but it is not immediately clear from where, or from whom, she bore her message. The "cosmic Principle or divine quality" may simply have been the Feminine Aspect of God.

Broad support exists among esotericists for belief in the World Mother. Yet it should be noted that Alice Bailey dismissed notions of a World Mother as purely symbolic, adding:

> Such an individual has never existed in our particular planetary life, though the avatars of a previous solar system, expressing itself through planetary life, always took this form. But not in this solar system.... This symbolism has come down from the far-off period of the Matriarchate, which had a religion that recalled the ancient ways of the earlier system and in which period of time Lilith symbolized the World Mother, until Eve took her place.[76]

Bailey's comments might not apply to the World Mother viewed as an office or position in the Planetary Hierarchy, held by a succession of human adepts.

Other Teachings

Rudolf Steiner and the Anthroposophists

Rudolf Steiner (1861–1925) served as head of the German section of the Theosophical Society, but his primary orientation was toward the western esoteric tradition, and eventually he left to form his own Anthroposophical Society.

In a lecture in 1908 Steiner commented, as we did in Chapter 1, that the *Gospel of John* describes incidents in which Mary was present but does not refer to her by name. His explanation was that the gospel's author wanted to avoid using Mary's "secular name" but was not at liberty to reveal her "esoteric name":

> He could not take the secular name, he had to express in the name the profound, world historic evolution. He does this by indicating that she cannot be called Mary and what is more, he places by her side her sister Mary, wife of Cleophas and calls her simply the

"Mother of Jesus." He shows thereby that he does not wish to mention her name, that it cannot be publicly revealed.[77]

Steiner claimed that in "esoteric circles, she [Mary] is always called the 'Virgin Sophia.' It was she who represented the 'Virgin Sophia' as an external historical personality."[78] It might assumed that Steiner was associating Mary with the Sophia of Hellenic Judaism, but he was actually referring to her stage of spiritual attainment. We learn that "Virgin Sophia" was the name he gave to the purified astral body.[79] Mary had attained mastery of the emotional and desire nature; indeed she was a living expression—"an external historical personality"—of that mastery.

Steiner continued:

> The author of the St John's Gospel regarded the physical, historic Mother of Jesus in her most prominent characteristics and asked himself—Where shall I find a name for her which will express most perfectly her real being? Then, because she had, by means of her earlier incarnations, reached those spiritual heights upon which she stood; and because she appeared in her external personality to be a counterpart, a revelation of what was called in esoteric Christianity, the Virgin Sophia, he called the Mother of Jesus the "Virgin Sophia;" and this is what she was always called in the esoteric places where esoteric Christianity was taught.[80]

Steiner did not identify the "places where esoteric Christianity was taught" in the first century CE. The "esoteric circles" in which Mary is currently called the "Virgin Sophia" presumably referred to his own Anthroposophical Society.

Steiner's claim that Mary had attained mastery of the astral nature would suggest that she was a second-degree initiate. We have suggested that she began her Palestinian lifetime as a third-degree initiate, more consistent with the "spiritual heights" to which Steiner referred.

An interesting comment appears in a work, *Meditations on the Tarot*, attributed to Hermeticist, and one-time student of Rudolf Steiner's, Valentin Tomberg: "One meets the Blessed Virgin inevitably when one attains a certain intensity of spiritual aspiration, when this aspiration is authentic and pure." In order to pass through the "sphere of mirages" or the "zone of illusion"—presumably the astral plane—one requires the protection of the Mantle of the Holy Theotokos.[81] The

"Mantle" was a reference to a tradition in the Eastern Orthodox churches in which Mary is revered as the protectress of the Byzantine and Slavic people.

The author of *Meditations* goes on to anticipate a time when the archetypal battle between St Michael and the dragon gives way to collaboration. It will be celebrated by a new feast in the liturgical calendar: "the festival of coronation of the Virgin on earth." "For then," he says, "the principle of opposition will be replaced on earth by that of collaboration.... And intellectuality will then bow before Wisdom (Sophia) and will unite with her."[82]

A sizable body of literature exists relating to the World Mother, but nowhere does it mention Sophia. An even larger body of literature has emerged in recent decades promoting Sophia as a goddess, but it does not mention the World Mother and rarely associates Sophia with Mary. The possibility of bridging these two bodies of literature and establishing a connection between Sophia and the World Mother is intriguing.

Corrine Heline

Corinne Heline's comments on Mary's transition to the deva evolution have already been noted. Heline was a student of Max Heindel, one-time associate of Rudolf Steiner and founder of The Rosicrucian Fellowship, one of several esoteric schools that sought to recover the teachings of Christian Rosencreutz and the Fraternity of the Rose Cross.[83] Thus she was grounded in the western esoteric tradition, but she also absorbed Theosophical and other modern esoteric teachings. Her best-known work was the seven-volume *The New Age Bible Interpretation* (1954). She also wrote *The Blessed Virgin Mary*, referenced herein.

Heline described a series of initiations Mary attained, linking them with the four elements. She identified the "Rite of the Annunciation" as Initiation by Water, the "Immaculate Conception" as Initiation by Fire,[84] the "Rite of Pentecost" as Initiation by Air, and the "Rite of the Assumption" as Initiation by Earth. Interestingly, Heline spoke of Marian initiations corresponding to all four elements; we recall that the Archangel Bethelda, in his communication to Hodson, mentioned Mary's association only with the Water element.

Water is important, nevertheless. Heline explained: "Water is the esoteric symbol of the emotional nature." By the time of the Annuncia-

Chapter 7. Mary in Esoteric Teachings

tion Mary had mastered her emotions and, under the guidance of the Archangel Gabriel, was able to foresee her mission and that of the child she was to bear:

> At this time Mary was given to understand the role she was destined to play in the mighty cosmic drama pertaining to heaven and earth. She was the vehicle chosen to become the mother of the most perfect Master ever the take embodiment in the human race.... The Master Jesus and the Blessed Mary were the purest and most advanced egos ever to come into incarnation... Hence it was that both Jesus and his mother were heralded by the angelic annunciation.[85]

Corinne Heline offered an esoteric interpretation of the Rosary, and also a series of twelve commentaries on Mary in relation to the astrological signs. To illustrate, Easter falls within the sign of Aries and the related commentary includes the following:

> On that first Easter morning and within her own sacred shrine Mary suddenly became aware that her sanctuary was filled with the same golden Light that surrounded the hills outside. Then, on pinions of love, the glorified body of the Resurrected Christ appeared before her. Thus Mary's eyes were the first to behold the Risen Lord.[86]

Heline's commentary on Cancer focused on the feast of the Visitation. At the time she wrote, the feast was celebrated on July 2, during the Sun's transit of Cancer (according to the tropical zodiac). In 1969 it was moved to May 31, which lies in Gemini.

Andrew Harvey

Anglo-Indian religious scholar and mystic Andrew Harvey (1952–) had a long association with Kamala Reddy ("Mother Meera"),[87] believed by devotees to be an incarnation of the Hindu goddess *Shakti*. Through that association he came to revere an entity whom he called the Divine Mother. In due course, a series of spiritual experiences persuaded Harvey that Mary was a true manifestation of the Divine Mother:

> In Mary the Divine Mother comes to earth and lives on earth and lives the passionate, strong, serious, simple and transforming life that shows us all how to live. Mary is the bridge between heaven

and earth, between the human and the divine worlds, between human and divine justice.[88]

Harvey also seemed to place Mary in the Trinity, in the hope of correcting gender imbalance within institutional Christianity:

> [S]eeing Mary as the Divine Mother would help us to see Christ too as every much the son of the Divine Mother as the Divine Father. Seeing that would release Christianity from its patriarchal stranglehold and restore the mystical purity of its passion for fraternity and sorority, for equality and social justice and service.[89]

Elsewhere, Harvey and a coauthor approved of the notion of Mary as mediatrix, noting that it is "the feminine principle of relationship that connects things to each other, for the supreme values of the heart."[90] They made another forceful point: "The extraordinary story of the elevation of Mary to the stature of Divine Mother shows the immense need of people to have the feminine principle at the heart of their religions."[91]

Mary's Ongoing Ministry

Corrine Heline affirmed that Mary's transition to the angelic kingdom did not mean that she had abandoned her human charges: "Although the Blessed Virgin now makes her home in the heaven world with the Angels, she spends much of her time on the earth plane working with humanity."[92] In a reference to Marian apparitions Heline added: "Many have testified to seeing her."

Geoffrey Hodson explained that Mary "entered the Angelic Hierarchy, being naturally moved to do so, knowing that with Her nature She could best help onward the evolution of human beings and animals as a Member of the Angelic Hosts."[93] Mary told Anna Raimondi: "I am here, as the other masters in spirit and the angels, to teach and enlighten my children and lead all to the kingdom. I pray that my messages will be heard and the world find love and peace."[94] In a message communicated during an apparition at Medjugorje in 2020 Mary reflected on her own service and called upon her audience to join her in service:

> [M]y body was the chalice of the God-man. I was in the service of truth, love and salvation, as I am now among you to call you, my children, apostles of my love, to be carriers of truth; to call you to

spread His words, the words of salvation, by your will and love for my Son: that with your actions you may show, to all those who have not come to know my Son, His love.[95]

Obstetric Ministry

Charles Leadbeater declared that Mary serves as a senior member of the Planetary Hierarchy, with a mission that embraces the protection of women during childbirth:

> As Queen of the Angels, She [Mary] is the leader of many thousands of angels, who are her representatives whom She sends down into the world. For She is present through Her representatives at every birth that takes place in the world. Never a child is born anywhere but the World Mother's representative stands by to give such strength, and such comfort, as karma may permit.[96]

Elsewhere Leadbeater affirmed: "[I]n a very real sense all the women of the world are under Her charge, and most especially so at the time of their greatest trial, when they are exercising the supreme function given to them by God, and thus becoming mothers."[97] Interestingly, Buddhists revere Kuan Yin as the protectress of women in childbirth.[98]

Annie Besant also commented on Mary's role as "Mother" to every child being born: "Hers is the tender mercy that presides at the birth of every child, whatever the rank or place of the mother."[99] In Hodson's *The Brotherhood of Angels and Men* (1927) Mary spoke through the Archangel Bethelda: "In the Name of Him whom long ago I bore, I come to your aid. I have taken every woman into my heart, to hold there a part of her that through it I may help her in her time of need."[100]

In a work Hodson published the following year Bethelda portrayed the World Mother in a priestly role, presiding over the "sacrament" of childbirth:

> The heavenly mother presides at every human birth. She is the High Priestess in Whose service every human mother makes her sacrifice that She, the Mother of the world, may be revealed in all Her splendor, all Her beauty, at the sacrament of birth. She is the heavenly woman of whom every woman is a part.[101]

He went on to affirm the bond that develops between the celestial Priestess and the human mother:

> At motherhood that sacred bond becomes a living line of light, as She descends from Her throne to stand beside the bed of birth. She knows the pain; she feels the agony; every cry pierces her heart and draws forth Her healing and protecting power upon the human mother in whom She sees Herself in miniature.[102]

The Miracle of Birth (1929) records Hodson's clairvoyant observations of pregnancy. Ranks of devic builders, he observed, construct the human vehicles and introduce the incarnating soul to its new habitat. The builders are part of the World Mother's operations:

> During investigations of the pre-natal life I constantly became aware of the presence and ministration of certain types of angels which were assisting in the dual process of construction of the new bodies—mental, emotional, etheric, and physical—and the induction into them of the reincarnating Ego.... A study of these angels revealed them as aspects of a great Intelligence which presides over and directs all maternal processes throughout Nature.[103]

In Theosophical literature, *Ego* (capitalized) denotes the soul.

By the 1970s Hodson was convinced that Mary was the World Mother. In *Light of the Sanctuary*, he focused on what it means for her to serve in that capacity:

> The Blessed Lady Mary ... moved by purest compassion and love, holds the whole of humanity in Her arms and at Her breast, nourishing it with spiritualizing life for the purpose of quickening the evolution of all sentient beings. The World Mother shares Herself with every mother—human and animal—throughout the periods of the gestation and delivery of her offspring. Impersonally, She is also present and Herself helps the mother during her labor.[104]

Through her legions of devic beings, Mary's mothering ministry extends even to the vegetable kingdom. Hodson wrote in his diary:

> The totality of Archangels on this planet concerned with every process of Nature in which procreation, interior growth, birth, childhood, youth, and motherhood, including that in the animal and plant kingdoms in which some form of pollinization and subsequent developments occur, is under the general and also very real directive "Rulership" of the Holder of the Office of World Mother.[105]

Chapter 7. Mary in Esoteric Teachings

Here, Hodson reaffirmed his belief that the World Mother is an office rather than a being. Again referring to the "Office of World Mother," Mary spoke about her ministry to all mothers, noting the special issues pertaining to pregnancy in the human kingdom:

> [My ministry] encompasses the whole of femininity throughout the animal and human kingdoms, the extremely subtle and sensitive procedures of Nature during pregnancies in both kingdoms and, more especially in the human, the actual procedure of the delivery of the child and the experiences through which every mother passes. In the animal kingdom this is reasonably natural, but in the human, for various reasons into which I will not go here—*karma* being the most important amongst them—assistance is necessary and is provided for the mental, astral, and physical bodies and nervous systems of every mother on earth. No single one is ever outside of the ministrations under Myself and sometimes by Myself supplied and applied by the angelic members associated with My Office of World Mother.[106]

The suggestion that karma complicates human childbirth might call to mind God's curse on Eve: "I will greatly multiply thy sorrow and thy conception; in sorrow thou shalt bring forth children."[107] But Hodson explained elsewhere that the cause is our lack of understanding of devic activity: "It is a lack of recognition of their [the building devas'] place and aid that has made childbirth ... a period of agony or death. When men invoke their aid, they will teach the human race how to bring forth their kind with joy."[108] Presumably women will have opportunities to do the same!

Mary acknowledged that only a few "mystics and occultists" know of her ministry on behalf of women in pregnancy. But "as the race evolves, humanity—especially women—will become more and more aware of these necessities and ministrations. Any published work, therefore, which draws attention to them now is of practical value to all mothers and mothers-to-be."[109] With the publication of Hodson's diary, and commentaries like this one, greater awareness of Mary's work should be possible.

Mary's "mothering" duties extend to the metaphorical birth of the Christ consciousness in the disciple's heart. Hodson explained: "Impersonally, She also is present and helps to bring about the mystical "birth" of the Christ consciousness within the Inner Self of every Ini-

273

tiate when admitted to membership of the Great White Brotherhood."[110] Earlier the Master Polidorus had remarked:

> To perceive the Gospel story of the Annunciation and Virgin birth as an account (a quite intimately descriptive and instructive one) of the awakening from relative "slumber" of the Christ-Principle within the consciousness of a human being. This applies especially to those who have begun to experience the interior "birth," and find themselves occasionally illumined, inspired, and increasingly interested in the living of the spiritual life amidst worldly activities.[111]

Healing Ministry

Mary ministers to women who are sick, as well as to those in pregnancy. As Besant declared:

> The sacredness of Motherhood brings Her beside the bed of suffering. Her compassion and Her tenderness, Her all-embracing Motherhood, know no differences of caste, color or rank. All, to Her, are Her children—the tenderest of all human movements and, because the most compassionate, the greatest power in the civilization.[112]

The recognition of Mary's concern for the sick was important to Hodson because of his healing ministry in the Liberal Catholic Church. Mary's first visitation to him in 1945 came after he sought her help in a healing: "I had invoked Her aid for a girl of nineteen during a healing service a few days previously and felt a response."[113] Three decades later Mary affirmed: "Though I am concerned for all mankind, I am especially concerned on behalf of all your female patients."[114]

In 1978 Hodson recorded a comment by the Master Kuthumi: "Cruelty in the treatment of women, children, and animals, its evil and sheer ugliness [would illustrate] the opposite of the ideal for which She [Mary] stands."[115] Two years later Mary herself added: "Amongst the evils of the world, always add, when speaking upon this subject, the degradation of and the consequent suffering of women."[116] Few human institution in recorded history can escape criticism for contributing to those "evils."

"Healing" may take the form of release from a physical body that can no longer sustain the indwelling life. Such an incident involved an initiated disciple of the Master Kuthumi "who had appealed to Geoffrey [Hodson] for help and guidance in the mental and spiritual aridity of later life." In response Kuthumi offered advice on preparing the woman for her death and eventual reincarnation:

> From the point of view of her membership of the Brotherhood and her close links with more than one Master and the Blessed Lady Mary, it is important that before she is freed from her body later on she endeavors, as far as possible mentally, to bring to life again her memory of her time under her Initiate Teacher and of any experiences she may have passed through.[117]

Kuthumi added that reawakening such memories would spare the woman "many of the experiences, some of them not pleasant, of astro-mental life after death." It would also "greatly affect her next life, both in the choice of parents and conditions and in the provision of opportunities to draw near to the Adept life of the planet ... and to the extremely important knowledge of both the existence of the Path and an opportunity to enter upon it once again."[118]

Women, the Family, and Society

Anna Kingsford and Annie Besant both saw a connection between the "return" of the World Mother and the empowerment of women in society. The increased frequency of Marian apparitions, and what appears to be Mary's desire to reveal more of herself, can be viewed in a similar light.

Geoffrey Hodson commented in *The Brotherhood of Angels and Men* (1927) that Mary "labors ever for the cause of human motherhood, and even now is bending all Her mighty strength and calling all Her Angel Court to labor for the upliftment of womanhood throughout the world."[119] He elaborated in an article also published in 1927:

> It is sufficient to say that the great orders of the angels stand ready to assist us in all our undertakings, providing that they are in accordance with the great plan: the power of the Lady Mary and Her hosts of angel servers is ready to be freely poured out in all work for the upliftment of the womanhood of the world and the exaltation of the ideals of love, marriage and parenthood.[120]

Two years later Hodson reaffirmed Mary's commitment to the cause of parenthood and the ideal of "true affection":

> She shares in all the joys of the first love; that all the happiness of true affection between man and maid finds an echo in Her heart, and that She adds to it from the boundless ocean of Her own perfected love and ardent joy. She seeks to increase, to bless, to enrich and to purify all that wondrous depth of love to which a woman's heart can give birth.

Hodson went on to speak of "the uplifting of the women of the world, the exaltation of human love, and the purification of the sacrament of parenthood." And he concluded his discussion with: "Thus does She fulfill Her great part in the Plan, and take Her place in the Hierarchy of Those Who, having learned to live in the Eternal, yet voluntarily submit to the imprisonment of time."[121]

In 1975 the Master Polidorus took up the cause of the World Mother Movement, originally proposed by Besant. In a message recorded by Hodson, Polidorus identified Roman Catholicism as fertile ground for the movement to take root:

> [A] World Mother Movement would at this time be of great benefit to humanity, and would offer Her increasing opportunities and channels for the helping of mankind. Such groupings do exist in certain Roman Catholic institutions, such as the monastery and chapel of Einzedelin. More and more are needed, particularly with greater freedom of religious thinking, even though within the Christian faith.[122]

While the World Mother Movement might have special significance for Christianity, it could also be embraced by multiple world religions. Polidorus continued:

> The same, of course, is equally true in other religions in which a Feminine Aspect of Deity and a representative thereof is accepted and believed in. Whilst all forms of ministration would be included in the activities of such groups, the underlying principle would be the furtherance throughout the world of compassionate humaneness in every walk of life—so overwhelmingly needed at the present time.[123]

Polidorus added: "Our Lady suggests inclusions in articles and books being newly reprinted for the Liberal Catholic Church, and certainly an article in *The Theosophist*, leaving all possible room for freedom of thought."[124]

Chapter 7. Mary in Esoteric Teachings

Marian Discipleship

The Christian vocation traditionally is envisioned as becoming a disciple of Jesus Christ. The Master Polidorus lent his full support to that ideal.[125] But he went on to say that becoming a disciple of Mary is equally valid: "Others may have found themselves also realizing beyond the slightest possible doubt, the existence of the Mother of Our Lord, the Blessed Lady Mary, and similarly devote themselves also to Her."[126] Again, both men and women may be eligible.

Earlier Geoffrey Hodson had written: "I now feel utterly sure and rededicate my life to Her service." And he encouraged others to do the same: "This ministration could become much more effective and general if increasing numbers of communities, groups, and individuals would especially recognize Our Lady, and both be gratefully recipient of Her benedictions and offer themselves as Her servers at the personal level."[127] Louis-Marie de Montfort might have reminded Hodson that the path to Mary leads ultimately to Christ; otherwise he would readily have agreed with him.

Service is the modus operandi at all levels. Mary, World Mother and "planetary Queen of the Angels," serves the Lord of the World, the Ancient of Days, "in what might be called, if one may so presume, His femininity-functions, extremely delicate and refined as they are in every kingdom."[128] For present purposes the Lord of the World can be identified with the Planetary Logos.[129] In service to her Logos, Mary has counterparts on other planets and in the solar system as a whole.

Correlating with the empowerment of women has been the desire to overcome patriarchy in institutional religion and to see the Divine in feminine as well as masculine terms. The impulse to explore the Feminine Aspect of Deity comes not just from the work of Christian and Jewish feminist theologians—though that work has contributed a great deal—but from a more general expansion of consciousness in both men and women across the human spectrum. Already raised to near-divine status in traditional Christianity and identified as the World Mother in esoteric Christianity, Mary clearly has a important place in any exploration of the Divine Feminine.

[1] For further information on western esotericism see John F. Nash, "Abraham Abulafia and the Ecstatic Kabbalah," *The Esoteric Quarterly* (Fall 2008), 51-64; "Hermeticism: Rise and Fall of an Esoteric System," Part I, *The Esoteric Quarterly* (Winter 2009), 39-51; Part II, *The Esoteric Quarterly* (Spring 2009), 33-42; "Occult Orders in Western Esotericism," *The Esoteric Quarterly* (Spring 2014), 75-104; "Themes in Western Esotericism," *The Esoteric Quarterly* (Fall 2014), 17-45.

[2] The major classical branches of yoga are *hatha yoga*, the yoga of physical postures; *pratyahara*, the withdrawal of consciousness from parts of the body; *pranayama*, yogic control of the breath; *bhakti yoga*, the yoga of devotion; *jnana yoga*, the yoga of knowledge; and *raja yoga*, the "kingly" yoga that integrates the other four. Some accounts replace pranayama by *laya yoga*, the dissolution of self into the supreme consciousness, or combine hatha yoga and pratyahara into one.

[3] John F. Nash, "Opportunities and Challenges of Christian Esotericism," *The Esoteric Quarterly* (Fall 2016), 21-44. See also: "Christianity's Role in a New World Religion," *The Esoteric Quarterly* (Spring 2006), 37-52.

[4] Here we use the terms interchangeably, though *adept* is the more general term for a fifth-degree initiate. Technically a *master* is an adept committed to working for the welfare of humankind; other adepts may be engaged in different kinds of work.

[5] Esoteric teachings make clear that the Hierarchy is concerned with souls, not personalities, and the Masters do not infringe upon freewill. Government, in the ordinary sense of the word, is left to human institutions.

[6] Geoffrey Hodson, *The Angelic Hosts*, Theosophical Publ. House, 1928, 38.

[7] Sandra Hodson (ed.), *Light of the Sanctuary: The Occult Diary of Geoffrey Hodson*, published posthumously, Theosophical Publishers, 1988, 413-414.

[8] See for example John F. Nash, "Origins and Evolution of the Tarot," *The Esoteric Quarterly* (Spring 2017), 67-98. Interestingly, Waite was raised Roman Catholic but left the church; Smith converted to Catholicism in her thirties.

[9] Helena I. Roerich, *Supermundane: The Inner Life*, Agni Yoga, book 1, 1938, §147.

[10] *Ibid.* The "mystery of His wanderings" may refer to the incident when the 12-year-old Jesus was found in the temple.

[11] *Ibid.*

[12] Charles Leadbeater, *Christian Gnosis*, Theosophical Publ. House, 1983/2011, 193. The work—originally targeted at the Liberal Catholic Church—was assembled from an incomplete manuscript and other papers in Leadbeater's files. The first edition appeared in 1983, nearly half

Chapter 7. Mary in Esoteric Teachings

a century after Leadbeater's death. Citations are from the current edition published in 2011. For a review of the book see: http://uriel.com/articles_etc/Misc%20files/EQ080112-End.pdf#page=5.

[13] S. Hodson (ed.), *Light of the Sanctuary*, 267.

[14] *Ibid.*, 115, 184, 210-212.

[15] Alice A. Bailey, *The Externalization of the Hierarchy*, Lucis Trust, 1957, 529.

[16] Anna Raimondi, *Conversations with Mary: Messages of Love, Healing, Hope, and Unity for Everyone*, New York: Atria, 2017, 63-64.

[17] The suggestion that Mary had already attained a major initiation could provide an esoteric interpretation of the Immaculate Conception.

[18] For example, Roger Bacon allegedly reincarnated as Francis Bacon. And according to Edgar Cayce, the Old Testament Joshua, famed warrior of the *Book of Joshua*, reincarnated as Yeshua the High Priest, mentioned in *Ezra* 3 and *Zechariah* 6:9–14, and then as Jesus of Nazareth. For further information on the previous lives of Jesus and Francis Bacon see Alice A. Bailey, *Initiation, Human & Solar*, Lucis Trust, 1922, 56, 58.

[19] S. Hodson (ed.), *Light of the Sanctuary*, 267-268. The monad, or "spirit," a fragment of the divine essence, is the highest element of the human constitution, transcending the personality and soul. See the discussion on human divinity later in the chapter.

[20] S. Hodson (ed.), *Light of the Sanctuary*, 267-268.

[21] See for example John F. Nash, "A Study of Gender, Part 1: Gender at the Human and Higher Levels, *The Esoteric Quarterly* (Fall 2017), 61-89.

[22] Today, many people take exception to the notion that the feminine polarity is "negative."

[23] S. Hodson (ed.), *Light of the Sanctuary*, 268.

[24] *Ibid.*

[25] *Ibid.*

[26] *Ibid.*, 283-284. "ALL ONENESS" was capitalized in the original. Note that in esoteric teachings *Logos* refers to God as a manifest being, not to Christ. The "Solar Logos" is God manifesting at the level of the solar system.

[27] Leadbeater, *Christian Gnosis*, 193.

[28] Charles W. Leadbeater, *The Masters and the Path*, Theosophical Publ. House, 1925, 288. Leadbeater made a similar point in *The World Mother as Symbol and Fact*, Theosophical Publishing House, 1928, 17-18.

[29] Leadbeater, *The World Mother as Symbol and Fact*, 1.

[30] Geoffrey Hodson, *The Brotherhood of Angels and Men*, Theosophical Publ. House, 1927, 5.

[31] *Ibid.*

[32] Corinne Heline, *The Blessed Virgin Mary: Her Life and Mission*, New Age Press, 1971, 106-107.

[33] *Ibid.*, 115.
[34] *Ibid.*, 78.
[35] S. Hodson (ed.), *Light of the Sanctuary*, 268.
[36] *Ibid..*
[37] Raimondi, *Conversations with Mary*, 32.
[38] Geoffrey Hodson, *The Angelic Hosts*, Theosophical Publ. House, 1928, 7.
[39] *Ibid.*, 20-21.
[40] *Ibid.*, 21.
[41] S. Hodson (ed.), *Light of the Sanctuary*, 421.
[42] *The Bahir* §104, (trans.: Aryeh Kaplan), Weiser, 1998, 39.
[43] A *principle* would not itself be a monad but would express the monadic life of the higher being of whom it was a manifestation.
[44] Here, *avatara* is used as the feminine form of the masculine *avatar*. In Hinduism and Buddhism, avatars and avataras typically are considered to be manifestations or incarnations of divine beings, carrying out specific missions on Earth. The Sanskrit word *avatar* literally means "descent."
[45] John F. Nash, "Great Esotericists of the Past: Anna Bonus Kingsford (1846-1888)," *The Esoteric Quarterly* (Winter 2012), 76-78.
[46] Anna Kingsford, *Clothed with the Sun*, 2/e, Watkins, 1889, 30.
[47] *Ibid.*, 31.
[48] Helena I. Roerich. *Leaves of Morya's Garden*, vol. II, §220. Agni Yoga Society, 1925, 69.
[49] *Ibid.*, §138, 36.
[50] See for example Bailey, *The Externalization of the Hierarchy*.
[51] Helena I. Roerich, *Agni Yoga*, § 20, §60, Agni Yoga Society, 1929, 20, 45
[52] Helena I. Roerich, *Fiery World*, vol. I, 663, Agni Yoga Society, 1933.
[53] Helena I. Roerich, "Mother of the World," *Letters of Helena I. Roerich*, vol. I, Agni Yoga Society, January 9, 1935. Roerich may have been referring specifically to her husband Nicholas' painting *Mother of the World* (1924), now at the Roerich Museum, Moscow, Russia.
[54] Annie W. Besant, *Esoteric Christianity or The Lesser Mysteries*, 2/e, Theosophical Publ House, 1905, 140. In the 2006 edition this quote appears on pp. 109-110.
[55] See for example *Proverbs* 8:22-30; *Wisdom of Solomon* 7:25-26, 29; *Ecclesiasticus* 24:13-16.
[56] Nibaran Chandra Basu, "Dhurga: The World-Mother Aspect of God." *The Theosophist* (January 1927), 433-440; February 1927, 537-545.
[57] Annie W. Besant, "The New Annunciation," *The Theosophist*, (vol. 49, June 1928), 278. See also Gregory Tillett, *The Elder Brother: A Biography of Charles Webster Leadbeater*, Routledge, 2016, 230.
[58] Besant, "The New Annunciation."

[59] Leadbeater, *The World Mother as Symbol and Fact*, 52-53.
[60] *Ibid.*, 1.
[61] Leadbeater, *Christian Gnosis*, 193,
[62] Hodson, *The Angelic Hosts*, 36-37. *Planetary Logos* might have been a better choice than Solar Logos, but members of the Theosophical Society paid little attention to the former.
[63] *Ibid.*, 37.
[64] S. Hodson (ed.), *Light of the Sanctuary*, 82.
[65] *Ibid.*, 116.
[66] *Ibid.*, 189 Italics in original.
[67] *Ibid.*, 268. The Hindu goddess' name more commonly is spelled *Parvati*. It is unclear what Hodson meant by "true Kwan [Kuan] Yin."
[68] *Ibid.*, 285.
[69] *Ibid.*, 284.
[70] Leadbeater, *The World Mother as Symbol and Fact*, 1.
[71] An organization chart of the Planetary Hierarchy is shown in Bailey, *Initiation, Human & Solar*, 49. A similar chart can be found in Leadbeater, *The Masters and the Path*, 286.
[72] Sandra Hodson (ed.), *Illuminations of the Mystery Tradition: Compiled from the Writings of Geoffrey Hodson*, Theosophical Publishing House, 1992, 70.
[73] Kuan Yin emerged as a female personage in Chinese Buddhism in about the 11th century CE, suggesting that she was a later avatara than Mary.
[74] Bailey, *The Externalization of the Hierarchy*, 291. Capitalization in original.
[75] *Ibid.*
[76] Alice A. Bailey, *Esoteric Healing*, Lucis, 1953, 362-363.
[77] Rudolf Steiner, "The Nature of the Virgin Sophia and of The Holy Spirit," lecture, Hamburg, Germany, May 31, 2008. Included in *The Gospel of St John* (transl.: M. B. Morges), ch. 12. Online: https://wn.rsarchive.org/Lectures/GA103/English/AP1962/19080531p01.html. Last accessed Feb. 20, 2021.
[78] *Ibid.*
[79] The astral body, sometimes referred to as the "sentient body," is the second of the three *bodies*, or vehicles, that comprise the personality. It is the seat of the emotions and desires.
[80] Steiner, "The Nature of the Virgin Sophia and of The Holy Spirit."
[81] Valentin Tomberg (attrib. to), *Meditations on the Tarot: a Journey into Christian Hermeticism* (transl.: R. Powell), Element, 1985/1993, 281.
[82] *Ibid.*, 282-283. Parenthesis original. Capitalization removed.
[83] John F. Nash, "Service Ideals in the Rosicrucian Movement," *The Esoteric Quarterly* (Winter 2005), 33-42.

[84] Heline seemed to confuse the Immaculate Conception with the Virgin Birth, despite a discussion of the terms earlier in the book. Compare Heline, *The Blessed Virgin Mary*, 52, 65-66, and 91ff.
[85] Heline, *The Blessed Virgin Mary*, 90.
[86] *Ibid.*, 142.
[87] "Mother Meera" (1960–) is not to be confused with Mirra Alfassa (1878–1973), known to her followers as "The Mother." The latter worked closely with Sri Aurobindo.
[88] Andrew Harvey, *Return of the Mother*, Tarcher/Putnam, 2001, 343.
[89] *Ibid.*
[90] Andrew Harvey & Anne Baring, *The Divine Feminine*, Conari Press, 1996, 104.
[91] *Ibid.*, 106.
[92] Heline, *The Blessed Virgin Mary*, 109.
[93] S. Hodson (ed.), *Light of the Sanctuary*, 268.
[94] Raimondi, *Conversations with Mary*, 32.
[95] "Our Lady's Latest Second-of-the-Month Message": https://www.medjugorje.com/medjugorje-messages/latest-2-message.html. Last accessed Feb. 13, 2020.
[96] Leadbeater, *Christian Gnosis*, 194.
[97] Leadbeater, *The World Mother as Symbol and Fact*, 1.
[98] See for example John H. Chamberlayne, "The Development of Kuan Yin: Chinese Goddess of Mercy," *Numen* (vol. 9, Jan., 1962), 45-52.
[99] Besant, "The New Annunciation."
[100] Hodson, *The Brotherhood of Angels and Men*, 5-6.
[101] Hodson, *The Angelic Hosts*, 38.
[102] *Ibid.*
[103] Hodson, *The Miracle of Birth*, 75-76.
[104] S. Hodson (ed.), *Light of the Sanctuary*, 414-415.
[105] *Ibid.*, 355.
[106] *Ibid.*, 284-285.
[107] *Genesis* 3:16.
[108] Hodson, *The Brotherhood of Angels and Men*, 5.
[109] S. Hodson (ed.), *Light of the Sanctuary*, 285
[110] *Ibid.*, 414-415.
[111] *Ibid.*, 375. Parenthesis in original.
[112] Besant, "The New Annunciation."
[113] S. Hodson (ed.), *Light of the Sanctuary*, 116.
[114] *Ibid.*, 365.
[115] *Ibid.*, 414.
[116] *Ibid.*, 460.
[117] *Ibid.*, 341.
[118] *Ibid.*

Chapter 7. Mary in Esoteric Teachings

---

[119] Hodson, *The Brotherhood of Angels and Men*, 5-6.
[120] Geoffrey Hodson, "The Radiation of Power," *The Theosophist* (vol. 49, Oct. 1927), 67ff.
[121] Hodson, *The Miracle of Birth*, 65.
[122] S. Hodson (ed.), *Light of the Sanctuary*, 269. "Einzedelin" is a reference to Einsiedeln Abbey, Switzerland, dedicated to Our Lady of the Hermits. Its Chapel of Our Lady, said to have been consecrated miraculously by Mary in 948, was a favored pilgrimage destination. A statue of the Madonna and Child, placed in the chapel in the 15th century, became a focus of great devotional attention.
[123] *Ibid.*
[124] *Ibid.* It does not seem that Hodson published anything in response to those exhortations.
[125] *Ibid.*, 375.
[126] *Ibid.*, 375-376.
[127] *Ibid.*, 268-269.
[128] *Ibid.*, 355.
[129] For a more detailed discussion of the Lord of the World see John F. Nash, "Sanat Kumara," *The Beacon* (March 2002), 13-20. Available online: http://uriel.com/articles_etc/Beacon%20files/Beacon20020304.pdf.

Mary: Adept, Queen, Mother, Priestess

Chapter 8
Mary and the Feminine Face of God

Chapter 8 explores humanity's hunger for a Feminine Aspect of Deity and asks whether Mary might have a connection to that Feminine Aspect. Institutional Judaism, Christianity and Islam envisioned God in purely masculine terms, distinguishing them from the religions that preceded and surrounded them. Yet the Divine Feminine survived in the shadows of biblical Judaism and took more definite form in Christianity. Modern esoteric teachings absorbed valuable concepts from Hinduism, which acknowledges feminine manifestations from the highest levels of the Godhead.

The Divine Feminine seems to be revealing more of herself to the modern world. She may soon lift her veil, allowing Mary's own position to take on new significance in the divine order. Among the topics discussed in this chapter are efforts to insert a feminine element into the Trinity, Mary and the feminine archetype, and the enigmatic personage of Sophia.

Introduction

This chapter seeks greater understanding of the Feminine Face of God—a topic that has received scant attention in two millennia of Christian doctrinal formulation. A major objective is to see if Mary has a gender-specific divine prototype, or a divine principle to whom she should aspire. Although precedents for feminine depictions of God can be found in Judeo-Christianity and elsewhere, they rarely enjoyed authoritative endorsement. Yet Mary is sometimes confused or conflated with the semidivine, or divine, personage Sophia. And Theosophical teachings give prominence to the World Mother.

What do We Mean by Divine?

Christian doctrine ostenseibly draws a sharp dichotomy between creature and creator, between human and divine. Yet the Eastern Orthodox doctrine of *theosis* envisions that, by virtue of the Incarnation, members of the human family can become "partakers of the divine nature."[1] Russian Orthodox theologian Sergei Bulgakov (1871–1944) affirmed that Mary, "has achieved perfect theosis."[2]

Esoteric teachings speak of a continuum of consciousness extending from the densest physical matter to the Godhead, the most transcendent aspect of Deity of which we can conceive. Evolutionary progress in every kingdom is marked by movement up that continuum. From this perspective "divine" is not a separate category from "human" but a position on the continuum significantly closer to the Godhead. We might be considered "divine" relative to an earthworm, while Christ is divine relative to us.

Investing all members of the human lifewave with divinity is an individualized *monad*, a divine spark, a unique fragment of divine essence. Each of us has—or at the very center of our being *is*—a divine monad. The monad is distinct from the *soul*. The soul is created when the monad descends into matter: the soul is "that entity which is brought into being when the spirit aspect and the matter aspect are related to each other."[3] It is "the form-building aspect," the "attractive factor" that enables us "to develop and grow so as to house more adequately the indwelling life, and which drives all God's creatures forward along the path of evolution, through one kingdom after another, towards an eventual goal and a glorious consummation."[4]

We are triune beings: body, soul and spirit. In the *Magnificat*, Mary referred to both soul and spirit: "My soul doth magnify the Lord, And my spirit hath rejoiced in God my Savior."[5] Paul prayed that "your whole spirit and soul and body be preserved blameless unto the coming of our Lord Jesus Christ."[6] In scripture, different Greek words were used for soul and spirit, showing the intention to distinguish between them. We are indeed triune beings,[7] made in the image of a triune God.

Disregarding the scriptural testimony, the Fourth Council of Constantinople (869) decreed that we are just body and soul; it also declared that the soul's purpose is merely to "animate the flesh."[8] The council's decree—one of the most unfortunate and ill-advised ever issued—was binding only on the Latin church, but it contaminated the whole of Christianity. The great majority of Christians today believe that we are nothing more than body and soul.

A few brave individuals in western Christianity defied persecution to teach the truth of the monad. For example, German theologian Meister Eckhart (c.1260–c.1328) spoke of the "tiny spark of the divine nature, a divine light, a ray and an imprint of the divine nature."[9] In a more relaxed theological environment American mystic Thomas Merton (1915–1968) spoke of "a point of nothingness" at the center of our being, "which belongs entirely to God." He likened it to "a pure diamond, blazing with the invisible light of heaven."[10]

Outside Christianity the concept enjoys wide acceptance. In esoteric Judaism the monad is equivalent to the *yehidah*; in Hinduism it corresponds to the *atman*. In esoteric teachings the monad is defined as "the focus or heart in any individual being, of all its divine, spiritual, and intellectual powers and attributes—the immortal part of its being."[11]

For most of us the monad, our God-given divinity, is hidden in the folds of the form life and our concerns with day-to-day existence. Spiritual progress allows more of that divinity to shine forth. A Hasidic Jewish writer explained: "Each of us possesses a Holy Spark, but not everyone exhibits it to the best advantage. It is like the diamond which cannot cast its luster if buried in the earth. But when disclosed in its appropriate setting, there is light."[12] Someone who has attained adeptship—which closely parallels theosis—expresses her or his divinity to a far greater degree than does humanity at large. Mary is a prime example. Adepts' divinity shines brightly, but it is still dim compared with that of beings like the Planetary or Solar Logos.

The monad is not only the investment of divinity in each of us; it is also our ultimate locus of identity. The human monad is the very heart of our being. No matter how many bodies we may incarnate in, or how many vehicles of other kinds we may inhabit, we shall be that monad throughout our entire evolutionary journey—until the end of the manvantara when all manifestation is withdrawn into the Godhead.

The Feminine Face of God

What precisely do we mean by the Feminine Face of God? It is God revealed as, and/or perceived as, feminine; in part it is God expressing the feminine archetypes of Queen and Mother.

In antiquity people may have perceived the Divine Feminine in the Moon, the sea, a forest, or the wind; or in a quality like fertility, nurturing or compassion. Perhaps the element or quality suggested femaleness, or female attributes were projected onto it. Over time it acquired a name and became a personage, an object of worship, a goddess. Many people viewed the Earth as the Great Mother.

Goddesses are created or discovered. This does not necessarily mean that deities are mere figments of primitive imagination. The Godhead ever seeks to reveal itself, and deities may emerge from the intersection of human aspiration and divine revelation. The divine essence can ensoul a form created by human aspiration.

Cultures with philosophical or theological traditions place less emphasis on the forms and greater emphasis on the Godhead and its manifestations. Christianity developed the sophisticated Trinitarian theology of the manifest God, but it lacked a feminine element. In Vedantic Hinduism the first manifestation of the Godhead is understood to be feminine. In the Kabbalah an early manifestation is a masculine–feminine duality. In these latter systems the Divine Feminine is interwoven with the very concept of God.

Pre-Christian Expressions of the Divine Feminine

Goddesses of Antiquity

The feminist movement of the 1970s and '80s popularized the belief that, in prehistory, the Great Goddess reigned supreme in a peaceful, matriarchal society. The Goddess was identified both with the Earth and with motherhood. Monica Sjöö and Barbara Mor declared that goddess worship emerged naturally from the child–mother relationship. Furthermore: "In matriarchal society ... there is a close identification with the collective group of mothers, with Mother Earth, and with the Cosmic Mother."[13] Lithuanian-American archaeologist Marija Gimbutas asserted that the goddess culture came to an end when invading Indo-European tribes from Central Asia imposed a warlike patriarchy.[14]

While the accuracy of the primeval scenario is now questioned, male warrior gods, like Indra, Yahweh, Ares, Mars and Odin, did gain ascendancy over the centuries. They represented physical strength and prowess in battle, to which men aspired and on which their own, their family's, and their tribe's survival often depended.

Even in increasingly male-dominated pantheons, some powerful goddesses held their own. A few reigned alone, like the Hindu Ushas, goddess of the dawn; the Assyrian Ishtar; the Greek Athena; and the Roman Cybele, known as *Magna Mater* ("Great Mother"). The Celtic Danu and the Aztec Coatlicue were the mothers of male gods. Others became their consorts.[15] In Egypt Osiris and Isis were both husband and wife and siblings. They and their son Horus were revered as the "holy family" of Egyptian religion. After Osiris' descent to the underworld, Isis was revered as a mother goddess, and artwork of her holding the infant Horus provided a prototype for the Christian Madonna and Child.

Of particular relevance to the present study was the ancient Sumerian fertility goddess Inanna. Inanna was known as the "Lady of Heaven," or "Queen of Heaven," and was associated with the planet Venus and the eight-pointed star.[16] Inanna had a sister, Ereshkigal, "Queen of the Underworld," whose characteristics were Inanna's polar opposites.[17] Inanna probably inspired the Chaldean–Hebrew goddess Asherah; Ereshkigal may have inspired another Hebrew personage, Lilith.

Asherah

Following a divine command Abraham and his family left their home in Ur of the Chaldees and journeyed to the Land of Canaan. His god was *El*, or *El Shaddai*, ("the High God", "God of the Mountain," or "Almighty God"). For example, "I am the Almighty God (*El Shaddai*); walk before me";[18] "I appeared unto Abraham, unto Isaac, and unto Jacob, by the name of God Almighty (*El Shaddai*)."[19]

El had a consort, Asherah. The mother goddess Asherah was worshipped in various parts of the Middle East; she and El allegedly gave birth to a pantheon of gods, from seventy to eighty-eight in number.[20] Asherah was also a goddess of the trees, or of forest groves, and her cult symbol was a stylistic tree: a wooden post. Asherah might have been related to the Semitic mother-goddess Ashtoreth, or Astarte, who also appears in the Old Testament.[21]

Around the time of Moses Judaism embraced a strict masculine monotheism. The name of the Israelite tribal deity was written: *YHWH*; we know it as Yahweh.[22] While El Shaddai was absorbed into Yahweh, the prophets and priests found no place for Asherah. Yet worship of Asherah seems to have continued below the surface of institutional Judaism, at least until the Exile.

Asherah appears some forty times in the Old Testament. The same word was used for the goddess and for one of her sacred trees, groves, or ritual posts; and since Hebrew has no capitals, distinguishing between them is not always easy. But at least five instances can been identified where the context clearly indicates a reference to the goddess.[23] Even then most translators hesitated to name her, instead rendering *asherah* as "the grove" or another cult symbol—or retaining the Hebrew word uncapitalized.[24]

The prophets and temple priests regarded the worship of Asherah as idolatrous and continually tried to suppress it by destroying her cult symbols. In *Judges* 8 Yahweh commanded Gideon to "cut down the grove [*asherah*]," next to an altar of Baal, and to "offer a burnt sacrifice with the wood."[25] Gideon had to destroy the shrine in the night to evade the people's wrath. Similarly, in *2 Chronicles* 14 Asa, king of Judah, found favor with God when he "took away the altars of the strange gods, and the high places, and brake down the images, and cut down the groves [*asherim*]."[26]

Many of Asherah's devotees seem to have been women, even royal women. In *1 Kings* 15 we read that Asa deposed Maachah, the queen mother, on grounds of idolatry and burned her statue of Asherah.[27] In *2 Kings* 23 King Josiah ordered Hilkiah the high priest to destroy cult objects, including asherim, in multiple locations.[28] The text also mentions that "women ... wove hangings for the grove [*asherah*]" and complains about "the high places that were before Jerusalem, which were on the right hand of the mount of corruption, which Solomon the king of Israel had builded for Ashtoreth."[29] A "high place" typically was a sacred mound, perhaps even a ziggurat, on which devotees conducted rituals and conversed with their deity.

Jeremiah the prophet complained about ritual sacrifices to a particular goddess as well as to unnamed deities:

Chapter 8. Mary and the Feminine Face of God

> Seest thou not what they do in the cities of Judah and in the streets of Jerusalem? The children gather wood, and the fathers kindle the fire, and the women knead their dough, to make cakes to the queen of heaven, and to pour out drink offerings unto other gods, that they may provoke me to anger."[30]

Jeremiah did not identify the "queen of heaven"; the title once belonged to Inanna but here, most likely, it referred to Asherah. A later chapter in *Jeremiah* records that the people defended the ritual sacrifices, claiming that Israel's fortunes had deteriorated after the prophet forbade them: "[E]ver since we stopped burning incense to the Queen of Heaven and pouring out drink offerings to her, we have had nothing and have been perishing by sword and famine."[31] The sacrificial offering of cakes to a goddess foreshadowed the rites of the Collyridians—and perhaps their Celtic successors—mentioned in Chapter 5.

The frequency with which priests and prophets spoke out against the cult of Asherah testifies to its broad extent and endurance. Some scholars have detected signs that Asherah survived in popular Judaic devotion until late biblical times, possibly as Yahweh's consort.[32]

Chokmah/Sophia

The grammatically feminine *chokmah* ("wisdom") began simply as the quality of being wise. By the late biblical period, however, it had become personified as a feminine individuality whom we can legitimately capitalize as Chokmah. He Greek name was *Sophia*. English translations render it as "Wisdom" and use the feminine pronoun.

Chokmah made several appearances in scripture. In *Proverbs* 8 she boldly declared:

> The Lord possessed me in the beginning of his way, before his works of old. I was set up from everlasting, from the beginning, or ever the earth was. When there were no depths, I was brought forth; when there were no fountains abounding with water. Before the mountains were settled, before the hills was I brought forth.... Then I was by him, as one brought up with him [Hebrew: *aman*]: and I was daily his delight [*riri*] rejoicing always before him."[33]

Some translations render *aman* as "master worker" or "architect," while others suggest "trusted confidante," even "darling." *Riri* generally means "object of delight, desire or pleasure." In the very next chapter of *Proverbs* Chokmah invited the townspeople to a proto-

Eucharist: "Come, eat of my bread, and drink of the wine which I have mingled."[34]

Proverbs is part of the canonical Hebrew Bible. The personified Chokmah is also conspicuous in the Old Testament Apocrypha, written after about 200 BCE.[35] For example we read in the *Wisdom of Solomon* 7: "[S]he is more beautiful than the sun, and above all the order of stars: being compared with the light, she is found before it.[36] In the next chapter the Lord declared: "I loved her, and sought her out from my youth, I desired to make her my spouse, and I was a lover of her beauty."[37] Yahweh may have succeeded in making Chokmah his consort. In Michelangelo's famous painting, *The Creation of Adam* (c.1508–1512), God the Father has his arm around a young woman; who could this be but Chokmah?[38]

The *Wisdom of Solomon*, like most of the Old Testament, was written in Hebrew. But *Ecclesiasticus*, also known as *Sirach*, was written in Greek, and there we see Chokmah confidently using her new name, Sophia. We also see a possible link with Asherah. In *Ecclesiasticus* 24, Sophia not only repeated the claim: "He [the Creator of all things] created me from the beginning before the world,"[39] she also declared her affinity for trees:

> I was exalted like a cedar in Libanus, and as a cypress tree upon the mountains of Hermon. I was exalted like a palm tree in Engaddi, and as a rose plant in Jericho, as a fair olive tree in a pleasant field, and grew up as a plane tree by the water.... As the turpentine tree I stretched out my branches, and my branches are the branches of honor and grace."[40]

Sophia even identified herself as a mother figure: "I am the mother of fair love, and fear, and knowledge, and holy hope: I therefore, being eternal, am given to all my children which are named of him [the Most High]."[41] Sophia bore Yahweh's sons and daughters, presumably the Jewish people.

Hellenic Jews seemed comfortable with the notion that Sophia might be a semidivine, or even divine, personage who helped God create the heavens and the earth. Psychologist Carl Jung saw Sophia as an archetypal goddess who softened Yahweh and helped him develop compassion.[42] We shall take up Sophia's story again later in the chapter.

Chapter 8. Mary and the Feminine Face of God

Other Expressions of the Divine Feminine

The grammatically feminine *ruach* ("spirit," "breath," "wind") appears frequently in the Hebrew Bible. We even find *ruach ha-kodesh* ("the holy spirit"); for example: "Cast me not away from thy presence; and take not thy holy spirit [*ruach ha-kodesh*] from me."[43] Ruach ha-kodesh was not a personage but a divine presence, force or activity. Notwithstanding, institutional Christianity would later adopt her, personify her, and change her gender.

In the Rabbinic period, following destruction of the temple, we find the feminine *shekinah*, the indwelling glory of God, contrasting with but also complementing *kavod*, the masculine transcendent glory. *Shekinah* was derived from the root verb *shakan* ("to dwell or abide"), often used to denote God's abiding presence in sacred locations like the Ark of the Covenant, the Holy of Holies, or Mount Sinai. For example in *Exodus* we read: "[T]the glory of the Lord abode [*shakan*] upon mount Sinai."[44] And in *Isaiah*: "For thus saith the high and lofty One that inhabiteth [shakan] eternity, whose name is Holy; I dwell [*shakan*] in the high and holy place."[45]

The Jewish nation was often personified. "Daughter of Zion" appears multiple times in the Old Testament; variants are "Daughter of Jerusalem," "Daughter of Judah," and even "Daughter of Babylon." In *Zephaniah* we read: "Sing, O daughter of Zion; shout, O Israel; be glad and rejoice with all the heart, O daughter of Jerusalem."[46] *Isaiah* comments on the daughter's virginity: "The virgin, the daughter of Zion, hath despised thee, and laughed thee to scorn; the daughter of Jerusalem hath shaken her head at thee."[47] In *Amos* and in *Jeremiah* we find "Virgin of Israel," for example, "Again I will build thee, and thou shalt be built, O virgin of Israel: thou shalt again be adorned with thy tabrets, and shalt go forth in the dances of them that make merry."[48] Israel is God's chosen one, the virgin betrothed to Yahweh, needing protection lest she go astray or be ravished by enemies.

The Divine Feminine in Christianity

This section will examine the divination of Mary in Christianity and also the evolution of Sophia to her modern status as a goddess. But we start with related issues associated with the Feminine Face of God in Christian doctrine.

The Godhead

In antiquity the Godhead was often envisioned as a divine ancestor or divine parent, or jointly as a divine father and mother. In biblical Judaism, which was not a theological religion, few people would have suggested that a more transcendent aspect of God lay beyond Yahweh, even though the latter was also their tribal deity. Christianity did become a theological religion, but, again, transcendence was sacrificed, and the concept of the Godhead remained largely undeveloped.

The Greek word *Theotes* ("Godhead") appears in the New Testament, and interestingly it is grammatically feminine.[49] The fourth-century First Council of Constantinople affirmed belief in "a single Godhead of Father and Son and holy Spirit."[50] The Athanasian Creed, which dates from the fifth or sixth century, affirmed that "the Godhead of the Father, of the Son, and of the Holy Ghost, is all one, the Glory equal, the Majesty co-eternal."[51]

Peter Lombard (c.1100–1160), bishop of Paris, interpreted "a single Godhead of Father and Son and holy Spirit" to mean that the Godhead is the *essence* of God, unifying but distinct from the three persons. Lombard was criticized by Joachim of Fiore on the grounds that he was turning the Trinity into a quaternity—strictly prohibited by doctrinal tradition but, as we shall see, possibly permitted by the Nicene Creed.[52] Today we might argue on Lombard's behalf that the divine essence pertains to the unmanifest God, while the persons of the Trinity comprise the manifest God; but Christian theology was, and remains, vague concerning any such distinction. In multiple respects "God" is a surprisingly vague concept in Christianity.[53]

Most Christians nominally accept the decrees of the First Council of Constantinople, and the Athanasian Creed is occasionally recited in the liturgy. But since Peter Lombard's time theologians have been reluctant to speak of the Godhead for fear of stumbling onto the minefields of heresy.

The Trinity

Christianity envisions God in triune form. Trinitarian doctrine emerged at a time when proto-institutional Christianity was becoming increasingly Greek in outlook. Plato had taught that an underlying "threeness" pervaded the whole of reality, and this threeness urged the construction of a trinity.

Chapter 8. Mary and the Feminine Face of God

The church readily identified the first two *hypostases* (Greek singular: *hypostasis*, or "person") of the Trinity as the Father and the Son but struggled to identify the third.[54] Eventually two candidates emerged. Theophilus, bishop of Antioch (c.117–c.181 CE), to whom we owe the very term "Trinity," nominated *Sophia*, the Greek name of the Hebrew *Chokmah*.[55] Irenaeus (c.130–c.202) and Paul of Samosata (200–275) also supported Sophia. But Justin Martyr (c.100–c.165) and Platonist philosopher Athenagoras of Athens (c.133–c.190) nominated *Pneuma Hagion* ("Holy Spirit"), the Greek translation of *ruach ha-kodesh*.

Both candidates had scriptural support, but ruach ha-kodesh had the advantage of its appearance at Pentecost, deemed to have been the birth event of Christianity. Pneuma Hagion was selected, creating the now-familiar Trinity of Father, Son, and Holy Spirit. That choice faced challenges, however, and much work remained to build a robust trinitarian doctrine.

One challenge was to explain how the impersonal *ruach ha-kodesh* could be placed in the same category as the anthropomorphic Father and Son. In the account of Pentecost, the Holy Spirit was perceived as "a sound from heaven as of a rushing mighty wind [that] filled all the house where they were sitting. And there appeared unto them cloven tongues like as of fire, and it sat upon each of them."[56] Nobody has suggested that a *person* descended on the apostles. Some commentators would argue that convincing personification of the Holy Spirit has still not been accomplished.

Then there was the issue of gender. *Ruach* was a feminine noun. And the extracanonical *Gospel of the Hebrews*, conventionally dated to the early second century, quotes Jesus as referring to "my mother the Holy Spirit."[57] But the Greek *Pneuma* was neuter; and its Latin form *Spiritus* was masculine. Institutional Christianity offered a trinity consisting of two obviously masculine components and a third that was at best neuter.[58]

The Nicene Creed, drafted by the Council of Nicaea (325) and finalized by the First Council of Constantinople (381),[59] decreed that God the Son was "begotten of the Father before all worlds." It then decreed belief "in the Holy Spirit, the Lord and Giver of life, who proceeds from the Father, who with the Father and the Son together is worshiped and glorified."[60] Interestingly, the Creed did not state that the Father, Son, and Holy Spirit were the *only* "persons" of divine manifestation. As worded, it did not exclude the possibility that additional persons remained unidentified; the notion of a Trinity was simply taken for granted, and Peter Lombard's contemporaries did not give him the benefit of the doubt.

The Nicene Creed did not give God the Son a mother, comparable to the Egyptian Isis. Choice of the masculinized ruach ha-kodesh as Third Person of the Trinity eliminated that possibility. But Sophia might not have provided a "God the Mother" either; she was also masculinized at times in the early church.

Trinitarian doctrine, as we know it today, is contained in the formula: God is three *hypostases* ("persons") in one *ousia* ("essence"). It built upon the Nicene Creed but primarily was the work of Athanasias of Alexandria (c.297–373) and the three Cappadocian Fathers: Basil the Great (330–379), his brother Gregory of Nyssa (c.335–c.395), and Gregory of Nazianzus (329–389). Their work is regarded as authoritative throughout most of Christianity.[61]

Reintroducing a Feminine Element into the Trinity

The Nicene Creed identified the Third Person of the Trinity, and linguistic and other factors conspired to ensure that the Third Person would not be feminine. But not everyone saw the matter as settled. Numerous attempts were made, and continue to be made, to reintroduce a feminine element into the Trinity.

In the sixth or seventh century "Mariamite" sects in Arabia allegedly believed in a trinity of God, Jesus and Mary. Muhammad may have come into contact with them, leading to a rebuke in the *Qur'an*: "And beware the Day when Allah will say, 'O Jesus, Son of Mary, did you say to the people: Take me and my mother as deities besides Allah?'"[62]

Another strategy was to project feminine qualities onto Christ or even onto God the Father. Anselm of Canterbury (1033–1109) prayed to Christ: "like a mother you gather your people to you; you are gentle with us as a mother with her children."[63] Anchorite Julian of Norwich (1342–c.1416) famously proclaimed: "[A]s truly as God is our Father, so truly is God our Mother."[64]

Renaissance physician and alchemist Paracelsus (c.1493–1541) was more specific. He suggested that the First Person of the Trinity was a male–female duality: "God made from himself from his person a woman." But this was no ordinary woman, she was a goddess (German: *ein Göttin*), "a Queen." In turn the Son and Holy Spirit proceeded from this divine duality: "[T]he Son is born of two persons, namely from God and the goddess, the Holy Spirit from God the Father and from the Son."[65] Commenting on Paracelsus' words, modern scholar Andrew Weeks concluded: "The intention here is clearly to establish a place in the divine family for a higher prototype of the Virgin Mary, a 'goddess,' with whom the Father generates the divine Son in heaven, prior to the birth of Jesus as God and man in the world."[66]

Apart perhaps from the Mariamites, few people have tried to incorporate Mary into the Trinity itself. But Lutheran theologian Ludwig Feuerbach (1804–1872) affirmed: "[T]he Virgin Mary fits in perfectly with the relations of the Trinity, since she conceives without man the Son whom the Father begets without woman; so that thus the Holy Virgin is a necessary, inherently requisite antithesis to the Father in the bosom of the Trinity."[67] He echoed the sentiments of Julian of Norwich in attributing feminine qualities to God the Son, but also declared: "the Son implicitly urges upon us the need of a real feminine being."[68]

Russian theologian and scientist Pavel Florensky (1882–1937) and Orthodox priest Sergei Bulgakov (1871–1944) tried to reintroduce Sophia into the Trinity, not to replace the Holy Spirit but as "a fourth, creaturely, and therefore nonconsubstantial Person."[69] Sophia "enters into the interior of the Trinity, and enters into communion with Divine Love."[70] Church authorities reacted negatively, complaining—as their western forebears had done in the case of Peter Lombard—that Florensky and Bulgakov were turning the Trinity into a quaternity.[71]

We shall see that Theosophist Annie Besant (1847–1933) had no qualms about turning the Trinity in to a quaternity. But Bulgakov retreated to a position that Sophia is the "nonhypostatic essence" of God... neither a fourth hypostasis nor an expression of any one of them to the exclusion of the others."[72] Sophia manifested through the three Trinitarian persons; her expression through the Son and Holy Spirit is "immediate," while the "relation of Sophia to the Father is mediated through his relation to the other hypostases."[73] Bulgakov's ecclesiastical superiors were still not satisfied.

A more cautious approach was to leave the Trinity intact and simply recast the Third Person as feminine. A twelfth-century fresco of the Trinity in the Chapel of St James, Urschalling, Upper Bavaria, depicts the Holy Spirit as female. A detail is shown in Figure 8.1.

Figure 8.1

Twelfth-century fresco of the Trinity in the Chapel of St James, Urschalling, Upper Bavaria, depicting the Holy Spirit as female.

In our own time Benedictine monk Bede Griffiths (1906–1993) confidently identified the Holy Spirit as the feminine aspect of Deity:

> It is in the Holy Spirit that the feminine aspect of the Godhead can be most clearly seen. She is ... immanent in all creation, the receptive power of the Godhead. The world comes forth from the Father, the eternal Ground of Being, in his Word.... In him the ideas and archetypes of all created beings are hidden, he is the exemplar of all creation. But it is the Spirit who conceives these "ideas" in her maternal womb and brings them forth in creation. She is the Great Mother ... who nourishes the seeds of all beings and makes them grow.[74]

Ingeniously, Griffiths managed to identify the Holy Spirit as the Divine Mother without needing to reorder the persons of the Trinity to "Father, Mother, Son." Bede also related the Mother directly to Mary: "Still more, she [the Holy Spirit] is the mothering Spirit in humankind, who receives the Word, the Wisdom of God, in her heart, of whom in the Christian tradition Mary is the figure, receiving the Word of God in her heart and bringing him forth in his earthly manifestation."[75] The British-born Griffiths settled in India and adopted the life of a Swami; his work showed the potential for incorporating South Asian religious concepts into Christian teachings.[76]

The Moravian Brethren and the Unity School of Christianity affirm that the Third Person of the Trinity is feminine. Even in mainline denominations, prominent individuals use the feminine pronoun to refer to the Holy Spirit, basing their stance on the feminine gender of the Hebrew *ruach*. The Church of Jesus Christ of Latter-Day Saints (Mormon) affirms belief in the "Mother in Heaven"; she and the Heavenly Father serve as the spiritual parents of all humanity.[77]

A Female Messiah

From the High Middle Ages onward, occasional suggestions were made that a divine female messenger or messiah would come to Earth. The Black Death, the Renaissance, the Reformation, and the Counter-Reformation provided unsettling environments in which such suggestions could take root. Sometimes the divine intervention was linked to a particular human woman.

Italian noblewoman Guglielma di Boemia ("Wilhelmina of Bohemia," 1210–1281) prophesied the end of time and the incarnation of the Holy Spirit in female form, possibly her own resurrected self. Her followers in Milan, known as "Guglielmites," planned to establish a female college of cardinals and elected a nun, Maifreda di Pirovano, pope. Maifreda began celebrating Mass. Needless to say, the sect was suppressed. The Inquisition charged thirty Guglielmites with heresy in 1300. Guglielma was condemned posthumously, and Maifreda and several followers were burned at the stake.

Italian writer and philosopher Dante Alighieri (c.1265–1321) had a lifelong obsession for Beatrice Portinari. Although Beatrice married another man, Dante used her as inspiration for the character "Beatrice" in his *Divine Comedy*.[78] As the representative of divine revelation, faith and grace, Beatrice is able to lead the pilgrim from purga-

Mary: Adept, Queen, Mother, Priestess

tory into heaven. Her very name suggests the incarnation of beatific love, and she leads the pilgrim into the beatific vision. British author William Anderson commented that Beatrice "mirrored to him [Dante] the Incarnation of Christ, and, in purifying his individual nature as a Christian, he found that the only way to the sight of God was through her as the revelation of his soul.... Through the love of her his love expands to become the love of God."[79]

Two generations later, Italian humanist poet Francesco Petrarca (1304–1374), "Petrarch," saw a woman in the church of Saint Clare in Avignon. He was captivated by her, and in his mind she became the perfect woman. He called her Laura and wrote more than 300 love poems about her over a period of twenty years.[80] It would be easy to dismiss such instances of unrequited love as emotional obsessions, but these were no ordinary men. Petrarch, Dante, and others like them recognized the divine origin of the feminine archetypes and may have glimpsed the Divine Feminine herself.

Most important, in terms of our present study, were the prophecies of the French scholar, diplomat and astronomer Guillaume Postel (1510–1581). In 1547, while working as chaplain at the Hospital of Ss John and Paul in Venice, Postel met an Italian woman named Joanna, whom he considered his spiritual mother. She foretold the beginning of a new age, a reformed church, a united world religion, and the moral perfection of humanity. Postel believed that she was the new Eve, a new incarnation of Christ, a new messiah who would redeem the world and usher in an age of universal concord. After her death in 1553 he believed that she entered his body, and he dedicated the rest of his life to serving as her prophet.[81]

Commenting, nineteenth-century esotericist Éliphas Levi declared: "Christianity, from Postel's standpoint, has been so far understood only by the reasoning mind and has not yet entered into the heart. The Word has been made man, but the world will only be saved when the Word shall be made woman."[82] Speaking for Postel, Levi continued: "Come therefore and come quickly, O mother-spirit, who appeared to me at Venice in the soul of a virgin inspired by god; descend and teach the women of the new world their redeeming mission and their apostolate of holy and spiritual life."[83]

Two other figures are significant to this discussion. One was Shaker "Mother" Ann Lee (1736–1784). Her followers believed that she was the Second Coming of Christ, embodying all the perfections of God in female form. The other remained more elusive. In the 1830s French social reformer Barthélemy Prosper Enfantin (1796–1864) sent emissaries to the Middle East looking for a female messiah and the mother of a new savior. Enfantin claimed that she would fulfill the prophecies of the "Daughter of Israel," mentioned in the Hebrew Bible. Although the quest was unsuccessful, believers emerged all over Europe. Whereas Lee imposed strict celibacy on the Shakers, Enfantin encouraged free love—whereupon the civil authorities suppressed his sect to protect public morals.[84]

Divination of Mary

The Archangel Gabriel told Mary: "[T]hou that art highly favored, the Lord is with thee: blessed art thou among women."[85] And for nine months, Christians affirm, she carried the Son of God in her womb. On her deathbed, according to the early Christian text, *Life of the Virgin*, Christ appeared to take her soul to heaven:

> [T]he Lord held forth his right hand, blessed his mother and said to her: "Let your heart rejoice and be glad, O Mary blessed among women, for every grace and gift has been given to you by my heavenly Father,... come forth to the eternal dwelling places, to unending peace and joy, to the treasure houses of my Father, so that you will see my glory and rejoice by the grace of the Holy Spirit.[86]

The text records that Mary's body was buried, but her tomb was found empty three days later. Another text relates that Christ instructed the Archangels Gabriel and Michael to take her body "up unto the cloud and to set it down in Paradise."[87] In a third text Mary passed through twelve gates on her way into "the heavenly Jerusalem." When she entered the tenth gate the "shining beings" worshipped her; at the eleventh the apostles worshipped her; and at the twelfth gate "the Child who was born of her, praised and blessed her."[88]

The Council of Ephesus (431) decreed that Mary was the *Theotokos*—understood in the West to mean "Mother of God." The decree might easily imply that Mary was herself divine. The institutional church stopped short of affirming her divinity. But it struggled to decide precisely what her status might be.

Cyril of Alexandria, architect of the Ephesus dogma, extolled Mary's magnificence: "It is you [Mary] through whom the Holy Trinity is glorified and adored throughout the earth; through whom the heavens exult; through whom the angels and archangels rejoice.'[89]

The Synod of Hieria (754) declared that Mary was "higher than every creature whether visible or invisible."[90] And the Second Council of Nicaea (787) stated that she deserved higher a level of reverence than did the saints. Mary was placed in a category of her own, somewhere between God and the rest of humanity.

Eleventh-century Peter of Damascus affirmed: "we confess that you are the Mother of God and we bless you, the ever-blessed. All generations proclaim you blessed as the only Mother of God, more honored than the cherubim and incomparably more glorious than the seraphim."[91] Peter's contemporary, Bernard of Clairvaux, associated Mary with the "woman clothed with the sun," mentioned in *Revelation*. For her role in Christ's Incarnation Bernard accorded Mary the very highest place in creation. Certainly Christ was higher still, but "So great a Mediator is Christ that we need another to mediate between Him and us."[92]

Twelfth-century abbess Hildegard of Bingen exclaimed: "Mary, you are the bright matter through which the Word breathed all the virtues forth, as once he led forth, in the primal matter of the world, the whole of creation."[93] Thomas à Kempis, German-Dutch author of *The Imitation of Christ* encouraged people to bow at the name of Mary, as they did at the name of Jesus.[94]

The Franciscan doctrine of the Primacy of Christ suggested the corollary that Mary was preordained, or predestined, to be Christ's mother—conceived in the Divine Mind at the very dawn of creation. The doctrine and its implications for Mary were discussed in Chapter 4, and highlights will be recalled later in the book. A major implication is that Mary occupies a special category of creation, above the level of humanity in general. Whether that category can be termed "divine" is a matter of definition.

The Collyridians were condemned for treating Mary as a goddess. But the institutional church raised Mary to a level which the masses could scarcely distinguish from divine. Mary not only took the place of pre-Christian goddesses; she met people's aspirational needs for a divine Queen and Mother. Clarification will come as we explore the Feminine Face of God in more detail and present Mary as the *expression* of that Feminine Face. Meanwhile another character demands attention.

Chapter 8. Mary and the Feminine Face of God

Sophia

Sophia is the direct Greek translation of Chokmah ("Wisdom"), the semidivine or divine personage of Hellenic Judaism, widely recognized as consort of Yahweh and co-creator of the world. Christ made one reference to her, rendered in English translation as: "[W]isdom is justified of all her children."[95] The feminine pronoun seems to confirm that he was using the name in the Judaic tradition.

Gnostic Christians accepted Sophia as a divine personage. In *Eugnostos the Blessed*, one of the Nag Hammadi texts, she is called "Mother of the Universe, whom some call 'Love.'"[96] Sophia is also mentioned in the *Book of Enoch* (*1 Enoch*) and the *Book of the Secrets of Enoch* (*2 Enoch*).[97] The latter presents a creation story in which God proclaimed: "On the sixth day I ordered My Wisdom to make man of seven substances ... and I made [Sophia] a ruler to rule upon the earth."[98]

Another Nag Hammadi text, *The Sophia of Jesus Christ*, suggests that Sophia was Christ's consort.[99] The prominent Gnostic teacher Basilides (d.140 CE) envisioned Sophia and Christ in a paired, complementary relationship.[100] But other Gnostic texts claim that Sophia fell from grace—perhaps echoing the story of Eve—and had to be rescued by Christ.

The most elaborate account of Sophia's fall and rescue is found in the *Pistis Sophia*, a text conventionally dated to the third or fourth century.[101] According to the *Pistis*, Sophia fell into the depths and was held captive for a long time, tormented by evil spirits, or *archons*. Christ eventually heard Sophia's cries for help and dispatched the Archangels Michael and Gabriel to bring her back to the heaven-world, or *Pleroma*. There "she rejoiced with a great joy." "I will give thanks to thee, O Light," she exclaimed, "for thou art a Savior.... I will speak this song of praise to the Light, for he has saved me from the height and depth of the chaos."[102]

Mainstream Christian apologists were reluctant to acknowledge Chokmah/Sophia's existence as a feminine personage, divine or otherwise, and tried to explain away the passages in *Proverbs* and elsewhere. The most common strategy was to interpret the passages as allegory or to overlook the feminine gender and associate the Sophianic passages with Christ. Despite their efforts, Sophia did attain an independent, if limited, existence in Christianity.

303

Abbess and mystic Hildegard of Bingen (1098–1179) wrote several poems on Sophia, whom she referred to by her Latin name *Sapientia*. One of the poems includes the following:

> O power of Wisdom [Sapientia]!
> You encompassed the cosmos,
> encircling and embracing all
> in one living orbit
> with your three wings:
> one soars on high,
> one distills the earth's essence,
> and the third hovers everywhere.
> Praise to you Wisdom, fitting praise![103]

Elsewhere Hildegard wrote:

> She is Divine Wisdom. She watches over all people and all things in heaven and on earth, being of such radiance and brightness that, for the measureless splendor that shines in Her, you cannot gaze on Her face or on the garments She wears. For She is awesome in terror as the Thunderer's lightening, and gentle in goodness as the sunshine. Hence, in Her terror and Her gentleness, She is incomprehensible to mortals, because of the dread radiance of divinity in Her face and the brightness that dwells in Her as the robe of Her beauty. She is like the Sun, which none can contemplate in its blazing face or in the glorious garment of its rays. For She is with all and in all, and of beauty so great in Her mystery that no one could know how sweetly She bears with people, and with what unfathomable mercy She spares them.[104]

Hildegard saw a close relationship between Sophia/Sapientia and *Caritas* (Latin: "Love"); indeed she regarded Caritas as Sapientia's "alter ego."[105] Although Hildegard's Caritas was feminine, perhaps we catch another glimpse of a bond between Christ and Sophia. Also, Hildegard's perception of a connection between love and wisdom anticipated by nearly a millennium the emergence of "Love–Wisdom" as the descriptor of the Second Aspect of Deity in trans-Himalayan esoteric teachings.[106]

A work attributed to Thomas Aquinas refers to Sapientia "[H]er fruit is more precious than all the riches of this world, and all the things that are desired are not to be compared with her.... She is the tree of life."[107] Her qualities are: "power, honor, strength, and dominion."[108]

Remarkable words for a cleric schooled in the patriarchal tradition! But allegedly he was writing shortly after a profound mystical experience, and he died soon thereafter.

Lutheran mystic Jakob Böhme (1575–1624) mentioned Sophia in a commentary on gender. He argued that "the masculine principle is predominantly anthropomorphic and creative, whereas the feminine principle is predominantly cosmic and birth-giving."[109] Böhme was one of several commentators who conflated Sophia and Mary. He also projected virginity onto Sophia. Böhme spoke of Sophia as the mother of Christ and the comforter of struggling humanity, offering himself as its representative: "[T]he Virgin, the divine Wisdom, has given me her promise not to leave me in any misery; she will come to help me in the Son of Wisdom."[110] Rudolf Steiner may have had Böhme's writings in mind when he claimed that Sophia was the "esoteric name" of Mary.

English mystic Jane Ward Lead (1624–1704), who was influenced by Böhme, had a number of visions. In one, a female figure told her:

> Behold I am God's Eternal Virgin-Wisdom, whom thou hast been enquiring after; I am to unseal the Treasures of God's deep Wisdom unto thee, and will be as Rebecca was unto Jacob, a true Natural Mother; for out of my Womb thou shalt be brought forth after the manner of a Spirit, Conceived and Born again."[111]

Sophia has always been revered in Eastern Orthodox Christianity, particularly in the Russian Orthodox Church. Her story merged with that of St Sophia of Rome. Allegedly the latter, along with her three daughters Faith, Hope and Love, was martyred under the Emperor Hadrian (r.117–138).[112] Sophia of Rome may have been legendary rather than real, but Russian Orthodoxy portrays the composite "St Sophia" as a figure transcending ordinary saints.

Sophia is the patroness of numerous Russian churches and has inspired numerous icons. The Russian Orthodox liturgy for the feast of Mary's Dormition includes a hymn with these words: "Let us behold the miraculous icon of the Wisdom of God.... I dare to sing in praise of the Patroness of the World, the most innocent Bride and Virgin.... Sophia, the Wisdom of God."[113] Use of this hymn on a Marian feast suggests another conflation of Sophia and Mary.

Russian émigré Vladimir Solovyov (1853–1900) described three visions of Sophia, the first when he was nine years old. He recalled his impressions many years later in a poem:

> Blue all around. Blue within my soul.
> Blue pierced with shafts of gold.
> In your hand a flower from other realms.
> You stood with radiant smile,
> Nodded to me and hid in the mist."[114]

This description is so similar to accounts of Marian apparitions that we suspect yet another conflation. Or perhaps it was actually Mary who appeared to Solovyov.

Sergei Bulgakov's attempts to reintroduce Sophia into the Trinity were mentioned earlier. Bulgakov also saw a close association between Sophia and the Glory of God, linking her with the shekinah and kavod. Sophia, he declared, "is the glory of God and either expression could be used indiscriminately of divine revelation within the Godhead, for they both refer to the same divine essence."[115] Commenting on the passage in *Proverbs* 8, Bulgakov identified Sophia as the "prototype of creation."[116]

From a different perspective, Bulgakov viewed Sophia as a symbol of the universal church, the *Ekklesia*; and he related both Sophia's and the Ekklesia's development to the doctrine of *theosis*: "The Church in the world is Sophia in process of becoming, according to the double impulse of creation and deification." Bulgakov added: "The Church is ... not only the body of Christ, but also the temple of the Holy Ghost.... This is what makes the Church the revelation, in terms of created Wisdom, of the divine."[117] Theosis normally is considered an individual goal; but Bulgakov envisioned deification of the whole Ekklesia, even the whole of humanity. That collective theosis would be the final manifestation of Sophia.

Sophia was a celestial figure; no suggestion has been made that she took physical incarnation, even as St Sophia of Rome. Yet writers from Theophilus of Antioch to Pavel Florensky had no doubts that she was female. Modern feminist theologians see Sophia as the closest approximation to a Christian goddess and have written a plethora of books to serve an eager readership.

Chapter 8. Mary and the Feminine Face of God

The Divine Feminine in Esoteric Teachings

Modern esoteric teachings drew upon precedents in the religions of South Asia and elsewhere to envision a feminine Principle at a level close to the Godhead. Correspondences between this Principle and Mary suggest that a relationship of profound significance may unite the two.

The Godhead

In Hinduism the Godhead, known as the *Brahman*, received great attention even in the *Vedas*, scriptural texts that date from the second millennium BCE. By the time of the *Upanishads*, which date from about 800–300 BCE, a sophisticated theology had emerged.

The Brahman was regarded as unmanifest, beyond attributes, utterly formless, unknown and unknowable, lying not only beyond the senses but beyond any kind of rational description: "Brahman is he whom speech cannot express, and from whom the mind, unable to reach him, comes away baffled."[118] The rishis were fond of saying that to make a positive statement about the infinite Brahman could only imply a limitation and would therefore be inappropriate. Instead, only negative statements or denials are acceptable: he is *neti neti*, "neither this, nor that."

The theology of the Brahman reached its apex in the philosophical school of Hinduism known as *Vedanta* (literally "conclusion of the Vedas"). In the Vedanta, the transcendence of the Brahman was often emphasized by use of the term *Para-Brahman*, or *Parabrahm*. Helena Blavatsky (1831–1891), co-founder of the Theosophical Society, studied under Vedantic scholar Tallapragada Subba Row (1856–1890), and thereby the notion of the Brahman, or Parabrahm, passed into modern esoteric teachings.

Meanwhile, a close equivalent to the Brahman appeared in esoteric Judaism. The *Zohar*, the foundational, thirteenth-century Kabbalistic text explains: "A spark of impenetrable darkness flashed within the concealed of the concealed from the head of Infinity—a cluster of vapor forming in formlessness ... not white, not black, not red, not green, no color at all."[119] What concealed that spark of impenetrable darkness were three veils: the *Ain* ("Ultimate"), the *Ain Soph* ("Limitless"), and the *Ain Soph Aur* ("Limitless Light"), collectively known for convenience simply as the *Ain Soph*.[120] Over time the Ain Soph came to mean not only the veils but what they veiled: the Godhead.

The concept of the Ain Soph passed into Hermeticism and the "Christian Kabbalah."[121] From there it and related elements of the Kabbalah passed into modern esotericism to support the concepts from Hinduism.

Cosmic Mother

In Vedantic Hinduism, the first manifestation of the Parabrahm is feminine. Subba Row called that first manifestation the "Cosmic Virgin," adding that she is the mother of the Logos.[122] Helena Blavatsky called her the "Celestial Virgin," or "the immaculate Virgin-Mother."[123] In her landmark text, *The Secret Doctrine* (1888), Blavatsky declared that the immaculate Virgin-Mother "is overshadowed, not impregnated, by the Universal Mystery [the Parabrahm]."[124] For comparison we could cite the creation story in *Genesis*: "[D]arkness was upon the face of the deep. And the Spirit of God moved upon the face of the waters."[125]

The Cosmic Virgin is not a *being*; rather she is to be understood as undifferentiated primal substance. Theosophical teachings borrowed another term from Hinduism to call her *Mulaprakriti* (Sanskrit: "Root of Nature"). The first manifestation is the "womb" from which Logoi and their worlds are born. To quote Blavatsky again: "Parabrahm manifests as Mulaprakriti and then as the Logos.... Mulaprakriti or Primordial Cosmic Substance, is the foundation of the object-side of things—the basis of all objective evolution and Cosmogenesis."[126] Significantly the astrological sign of Virgo is an Earth sign, and the goddess Virgo was usually considered a goddess of the Earth, of fertility.

Annie Besant embraced the notion of the Cosmic Mother and, without hesitation, sought to incorporate her into the Trinity: "[T]here is a fourth fundamental manifestation, the Power of the God, and this has always a feminine form."[127] In some religions the feminine manifestation might be described by a parallel trinity or *trimurti*, but in Christianity—with which Besant identified—the Trinity must be expanded to a "sacred Quaternary."[128] Besant added:

> [W]e saw that there was a Fourth Person ... feminine, the Mother.... That which makes manifestation possible. That which eternally in the One is the root of limitation and division, and

Chapter 8. Mary and the Feminine Face of God

which, when manifested, is called Matter.... She is the Fourth, making possible the activity of the Three, the Field of Their operations by virtue of Her infinite divisibility, at once the "Handmaid of the Lord," and also His Mother, yielding of Her substance to form His Body, the universe, when overshadowed by His power.[129]

Descriptors like "Cosmic Virgin," "Celestial Virgin," "immaculate Virgin-Mother," and "Handmaid of the Lord" urge us to inquire what parallels, correspondences, or actual connections, might exist between the cosmic Feminine Principle and Mary.[130] We note that Mary gave birth to the one whom Christianity calls the "Logos." And the notion of a procreatrix of Logoi calls to mind Mary's designation as Theotokos, or "Mother of God."

Esoteric teachings envision chains or hierarchies of Logoi extending from the unmanifest Godhead "down" into successively denser levels of form. At each level a Logos shares in the life of the one above, while investing part of its own life in the Logoi below. At its particular level a Logos creates and ensouls a "body," which may be a galaxy, a star, or a planet; our Solar Logos and Planetary Logos create and ensoul the Sun and the Earth, respectively. Yet, the Logoi on a chain should not be viewed as "separate gods"; separation does not exist at those levels of consciousness.

The Solar and Planetary Logoi—and probably others—are triune, expressing Will or Power, Love–Wisdom, and Active Intelligence.[131] The three Logoic aspects could be regarded as *hypostases*, and correspondences with the Father, Son, and Holy Spirit are close but not exact. Separately, or as part of a triune structure, a Logos may have both a masculine and a feminine face. We are reminded of Geoffrey Hodson's comment that "Mary, World Mother and "planetary Queen of the Angels," serves the Lord of the World, the Ancient of Days, "in what might be called, if one may so presume, His femininity-functions."[132]

Blavatsky's contemporary, Anna Kingsford, described the relationship between Mary—or at least a higher proto-Mary—and the Godhead: "She appears as the Daughter, Mother, and Spouse of God.... In Her subsist inherently all the feminine qualities of the Godhead."[133] Interestingly, the phrase "Daughter, Mother, and Spouse of God" also appears in a Marian devotion promoted by the conservative Roman Catholic prelature Opus Dei.[134] Kingsford continued:

Mary: Adept, Queen, Mother, Priestess

> As Venus, the brightest of the mystic seven who represent the Elohim of God, She [the proto-Mary] corresponds to the third, the spirit of counsel, in that counsel is wisdom, and love and wisdom are one. Thus, in mystical art, She is portrayed as Aphrodite the Sea-Queen, and Mary the Star of the Sea, and as the soul from whose pure intuition of God proceeds the perfected man.... As Pallas or Minerva, She is "Our Lady of Victories," adversary of demons and dragons, wearing the panoply of heaven, and the insignia of wisdom and righteous war. As Isis or Artemis, She is pre-eminently the Initiator, the Virgin clothed in white, standing on the Moon, and ruling the waters.[135]

Kingsford was fascinated by the concept of the Immaculate Conception, raising it above the narrow meaning it had in Roman Catholicism (to which she converted):

> [T]he Immaculate Conception is none other than the prophecy of the means whereby the universe shall at last be redeemed. Maria—the sea of limitless space—Maria the Virgin, born herself immaculate and without spot, of the womb of the ages, shall in the fullness of time bring forth the perfect man, who shall redeem the race.[136]

This "perfect man," made in the likeness of the son Mary bore in Palestine, will be redeemed humankind, or at least a significant portion of it.

Alice Bailey considered Eve, Isis and Mary to be the three "mothers" of Christ:

> Eve has no child in her arms; the germ of the Christ life is as yet too small to make its presence felt; the involutionary process is yet too close; but in Isis the midway point is reached; the quickening of that which is desired (the Desire of all nations, as it is called in the Bible) has taken place and Isis consequently stands in the ancient zodiacs for fertility, for motherhood and as the guardian of the child. Mary carries the process down to the plane or place of incarnation, the physical plane, and there gives birth to the Christ child.[137]

Bailey also saw the three mothers as expressions of the constellation Virgo—and the great Life that lies behind it:

> In these three Virgins and these three Mothers of the Christ, you have the history of the formation and the function of the three as-

Chapter 8. Mary and the Feminine Face of God

pects of the personality through which the Christ must find expression. The sign of Virgo itself stands for a synthesis of these three feminine aspects.... She [Virgo] is the Virgin Mother, providing that which is needed for the mental, emotional and physical expression of the hidden but ever present divinity."[138]

Interestingly, Bailey included Eve in her list of Virgin Mothers, despite the usual assumption that she and Adam had sexual relations. Conversely, she omitted Athena and other traditional virgin goddesses from the list of expressions of Virgo's procreative power.

The notion of a hierarchy of Logoi extending down from the Godhead to the planetary level suggests the possibility of a parallel channel of divine femininity—perhaps a hierarchy of Mothers—extending from the cosmic Virgin Mother to Mary.

The World Mother may be the member of that hierarchy of motherhood serving at the planetary level. As noted in Chapter 7, the early Theosophists regarded the World Mother as a *being*. In his early writings Geoffrey Hodson commented: "The teachings ... relate this Being to the Divine Feminine or Mother Aspect of the Deity, of which she is a manifestation or representation."[139] In *The Kingdom of the Gods*, Hodson commented: "The planetary World Mother is conceived ... as a highly-evolved Archangel Representative and Embodiment on earth of the Feminine Aspect of the Deity ... in whom all the highest qualities of womanhood and motherhood shine forth in their fullest perfection."[140]

Initially, Annie Besant, Charles Leadbeater, and Hodson all believed that the World Mother sent multiple avataras to Earth, including Isis, Kuan Yin, and Mary. Eventually, Leadbeater and Hodson offered the alternative suggestion that "World Mother" is an office in the Planetary Hierarchy, and Mary currently holds that office. Indeed, Mary herself explained to Hodson: "I ... serve as far as I am capable in the Department known as 'World Mother.'"[141]

When Hodson was still open to the possibility that the World Mother was an entity who sent avataras to Earth, he posed the question of where Isis lay on the continuum that unites human mothers with the Cosmic Mother: "Shall we kneel before the throne of Isis and beseech the heavenly Mother, surrounded by Her court of queens, whence was She born, has She Herself a mother, or is the mighty scale of motherhood complete in Her?"[142]

Mary: Adept, Queen, Mother, Priestess

Even then Hodson would probably have permitted us to ask a similar question: "Shall we kneel before the throne of Mary...?" And the answer again would have been "no, the scale of motherhood is not complete in Her." Fifty years later, Hodson referred to Mary as an "incarnation of the Maternal Spirit of the Godhead."[143]

The Feminine Archetype

The Apostle Paul famously announced that the man "is the image and glory of God; but the woman is the glory of the man."[144] Several of the church fathers complained that Eve brought sin into the world, and women posed a continued threat to men's morals.[145]

Not surprisingly Hildegard of Bingen (1098–1179), a strong feminist for her time, took issue with such characterizations.[146] Women's procreative abilities made them not only co-creators with God but also co-revealers of divine reality. The daughters of Eve played as important a role in Christ's Incarnation as did the sons of Adam. Summarizing Hildegard's views religious historian Barbara Newman commented: "Woman's primary significance in the divine scheme of things is to reveal the hidden God by giving him birth. In the meantime, she gives birth to his image in every child that she bears."[147]

The feminine archetype may be an expression of the Godhead. Motherhood is an important element of the archetype, queen is a second, and revealer of mysteries may be a third. But what precisely are the elements that make up the composite feminine archetype?

Katherine Tingley, head of the American Theosophical Society, was by any standard a strong and capable woman. In 1911 she declared that woman needed to "find Herself," to "release from bondage ... the Real Woman within."[148] And: "We want Divine Fire, the Divine Life, the splendid, royal warriorship of men and women."[149] Yet Tingley also encouraged "the devotional spirit" in women, "for it opens a path to the soul."[150] Speaking to a group of women she confided:

> The greatest work that woman can do today is to become so sweetly feminine, so sweetly spiritual and strong, so grandly compassionate and helpful, that she will hold the whole human family in her keeping. She will make the home her altar, her kingdom; and from that altar, from that kingdom, she be sent out the gospel of life to all people.[151]

Chapter 8. Mary and the Feminine Face of God

In Geoffrey Hodson's work the "Eternal Woman" took the place of Tingley's "Real Woman." Writing in 1941, he affirmed: "Behind all womanhood exists the Eternal Woman, the one divine manifestation as femininity."[152] Hodson added:

> Within and through the feminine personality is made manifest the spirit of femininity, the archetypal woman. This is the highest in every woman. Perpetually this is seeking ever fuller, ever more radiant, more tender, more fragrant expression through the wondrous flower which is an individual woman.[153]

The Eternal Woman's qualities, Hodson wrote, are:

> sacrifice, tenderness, graciousness, divine radiance, heavenly fragrance, beauty, and grace. They are wisdom, fathomless as a still dark pool of infinite depth, profound compassion and intimate concern for all living things, ministration, healing love. They are joyous radiant girlhood, graceful womanhood, creative, preserving, and transforming motherhood.[154]

Those qualities read much like the image of Mary built from centuries of devotion. Not incidentally, in one visitation Mary spoke to Hodson "in a voice of compelling sweetness and beauty and with the most engaging charm."[155]

Hodson claimed that the Eternal Woman archetype is partially realized in every woman; therein lies the potential to develop an intimate relationship with the cosmic Feminine Principle. Borrowing a term from Christology, he stated:

> The potentiality of this *hypostatic union* exists in every woman and is frequently foreshadowed throughout successive human lives as interior illuminations, wondrous yet indescribable in visions ever beyond the possibility of communication to another. This is in part the mystery of womanhood, this the secret life of every woman, that on occasion she knows and is one with the Eternal Woman and has her mysterious life in that realm wherein She abides.[156]

Mary is able to express the archetypal qualities to the full, and in her the hypostatic union is fully realized:

> In the holder of the divine Office of World Mother, a conscious union occurs between the archetypal woman fully manifest in the woman Adept and the cosmic principle of womanhood. This con-

stitutes a descent, fiery, pentecostal, of the Eternal Woman into its own purified and exalted superhuman manifestation in time and space.[157]

That last sentence is enigmatic. Hodson's Eternal Woman was defined primarily by tenderness and grace. Yet here we read of the "fiery, pentecostal" descent of the Eternal Woman, calling to mind the passage in the extracanonical *Gospel of Bartholomew* when "fire issued out of her [Mary's] mouth; and the world was at the point to come to an end."[158] Perhaps Hodson glimpsed something more in the feminine archetype.

The authentic feminine archetype, discerned from the world's mythologies, seems to be quite complex; Jungian psychologists identify seven major forms: the Maiden, the Mother, the Queen, the Huntress, the Wise Woman, the Mystic, and the Lover. Most people would have difficulty visualizing Mary as a huntress or a lover—even as fiery or "pentecostal." But we have already seen that the historical Mary was a strong woman. Andrew Harvey (1952–) described her life as "passionate, strong, serious, simple and transforming."[159]

The Mother Archetype

Earlier we saw the cosmic Virgin Mother associated with Mulaprakriti and the Earth element. Yet the Archangel Bethelda associated Mary and the World Mother with the Water element. Geoffrey Hodson's early book *The Angelic Hosts* (1928) records Bethelda's words:

> [T]he divine Mother is for ever giving birth and, through Her, the life of the system is eternally renewed. The element of water is the eternal mother, the heavenly woman, the Virgin Mary, ever producing, yet ever immaculate, the Universal Isis, the goddess queen of the solar system, the spouse of the solar deity. Her life is outpoured freely for the sustenance and nutrition of the system. She is the eternal and unsolvable mystery, for, remaining virginal and immaculate, yet is She ever pregnant and ever giving birth. The solar system is Her child which She nourishes upon Her bosom.[160]

In the same work Hodson delved deeper into the Water element, seeing it as a reflection of the Divine Mother:

> [W]ater is an expression of the one all-pervasive element which is the vehicle of the feminine aspect of the Logos, the mother of all worlds, of all angels and of all men. Water, therefore, is sacred.

Chapter 8. Mary and the Feminine Face of God

When drinking it, Her life is received; when it irrigates the fields, it is a token of Her beneficence; when men bathe in water, it is She Who makes them clean; when they ride upon the ocean, it is She Who bears them on Her bosom.[161]

Anna Kingsford would have agreed with him. Hodson continued:

At sunrise the glory of the rosy clouds is Hers [the Mother's]; the beauty of the sunset sky is a reflection of Her immortal loveliness. The blood within men's veins is Hers; the sap within the trees and plants, Her life; the dew which bejewels the meadow and the lawn, which cools and refreshes the parched soil, is an example of the boundless generosity and selfless sacrifice with which She supports and nourishes the world. The rainbow is Her message to angels and to men that their Mother broods over them with ever watchful and maternal care and reveals to them Her glorious sevenfold beauty which encircles all the world.[162]

During his clairvoyant study of a woman's pregnancy, published in 1929, Hodson had the vision mentioned in Chapter 6: "She is radiant and beautiful beyond description...." While the figure shared all the characteristics of the Marian apparitions, Hodson initially identified it only as "that personification of the feminine principle in divinity, which was recognized among earlier peoples as Isis, Venus and Ishtar, and in more modern times as the Virgin Mary."[163] A few pages later, he seemed to concede that it *was* Mary.

In 1978 Hodson recorded another communication from the Archangel Bethelda declaring that, as World Mother, Mary "is to be revered most deeply and humbly."[164] Significantly, the archangel acknowledged that age-old worship of the Divine Feminine was not only condoned, but was actually promoted, by the Planetary Hierarchy: "Throughout the ages, Adept and Archangelic Teachers have placed before—and even caused to be built within—the human mind the concept and therefore the worship of a Feminine Aspect of Deity."[165]

Worship of the Divine Feminine, Bethelda suggested, would inspire not only an important change in human consciousness but awareness of the universal dimensions of femininity:

One purpose for this teaching is to inspire devotion leading to the adoption of the concept of a perfect Divine Woman. The states of consciousness brought about in those who thus respond inwardly can grow towards the more abstract Feminine Principle in Nature.

This principle pervades all creation from the mineral of the dense world to the formless aspects of Solar Systems, Universes, and Cosmoi.[166]

An important insight into the feminine archetype appeared in a comment on a social media platform; it said: "Some of us see women as points of light within a greater light, as various expressions at various degrees of development of the Mother of the World."[167]

To summarize the esoteric teachings, a cosmic Divine Feminine Principle emerged as the first manifestation, or at least as an early manifestation, from the transcendent Godhead. Among much else this Principle embodies the feminine archetypes, which include Queen and Mother. Mary who rose to be Queen of the Angels and Mother of the World, expresses these archetypes more than any other woman. Thus, and possibly in other ways, Mary has established a connection with the Divine Feminine and serves as an expression of the Feminine Face of God.

---

[1] *2 Peter* 1:2-4.
[2] Boris Jakim, "Sergius Bulgakov: Russian *Theosis*," Michael J. Christensen & Jeffery A. Wittung (eds.), *Partakers of the Divine Nature*, Baker Academic, 2008, 253.
[3] Alice A. Bailey, *A Treatise on White Magic*, Lucis Trust, 1934, 34.
[4] *Ibid.*, 35.
[5] *Luke* 1:46-47. Mary's reference to her "spirit"—her monad—may have a bearing on the question, addressed later in the chapter, of whether the historical Mary was the manifestation of a higher being or a member of the human lifewave.
[6] *1 Thessalonians* 5:23
[7] Alice A. Bailey, *A Treatise on Cosmic Fire*, Lucis Trust, 1925, 4.
[8] Source: https://www.papalencyclicals.net/councils/ecum08.htm. Last accessed Feb. 16, 2020. Esotericists would recognize the "soul," as described by the council, as the etheric body. Some writers have suggested a political motive for the council's decree: by stripping humanity of its divinity, the church positioned itself as the intermediary between us and God. The eastern churches held their own "Fourth Council" several years later, and do not recognize the legitimacy of the one in 869 CE.
[9] Meister Eckhart, Sermon 31, "Vir Meus Servus Tuus Mortuus Est" on *2 Kings* 4:1ff., *The Complete Mystical Works of Meister Eckhart* (transl.: M. O'C. Walshe), Crossroad, 1979, 187. Eckhart was condemned as a

heretic—for this and other matters—but fortunately died before the papal agent arrived with the articles of condemnation.

[10] Thomas Merton, *Conjectures of a Guilty Bystander*, Image Books, 1965, 155.

[11] Gottfried de Purucker, *Encyclopedic Theosophical Glossary*. Online: https://www.theosociety.org/pasadena/etgloss/mi-mo.htm. Last accessed May 7, 2021. The definition of the monad in esoteric teachings is not altogether different from the way Gottfried Wilhelm Leibniz (1646–1716) understood it.

[12] I. (Isaac?) Berger, *Esser Oroth*, 1913. Quoted in Louis I. Newman, *The Hasidic Anthology*, Schoken Books, 1963, 172.

[13] Monica Sjöö & Barbara Mor, *The Great Cosmic Mother: Rediscovering the Religion of the Earth*, San Francisco: Harper & Row, 1987, 67.

[14] Marija Gimbutas, *The Language of the Goddess: Unearthing the Hidden Symbols of Western Civilization*. San Francisco: Harper & Row, 1989.

[15] All three persons of the Hindu *trimurti* had consorts: Brahma's consort was Vidya, or Saraswati; Vishnu's was Lakshmi; and Shiva's took various forms, including Kali and Shakti.

[16] Paul Collins, "The Sumerian Goddess Inanna (3400–2200 BC)," *Papers from the Institute of Archaeology*, (Nov. 15, 1994), 103–118. The flag of Iraq bore the image of the Star of Inanna from 1959 to 1963.

[17] The Burney Relief, currently displayed in the British Museum in London, may be a representation of Inanna or Ereshkigal, or possibly the two combined. The terracotta relief, dated to between 1800 and 1750 BCE, shows a nude, female figure with bird's wings, dewclaws on her lower legs, and talons instead of feet.

[18] *Genesis* 17:1.

[19] *Exodus* 6:3.

[20] Susan Ackerman, "Asherah/Asherim: Bible," Jewish Women's Archive. Online: https://jwa.org/encyclopedia/article/asherahasherim-bible. Last accessed Aug. 2, 2020.

[21] *1 Kings* 11:5, 33; *2 Kings* 23:13.

[22] The divine name was never uttered outside the Holy of Holies, and since biblical Hebrew has no vowels, we do not know how the name was pronounced. The Gentile creation *Yahweh* is probably a closer approximation than the now-anachronistic *Jehovah*.

[23] "Asherah and Ashtoreth." Online: http://oldtestamentstudies.datascenesdev.com/languages/asherahandashtoreth.asp?item=4&variant=0. Last accessed Aug. 20, 2020.

[24] See for example *1 Kings* 18:19; *2 Kings* 21:7.

[25] *Judges* 6:25-26.

[26] *2 Chronicles* 14:3. *Asherim* is the irregular (masculine) plural form of the grammatically feminine *asherah*.

[27] *1 Kings* 15:13.
[28] *2 Kings* 23:1-16.
[29] *Ibid.* 23:13. It will be recalled that "Solomon loved many strange women" and "went after Ashtoreth the goddess of the Zidonians" (*1 Kings* 11:1, 5).
[30] *Jeremiah* 7:17-18
[31] *Ibid.* 44:18, New International Version. The King James translation is "But since we left off to burn incense to the queen of heaven, and to pour out drink offerings unto her, we have wanted all things, and have been consumed by the sword and by the famine."
[32] Ackerman, "Asherah/Asherim: Bible."
[33] *Proverbs* 8:22-30. For more on Sophia see John F. Nash, "Sophia: the Gnostic Heritage," *The Esoteric Quarterly* (Fall 2009), 29-39.
[34] *Proverbs* 9:5.
[35] The *Septuagint* contains Greek translations of the books of the canonical Hebrew Bible and the additional books referred to as "apocryphal" or "deuterocanonical." Some of the apocryphal books were originally written in Hebrew and translated into Greek; others were written in Greek. Christian denominations disagree on which of the apocryphal books should be included in the Old Testament
[36] *Wisdom of Solomon* 7: 29.
[37] *Ibid.* 8:2.
[38] Attempts to identify the female figure as Eve fail because, according to *Genesis*, she was created after Adam.
[39] *Ecclesiasticus* 24:9.
[40] *Ibid.* 24:13-16.
[41] *Ibid.* 24:18.
[42] Bernice H. Hill, "Sophia and Sustainability," 2006. Online: http://www.cgjungpage.org/learn/articles/technology-and-environment/810-sophia-and-sustainability. Last accessed Nov. 26, 2019.
[43] *Psalm* 51:11.
[44] *Exodus* 24:16.
[45] *Isaiah* 57:15. For more information on the Shekinah see John F. Nash, "The Shekinah: the Indwelling Glory of God," *The Esoteric Quarterly* (Summer 2005), 33-40.
[46] *Zephaniah* 3:14.
[47] *Isaiah* 37:22.
[48] *Jeremiah* 31:4. A tabret is a timbrel or tambourine.
[49] *Colossians* 2:9. The possible theological implications of the feminine gender have never been explored. It could be argued that grammatical gender is of no consequence, but the author of *Colossians* evidently preferred a feminine noun to a neuter or masculine one.
[50] First Council of Constantinople, Canon 5.

Chapter 8. Mary and the Feminine Face of God

[51] See for example The Episcopal Church, *Book of Common Prayer*, 1979, 864. Originally attributed to Athanasius of Alexandria, the creed is now believed to have been written at least a century after his death. Its authorship remains in doubt.

[52] Lombard was condemned by his contemporaries but exonerated by Canon 2, of the Fourth Lateran Council (1215), 55 years after his death.

[53] The concept of God varies greatly among theologians, from the Pseudo-Dionysius to Thomas Aquinas, to Paul Tillich, to Vladimir Lossky, to John Robinson. It varies even more from the theologians to the average preacher at a Sunday service. The greatest coherence is among the mystics, from Hildegard of Bingen and Teresa of Ávila to Seraphim of Sarov and Thomas Merton; but their experience of God cannot be captured by formulas like Unmoved Mover or Ground of Being.

[54] *Hypostasis* originally meant "underlying reality" but was honed over a period of centuries to contrast with *Ousia* ("substance"). Its final meaning became "individual, or distinct, reality"—imperfectly translated as "person"—providing the trinitarian formula: "three Hypostases in one Ousia," or "three Persons in one [substance of] God."

[55] Theophilus of Antioch, *Epistle to Autolychum*, II, 15. Theophilus of Antioch—not to be confused with the fourth-century Theophilus, patriarch of Alexandria—first coined the term *trinitas* (Greek: "three"), from which "Trinity" is derived.

[56] *Acts* 2:2-3.

[57] *Gospel of the Hebrews*, fragments 2 &3, quoted by Origen in *Commentary on John*, ii. 12; and *On Jeremiah*, homily xv.4. The *Gospel of the Hebrews* is not to be confused with the canonical *Epistle to the Hebrews*.

[58] Given the misogyny of early Christianity, the gender imbalance probably may not have been considered a disadvantage at the time. From our perspective we can see that the all-male (or male-neuter) trinity had far-reaching consequences in denying women—even Mary—a divine prototype.

[59] First Council of Constantinople, "A letter of the bishops gathered in Constantinople." Online: https://www.papalencyclicals.net/councils/ecum02.htm. Last accessed Feb. 24, 2021.

[60] Note that the statement relating to the Holy Spirit did not include the *filioque* clause "proceeds from the Father *and from the Son*." That was a later interpolation by the Latin church, the primary theological issue leading to the East–West schism of 1054. Nor did the original Nicene Creed use the male pronoun that appears in modern versions: "*He* has spoken through the Prophets."

[61] Denominations that reject the Trinity include Unitarians, Mormons, and Christian Scientists.

[62] *Qur'an* 5:116. Whether the Mariamites ever existed is unclear, but significantly the *Qur'an* was written at a time when Mary was being raised to near-divine status.
[63] "A Song of Anselm," *Common Worship: Daily Prayer*, Church House, 2005.
[64] Julian of Norwich, "Third Meditation," *Showings: the Long Text*, ch. 59.
[65] Quoted in English translation by Andrew Weeks, *Paracelsus: Speculative Theory and the Crisis of the Early Reformation*, State Univ. of New York Press, 1997, 83-84.
[66] *Ibid.*, 83.
[67] Ludwig Feuerbach, *The Essence of Christianity* (transl.: G. Eliot), 1843, part 1, ch. 4.
[68] *Ibid.*
[69] Pavel Florensky, *The Pillar and the Ground of Truth*, (transl: B. Jakim), Princeton University Press, 1997, 239, 252. Sergei Bulgakov, *Sophia: the Wisdom of God* (transl: P. Thompson *et al.*), Lindisfarne, 1993, 252. Italicization removed. The Son and Holy Spirit are deemed to be *consubstantial* with, or are of the same substance as, the Father; the "creaturely" fourth person enjoyed a lower status
[70] Bulgakov, *Sophia: the Wisdom of God,* 252.
[71] Florensky was arrested and executed in 1937 on charges of anti-Soviet activities. Bulgakov escaped to Paris after the Russian Revolution, only to experience tension with the Russian Orthodox authorities in exile.
[72] Bulgakov *Sophia: the Wisdom of God*, 35-37.
[73] *Ibid.*, 52.
[74] Bede Griffiths, *Marriage of East and West*, Medio Media, 1982, 192.
[75] *Ibid.*
[76] Fr Griffiths continued his priestly duties in an environment that may have been familiar to the Apostle Thomas but was unfamiliar to most western Christians. Importantly, he worked within the framework of the Church of Rome, giving his ideas credibility in circles that might otherwise have dismissed his comments out of hand.
[77] Source: "Mother in Heaven." Online: https://www.churchofjesuschrist.org/study/manual/gospel-topics-essays/mother-in-heaven?lang=eng. Last accessed July 29, 2021.
[78] Dante Alighieri, *The Divine Comedy: The Vision of Paradise, Purgatory, and Hell*. Online: https://www.gutenberg.org/files/8800/8800-h/8800-h.htm. Last accessed May 14, 2021.
[79] William Anderson, *Dante, The Maker*, Routledge & Kegan Paul, 1980. 416.
[80] Petrarch, *The Complete Canzoniere*. Online: https://www.poetryintranslation.com/PITBR/Italian/Petrarchhome.php. Last accessed May 14, 2021.

[81] Yvonne Petry, "Gender, Kabbalah and the Catholic Reformation: A Study of the Mystical Theology of Guillaume Postel," PhD Thesis, Department of History, University of Manitoba, Winnipeg, Sept., 1997.

[82] Éliphas Levi, *A History of Magic* (transl. A. E. Waite), Weiser, 1913/1969, 253.

[83] *Ibid.*, 254.

[84] Source: Barthélemy-Prosper Enfantin, https://www.nndb.com/people/882/000095597/. Last accessed March 25, 2021. See also Paola Ferruta, "Constantinople and the Saint-Simonian Search for the Female Messiah: Theoretical Premises and Travel Account from 1833," *International Journal of the Humanities* (January 2009), 67-72.

[85] *Luke* 1:28.

[86] *Life of the Virgin* (transl.: S. J. Shoemaker), New Haven, CT: Yale Univ. Press, 2012, §111, 136.

[87] *Narrative of John the Theologian and Evangelist, concerning the Dormition of the Most Holy Theotokos and how the Undefiled Mother of Our Lord was Translated*. Appendix B of Stephen J. Shoemaker, *Ancient Traditions of the Virgin Mary's Dormition and Assumption*, Oxford Univ. Press, 2002, 369.

[88] *Transitus Mariae*, book V. Reproduced in Agnes Smith Lewis (ed.), *Apocrypha Syriaca*, Clay and Sons, 1909. Reprint: Cambridge University Press, 2012, 66. "Shining being" is a precise translation of the Sanskrit *deva*; the deva evolution includes the choirs of angels of Christian tradition.

[89] Cyril of Alexandria, "In Defense of the Theotokos," homily, Council of Ephesus, June 22, 431. Emphasis added.

[90] Synod of Hieria, Canon 15. Online: https://sourcebooks.fordham.edu/source/icono-cncl754.asp. In the nineteenth century Pope Pius IX used similar language in his *ex cathedra* pronouncement *Ineffabilis Deus*.

[91] Peter of Damascus, "A Treasury of Divine Knowledge," *Philokalia*, (transl: G. Palmer *et al.*), Eling Trust, 1977, vol. 3, 130.

[92] Bernard of Clairvaux, "Sermon for the Sunday within the Octave of the Assumption," *Sermons on the Blessed Virgin Mary*, Augustine Publ., 1987, 207.

[93] Hildegard of Bingen, Antiphon "O Splendidissima Gemma," *Symphonia*, (transl: M. Atherton), *Hildegard Selected Readings*, Penguin Books, 2001, 117.

[94] Thomas à Kempis, *Founders of the New Devotion: Being the Lives of Gerard Groote, Florentius Radewin and Their Followers*, English translation, Kegan Paul, 1905, 64.

[95] *Luke* 7:35.

[96] *Eugnostos the Blessed.* III, 80, James M. Robinson (ed.), *Nag Hammadi Library*, revised edition, Harper-San Francisco, 1988, 231.

[97] The two books were not included in the canonical Bible, but *1 Enoch* was widely referenced by the early Christian fathers. Tertullian referred to it as "scripture," and there is even a reference to it in *Hebrews* 11:5. The authors—probably more than one—were not the biblical Enoch, the grandfather of Noah; but they describe Enoch's visions. They were probably Hellenic Jews writing somewhere between 200 BCE and 100 CE. The books seem to have been written in a mixture of Aramaic, Hebrew and Greek.

[98] *The Book of the Secrets of Enoch*, XXX:8, 12, (transl: W. Morfill), Clarendon, 1896/1999, 39-40.

[99] *The Sophia of Jesus Christ* (transl.: D. M. Parrott), Gnostic Society Library. Online: http://gnosis.org/naghamm/sjc.html.

[100] Kurt Rudolph, *Gnosis*, (transl: R. Wilson), Harper, 1977/1984, 311.

[101] Violet MacDermot, Introduction to *The Fall of Sophia* (transl: V. MacDermot), Lindisfarne, 2001, 22-25. *Pistis* is usually translated as "faith" or "faithful;" but another meaning, more appropriate in the circumstances, would be "hostage." For an interpretation of the symbolism of the *Pistis Sophia* see: https://www.theosophical.org/publications/quest-magazine/2395-the-pistis-sophia-an-introduction? Last accessed Aug. 20, 2020.

[102] MacDermot (ed.), *The Fall of Sophia*, book 2, § 81, 174.

[103] Barbara Newman, *Sister of Wisdom: St. Hildegard's Theology of the Feminine*, Univ. of California Press, 1978, 64. See also Peter Dronke, *Poetic Individuality in the Middle Ages*, Oxford Univ. Press, 1970, 157. Like the Hebrew *Chokmah* and the Greek *Sophia*, *Sapientia* is a feminine noun in Latin.

[104] "Writings of St. Hildegard von Bingen ... on the Holy Spirit." Online: http://holyspirit-shekinah.org/_/writings_of_st_hildegard_von_bingen.htm. Last accessed July 25, 2020.

[105] Newman, *Sister of Wisdom*, 49. We do not know whether Hildegard was aware of the comment in *Eugnostos the Blessed* cited earlier.

[106] See for example Alice A. Bailey, *Initiation, Human & Solar* (New York: Lucis, 1922), xv.

[107] Thomas Aquinas (attributed to), *Aurora Consurgens*, I: 20-25, (transl.: Marie-Louise von Franz). Inner City, 2000, 35.

[108] *Ibid*, V: 13, 53-55.

[109] Jakob Böhme, *The Threefold Life of Man*, (transl: S. Janos), Quoted in: N. Berdyaev, *Studies Concerning Jacob Boehme*, etude II, 1930, 34-62.

[110] Jakob Boehme, *Confessions* (transl: W. S. Palmer), Harper and Bros., 1954, 97.

Chapter 8. Mary and the Feminine Face of God

[111] Jane Lead, *A Fountain of Gardens*, Journal Entries: 1670-1675, Bradford, 1696. See also: Julie Hirst, "The Divine Ark: Jane Lead's Vision of the Second Noah's Ark, *Esoterica* (vol. VI), 16-25. Lead's work was central to the Philadelphian Society for the Advancement of Piety and Divine Philosophy (the Philadelphians). "Lead" is sometimes spelled "Leade."

[112] "Martyr Sophia and her three daughters at Rome," Orthodox Church in America. Online: https://www.oca.org/saints/lives/2017/09/17/102638-martyr-sophia-and-her-three-daughters-at-rome. Last accessed Nov. 22, 2019. According to some accounts, only the three daughters were martyred. Other accounts identify this Sophia with the fourth-century St Sophia of Milan.

[113] Liturgy for the feast of the Dormition of Mary, August 15. Source: Sophia Foundation of North America. Translated from Old Church Slavonic by Natalia Bonetskaya.

[114] Quoted in Eugenia Gourvitch, *Vladimir Solovyov: the Man and the Prophet*, Rudolf Steiner Press, 1992, 25.

[115] Bulgakov *Sophia: the Wisdom of God*, 50.

[116] *Ibid.*, 65.

[117] *Ibid.*, 138-139.

[118] *Tattiriya Upanishad*, II, 4 (transl: Swami Prabhavananda), *The Spiritual Heritage of India*, Doubleday, 1962, 44.

[119] Moses de León (attrib. to), *Zohar*, "Parashat Bereshit," Pritzker Edition, vol. 1, Stanford Univ. Press, 2003, 107-108.

[120] John F. Nash, "From the Zohar to Safed: Development of the Theoretical Kabbalah," *The Esoteric Quarterly* (Summer 2009), 21-46.

[121] John F. Nash, "Origins of the Christian Kabbalah," *The Esoteric Quarterly* (Spring 2008), 43-58.

[122] T. Subba Row, "The Virgin of the World," *Esoteric Writings*, Theosophical Publishing House, 1895, 230ff.

[123] These terms drew upon the mythology of virgin mothers, but in Blavatsky's case they also drew heavily on Mariology. Like many esotericists she disposed of a real Mary by turning her into a set of symbols, which could then be distributed as needed to other realities.

[124] Helena P. Blavatsky, *The Secret Doctrine*, vol. I, Theosophical University Press, 1888, 88, 215. Emphasis removed.

[125] *Genesis* 1:2.

[126] Blavatsky, *The Secret Doctrine*, vol. II, 24. Capitalization of "object" removed.

[127] Annie W. Besant, *Esoteric Christianity or The Lesser Mysteries*, 2/e, Theosophical Publ House, 1905/1966, 178. In the 2006 edition this quote appears on p. 139.

[128] *Ibid.*

[129] *Ibid.*, 180. (2006 ed., 140.)

[130] Subba Row gave Isis a higher status than Mary, claiming that the former could be identified with the Cosmic Virgin, whereas Mary was an incarnation of the "Virgin of the World."

[131] Alice A. Bailey, *Initiation: Human and Solar*, Lucis Trust, 1922, xv, 3.

[132] Sandra Hodson (ed.), *Light of the Sanctuary: The Occult Diary of Geoffrey Hodson*, Theosophical Publishers, 1988, 355.

[133] Anna Kingsford & Edward Maitland, *The Perfect Way, or the Finding of Christ*, 3/e, Field & Tuer, 1890, 55. The quote appears in a slightly different form in Kingsford, (same title), Cambridge Univ. Press, 1882/2011, 56.

[134] Source: https://opusdei.org/en-us/dailytext/mother-daughter-and-spouse-of-god/. Last accessed Nov. 2, 2019. The phrase may have been inspired by a Marian antiphon by Francis of Assisi, mentioned in Chapter 4.

[135] Kingsford & Maitland, *The Perfect Way*, 54-55.

[136] Anna B. Kingsford, *Clothed with the Sun*, 2/e, Watkins, 1889, 32.

[137] Alice A. Bailey, *Esoteric Astrology*, Lucis Trust, 1951, 253. Parenthesis in original.

[138] *Ibid.*, 253-254. Capitalization in original.

[139] Geoffrey Hodson, *The Miracle of Birth*, Theosophical Publishing House, 1929/1981, 75-76

[140] Geoffrey Hodson, *The Kingdom of the Gods*, Theosophical Publishing House, 1952, 244.

[141] S. Hodson (ed.), *Light of the Sanctuary*, 284.

[142] Geoffrey Hodson, *The Angelic Hosts*, Theosophical Publishing House, 1928, 65. Online: http://hpb.narod.ru/AngelicHosts.htm. Last accessed Mar. 3, 2021

[143] S. Hodson (ed.), *Light of the Sanctuary*, 414-415. That entry is dated September 2, 1978.

[144] *1 Corinthians* 11:7.

[145] However there seems to be no truth in the legend that the Synod of Mâcon (585) decreed that women do not have souls.

[146] Hildegard's reaction would have been even stronger a century later when Thomas Aquinas (1225–1274) quoted Aristotle to support the view that a woman is born from a defect in the male sperm. See his *Summa Theologiae*, Part 1, Question 92, Objection 1. The key phrase in Latin is *deficiens et occasionatus*; usually translated as "deficient and misbegotten," it can also mean "unfinished and caused accidentally."

[147] Newman, *Sister of Wisdom*, 93.

[148] Katherine Tingley, *Theosophy: the Path of the Mystic*, 2/e, Theosophical Publ. Co., 1922, 125. Capitalization in original. This and the following quotes are "From a Lecture to Women Only, in a series delivered early in 1911."

[149] *Ibid.*, 126.
[150] *Ibid.*, 123.
[151] *Ibid.*, 125.
[152] S. Hodson (ed.), *Light of the Sanctuary*, 81.
[153] *Ibid.*
[154] *Ibid.*, 81-82. Lest it be thought that this was written by a lovestruck teenager, Hodson was then 55 years old—halfway through a 40-year-long marriage to his first wife Jane, who suffered from multiple sclerosis.
[155] *Ibid.*, 115-116.
[156] *Ibid.* Emphasis added. In Christian doctrine "hypostatic union" refers to the union of the human and divine natures in the *hypostasis*, or "person," of Jesus Christ.
[157] *Ibid.*, 82.
[158] *Gospel of Bartholomew* II:22 (transl.: M. R. James), Gnostic Society Library.
[159] Andrew Harvey, *Return of the Mother*, Tarcher/Putnam, 2001, 343. Hodson did list "transforming motherhood" among his list of archetypal qualities.
[160] Hodson, *The Angelic Hosts*, 36-37..
[161] *Ibid.*, 38.
[162] *Ibid.*
[163] Hodson, *The Miracle of Birth*, 62. Oddly, however, the chapter is titled "Our Lady," and he used that very term later in the chapter.
[164] S. Hodson (ed.), *Light of the Sanctuary*, 419.
[165] *Ibid.*, 420.
[166] *Ibid.*
[167] John O'Neill, FaceBook comment, June 30, 2021.

Mary: Adept, Queen, Mother, Priestess

Chapter 9
Synthesis and Reflections: The Historical Mary

Chapters 9 and 10 synthesize and reflect upon what we have learned about Mary. Together, they present Mary as Adept, Queen, Mother, Priestess; as an expression of the Feminine Aspect of Deity; as a role model for our time and all time. Chapter 9 focuses on the historical Mary, Chapter 10 on the "celestial" Mary.

The purpose of this chapter is to create a consensus biographical sketch of the historical Mary from the scriptural testimony, other writings, and where possible Mary's own words. It is also to reflect upon the impact this remarkable Jewish woman had on the Redemption, the spiritual community in Jerusalem, and the emerging religion we now know as Christianity.

The miraculous events surrounding her death provide the link between the historical and the celestial Mary. Not long after Mary's death, the Jerusalem community came to an end, and the city was destroyed by the Roman army. By then Christianity's Judaic roots were fading from memory, the church was taking on a Greco-Roman character, and new centers of ecclesiastical power were emerging.

The chapter ends with a discussion of Mary's spiritual status. The belief that the historical Mary was an "ordinary" member of the human family is defended against serious suggestions that she was the manifestation of a deity, in the tradition of Aphrodite, Isis, or Kuan Yin.

The Historical Mary
Mary's Birth and Early Life

The canonical New Testament is silent on Mary's birth and childhood and provides few details of her later life. French priest and saint

Louis-Marie de Montfort (1673–1716) claimed that the lack of information was intentional: "[T]he Holy Ghost ... consented that the Apostles and Evangelists should speak very little of her, and no more than was necessary to make Jesus Christ known."[1] Fortunately, others—from the second century to more recent times—felt no such reticence and wrote a great deal about Mary.

In the account given by Anne Catherine Emmerich, an Essene elder prophesied that the lineal descendent of a devout couple, Stolanus and Emeron, would be the mother of the Redeemer.[2] Their daughter Ismeria and granddaughter Hannah bore the identifying mark, but Hannah's first child, Maria Heli, did not. So Hannah her husband, Joachim, waited for a second child. Years of devotion and ascetic practices went by until Hannah passed normal childbearing age. Alas, she and Joachim had not fulfilled the prophecy. Yet all things are possible with God, and finally an angel announced that they would be blessed with the promised child. Their child would be Mary.

A medieval tradition, endorsed by Emmerich, insisted that Hannah and Joachim came together at, or under, the Golden Gate of the temple in Jerusalem. Another tradition pointed to Joachim's absence in the wilderness to suggest that Mary's conception might have been unaided by her father. Perhaps aware of the latter tradition, Anselm of Canterbury (c.1033–1109) proposed that Mary was conceived without original sin; in 1854 Pope Pius IX declared the Immaculate Conception to be infallible dogma. From whatever perspective, Mary's conception was unusual, and Mary was a special child.

Mary was born in about 22–20 BCE. Emmerich claimed that her birth was premature. Hannah had an ecstatic experience before her child was due. The "Blessed Virgin's soul was united to her body five days earlier than with other children, and ... her birth was twelve days earlier."[3]

The *Infancy Gospel of James* explains that, in gratitude for the birth of their child, Hannah and Joachim offered their daughter to be raised as a temple virgin. Mary was duly presented to the temple when she was three years old. At the presentation ceremony the high priest exclaimed:

> The Lord has magnified thy name in all generations. In thee, on the last of the days, the Lord will manifest His redemption to the sons of Israel. And he set her down upon the third step of the altar,

Chapter 9. Synthesis and Reflections: The Historical Mary

and the Lord God sent grace upon her; and she danced with her feet, and all the house of Israel loved her.[4]

Temple virgins attended a "boarding school" within the temple precinct, a protected environment in which they learned practical skills like knitting, weaving and embroidery. They also made and cared for priestly vestments. We do not know whether the girls were taught to read and write, but they received a commendable education for the time; importantly, they witnessed and probably memorized much of the temple liturgy. Mary told Anna Raimondi: "I was given to the temple ... to be raised by the priests in the ways of my religion and my people."[5]

Mary seems to have had two mentors in the temple. According to Emmerich, Mary's education was entrusted to Noemi, an Essene and "sister of Lazarus' mother." The *Qur'an* relates that her upbringing was entrusted to Zachariah, later to become the father of John the Baptist. "Whenever Zachariah entered in upon her in the sanctuary, he found food by her side. He said: 'Mary, from where do you have this?' She said: 'It is from Allah. Allah provides for whomever He wills, without beckoning.'"[6] The *Infancy Gospel of James* confirmed that Mary lived "as if she were a dove [and] received food from the hand of an angel."[7]

The *Gospel of Bartholomew* testifies that Mary had an ecstatic experience while still in the temple. An angel appeared to her—evidently some years before the more familiar Annunciation—and told her that she was "highly favored, the chosen vessel, grace inexhaustible," and was to bear the Messiah. The angel also enacted a proto-Eucharist:

> And he [the angel] smote his garment upon the right hand and there came a very great loaf, and he set it upon the altar of the temple and did eat of it first himself, and gave unto me [Mary] also. And ... there came a very great cup full of wine: and he set it upon the altar of the temple and did drink of it first himself, and gave also unto me. And I beheld and saw the bread and the cup whole as they were.[8]

Clearly this was a prophecy of Mary's future eucharistic ministry. It may also have communicated divine authorization to participate in institution of the Eucharist at the Last Supper.[9] We shall return to that possibility later in the chapter.

When Mary's tenure in the temple came to an end, sometime between the ages of twelve and fifteen, the priests decided that she should marry. Emmerich mentioned an interested suitor: "a devout youth from the region of Bethlehem" who had "an ardent longing in his heart to become Mary's husband."[10] But he did not receive the desired sign from heaven. Instead the responsibility to serve as Mary's husband, and foster-father of Jesus, fell to a reluctant Joseph. Mary's own wishes were not recorded and do not seem to have been considered; she was the property of the temple, and this was an arranged marriage.

The *Infancy Gospel of James* describes Joseph as advanced in age and with grown children. He seems to have been raised in Bethlehem but may have moved north, to Samaria, by the time he was selected to be Mary's husband.

Emmerich described a lavish wedding at the Mount Sinai, Jerusalem, home of her mother Hannah and Hannah's second husband; Joachim had died during Mary's stay in the temple. Other sources claim that both Hannah and Joachim died before Mary left the temple. And Mary herself told Raimondi: "They passed prior to my betrothal to Joseph, well before the birth of my son."[11]

Mary's Appearance and Personality

Scripture is silent on Mary's physical characteristics and personality. It offers few insights into how she came across to other people or how others related to her. Even if some of the evangelists knew her personally, none felt moved to discuss such matters in their writings.

A medieval legend claimed that Luke the Evangelist was an artist and painted Mary's portrait.[12] Allegedly he listened to her stories while she posed for him, accounting for the relatively high number of references to her—twelve—in his gospel. The legend assert that Luke painted three, or even seven, portraits, all on wooden boards in the style of Eastern Christian icons. Multiple churches, cathedrals and monasteries claim to have one of those icons, but none can be traced back reliably before the fifth century.[13] The one shown in Figure 9.1 may date from the twelfth century.

Anne Catherine Emmerich, who seems to have been able to observe biblical scenes in minute detail, described the three-year-old Mary as "very delicately formed," with "reddish-fair hair, smooth but curly at the ends."[14]

Chapter 9. Synthesis and Reflections: The Historical Mary

Figure 9.1

The Theotokos of Vladimir. One of several portraits of Mary claimed to have been painted by Luke the Evangelist.

Mary evidently developed into a strikingly beautiful young woman. Emmerich offered this description of Mary at her wedding to Joseph:

> The Blessed Virgin had very abundant hair, reddish-gold in color. Her high, delicately traced eyebrows were black; she had a very high forehead, large downcast eyes with long black lashes, a rather long straight nose, delicately shaped, a noble and lovely mouth, and a pointed chin. She was of middle height.[15]

Another detailed description of the adult Mary is attributed to Epiphanius, fourth-century bishop of Salamis:

> She was of middle stature, but some say that she was of more than middle height.... Her complexion was of the color of ripe wheat, and her hair was auburn (or reddish). Her eyes were bright and keen, and light brown in color, and the pupils thereof were of an olive-green tint. Her eyebrows were arched (or semicircular) and deep black. Her nose was long, her lips were red and full, and overflowing with the sweetness of her words. Her face was not

Mary: Adept, Queen, Mother, Priestess

round, but somewhat oblong (i.e. oval). Her hand was long and her fingers were long.... She wore garments of natural colors (i.e. un-dyed homespun), and was content with them, a fact which is even now proved by her holy head-cloth.[16]

Mary explained that, in her apparitions, she can assume whatever physical form witnesses might expect or be receptive to; so the reports of apparition witnesses generally do not provide reliable insights into the appearance of the historical Mary. One exception may be the vision Anna Raimondi had when she was a child; on that occasion Mary seemed to replicate her Palestinian characteristics:

> She was dressed in a well-worn brown robe, the fabric appeared rough, but radiated warmth. There was a light brown dress underneath. She had olive skin, wide, soft mahogany-colored eyes and coffee-colored hair that hung to her waist where a hemp belt was tied and held her dress together. She wore a tan-colored covering adorning the top of her head, but no hood. Her face stood out in repose. Her penetrating eyes captured my attention.[17]

Later, Mary told Raimondi: "[A]s a Middle Eastern woman, my skin was dark, my eyes a deep brown, and I was small in stature.... My dark wavy hair came down to my waist."[18]

The lack of agreement on Mary's height is interesting, but we must remember that people generally were shorter in stature 2,000 years ago than they are now. "Observers" like Epiphanius may have compared Mary to women of her time, while Mary may have described herself to Raimondi in terms meaningful today.

Mary was introduced to sacred ritual at an early age and seems to have enjoyed it. Emmerich described the scene at Mary's presentation to the temple:

> Mary was taken [to the temple] by her mother Hannah in a festal procession. First came Hannah and her elder daughter Mary Heli, with the latter's little daughter Mary Cleophas, then the holy child Mary followed in her sky-blue dress and robe with wreaths round her arms and neck; in her hand she held a candle or torch entwined with flowers. Decorated candles like this were also carried by three maidens on each side of her, wearing white dresses, embroidered with gold.[19]

Chapter 9. Synthesis and Reflections: The Historical Mary

After the induction ceremony, Mary danced with the other temple virgins:

> They stood opposite each other in pairs, and danced in various figures and crossings.... [I]t was like a minuet. Sometimes there was a swaying, circular motion of the body, like the movement of the Jews when they pray. Some of the young girls accompanied the dancing with flutes, triangles, and bells.[20]

One early Christian writer insisted that "Mary did not ever adorn herself"—or even bathe![21] Yet Emmerich's account of Mary and Joseph's wedding gives the impression that Mary was not averse to dressing in fine clothes, having an elaborate hair style, or wearing "a jewel-encrusted crown" when the occasion warranted.[22]

Epiphanius envisioned a rather dour figure, ever mindful of the burden of her mission:

> She [Mary] was grave and dignified in all her actions. She spoke little and only when it was necessary to do so. She listened readily and could be addressed easily. She paid honor and respect (i.e. she saluted) everyone.... She was wont to speak to every one fearlessly and clearly, without laughter, and without agitation, and she was specially slow to anger.... She was wholly free from all ostentatious pride, and she was simple, unpretentious, and inclined to excessive humility. She ... was filled with divine grace in all her ways.[23]

Mary described herself in somewhat different terms in her conversations with Raimondi: "When I was a girl, I played, laughed, and cried as girls do. My life as a child was not extraordinary although my faith and love for God was always foremost."[24] Mary added, however, that her carefree attitude changed as she saw Jesus grow up and undertake his redemptive mission. Her suffering during the Passion and Crucifixion will be discussed later in the chapter.

Many sentimental Christmas carols present Mary singing lullabies to the infant Jesus, and invite us to join her.[25] Russian esotericist Helena Roerich (1879–1955) spoke of Mary singing a lullaby "in which She foretold His miraculous future."[26] Roerich also presented Mary as a gifted, educated woman, equipped to help Jesus as he grew up; for example: "She knew several languages, and thus made the path easier for Him."[27]

Should Mary's appearance and personality be of any concern to us? Should we not be content to learn of her activities, accomplishments and ministry? Certainly we must not allow an image to become a distraction, still less an idol. That said, for those who aspire to a relationship with Mary, a visual or mental image—a *living* image, more than a statue or picture—may be important. Equally important may be the need to know if the image has some basis in reality, historical or otherwise; or whether it is simply a creation of our own imagination or desire.

Mary and the Incarnation

Mary was humanity's representative, chosen to facilitate what Christianity calls "the Incarnation." But even she could not have understood the enormity of what was in progress. Similarly, those who wrote the gospel stories and other accounts sought to put words to what lay beyond human comprehension. They drew upon Old Testament prophecy, mythology and story, as well as on what scant historical information might have survived to the latter decades of the first century CE, when the first canonical gospels scriptures were written.

The Annunciation and Visitation

The Annunciation and Visitation were key events in Mary's early adult life. Probably Mary already knew that she would bear the Redeemer; but at the Annunciation, as recorded in *Luke*, the Archangel Gabriel announced the beginning of her pregnancy:

> [T]he angel came in unto her, and said, Hail, thou that art highly favored, the Lord is with thee: blessed art thou among women.... Fear not, Mary: for thou hast found favor with God. And, behold, thou shalt conceive in thy womb, and bring forth a son, and shalt call his name Jesus.[28]

Gabriel may also have given Mary instructions or information about her child's and her own futures, beyond the few words recorded in the gospels.

The scene at the Annunciation is captured sensitively in *Mary and Gabriel* (1912) by English poet Rupert Brooke. Part of it reads:

> He [Gabriel] knelt unmoved, immortal; with his eyes
> Gazing beyond her, calm to the calm skies;
> Radiant, untroubled in his wisdom, kind.

Chapter 9. Synthesis and Reflections: The Historical Mary

His sheaf of lilies stirred not in the wind.
How should she, pitiful with mortality,
Try the wide peace of that felicity
With ripples of her perplexed shaken heart,
And hints of human ecstasy, human smart,
And whispers of the lonely weight she bore,
And how her womb within was hers no more
And at length hers?[29]

Reinforcing the account in *Luke*, Mary shared her experience of the Annunciation with Bridget of Sweden (c.1303–1373)::

> When the angel announced to me that I should bear a Son, as soon as I consented, I felt something amazing and inexplicable in me, so that greatly wondering, I at once went up to my cousin Elizabeth to console her in her pregnancy and confer with her on what the angel had announced to me.[30]

The fact that Mary journeyed to see Elizabeth, seeking advice on what the angel had told her, provides strong evidence that her mother Hannah was no longer alive. A cousin—perhaps one she barely knew—was the only person Mary could confide in.[31]

Elizabeth would soon give birth to John the Baptist. The Visitation reinforced family connections between the mothers and their offspring. The two women's joyous exchange gave us the *Magnificat* and part of the *Ave Maria*. Elizabeth greeted Mary thus: "Blessed art thou among women, and blessed is the fruit of thy womb. And whence is this to me, that the mother of my Lord should come to me? ... And blessed is she that believed: for there shall be a performance of those things which were told her from the Lord."[32]

Mary's ecstatic utterance, now known as the *Magnificat*, began with words that have echoed down the centuries:

> My soul doth magnify the Lord, and my spirit hath rejoiced in God my Savior. For he hath regarded the low estate of his handmaiden: for, behold, from henceforth all generations shall call me blessed. For he that is mighty hath done to me great things; and holy is his name. And his mercy is on them that fear him from generation to generation.[33]

It is one of the most beautiful canticles in the liturgy, and—like the *Ave Maria*—the inspiration for numerous musical settings. Not incidentally, the *Magnificat* also affirmed the threefold human constitution of body (or personality), soul and spirit;[34] Mary affirmed that we are made in the image of a triune God.

The *Magnificat* continued with a protest against social, economic and political inequalities: "He hath shewed strength with his arm; he hath scattered the proud in the imagination of their hearts. He hath put down the mighty from their seats, and exalted them of low degree. He hath filled the hungry with good things; and the rich he hath sent empty away."[35] German Lutheran pastor and martyr Dietrich Bonhoeffer (1906–1945) described Mary's message as "revolutionary" and praised the courageous teenager who spoke out:

> It is not the gentle, sweet, dreamy Mary that we so often see portrayed in pictures, but the passionate, powerful, proud, enthusiastic Mary, who speaks here. None of the sweet, sugary, or childish tones that we find so often in our Christmas hymns, but a hard, strong, uncompromising song of bringing down rulers from their thrones and humbling the lords of this world, of God's power and of the powerlessness of men. These are the tones of the prophetic women of the Old Testament: Deborah, Judith, Miriam, coming alive in the mouth of Mary.[36]

Perhaps we can trace Mary's ministry back to that moment—when she was about fifteen years old.

Jesus' Birth

"Jesus was born in Bethlehem of Judaea in the days of Herod the king."[37] That terse comment is the most *Matthew* has to say about the Nativity; *Mark* and *John* do not mention it at all. Only *Luke*, among the canonical scriptures, tells us of the census, the journey to Bethlehem, and the desperate search for a resting place where Mary could give birth to Jesus.

Endless discussion has occurred over whether the Nativity actually occurred in Bethlehem, or whether the gospel story was simply made to conform to Old Testament prophecy. Joseph seems to have come from the Bethlehem area but may have moved to Nazareth after his marriage to Mary. Accordingly, if indeed there was a census requiring every man to register in his hometown, Joseph was required to return to Bethlehem. Women were not subject to the census, so Mary could have been left in the care of her family. But we are told that an angel instructed Joseph to take her with him—at a late stage of pregnancy.[38]

Chapter 9. Synthesis and Reflections: The Historical Mary

Mary gave birth to Jesus in the lowliest of environments: a stable, a cave, perhaps a house, even the shade of a palm tree; for "there was no room for them in the inn."[39] Bridget described the scene: "When I was at the crib of Bethlehem I beheld a most beautiful Virgin with child, in a white mantle and tunic, evidently about to be delivered."[40] With her were "a most venerable old man," an ox and an ass. The old man, presumably Joseph, withdrew, leaving Mary to disrobe and prepare for the birth. In due course:

> She stood with uplifted hands, and eyes fixed on Heaven, rapt as it were, in an ecstasy of contemplation, inebriated with the divine sweetness. And while she thus stood in prayer, I beheld her Child move in her womb, and ... in the twinkling of an eye, she brought forth her Son, from whom such ineffable light and splendor radiated, that the sun could not be compared to it.[41]

The first witnesses to the auspicious birth were not priests or kings but ordinary people. Hebrew midwives may have helped with the delivery. Then shepherds came, alerted to the auspicious birth by angelic beings: "And suddenly there was with the angel a multitude of the heavenly host praising God, and saying, Glory to God in the highest, and on earth peace, good will toward men."[42] The Magi came later, as recorded in *Matthew*:

> [T]here came wise men from the east to Jerusalem, saying, Where is he that is born King of the Jews? for we have seen his star in the east, and are come to worship him.... And when they were come into the house, they saw the young child with Mary his mother, and fell down, and worshipped him: and ... they presented unto him gifts; gold, and frankincense and myrrh.[43]

A fifth- or early sixth-century mosaic in the Basilica of Sant'Apollinare Nuovo in Ravenna, Italy, shows the three Magi approaching the Madonna and Child, followed by a procession of twenty-two virgins bearing offerings.[44] Why twenty-two? It may be a reference to the twenty-two letters in the Hebrew alphabet. Esotericists Harriette and Homer Curtiss described the twenty-second letter, *tau*, thus: "Its meaning is 'The Sign of the Cross'.... It is a double letter just as the cross is both crucifixion and redemption.... This letter is assigned also to Beauty, i.e., the Beauty of Holiness."[45]

Herod sought to kill the child, serving as a forerunner of those who would crucify Jesus three decades later. Mary was no doubt aware that she would live to see her son suffer and die. Simeon's prophecy confirmed what she already knew: "Behold, this child is set for the fall and rising again of many in Israel.... Yea, a sword shall pierce through thy own soul also."[46] Simeon's prophecy is counted as the first of Mary's Seven Sorrows.[47] It also reinforced the message of the Magi: Christ would be "A light to lighten the Gentiles."[48] Anna, the prophetess, gave thanks for Jesus' birth "and spake of him to all them that looked for redemption in Jerusalem."[49]

The flight into Egypt, whether it occurred as soon as the Magi departed or several months later, may have been the first of several visits by both Mary and Jesus. Jesus may well have gone there during his "silent years," and Mary's initiation into the Egyptian Mysteries may also have taken her there.

Reflections on the Incarnation

The Annunciation, when Mary "felt something amazing and inexplicable" in her, is believed to have been the moment when Jesus was conceived "by the power of the Holy Spirit."[50] It was the moment when "the Word was made flesh, and dwelt among us."[51]

Former Archbishop of Canterbury Rowan Williams (1950–) pondered the awesome significance of Mary's pregnancy: "Mary carrying the Christ child is carrying what no one can carry.... The terrible weight of divine love."[52] Williams also noted the significance "of the Word growing silently in Mary's body." During that time, he added,

> the presence of God incarnate in the world was not in visible action or speech, but wholly in secrecy. The Divine Word prays to the Father, loves and adores the Father as throughout eternity the Word must do, and, in the pregnancy of Mary, does so in the human medium of a developing organism not yet active and distinct.[53]

An earlier Anglican clergyman, Lancelot Andrewes (1555–1626), boldly modified *Psalm* 2:7 to create an affirmative exclamation for Mary: "Thou art my Son, this day I brought Thee into the world."[54]

Christian Kabbalist Johann Reuchlin (1455–1522) noted that the Hebrew form of Jesus' name, *Yehoshuah* (transliterated as YHShVH), was formed by the insertion of the letter *shin* (Sh) into YHVH, the unutterable name of God; by completing the divine name, Jesus fulfilled the Jewish covenant.[55] Furthermore, Reuchlin noted, shin is one

Chapter 9. Synthesis and Reflections: The Historical Mary

of the three mother letters in the Hebrew alphabet, providing an affirmation that God had incarnated through a woman. The very name of Jesus encoded the doctrine of the Incarnation.

Swiss theologian Hans Urs von Balthasar (1905–1988) exclaimed: "Christmas is not an event within history but is rather the invasion of time by eternity."[56] Anglo-Catholic writer Evelyn Underhill (1875–1941) emphasized the ongoing reality of the Incarnation:

> The incarnation, which is for popular Christianity synonymous with the historical birth and earthly life of Christ, is for the mystic not only this but also a perpetual Cosmic and personal process. It is an everlasting bringing forth, in the universe and also in the individual ascending soul, of the divine and perfect Life, the pure character of God, of which the one historical life dramatized the essential constituents.[57]

The Star of Bethlehem had great significance. It may have been a comet, or a Jupiter–Saturn or Jupiter–Regulus conjunction. But perhaps it was Christ's monad, or divine spark, hovering over the child into whom it would descend. American author Baird Spalding (1872–1953) wrote that the star "shone brighter at Jesus' birth than it had before, but soon its brightness will be like the noonday sun, for this new light foretells the day when the Christ is born in the hearts of all men."[58] Clearly the Christ was born in the hearts of the Magi, who served as representatives of the Gentiles—and also of the ancient mystery traditions.

The predominant view in Western Christianity is that the Incarnation was designed to atone for man's sins; humankind had disobeyed God's commandments, and Christ came on a repair mission.[59] Yet in Chapter 4 we examined the more optimistic Scotist position that the Incarnation was ordained before the fall of man as part of God's self-revelation: the doctrine of the absolute primacy of Christ.[60] A possible, but not necessary, corollary of the doctrine was that Mary was preordained, or predestined, "from the beginning" to be the mother of Christ.

In the eastern churches, the Incarnation is seen as the means by which Christ unlocked humanity's potential to attain theosis, or "deification." That again was part of the Divine Plan, ordained from the beginning of the world.[61] When Orthodox theologians consider the redemptive aspects of the Incarnation they emphasize the healing of human weakness rather than expiation for sin.

Esotericists claim that Christ ushered the planet through a major initiation. To quote Alice Bailey (1880–1949), scribe for the Master Djwhal Khul, Christ "established for the first time in planetary history a contact between the Hierarchy, Humanity, Shamballa, and the Spirit of Peace."[62] Shamballa is the name given to be the divine center of the planet; the Spirit of Peace is believed to be an exalted entity coming from beyond the bounds of Earth.

Bailey noted that Christ's "first recorded utterance" was that "He must be about His Father's business"—and that, at the end of his life, he reiterated the same thought in the words: "Father, not my will but Thine be done."[63] Bailey commented: "This achievement enabled Him [Christ] to put Humanity in touch with the Spirit of Peace. He ... Himself became the Light of the World and the Prince of Peace."[64]

Mary's Virginity

Becoming a temple virgin was not the same as taking a vow of lifetime chastity. Mary entered the temple before she could give informed consent and was dismissed when she reached puberty.[65] Temple "virgin" should be understood in terms of the Hebrew word *almah*. The word appears in *Isaiah* 7:14, famously translated as "A *virgin* shall conceive and bear a son." More generally, *almah* simply meant "a girl" or "young woman."

Christian teachings assert that Mary was a virgin, at least up to the time she bore Jesus and possibly thereafter. Mary may well have chosen a life of celibacy. That choice would have been unusual in her culture; Judaic custom generally favored large families, and celibacy was rarely esteemed, even among the ascetic sects of Judaism. The Nazarites, who may have numbered John the Baptist among their members, took other vows of renunciation but did not take an explicit vow of celibacy. Yet we do find celibacy in the ranks of the Essene priesthood, and Anne Catherine Emmerich claimed that Mary's maternal great-grandparents were Essenes. Emmerich also claimed that Mary's education in the temple was entrusted to an Essene, Noemi.

A more immediate factor supporting Mary's perpetual virginity was Joseph's age. Maximus the Confessor commented that, at the time of her betrothal, Joseph was "more than seventy years old, so that no one could raise any suspicions whatsoever of marriage."[66]

Chapter 9. Synthesis and Reflections: The Historical Mary

Jesus' four "brothers" and two "sisters" may not have been Mary's children. Epiphanius of Salamis made the insightful comment that Jesus would not have entrusted Mary to John the Beloved if she had other children.[67] That said, the early text *Life of the Virgin* reveals that, when John departed for Ephesus. the care of Mary fell to "the blessed James the son of Joseph, who was called the brother of the Lord."[68] One of Jesus' "brothers" listed in *Mark* 6:3 and *Matthew* 13:55-56 was named James.

Much of the debate over Mary's virginity took place when Christianity was expanding into a polytheistic world. Possibly Mary's persona was being fashioned to compete with other virgin mothers of antiquity; Perseus, Romulus, Mithras, Horus and Krishna were just a few of the personages said to be the products of virgin births. Allegedly the Druids worshiped the *Virgo paritura* ("Virgin who will give birth") in Chartres, France, before the first cathedral—dedicated to Mary—was built on the site in the fourth century.[69]

"Virgin Mother" also connects Mary to the constellation Virgo. Significantly, her birth is celebrated September 8, when the Sun is in the sign of Virgo. In esoteric astrology Virgo is considered "the emanator of energies which nourish and aid the growth of the Christ consciousness."[70]

Moreover, the debate took place in an era of deteriorating attitudes toward women and toward the human body. The impulse to decree Mary's perpetual virginity probably came at least in part from a desire to present her as a suitable object of devotion and model of "purity." One positive result: as converts projected attributes of their pre-Christian goddesses onto Mary, emphasis on her virginity may have saved her from being seen as a fertility goddess.

It is important to note that Christianity's emphasis on Mary's virginity reflects a surprisingly strong focus on physical, rather than spiritual, reality—another example being emphasis on the resurrection of the body.[71]

The excessive—even prurient—attention to Mary's virginity can be countered by choice of honorific. "The Virgin Mary" and "St Mary the Virgin"[72] can be replaced by "the Lady Mary," found in several early Christian texts and linking her with the ancient mysteries. Other appropriate titles are: "Holy Mother Mary," "Mary, the Mother of Jesus," "Mary, Queen of Heaven," and "Mary, Queen of the Angels."

Meanwhile, in light of the broad meaning of *almah*, "perpetual virginity" can be reinterpreted as Mary's eternal youthfulness.

Mary During Jesus' Lifetime

Scripture tells us nothing about the kind of life Mary and her family lived. But a modern writer offered insightful comments:

> The picture of the Holy Family as a tiny group of three living in a tranquil, monastic-like carpenter's shop is highly improbable. Like most people at that time, they probably lived in an extended family unit, where three or four houses of one or two rooms each were built around an open courtyard, in which relatives shared an oven, a cistern and a millstone for grinding grain, and where domestic animals also lived. Like women in many parts of the world today, Mary most likely spent, on the average, 10 hours a day on domestic chores like carrying water from a nearby well or stream, gathering wood for the fire, cooking meals and washing utensils and clothes.[73]

Raising the child Jesus obviously posed unique challenges. Mary and Joseph lost the twelve-year-old boy for three days—the length of time is significant—when he tarried in the temple after the Feast of Passover. And the apocryphal *Infancy Gospel of Thomas* describes a number of mischievous incidents as Jesus explored his divine powers. Mary must have kept many things in her heart.

Mary seems to have been present at Jesus' baptism. And she may have accompanied him on many of his journeys around Galilee and surrounding areas during his ministry.

Helena Roerich renounced Christianity to become a Buddhist, but she expressed remarkable insight into Mary's involvement in Jesus' ministry. Writing for the Master Morya she described Jesus as "the Great Pilgrim," perhaps a reference to his travels during his "silent years" and his itinerant ministry.

Roerich insisted that Mary had an instinctual grasp of her son's mission. Mary did not "object to His long pilgrimages, and gathered all that was necessary to make the travels easier"; she "understood the mystery of His wanderings."[74] Roerich also presented Mary as fully participating in Jesus' mission: She recognized "the grandeur" of his total renunciation, "and thus could give heart to those of diverse char-

Chapter 9. Synthesis and Reflections: The Historical Mary

acter who were weakened by doubt and rejection. She was prepared to experience the same achievement as Her Son, and He entrusted to Her His decision."[75] "His decision" was commitment to a ministry that he knew would lead to the Crucifixion.

The Marriage Feast of Cana traditionally is recognized as the occasion of Jesus' first miracle. The story raises questions about his reluctance to get involved, and his reaction to his mother's prompting: "Woman, what have I to do with thee? Mine hour is not yet come."[76] Throughout the centuries writers have tried to soften, or at least understand those words. Anne Catherine Emmerich suggested that the whole situation arose because Jesus had promised to bring wine for the banquet. Pope John Paul II suggested that Mary's instruction to the servants: "Whatsoever he saith unto you, do it,"[77] were prophetic of the institution of the Eucharist. And "the role she assumed at Cana in some way accompanies Christ throughout his ministry."[78] In consequence Mary "has a profound relationship" with the Eucharist.[79]

The canonical gospels are silent on the presence of Mary, or indeed any women, at the Last Supper. But a plausible translation of an early Christian text indicates that Mary was not only present but participated in some of the rituals:

> [W]hen the great mystery, the supper, took place, she [Mary] sacrificed herself as the priest and was sacrificed; she offered and was offered. Then, the Lord Jesus presided over the twelve apostles and those he wanted, and he delivered the sublime mysteries and signs of God's Passover, he gave them some of his precious body and blood as the bread and the drink.[80]

This passage—if we the translation is accurate—raises the tantalizing possibility that Mary participated in the institution of the Eucharist. We recall that she may have received authorization to perform eucharistic rites, while still in the temple. Moreover, her ecstatic experience in the temple and her presence at the Last Supper laid a strong foundation for her later involvement in the evolving Eucharistic liturgy.

Mary at the Crucifixion

Mary witnessed Jesus' Passion and Crucifixion. Several accounts testify that she was present during the trial and its immediate aftermath. A tradition dating from the Middle Ages alleges that Mary met Jesus as he carried the Cross on the road to Calvary. The incident is now enshrined in the fourth Station of the Cross and the fourth Sorrowful Mystery of Roman Catholic devotion.

The fourth gospel places Mary at the foot of the cross. Jesus spoke from the cross to entrust Mary to the care of the Beloved Disciple: "[H]e saith unto his mother, Woman, behold thy son! Then saith he to the disciple, Behold thy mother! And from that hour that disciple took her unto his own home."[81] By contrast, *Mark* comments only that "There were ... women looking on afar off."[82] Three of the women are named, but Mary is not listed as being among them. Nor is Mary's presence mentioned in the other synoptic gospels.[83]

According to tradition Mary remained at the cross until Jesus died and then received his body into her arms. That moment of extreme pathos inspired the artistic theme of the *Pietà*, which began no later than the twelfth century and continues to our own time.[84] Famous renderings of the *Pietà* theme are Michelangelo Buonarroti's sculpture (c.1498), displayed in St Peter's Basilica, Rome, and the paintings by El Greco (c.1574) and Annibale Carracci (c.1600).

It was Mary's destiny, both as a mother and as a representative of humanity, to share in the suffering and death of her son. According to Anne Catherine Emmerich, Jesus had told Mary that "she would suffer with Him all the cruel torture of His death, that with Him, she would die His bitter death."[85] Maximus the Confessor pondered her suffering during the Passion:

> [I]t is neither in our power nor anyone else's power to describe the holy Virgin's sufferings and tears and groanings of her heart at each moment, for they are beyond nature, and as her birthing was beyond nature, so also her sorrow.... But she who suffers alone knows, and she alone completely understands the Lord who was born from her.... How did the immaculate mother endure the pain? How did she not give up her spirit as well?[86]

Mary told Bridget of Sweden of her shock at seeing Jesus scourged: "At the first blow, I who stood nearest, fell as if dead, and on recovering my senses I beheld his body bruised and beaten to the very ribs."[87] And later: "[M]y heart was scourged and pierced when my Son was. I was nigher to Him in His Passion, and did not leave him. I stood nearer to His cross, and as what is nearer the heart wounds more keenly, so the pain of it was keener to me than to others."[88] Mary continued, reiterating her participation in her son's agony: "[W]hen He

Chapter 9. Synthesis and Reflections: The Historical Mary

looked upon me from the cross, and I on Him, then tears streamed from my eyes." The account supports the testimony in *John* that Mary stood close enough to the cross to interact with Jesus.

The hymn *Stabat Mater* attempts to capture Mary's suffering at the cross:

> At the cross her station keeping,
> Stood the mournful Mother weeping,
> Close to Jesus to the last.
> Through her heart, his sorrow sharing,
> All his bitter anguish bearing,
> Now at length the sword has passed....[89]

In her communications with Anna Raimondi, Mary placed her sufferings in a larger context:

> I endured great emotional pain during my son's last days and during his persecution. I witnessed the purity of his love as he spread it to all people even as he was rejected. As a mother and a person who loved him and his message, the way people treated him caused me great pain. I didn't understand fully the true reason for the circumstances of my son's suffering for it wasn't revealed to me until later.... As his mother, the one who brought him into the world and love him as only a mother could, the pain my son endured tore at me.[90]

Maximus and Emmerich both placed Mary at the sepulcher after Jesus' burial. In a spirit of modern-day *midrash*, American poet Velma West Sykes (1893-1976) created a poignant scene in which Mary met another grieving woman there:

> The city slept, and in the burial place
> Slept still more soundly its inhabitants,
> Indifferent to the early morning calls...
> Two women met. Both paused, for each well knew
> Some great emotion brought the other forth
> Like as herself, at this hour of the dawn.[91]

The other woman quickly recognized Mary as the mother of Jesus who was crucified. She commented that Jesus "had many friends who suffered with him on his way to death," while her own son took his life without "a single friend to stay his hand." The poem ends thus:

"Tell me," said Mary, clutching at the hand
That grasped the woman's shawl. "Who was your son?"
The other bowed her head and slowly spoke,
"His name was Judas—Judas Iscariot!"[92]

Priestess at the Cross

If, as the *Qur'an* asserts and *Luke* hints, Mary was a descendent of Aaron, she belonged to the priestly caste of biblical Judaism. We have already seen that her priestly role may have been reaffirmed by the angel in the temple and demonstrated at the Last Supper.

A tradition dating from the Middle Ages related Mary's priestly status to her participation in the Sacrifice of the Cross. An unnamed homilist affirmed: "She [Mary] offers with the chalice of her blessed hands ... the most blessed body and blood, with which the High Godhead had clothed himself through her."[93] In the same sermon the homilist made the insightful remark: "She offered ... the Son to the Father, and herself completely in it, so that we all should become divine therein."[94] Mary, who we understand achieved theosis herself, evidently played a role in extending it to humanity at large.

French priest Julien Loriot (1633–1715) declared: "Mary is a divine priestess, she is a great sacrificer who takes the place of all people and offers to God in their name the greatest and most worthy sacrifice that has ever been offered, presenting to him his unique Son ... the most perfect sacrifice which the earth has ever offered."[95] Lest his readers misunderstood him, he repeated the word "priestess."

Cardinal Nicholas Wiseman (1802–1865), Roman Catholic primate of England and Wales, was also unequivocal in his use of the term priestess. He compared Mary with an Old Testament forerunner: Mary "became the priestess on the part of all mankind, who was allowed to accomplish the holocaust, which was considered too difficult and painful for Father Abraham, the sacrifice of a beloved child."[96] In 1914 Armenian Catholic Bishop Jean Nazlian went so far as to say: "More than any priest she can point at her crucified Son and say: 'This is my body!' Mary is therefore not a priest who does not share in the sacrifice, but a priest who puts herself into the victim who is the heavenly bread."[97]

We saw that Mary may have participated in the institution of the Eucharist. Now, in the words of high churchmen, we have affirmation that she participated, in a priestly role, in its fulfillment on Calvary. With the *Pietà* and Nazlian's words in mind, we can easily envision Mary saying: "This is my body, this is my blood."

An early Christian text, known as the "Homily of John the Son of Zebedee," records that Mary had an ecstatic experience on Calvary, which she described to John:

> Hearken and I will tell thee an astounding and hidden mystery, which cannot be known by the heart (or mind) and cannot be comprehended by the understanding, which my Lord and my Son, Jesus Christ my beloved one and my Redeemer, revealed unto me at Golgotha, at the time of the sixth hour, which is noon, on the day of the Eve of the Sabbath. A shining cloud came and bore me along and took me up into the third heaven, and it set me down at the boundary of the earth, and my Son appeared unto me. And He said unto me, "Peace be unto thee, O Mary, My mother, thou dwelling-place of God. Peace be unto thee, O virgin, who gavest birth to Me. From thy womb hath gone forth the river of peace. I will reveal unto thee an astounding wonder." [98]

Esotericists would readily agree that Mary earned the title of Priestess. They would also affirm that she attained the fourth initiation at the foot of the cross, in preparation for attaining the fifth initiation by the end of her Palestinian lifetime.

Mary at the Resurrection

Mary Magdalene is acclaimed as the first witness to the Resurrection, meeting the risen Jesus early on the first Easter Sunday.[99] Multiple appearances followed, and Paul commented on the sheer numbers of people who were thus blessed: "[H]e was seen of Cephas [Peter], then of the twelve: After that, he was seen of above five hundred brethren at once; of whom the greater part remain unto this present.... After that, he was seen of James; then of all the apostles. And last of all he was seen of me [Paul]."[100]

Nowhere, however, do the canonical scriptures record that Christ appeared to his mother. Not even John the Beloved, who alone of the evangelists, placed Mary at the cross, gave her a glimpse of the Resurrection. Is it possible that Mary, who had shared in the agony of Jesus' death, would only learn from third parties that he had risen again? Is it likely that Christ would not have shared news of the Resurrection, the climax of his mission on Earth, with the one who made the Incarnation possible?

Fortunately, a few other texts are more generous. Maximus the Confessor recalled that Mary kept watch at the tomb, "a witness to everything until she saw even his glorious Resurrection." The other women did not understand what they were seeing. "Only the immaculate mother of the Lord standing there knew everything. And because of this, she received the good news of the Resurrection before anyone else, and before anyone else she became worthy of the ... divinely beautiful vision of her Lord and son."[101]

Emmerich testified that, at about nine o'clock on the Saturday evening Mary had a vision:

> Floating down toward her in the midst of a great multitude of souls of the ancient Patriarchs, I [Emmerich] saw the most holy soul of Jesus, resplendent with light and without a trace of wound. Turning to the Patriarchs and pointing to the Blessed Virgin, He uttered the words "Mary, My Mother."[102]

And in a text attributed to "Bartholomew the Apostle":

> Christ Himself, when He rose from the dead and appeared to her and the other women at the tomb mounted on the chariot of the Father of the Universe, cried out, saying ... "All Paradise rejoiceth in thee. I say unto thee, O My Mother, He who loveth thee loveth Life. Hail, thou who didst sustain the Life of the Universe in thy womb! .... I will give My peace, which I have received from My Holy Father, to My disciples, and to every one who shall believe in My Name and in Mary."[103]

So far as is known, Mary has never commented on her experiences at the Resurrection in any of her communications with apparition witnesses or other contacts.

Mary's Later Life

Mary's Ministry in Jerusalem

Ann Catherine Emmerich testified that sometime prior to the Ascension, Mary, Jesus' disciples, Joseph of Arimathea, the "holy women," and others were assembled for prayer. Mary assumed a leadership role that would play out over the next several decades:

Chapter 9. Synthesis and Reflections: The Historical Mary

> They spoke in words full of mystery of their relationship to the Mother of the Lord and what she should be to them.... I saw the Blessed Virgin hovering over the assembly in a shining and outspread mantle whose folds embraced them all, and on her head descended a crown from the Most Holy Trinity.... I had the conviction that Mary was the legitimate head of them all, the temple that enclosed them all.[104]

Another scene unfolded after the Ascension. Jesus' followers, who were observant Jews, gathered in the upper room to observe the traditional Jewish feast of Pentecost. *Acts* records that Mary was there with them.[105] Again, as their "legitimate head," she may have been the central figure in the group. Many works of art depicting the event show the disciples gathered around Mary; examples are *Pentecost* by Duccio di Buoninsegna (c.1309) and a work of the same name by Jan Joest van Kalkar (c.1506).

That Pentecost feast was interrupted. "[S]uddenly there came a sound from heaven as of a rushing mighty wind .... And there appeared unto them cloven tongues like as of fire, and it sat upon each of them."[106] Pope Pius XII suggested that Mary was instrumental in securing the descent of the Holy Spirit: "She it was through her powerful prayers obtained that the spirit of our Divine Redeemer, already given on the Cross, should be bestowed, accompanied by miraculous gifts, on the newly founded Church at Pentecost."[107]

Along with the others present, Mary received the gifts of the Holy Spirit:

> For to one is given by the Spirit the word of wisdom; to another the word of knowledge by the same Spirit; to another faith ... to another the gifts of healing ... to another the working of miracles; to another prophecy; to another discerning of spirits; to another divers kinds of tongues; to another the interpretation of tongues.[108]

Mary put several of those gifts to good use in her ministry.

The community of Jesus' followers that formed after Pentecost, in and around Jerusalem, functioned as a kind of spiritual commune in which everything was shared:

> And all that believed were together, and had all things common; And sold their possessions and goods, and parted them to all men, as every man had need. And they, continuing daily with one ac-

cord in the temple, and breaking bread from house to house, did eat their meat with gladness and singleness of heart, Praising God, and having favor with all the people. And the Lord added to the church daily such as should be saved.[109]

Mary was in every way a Jewish woman. She was born into a Jewish family, raised in the temple, and probably followed traditional observances throughout her life. The community retained much of its Judaic identity too. The teachings of Jesus were grafted onto the long traditions of Judaism, rather than viewed as the beginning of a new religion. Indeed, the very term *Christian* was not used until about 41 CE, and the term *Christianity* not until the second century.

No elaborate body of doctrine had yet developed. Jesus' followers did not debate whether he was co-equal with the Father, begotten of the Father before all ages; the formulation of Christological and Trinitarian doctrine lay centuries in the future. Most people probably saw Jesus as a prophet in the tradition of Moses, Isaiah, and John the Baptist. What mattered were their *experiences*. The Sermon on the Mount, the Crucifixion, the Resurrection, the Ascension, and now Pentecost were powerful, transformative experiences— experiences that shook them to the core of their being.

Mary's training in the temple, her unique experience of giving birth to Jesus, and perhaps the authority that came from higher consciousness ensured her position of prominence and the community's trust. The disciples turned to her for consolation, inspiration and counseling. *Life of the Virgin* declares that Mary "was not only an inspiration and a teacher of endurance and ministry to the blessed apostles and the other believers, she was also a co-minister with the disciples of the Lord. She helped with the preaching, and she shared mentally in their struggles and torments and imprisonments."[110] *The Ethiopic Six Books* testifies:

> [M]any men and women came to Mary, and they prostrated themselves before her, saying, "Have mercy on us and forgive us, and do not cast us away, O master." And the Blessed One, having extended her arms, blessed them and said, "May the Lord receive your prayer and your petition."[111]

The blessing, which was mentioned in the Old Testament and also in the writings of Christian church father John Chrysostom, signified ecclesiastical authority.[112]

Chapter 9. Synthesis and Reflections: The Historical Mary

Numerous works of sacred art from late antiquity show Mary with hands raised in blessing. A detail from an illumination in the *Rabbula Gospels*, dated to 485 CE, is shown in Figure 9.2. In its entirety, the image shows Mary flanked by archangels and Jesus' disciples; the transcendent Christ hovers above her.[113] Mary is wearing the blue *maphorion*, which iconographers associate with the mother of Jesus. From her waistband hangs the fringed *enchirion*, or "Eucharistic cloth," signifying high priestly status. Ally Kateusz commented on the image:

> [T]his illuminator depicted Mary as the focal point of the scene—she stands in the center with her arms raised. Additionally, signifying her headship of the male apostles who stand on either side of her, Mary was painted taller than they. Her posture is erect and powerful, her gaze direct. Signifying her elevated spirituality, she is flanked by archangels, and only she, Jesus above her, and the angels have halos.[114]

Figure 9.2

Mary, flanked by archangels, blessing her followers.

Detail from an illustration in the *Rabbula Gospels* (sixth century). This image contrasts with later western artwork depicting a submissive Mary with eyes lowered and hands clasped in prayer.

351

Mary: Adept, Queen, Mother, Priestess

The Roman Catholic religious order known as the Society of Mary (Marists) has an interesting maxim, which affirms the importance of Mary's post-Pentecostal ministry and also hints at her ongoing ministry in the world today: "I [Mary] was the mainstay of the new-born Church; I shall be again at the end of time."[115] Pope John Paul II may have had that maxim in mind when he commented on Mary's contribution to the early church:

> [A]t the first dawn of the Church, at the beginning of the long journey through faith which began at Pentecost in Jerusalem, Mary was with all those who were the seed of the "new Israel." She was present among them as an exceptional witness to the mystery of Christ. And the Church was assiduous in prayer together with her, and at the same time "contemplated her in the light of the Word made man." It was always to be so.[116]

Incidents in Mary's Ministry

John the Beloved reportedly took Mary "unto his own home" in Jerusalem. That arrangement seems to have lasted about ten years. What happened then is unclear. A late tradition, echoed by Emmerich, claimed that John took her with him to Ephesus, in Asia Minor. According to one source Mary not only went to Ephesus but even spent time in Cyprus and Greece:

> During the persecution initiated by King Herod against the young Church of Christ (*Acts* 12:1-3), the Most Holy Virgin and the Apostle John [the Beloved] withdrew to Ephesus in the year 43.... The Mother of God was on Cyprus with Saint Lazarus ... where he was bishop. She was also on Holy Mount Athos.[117]

The consensus of the early texts, however, is that John left for Ephesus without her. Several texts attest that Mary moved from Jerusalem to Bethlehem, a distance of a few miles or kilometers. They explain that the authorities in Jerusalem were becoming concerned that her presence in the capital was attracting too much attention. But Mary did not go into retirement.

The fifth-century *Transitus Mariae* relates that Mary taught, healed the sick, baptized, and cast out demons. High-ranking women came, "year by year," from Rome, Athens, Alexandria, and other "distant regions" seeking counsel and healing. During one religious festival, "two thousand eight hundred souls, men, and women, and children" were healed.[118]

Chapter 9. Synthesis and Reflections: The Historical Mary

One group of women asked her: 'Tell us, O Lady, mistress of the world, how our Lord Jesus the Christ was born of thee without intercourse with man' And the Lady Mary told them everything that they sought from her."[119] Evidently Mary felt comfortable speaking to the women about the Nativity.

By contrast, the extracanonical *Gospel of Bartholomew* records an incident when the male disciples asked a similar question. Her response was: "If I should begin to tell you, fire will issue forth out of my mouth and consume all the world."[120] It almost did later, when Mary began to tell the disciples of the prophecy of Jesus' birth, uttered by the angel when she lived in the temple: "[A]s she was saying this, fire issued out of her mouth; and the world was at the point to come to an end." But Jesus appeared "and said unto Mary: Utter not this mystery, or this day my whole creation will come to an end."[121]

Clearly, Mary had knowledge that was of exceedingly great power, and the gospel's author was suggesting that she had to learn to discern between what could be revealed and what must forever be held in her heart.[122] The translation of the *Gospel of Bartholomew* continues, in a masterly twentieth-century revival of King James English: "[T]he apostles were taken with fear lest haply the Lord should be wroth with them."[123]

Artwork attests to Mary's involvement in the emerging Eucharistic ritual. Multiple artifacts from the early centuries of the Common Era depict her in Eucharistic vestments, and a notable example from fifteenth-century France is illustrated in Chapter 10. In celebrating the Eucharist, Mary no doubt made good use of the liturgical training she had received in the temple, as well as her memory of the angel's prophecy and even her participation in the ritual of the Last Supper. Whether in Jerusalem or Bethlehem Mary helped mold the sacrament and sacrifice of Bread and Wine for later generations of Christians.

Mary pursued her ministry for at least eleven, and possibly as many as thirty, years after the death of her son. Bridget of Sweden recorded Mary's comment: "[T]he natural constitution of my body required that I should live longer, that my crown might be increased."[124] The crown clearly referred to Mary's queenship. But it may also have referred to her initiatory status. Esotericists could interpret the "increase" in her crown as step forward on the path toward adeptship. Mary's initiatory path will be discussed later in the chapter.

The Conclusion of Mary's Earthly Life

Dormition and Assumption

According to the *Transitus Mariae*, Mary was alerted to her approaching death by the Archangel Gabriel: "Hail to thee, mother of God! Thy prayer has been accepted to heaven before thy Son, our Lord Jesus Christ. And therefore thou shalt depart from this world unto life everlasting."[125] Mary confirmed the essence of that prophecy in a communications with Bridget of Sweden: "I beheld a radiant angel, such as I had before seen, who said to me: 'Thy Son, who is our Lord and God, sent me to announce to thee, that the time is at hand, when thou shalt come bodily to him, to receive the crown prepared for thee.'"[126] By then, Mary was expected to have earned her awaited crown.

What happened next is confused by conflicting stories in the early Christian texts about Mary's location, Jerusalem or Bethlehem; her interaction with the angel; and her performance of ritual offerings.

In some texts the angel gave Mary a palm-staff, which she carried to the Mount of Olives "with the Angel's light shining ahead of her." Then Mary cried out to her son: "I have painfully given birth first to you and them to all who hope in you. Hear the prayer of your mother Mary crying out to you."[127]

Other texts describe a more composed Mary consoling her followers and assuring them that death will not separate them from her care: "[W]hen I stand before him [the Father], I will not cease to pray and intercede on behalf of you and all Christians and the entire world."[128] This statement is significant in the light of belief in the celestial Mary's response to intercessory prayer.

We also find Mary confidently making offerings of incense—a traditional Jewish ritual. For example, "one Friday," Mary asked for incense to be brought to her, "for I wish to pray to my Master the Christ whom I have in heaven." She then prayed thus: "My Master, the Christ, listen to the voice of Thy mother. And send me Mar ['my lord'] John, that I may see him. And I thank Thee for Thy goodness. I know that Thou hearest me in what I ask from Thee."[129] Upon John's arrival, Mary asked him: "Put incense in the censer and pray." He did so, calling on Christ: "Grant that she see you while still living.'"[130]

Chapter 9. Synthesis and Reflections: The Historical Mary

Soon thereafter, Jesus' other disciples were summoned from the mission fields and transported miraculously to Mary's bedside. She blessed the disciples and the women who had cared for her. Whether Paul was among the disciples is disputed, and there is disagreement over the timing of Thomas' arrival.

Christ himself came. Mary "made an offering for the entire world and for every soul that calls upon the Lord and calls upon the name of his mother." Finally,

> the Lord held forth his right hand, blessed his mother and said to her: "Let your heart rejoice and be glad, O Mary blessed among women, for every grace and gift has been given to you by my heavenly Father, and every soul that calls on your name with holiness will not be put to shame but will find mercy and comfort both in this life and in the age to come. You, however, come forth to the eternal dwelling places, to unending peace and joy, to the treasure houses of my Father, so that you will see my glory and rejoice by the grace of the Holy Spirit.[131]

Mary's soul was taken up and transported to Paradise.

Those in attendance proceeded to prepare Mary's body for burial. In some texts concerns were expressed that her remains might be seized by the authorities as the funeral procession made its way to the tomb in Jerusalem; but "the Holy Spirit came, and he snatched them up and brought them to Jerusalem."[132] Mary's body was placed in the tomb, and the tomb was sealed.

Several texts assert that Thomas, who had been in India, was unable to reach Mary's bedside before she died. He arrived at the grave site "on the third day" and pleaded with the disciples to open the tomb so he could pay homage. When they did so they found it empty:

> [T]hey did not find the glorious body of the holy mother of Christ, for it had been translated wherever her son and God wished.... They found only the burial wrappings and the shroud in which they had laid her to rest .... [T]he body of the immaculate Virgin was not there ... it had been raised up to her son and God.[133]

In her communications with Bridget, Mary was ambiguous about the length of time her body lay in the grave. In one instance she stated: "For fifteen days my body lay buried in the earth; then, with a multitude of angels, it was assumed into heaven."[134] But a sentence or two later Mary commented: "And when dead, I lay in the sepulcher three days; then I was taken up to heaven with infinite honor and joy."[135]

Eastern Orthodox tradition recalls that Mary appeared to the disciples on the evening following the discovery of her empty tomb:

> On the evening of the same day, when the Apostles had gathered at a house to strengthen themselves with food, the Mother of God appeared to them and said: "Rejoice! I am with you all the days of your lives." This so gladdened the Apostles and everyone with them, that they took a portion of the bread, set aside at the meal in memory of the Savior ("the Lord's Portion"), and they exclaimed: "Most Holy Theotokos, save us."[136]

The early Christian texts do not agree on whether Mary's body and soul were reunited. They do agree, however, that Mary died. The belief—encouraged, though not mandated, by the Roman dogma of the Assumption—that Mary's body and soul were assumed into heaven before she died receives no support from the early texts. It seems to have arisen solely from the pious desire to spare Mary the ignominy of death.

Demise of the Church of Jerusalem

We do not know definitively when Mary passed away, but it was unlikely to have been later than 60 CE. Mercifully, she was spared the demise of the Christian community she served and the destruction of Jerusalem, a city of so many memories, bitter and sweet. The circumstances of Jerusalem's destruction involve the Christian community, the larger Jewish community, and the Roman occupation forces.

The Christian community in Jerusalem viewed itself as Jewish. It was a sect within Judaism: the "Jesus sect," and its members participated in temple and synagogue rites. Pentecost was a Jewish feast, and Christians probably continued to observe it for its traditional significance as well as for the descent of the Holy Spirit on that notable occasion. We learn that Paul hastened on one of his journeys, hoping "to be at Jerusalem the day of Pentecost."[137] Other traditional holy days were also observed. *Acts* 12 records that Peter was freed from Herod's prison during "the days of unleavened bread."[138] The days of unleavened bread, recalling the Israelite's deliverance from Egypt, are mentioned again in *Acts* 20. *Acts* 27 mentions "the fast," a reference to the Day of Atonement.[139]

Chapter 9. Synthesis and Reflections: The Historical Mary

Organizational leadership of the Jerusalem community was the responsibility of James, "brother of the Lord. Retroactively he was described as "first bishop of Jerusalem," though he would not have recognized the term. Especially after Mary's death the community turned to James for spiritual leadership too.

The "Jesus sect" competed with other branches of Judaism for the hearts and minds of the people. Tensions between the Christianity community and the Jewish establishment mounted. Sometime in the 60s, CE James was assassinated.[140] According to Christian historian and polemicist Eusebius (c.265– 339), the Jews "were unable to bear longer the testimony of the man who, on account of the excellence of ascetic virtue and of piety which he exhibited in his life, was esteemed by all as the most just of men." James "was thrown from the pinnacle of the temple [and] beaten to death with a club."[141]

For unrelated reasons, Jews throughout Judaea rose up in open rebellion against the Roman occupation in 66 CE. The Jews scored some early victories, but the Emperor Nero ordered the Roman army to crush the revolt; command was entrusted to Vespasian1and then to Titus, both of whom would themselves become emperors. Roman forces laid siege to the heavily defended Jerusalem, and it fell in 70 CE. The Romans destroyed the city and the Jewish temple. The last vestige of the rebellion ended with the fall of Masada in 74 CE.

Eusebius claimed that the Christian community was warned "by a revelation" of the impending siege and took refuge in Pella, across the Jordan River.[142] Also, after the martyrdom of James "the apostles and disciples of the Lord that were still living came together from all directions with those that were related to the Lord according to the flesh (for the majority of them also were still alive)" to choose a successor. Unanimously they selected "Symeon, the son of Clopas, of whom the Gospel also makes mention.... He was a cousin, as they say, of the Savior.... Clopas was a brother of Joseph."[143] Some writers have suggested that Symeon was the younger brother of James: the "Simon" mentioned in two of the canonical gospels as another "brother" of Jesus.[144]

Symeon is listed as the second bishop of Jerusalem. Evidently he returned to Judaea, because the Roman authorities crucified him there, early in the second century. Many members of the original Christian community may have stayed in Pella, however, or migrated east to present-day Syria and beyond. After further rebellions in 115–117 and 132–136 CE, Jerusalem was turned into a Roman city and renamed Aelia Capitolina; a temple to Jupiter was built on the Temple Mount. The great majority of Jews in Judaea were slain, died of privation, or were sold into slavery. Christians were persecuted too, and few lived in Jerusalem from the time of the first rebellion until the fourth century.

The only Christian proto-scriptures written prior to 70 CE were the epistles of Paul and possibly the extracanonical *Gospel of Thomas*. *Mark*, the earliest canonical gospel, was written shortly after 70 CE, and the other canonical gospels in the latter years of the first century; the *Acts of the Apostles* may have been written early in the second century. Thus, the gospels and *Acts* were written at a time when Jews in Palestine faced great hostility from the Roman authorities.

The New Testament betrays anti-Semitic bias. For example, the gospels attempt to shift responsibility for Jesus' death from the Romans, who actually carried out his execution, onto the Jewish authorities; Pontius Pilate is depicted as a weak ruler, swayed in his judgments by a Jewish mob. Late-first-century Christians may have been trying to distance themselves from the Jews and gain Roman sympathy. Some writers assert that the Jewish establishment expelled Christians from the synagogues in retaliation for complicity with the Romans; others assert that Christians themselves gradually disengaged from the synagogues and established their own places of worship.

Not surprisingly, the New Testament authors felt disinclined to write about the Judaic Christian community in Jerusalem. Mary's post-Pentecostal ministry was not recorded and would soon be forgotten. Some of the liturgical rites Mary practiced—rites that she learned in the temple and which provided continuity between Judaic and Christian worship—may have been lost. Christianity increasingly severed its Judaic cultural roots. Judaic Christianity survived for a while in some marginalized groups, referred to as "Ebionites," or "Nazarenes";[145] but it was completely gone by the end of the fourth century.

The Christianity we know is the Christianity of Paul. Paul never met Jesus and clearly had little interest in his earthly life; he never mentioned Mary and made only one reference to James.[146] It is also clear from the Council of Jerusalem that he was taking Christianity in a new direction, targeted at the Greco-Roman world. The official history of nascent Christianity, presented in the New Testament, with the

Chapter 9. Synthesis and Reflections: The Historical Mary

possible exception of *Matthew*,[147] embodies a Pauline vision of the new religion.

When the Emperor Constantine embraced Christianity in the fourth century it was Greco-Roman Christianity. The Jerusalem community had already faded from memory. New centers of ecclesiastical power were emerging: Antioch, Alexandria, Rome, and eventually Constantinople. Constantine and his mother Helen restored some of the sacred sites in Jerusalem, and the city became a pilgrimage destination; but it never regained political importance in the church or its standing in the Christian world.

Also forgotten were the ideals of sharing within the Christian community—ideals that Mary herself had promoted even before Jesus was born. In the church of the Roman Empire, and beyond, wealth inequality was no longer considered antithetical with Christianity. Among the first to avail themselves of that new freedom were the bishops.

Mary's Spiritual Status

In this chapter, and most of the earlier chapters, the implicit assumption was made that the historical Mary belonged to the human lifewave—that she was an "ordinary" member of the human family, albeit one who made extraordinary progress on the spiritual path. We believe this to be the correct assumption, supported by the great weight of evidence.

For completeness, however, we must acknowledge an alternative theory: that the historical Mary was an *avatara*, as the term is used in the religions of South Asia. *Avataras* therein are believed to be manifestations or incarnations of deities, sent to Earth to carry out prescribed missions. They have no individual monad or incarnational history.

Mary as Avatara

The avatara theory received support in discussions of the World Mother by Theosophists and others, and discussants used the term in the traditional sense. The Theosophists were unsure whether the World Mother was an office in the Planetary Hierarchy or was a divine being or entity. But those who took the latter view declared that she sent avataras to Earth, and the Christian Theosophists identified Mary as one of those avataras.

For example, Geoffrey Hodson made the statement that the World Mother chose "to minister to mankind under the Parviti [sic], true Kwan [sic] Yin, Ishtar, Hathor-Isis, Lady Mary Individualities."[148]

Mary's own words strongly suggest that she holds the *office* of World Mother: "I ... serve as far as I am capable in the Department known as 'World Mother.'"[149] So the issue of avataras may be moot. But the avatara theory is also weak in placing Mary in the same category as the other cited personages.

Ishtar, Parvati, Ishtar, Hathar and Isis were envisioned by their respective cultures as mythological rather than historical figures. One legend identified Kuan Yin with the princess Miao Shan,[150] while other legends assign her different identities. It is unclear what Hodson meant by the "true Kwan Yin."

Although Mary was the subject of many legends, nowhere does the account of her life suggest that she was purely mythological. In a biography extending from her conception to her physical death, she comes across as a "flesh and blood" human being. Accordingly, we reaffirm the belief that Mary was a member of the human family.

Future revelation may resolve the conflicting theories into a larger synthesis. Even now, limited common ground can be found. Esoteric teacher Alice Bailey offered a broader definition of *avatara* that may allow the term to extend to a human Mary. Writing for the Master Djwhal Khul, Bailey defined an *avatar* (we are using *avatara* as the feminine form) as:

> a Being Who—having first developed His Own nature, human and divine, and then transcended it—is capable of reflecting some cosmic Principle or divine quality and energy which will produce the desired effect upon humanity, evoking a reaction, producing a needed stimulation and, as it is esoterically called, "leading to the rending of a veil and the permeation of light."[151]

Bailey added: "The response or reaction of humanity ... establishes in due time the recognition of something transcendent, something to be desired and striven for, something which indicates a vision which is first a possibility and later an achievement."[152]

Mary's mission to serve as the mother of Jesus certainly reflected "divine quality and energy." It "produced the desired effect upon humanity," rent a veil and permeated light, and evoked "the recognition of

Chapter 9. Synthesis and Reflections: The Historical Mary

something transcendent ... a possibility and later an achievement." Based on Bailey's definition we can preserve the notion that Mary was an avatara, in the sense of carrying out a divine mission, while avoiding the need to abandon the belief that she was a member of the human family.

Preparation for Mary's Palestinian Lifetime

A member of the human lifewave has, or *is*, an individualized monad and has an incarnational history. The conclusion that the historical Mary was truly human allows us to speak of her monad and her incarnations prior to birth in late-first century BCE Palestine.

The monad that incarnated as the historical Mary may have been identified as the future mother of Jesus thousands of years earlier—perhaps even at what Christianity terms "the beginning." Bernard of Clairvaux (1090–1153) affirmed: "Now, when the Creator of men willed to become man and to be born in the human way, it was necessary for Him to select, or rather to create for Himself, out of all possible women, such a Mother as He foreknew would be worthy of Him and deserving of His esteem."[153] Anne Catherine Emmerich (1774–1824) commented:

> The Blessed Virgin was the one and only pure blossom of the human race, flowering in the fullness of time.... She alone was the pure immaculate flesh and blood of the whole human race, prepared and purified and ordained and consecrated through all the generations of her ancestors.... She was preordained in eternity and passed through time as the Mother of the Eternal.[154]

Mary's soul no doubt was groomed for her Palestinian mission over the course of multiple lifetimes. The *Qur'an* traces her lineage, on her mother's side, back to Moses and Aaron. Aaron was chosen by God to be the first high priest, and his descendents formed a priestly lineage.[155] Mary may have attained the third initiation as Miriam the Prophetess, sister of Moses and Aaron.

From *Exodus* we learn that Miriam kept watch while Moses lay in an "ark of bulrushes" on the edge of the Nile. and when he was rescued by Pharaoh's daughter she fetched her mother to serve as his "nurse."[156] Much later, after Moses led the Israelites across the Red Sea, Miriam "took a timbrel in her hand; and all the women went out after her with timbrels and with dances. And Miriam answered them,

Sing ye to the Lord, for he hath triumphed gloriously; the horse and his rider hath he thrown into the sea."[157]

Mary as Adept

As a member of the human family, Mary's adeptship would have been the culmination of a long journey on the initiatory path, extending over multiple incarnations. But it is not unusual for an individual to attain two major initiations in the same lifetime. Mary's participation in the Sacrifice of the Cross likely offered the setting in which she attained the fourth initiation. Mary then continued Christ's ministry—counseling, teaching, healing, and enacting sacred ritual—making it her own. She assumed a leadership position in the Christian community of Jerusalem, recognized as a Priestess who spanned Judaic and nascent Christian traditions. Pope Pius XII's suggestion that Mary's invocation secured the descent of the Holy Spirit on the disciples at the first "Christian" Pentecost implies considerable spiritual authority.[158] Mary was already a fourth-degree initiate and was preparing for the fifth initiation.

Mary commented: "[T]he natural constitution of my body required that I should live longer, that my crown might be increased." In due course the angel told her: "[T]he time is at hand ... to receive the crown prepared for thee." The crown not only signified her queenship, it was also the fifth initiation. And she may have been crowned on her deathbed, or shortly thereafter, when her soul was transported to heaven.[159] Christ's words immediately before her death: "[F]or every grace and gift has been given to you by my heavenly Father," are significant in that regard. According to Alice Bailey, the initiator, or hierophant, for the fifth initiation is the Planetary Logos,[160] but Christ would have served as Mary's sponsor.

Writing in the 1920s, Charles Leadbeater declared that Mary "became, indeed, an adept" during her Palestinian lifetime.[161] Many years later Geoffrey Hodson reaffirmed that Mary attained the fifth initiation, overcoming unusual challenges related to her gender:

> Having been ... the Mother of Jesus ... She did Herself attain to Adeptship, took the Fifth Initiation in the Egyptian Mysteries, having also been trained in their Chaldean form, as a woman, meaning in a female body. The tests were very severe in those days, especially for beginners, even for males, but She passed through them all successfully, almost overriding them as it were,

Chapter 9. Synthesis and Reflections: The Historical Mary

instead of being subjected to them. She was then one of earth's Adepts.[162]

Theosophist Annie Besant declared that the "Mysteries of Egypt were the glory of that ancient land, and the noblest sons of Greece, such as Plato, went to Saïs and to Thebes to be initiated by Egyptian Teachers of Wisdom."[163] The Egyptian mysteries are believed to have developed as "sects" focused on the deities of particular regions and eras. Historians identify the Mysteries of Osiris and Isis as two principal forms.[164] The Master Polidorus explained that the former, which had a masculine polarity, were associated more strongly with the human kingdom, and the latter, which had a feminine polarity, with the devic kingdom.[165] If the Mysteries of Isis were still in existence in the first century CE, they would have offered an attractive option for Mary.

Having completed her incarnational journey on Earth Mary was free to choose her next phase of service. "Each Adept," she explained to Hodson,

> pursues both a particular path of Self-expression that is decided largely by the nature of the Monad, and fulfils the associated duties sometimes but not always as an Adept Official.... I in My turn, continuing to express innate Monadic accentuations, serve as far as I am capable in the Department known as "World Mother."[166]

"Monadic accentuations" is interpreted to mean Mary's femininity, insofar as it extends to the monadic level.

Hodson also reported that, after her death, Mary "left the human kingdom ... and entered the Angelic Hierarchy, being naturally moved to do so, knowing that with Her nature She could best help onward the evolution of human beings and animals as a Member of the Angelic Hosts."[167]

---

[1] Louis-Marie de Montfort, *True Devotion to Mary* (transl.: F. W. Faber), Tan Books, 1712/2010, 2. Perhaps that intent explains the failure of the synoptic gospels to place Mary at the cross and the oblique reference to her at the tomb in *Matthew* 27:61.

[2] Clemens W. Brentano (ed.), *The Life of the Blessed Virgin Mary: From the Visions of Ven. Anne Catherine Emmerich* (transl.: M. Palairet), Tan Books, 1954/1970, 15-16.

[3] *Ibid.*, 72-73.
[4] *Infancy Gospel of James* 1-3, (transl.: A. Roberts & J. Donaldson), *Early Christian Writings*, 7.
[5] Anna Raimondi, *Conversations with Mary: Messages of Love, Healing, Hope, and Unity for Everyone*, Atria, 2017, 22.
[6] *Qur'an* 3:37 (transl: T. Khalidi), Viking Press, 2008. "Allah" is restored to conform to other translations. Note that, to this today, Arab Christians refer to God as "Allah."
[7] *Infancy Gospel of James* 8.
[8] *Gospel of Bartholomew* II:4-5 (transl.: M. R. James), Gnostic Society Library, 18-19.
[9] See the discussion in Ally Katseusz, "She Sacrificed Herself as the Priest," *Journal of Feminist Studies in Religion* (Spring 2017), 45-67.
[10] Brentano (ed.), *The Life of the Blessed Virgin Mary*, 131.
[11] Raimondi, *Conversations with Mary*, 22.
[12] Luke is also thought to have been a physician.
[13] The Hodegon Monastery in present-day Istanbul is said to have been founded by St Pulcheria (399–453) to house one of the icons she brought from Antioch.
[14] Brentano (ed.), *The Life of the Blessed Virgin Mary*, 94.
[15] *Ibid.*, 136.
[16] "Epiphanius of Salamis," *Legends of Our Lady Mary the Perpetual Virgin and her Mother Hanna*, Medici Press, 1922, xxiii. Parenthetical inserts presumably by the translator. *the Perpetual Virgin and her Mother Hanna*, xxiii. Parenthetical inserts presumably by the translator. Other writers attribute this statement to another Epiphanius, Epiphanius the Monk, who lived in the eighth or ninth century. See for example Geoffrey Ashe, *The Virgin: Mary's Cult and the Re-Emergence of the Goddess*, Arkana, 1976/1988, 79.
[17] Raimondi, *Conversations with Mary*, 2.
[18] *Ibid.*, 17.
[19] Brentano (ed.), *The Life of the Blessed Virgin Mary*, 110.
[20] *Ibid.*, 115.
[21] "Sahidic Fragments of the Life of the Virgin," vol. I. 15, fragment II A, vv. 13-17. J. Armitage Robinson (ed.), *Texts and Studies: Contributions to Biblical and Patristic Literature*, Cambridge Univ. Press, 1896.
[22] Brentano (ed.), *The Life of the Blessed Virgin Mary*, 136.
[23] "Epiphanius of Salamis," *Legends of Our Lady Mary the Perpetual Virgin and her Mother Hanna*, xxiii. Parenthetical inserts presumably by the translator.
[24] Raimondi, *Conversations with Mary*, 17.
[25] A famous example is the Coventry Carol, which begins: "Lullay, thou little tiny child. Sleep well, lully, lullay."

Chapter 9. Synthesis and Reflections: The Historical Mary

[26] Helena I. Roerich, *Supermundane: The Inner Life*, Agni Yoga, book 1, 1938, §147.
[27] *Ibid.* Mary grew up speaking Aramaic and no doubt learned Hebrew in the temple. She may also have acquired some knowledge of Latin, Greek or Coptic. She and Joseph would have been exposed to Coptic during their stay in Egypt.
[28] *Luke* 1:28, 30-31.
[29] https://www.rupertbrooke.com/poems/1912-1913/mary_and_gabriel/. Last accessed March 25, 2020.
[30] Bridget of Sweden, *Revelations of St Bridget*, Tan Books, 1862/2015, 21.
[31] Anne Catherine Emmerich claimed that Mary had never met Elizabeth.
[32] *Luke* 1:42-43, 45.
[33] *Ibid.* 1:46-50.
[34] Paul made a similar affirmation in *1 Thessalonians* 5:23. But the Fourth Council of Constantinople (869) ignored the scriptural record and decreed that we are no more than body and soul.
[35] *Luke* 51-53.
[36] Dietrich Bonhoeffer, Sermon on the Third Sunday of Advent, 1933. Online: http://locusthoney.blogspot.com/2011/12/sermon-on-magnificat-by-dietrich.html.
[37] *Matthew* 2:1.
[38] Brentano (ed.), *The Life of the Blessed Virgin Mary*, 170.
[39] *Luke* 2:7.
[40] Bridget of Sweden, *Revelations of St Bridget*, 25.
[41] *Ibid.*, 26.
[42] *Luke* 2:13-14.
[43] *Matthew* 2:1-2, 11.
[44] Basilica of Sant'Apollinare Nuovo, Ravenna, left lateral wall mosaic: https://en.wikipedia.org/wiki/Basilica_of_Sant%27Apollinare_Nuovo#/media/File:Sant_Apollinare_Nuovo_North_Wall_Panorama_01.jpg. Last accessed Sept. 17, 2021.
[45] Harriette A. & F. Homer Curtiss, *The Key of Destiny*, Sun Books, 1923, 319. In numerology 22 is considered a "master number," it is sometimes called the "angel number."
[46] *Ibid.* 2:34-35.
[47] The Seven Sorrows are: The prophecy of Simeon; The flight into Egypt (*Matthew* 2:13, 14); the loss of the Child Jesus in the temple (*Luke* 2: 43-45); the meeting of Jesus and Mary on the Way of the Cross; the Crucifixion; the descent from the Cross; and the burial of Jesus.
[48] *Luke* 2:32.
[49] *Ibid.* 2:36-38.

[50] Nicene Creed. "For us and for our salvation he came down from heaven: by the power of the Holy Spirit he became incarnate from the Virgin Mary, and was made man." *Book of Common Prayer*, 1979, 358.

[51] John 1:14.

[52] Rowan Williams, *Ponder these Things: Praying with Icons of the Virgin*," Sheed and Ward, 2002, 31.

[53] *Ibid.*, 45.

[54] Quoted in Marianne Dorman, "Andrewes and the Caroline Divines: Teachings on the Blessed Virgin Mary," Ecumenical Society of the Blessed Virgin Mary, 2000.

[55] Reuchlin's arguments were presented in his book *De Verbo Mirifico* ("On the Miraculous Word"). See, for example: Gershom Scholem, *Kabbalah*, Meridian, 1974, 198. See also the Introduction to Johann Reuchlin, *On the Art of the Kabbalah*, Univ. of Nebraska Press, 1993, xix-xxi.

[56] Hans Urs von Balthasar, *Light of the Word: Brief Reflections on the Sunday Readings*, Ignatius, 1993, reading for Christmas, Mass during the day.

[57] Evelyn Underhill, *Mysticism: A Study in the Nature and Development of Spiritual Consciousness*, 3/e, Dutton, 1912, 141.

[58] Baird T. Spanding, *Life and Teachings of the Masters of the Far East*, vol. II, DeVorss, 1927, 71-72.

[59] Some commentators have seen a correspondence with the *Tikkun Olam* of esoteric Judaism. In particular, the Safed Kabbalists wrote of repairing the world after the shattering of the vessels. See for example John F. Nash "From the Zohar to Safed: Development of the Theoretical Kabbalah," *The Esoteric Quarterly* (Summer 2009), 21-46.

[60] The Scotist position is named after its chief exponent: Scottish Franciscan theologian John Duns Scotus (c.1266–1308).

[61] J. A. McGuckin, "The Strategic Adaptation of Deification," *Partakers of the Divine Nature*, Baker Academic, 2008, 105-107.

[62] Alice A. Bailey, *The Externalization of the Hierarchy*, Lucis Trust, 1957, 161-162. The Spirit of Peace is described as a "mysterious and divine Entity" who may, at some time in the future send "an Avatar or Messenger of Peace to lead the nations to right action; perhaps some happening will take place of such significance that its import will be immediately recognized by humanity as a whole, leading them to take all the needed steps to restore right human relations," 159, 161.

[63] *Ibid.*, 162.

[64] *Ibid.*

[65] By contrast, the Vestal Virgins of ancient Rome took a 30-year vow of celibacy and performed liturgical duties in adulthood.

Chapter 9. Synthesis and Reflections: The Historical Mary

[66] *Life of the Virgin* (transl.: S. J. Shoemaker), New Haven, CT: Yale Univ. Press, 2012, §17, 48. Clearly, Maximus was questioning Joseph's potency.

[67] "Against Antidicomarians," *The Panarion of Epiphanius of Salamis* (transl.: F. Williams) 2/e, Nag Hammadi and Manichaean Studies, §10, 10.

[68] *Life of the Virgin* §97, 124-125. Maximus the Confessor, to whom *Life* is attributed, would only say that James "was called the brother of the Lord on account of his great virtue."

[69] Vincent Sablon, *Histoire de l'Auguste et Vénérable Église*, 1671; extract in Robert Branner (ed.), *Chartres Cathedral*, Norton & Co., 1969, 107-114. At least five earlier cathedrals occupied the site since the Diocese of Chartres was formed in the 4th century. All were destroyed by fire. The present cathedral of Our Lady of Chartres was constructed between 1194 and 1220.

[70] Bailey, *The Externalization of the Hierarchy*, 155.

[71] The inextinguishability of life can be assured in other ways than the resuscitation of a corpse. One does not have to deny the Incarnation in order to react against a pervasive reluctance to see beyond physical reality.

[72] Was that her defining characteristic? We are reminded of the unfortunate monikers hung on other historical figures, like "Charles the Bald," "Piero the Gouty," "Henry the Impotent," and "Ludwig the Mad."

[73] Robert P. Maloney, "The Historical Mary," *America, the Jesuit Review* (December 19), 2005.

[74] Roerich, *Supermundane*, book 1, §147.

[75] *Ibid.*

[76] *John* 2:4.

[77] *Ibid.* 2:5.

[78] John Paul II, *Rosarium Virginis Mariae*, Apostolic Letter, Vatican, October 16, 2002, §21.

[79] John Paul II, *Ecclesia de Eucharistia*, Encyclical Letter, Vatican, April 17, 2003, ch.6, §53.

[80] Ally Kateusz, *Mary and Early Christian Women: Hidden Leadership*, Palgrave, 2019, 132-133.

[81] *John* 19:25-27.

[82] *Mark* 15:40.

[83] *Matthew* 27:55-56, *Luke* 23:49. The claim is sometimes made that "Mary the mother of James the less and of Joses" was actually Mary the mother of Jesus; but why her more obvious identity would be concealed is unclear. It should be noted that the authors of the synoptic gospels made no claim to have witnessed the Crucifixion.

[84] The Polish artist Bogdan Cierpisz painted a *Pietà* in 1980, inspired by a 15th-century work.

[85] Carl E. Schmöger (ed.), *The Life Jesus Christ and Biblical Revelations: From the Visions of Ven. Anne Catherine Emmerich*, vol. IV (transl.: "an American nun"), Tan Books, 1914/2011, 42.
[86] *Life of the Virgin* §84, 111.
[87] Bridget of Sweden, *Revelations of St Bridget*, 44. The rest of the description is graphic.
[88] *Ibid.*, 63.
[89] *Stabat Mater*, by Jacopone di Benedetti (13th century). Translation by Edward Caswall.
[90] Raimondi, *Conversations with Mary*, 63-64.
[91] Velma W. Sykes, "Two Mothers." A native of Garnett, Kansas, Velma West Sykes (1893-1976) published poetry in the *Saturday Evening Post, Science Monthly, Harp*, and *Kansas Magazine. Midrash* is a literary style, notably used during the rabbinic period of Judaism, consisting of commentary on, interpretation of, and embellishment of scriptural texts. In recent decades it has become popular among Jewish feminist writers like Rabbi Jill Hammer.
[92] *Ibid.*
[93] Sermon 138. Quoted in Ineke Cornet, *The Arnhem Mystical Sermons*, 211. The manuscripts date from the sixteenth-century, but the sermons themselves may be earlier. The names of the homilists are not listed.
[94] *Ibid.*
[95] Julien Loriot, Sermon 10 on the Purification, ib. 316. Cited in http://www.womenpriests.org/mrpriest/loriot.asp. Last accessed Nov. 22, 2018.
[96] Nicholas Wiseman, *Sermons on our Lord Jesus Christ and his Blessed Mother*, 2/e, Duffy, 1866, 342-343. http://www.womenpriests.org/mrpriest/m_sacrif.asp. Last accessed Nov. 22, 2018.
[97] Jean Nazlian (or Naslian), Proceedings of the 25th Congrès Eucharistique International, Lourdes, Secretariat General, 1914. Online: https://archive.org/details/xxvecongreseucha00inte/page/36/mode/2up. Last accessed Jan. 14, 2020.
[98] "Homily of John the Son of Zebedee," E. A. Wallis Budge, *Legends of Our Lady Mary the Perpetual Virgin and her Mother Hanna*, Medici Press, 1922, 245ff.
[99] *John* 20:1-10
[100] *1 Corinthians* 15:5-8.
[101] *Life of the Virgin* §92, 119.
[102] Brentano (ed.), *The Life of the Blessed Virgin Mary*, 357.
[103] "Bartholomew the Apostle." E. A. Wallis Budge, *Legends of Our Lady Mary the Perpetual Virgin and her Mother Hanna*, Medici Press, 1922, xxxvii-xxxix.

Chapter 9. Synthesis and Reflections: The Historical Mary

[104] Brentano (ed.), *The Life of the Blessed Virgin Mary*, 412.
[105] *Acts* 1:14.
[106] *Acts* 2:2-3.
[107] Pius XII, Encyclical letter *Mystici Corporis Christi*, ("The Mystical Body of Christ"), Vatican, June 29, 1943, §110. Pius may have based his observation on the comment in *Acts* 1:14 that the disciples "continued with one accord in prayer and supplication, with the women, and Mary the mother of Jesus, and with his brethren."
[108] *1 Corinthians* 12:8-10.
[109] *Acts* 2:44-47.
[110] *Life of the Virgin* §97, 124.
[111] *The Ethiopic Six Books*. Appendix D of S. J. Shoemaker, *Ancient Traditions of the Virgin Mary's Dormition and Assumption*, Oxford Univ. Press, 2002, 378.
[112] Kateusz, *Mary and Early Christian Women*, 70.
[113] The complete image can be seen at http://teca.bmlonline.it/ImageViewer/servlet/ImageViewer?idr=TECA0000025956&keyworks=Plut.01.56#page/37/mode/1up. Last accessed Sept. 9, 2019. Therein, and sometimes elsewhere, it is titled "the Resurrection," missing the point that Mary is the central character. The image of Mary in the *Rabbula Gospels* illumination seems to have inspired a twelfth-century mosaic in the Duomo di Cefalù, Sicily. The similarities are striking: Mary's hands are raised in blessing, the enchirion hangs from her girdle, even the color of her shoes and the placement of her feet are the same.
[114] Kateusz, *Mary and Early Christian Women*, 71.
[115] François Drouilly, *15 Days of Prayer with Jean-Claude Colin* (transl.: P. Gage), New City, 2002, 114.
[116] John Paul II, Encyclical letter *Redemptoris Mater*, part 2, §27, March 25, 1987.
[117] "The Dormition of our Most Holy Lady the Mother of God and Ever-Virgin Mary," Orthodox Church in America. Online: https://www.oca.org/saints/lives/2013/08/15/102302-the-dormition-of-our-most-holy-lady-the-mother-of-god-and-ever-v. Last accessed May 19, 2021. Parenthesis in original. *Acts* 12 records that Herod killed James the Apostle and imprisoned Peter.
[118] *Transitus Mariae*. Reproduced in Agnes Smith Lewis (ed.), *Apocrypha Syriaca*, Clay & Sons, 1909. Reprint: Cambridge Univ. Press, 2012, 35.
[119] *Ibid.*, 34.
[120] *Gospel of Bartholomew* II:4-5 (transl.: M. R. James), Gnostic Society Library.
[121] *Ibid.* 22.

[122] On a separate issue, Jesus' reference to "my creation" suggests that the *Gospel of Bartholomew*—or at least that passage—was written after the Christological concepts of the Nicene Creed had begun to take shape. Earlier, the author would probably have recorded Jesus' words as "my Father's creation."

[123] Note: this translation was published in 1924! The translator, Montague Rhodes James, provost of King's College, Cambridge, and vice-chancellor of the University of Cambridge, clearly sought to imitate the timeless English of the King James Bible.

[124] Bridget of Sweden, *Revelations of St Bridget*, 67.

[125] *Transitus Mariae*, 20.

[126] Bridget of Sweden, *Revelations of St Bridget*, 68.

[127] *Narrative of John the Theologian and Evangelist, concerning the Dormition of the Most Holy Theotokos and how the Undefiled Mother of Our Lord was Translated.* Appendix B of S. J. Shoemaker, *Ancient Traditions of the Virgin Mary's Dormition and Assumption*, 356-357.

[128] *Life of the Virgin* §106, 132.

[129] *Transitus Mariae*, 25.

[130] *The Ethiopic Six Books*, 380.

[131] *Life of the Virgin* §111,136.

[132] "The Ethiopic Six Books," 386.

[133] *Life of the Virgin* §117, 141.

[134] Bridget of Sweden, *Revelations of St Bridget*, 86.

[135] *Ibid.*, 86-87.

[136] "The Dormition of our Most Holy Lady the Mother of God and Ever-Virgin Mary." Parenthesis in original.

[137] *Acts* 20:16.

[138] *Ibid.* 12:3-11.

[139] *Ibid.* 27:9. The Day of Atonement is the only day in Scripture commanded by God to be a day of fasting (*Leviticus* 23:27).

[140] Historians disagree on whether James was murdered in 62 or 69 CE. Also, traditional Judaism was itself fragmented, and some historians question whether there was a "Jewish establishment" at the time; James may have been killed by one or other of the competing Jewish factions. The assassination of this James should be distinguished from the slaying of "James the brother of John with the sword." The latter incident, recorded in *Acts* 12:2, took place some two decades earlier.

[141] Eusebius of Caesarea, *Church History*, book II, ch. 23:2-3.

[142] *Ibid.*, book III, ch. 5:3.

[143] *Ibid.*, book III, ch. 11:1-2. Parenthesis in original or translation. We recall that Anne Catherine Emmerich mentioned a "Cleophas," husband of Mary's aunt Maria Heli.

[144] *Mark* 6:3; *Matthew* 13:55-56.

Chapter 9. Synthesis and Reflections: The Historical Mary

[145] *Ebionite* means "poor one." It may refer to the ascetic lifestyles of the later sect, but it also recalls the socialist principles of the Jerusalem church, suggesting the possibility of direct lineage.

[146] Paul did, however, call James a "pillar" of the church (*Galatians* 2:9).

[147] The Ebionites are alleged to have used a Hebrew or Aramaic version of *Matthew* that omitted the genealogy and reference to the virgin birth. Some writers have theorized that the New Testament *Matthew* was based on that original.

[148] Sandra Hodson (ed.), *Light of the Sanctuary: The Occult Diary of Geoffrey Hodson*, published posthumously, Theosophical Publishers, 1988, 268. Those personages extend over a period of more than 5,000 years. A cult of Ishtar existed in Mesopotamia in the fourth millennium BCE, while a female Kuan Yin emerged in Chinese Buddhism in the eleventh century CE—a thousand years after Mary. Note that Charles Leadbeater and Hodson also wrote in support of the alternative view that Mary belonged to the human kingdom.

[149] S. Hodson (ed.), *Light of the Sanctuary*, 284.

[150] Martin Palmer, *et al.*, *The Kuan Yin Chronicles: The Myths and Prophecies of the Chinese Goddess of Compassion*, Hampton Roads, 2009.

[151] Bailey, *The Externalization of the Hierarchy*, 291. Capitalization in original.

[152] *Ibid.*

[153] Bernard of Clairvaux, Second Sermon on the Glories of the Virgin Mother" (transl.: "a priest"), *St Bernard's Sermons on the Blessed Virgin Mary*, Mount Melleray Abbey, 1987, 15.

[154] Brentano (ed.), *The Life of the Blessed Virgin Mary*, 147.

[155] *Exodus* 28:1. The priestly lineage has always been understood to flow through Aaron's male descendents, but Mary—and Christ—established a new dispensation.

[156] *Exodus* 2:3-9.

[157] *Ibid.* 15:20-21.

[158] Pius XII, Encyclical letter *Mystici Corporis Christi*, ("The Mystical Body of Christ"), Vatican, June 29, 1943, §110.

[159] Some of the early texts claim that Mary's body was raised from the dead. Christian esotericists typically associate the fifth initiation with Christ's Resurrection, though Alice Bailey insisted: "the seventh initiation ... is the true resurrection. The correct name for the fifth initiation is the Initiation of Revelation." *The Rays and The Initiations*, Lucis Trust, 1960, 643.

[160] Bailey, *The Rays and The Initiations*, 56.

[161] Charles Leadbeater, *Christian Gnosis*, Theosophical Publishing House, 1983/2011, 193.

[162] S. Hodson (ed.), *Light of the Sanctuary*, 267.

[163] Annie W. Besant, *Esoteric Christianity or The Lesser Mysteries*, 2/e, Theosophical Publ House, 1905/1966, 14. In the 2006 edition this quote appears on p. 11.
[164] See for example the works of Egyptologist Ernest A. Wallis Budge (1857–1934).
[165] S. Hodson (ed.), *Light of the Sanctuary*, 414.
[166] *Ibid.*, 284.
[167] *Ibid.*, 268.

Chapter 10
Synthesis and Reflections: The Celestial Mary

Chapter 10 identifies and examines the qualities of the "celestial Mary": the subject of Christian devotion and doctrine and of modern esoteric teachings. Along with Chapter 9 it presents Mary as Adept, Queen, Mother, Priestess; an expression of the Feminine Aspect of Deity; a role model for our time and all time.

The discussion of Mary's spiritual status continues. This chapter affirms monadic continuity between a human historical Mary and the celestial Mary, and rejects claims that a celestial Mary existed before the historical Mary was born. The chapter concludes with some comments on Mary's influence in the church and the world.

The Celestial Mary

Except perhaps in segments of Protestantism, Mary is seen not just as an historical figure but also as a living being, continuing to play a vital role in Christianity and the world— today's world. Christian devotion and theological speculation developed an image of this "celestial" Mary, and esoteric teachings added new dimensions to that image. Her characteristics differ in important ways from those of the historical Mary, raising questions about the spiritual status of each and even the relationship between them.

The historical Mary was an assertive Middle Eastern woman steeped in Judaic tradition. The celestial Mary became a "European," "Christian" woman of high social status and mild manners. She was named *Theotokos* (interpreted in the West as "Mother of God"), Queen of Heaven, Star of the Sea, and eventually Mother of the World. The celestial Mary is a figure of power and glory.

We might ask whether the celestial Mary is simply the product of human imagination. But she is revealing more of herself, through ap-

373

paritions and other communications, offering reassurance that she is real. Her communications and modern esoteric teachings have also provided new insights into her relationship with the historical Mary.

The Collyridians were criticized for worshipping Mary. Later, Protestants accused Roman Catholics of doing the same, and in the 1960s the Church of Rome became self-conscious about its "Marian cult." At times Mary became a goddess in the mass consciousness, though the medieval church and its Roman and Orthodox successors tried to keep her just below the divine level.

The celestial Mary has played a major role in Christianity. Why is she so important? Institutional Judaism and Christianity projected masculine characteristics onto their God, leaving people with hunger for an expression of the Feminine Face of God. Contemporary Sufi teacher Llewellyn Vaughan-Lee reflected on the unfilled need:

> The feminine is the matrix of creation.... Out of the substance of her very being life comes forth. She can conceive and give birth, participate in the greatest mystery of bringing a soul into life. And yet we have forgotten, or been denied, the depths of this mystery, of how the divine light of the soul creates a body in the womb of a woman, and how the mother shares in this wonder, giving her own blood, her own body, to what will be born. Our culture's focus on a disembodied, transcendent God has left women bereft, denying them the sacredness of this simple mystery of divine love.[1]

Perhaps it has left men similarly bereft.

The priests and prophets of pre-Exile Judaism continually confronted an undercurrent of goddess worship among the masses—and sometimes by royalty. In Christianity people turned to Mary. With the spread of Christianity into the pagan world, Mary took the place of popular goddesses. She often assumed characteristics of earlier deities, especially Queen and Mother. Fortunately, Mary was never seen as a war goddess, and over-emphasis on her virginity—regrettable in many other ways—may have saved her from becoming a fertility goddess.

Church leaders capitalized on Mary's potential to lure people away from their pagan goddesses. And, from pastoral concerns, they recognized people's need for a female spiritual role model. They allowed her to be revered as Queen, first in a devotional context and eventually as possible doctrine.

Chapter 10. Synthesis and Reflections: The Celestial Mary

As Queen, Mary captured people's need for a female deity whom they could worship—or come as close to worship as the church would allow. As Mother she served as one to whom they could turn in their troubles and sorrows. Mary, who had been Jesus' mother and then spiritual mother of the Jerusalem community, became mother to all Christians who needed her.

Marian devotion may have started at a grassroots level, but it was soon embraced by prominent clergy, from Cyril of Alexandria to Thomas à Kempis, to Louis-Marie de Montfort. The western church struggled to define acceptable limits of devotion. If the Collyridians went too far in one direction, certainly the Protestants went too far in the other. The Eastern churches were less self-conscious, preferring to focus on liturgical elegance; for example, we find Marian titles like "Mother of an unsetting star," "Dawn of the mystic day," and "Ray of the spiritual Sun."[2]

Medieval art depicted the celestial Mary as an unworldly figure, and the icons of the Eastern churches continue to show her thus. Western artists increasingly presented Mary as a more accessible, human figure—albeit of their patrons' social standing and occasionally resembling patrons' family members. Mary was also presented as a demure, submissive figure, contrasting with the assertive leader of the Jerusalem church. The church tried to reconcile the submissive image with the theological status it accorded her, like "Mother of God," by insisting that her status came entirely through the grace of her son.

Music added an important dimension to Marian devotion and intercession, as it did to the whole Christian liturgy. Music can express, sometimes better than words, the heights and lows of emotion, soaring adoration and bitter lamentation. Not surprisingly, Marian themes—notably the *Magnificat* and the *Ave Maria*—inspired much of our sacred musical heritage.

Mariology, the branch of theology devoted to Mary, faced some interesting challenges. The church had declared Mary to be the mother of God—perhaps without considering the implications of its decree—but stopped short of affirming her divinity. It was hamstrung by the insistence on a strict metaphysical dichotomy between "divine" and "non-divine." Had the theologians recognized divinity in the whole of creation, expressed more by some entities than by others, they would have felt more freedom to acknowledge Mary's divinity.

Instead, dogmatic development focused on Mary's virginity and then, in the Church of Rome, on her Immaculate Conception and Assumption into heaven. Doctrinal discussion also continued on a broad front, below the level of dogma, exploring her role in the Redemption and in the dispensation of grace. Another line of inquiry explored the possibility that Mary had been chosen "in the beginning"— predestined—to be the mother of Christ.

Mary Revealing Herself

The celestial Mary is reaching out to humanity though apparitions, visitations, locutions, and communications with selected individuals. Chapter 6 studied the apparitions at Guadalupe, Lourdes, Fátima, Zeitoun and Medjugorje. It also studied one-on-one communications with Bridget of Sweden in the fourteenth century and with Geoffrey Hodson and Anna Raimondi in our own time. Mary may also be revealing herself in a more general way through the empowerment of women—where it has been permitted—in public life and in the church.

Mary's physical appearance, in both her historical and her celestial phases, has long been a matter for discussion. She seems to have considerable freedom in how she presents herself in apparitions and visitations. Geoffrey Hodson (1886–1983) suggested that Mary assumes a form that people will recognize: she "responds to and permits Herself to be mentally molded by our religious conceptions, and Who permits Herself to be seen in forms acceptable and helpful to those who are accorded the appropriate vision."[3] Mary herself confirmed that assertion in a communication to Anna Raimondi:

> I look like what the beholder wants me to look like. If one wants me to be of fair skin and light eyes, so be it. If that brings comfort, so be it.... I am a being now of love and comfort. I have no skin color and all skin colors. I have no distinguishing features and yet carry the beauty of all the world as I embrace your energies and raise your vibrations.[4]

Evidently Mary approves of representations of herself in any ethnicity, or according to any cultural norms, that may inspire viewers or artists. All must understand, however, that the particular ethnicity or culture is not the only appropriate one, or that it might be superior to another.

Chapter 10. Synthesis and Reflections: The Celestial Mary

We must also understand that few icons, paintings or statues are intended to resemble the historical Mary.[5] Our culture generally demands that religious images look old, but not too old; we want them to display hallowed archaism but to avoid a level of historical accuracy that would make them unrecognizable or disturbing.[6] A parallel impulse may explain the popularity of the King James Bible: its language evokes a sense of archaic reverence, but it is still English and not so archaic as to be unintelligible.[7]

Chapter 3 cited an early-Christian writer's forty-two "salutations" to the parts of Mary's body, which included: "Salutation to thine arms, and to thy forearms, and to thy bosom wherewith thou hast embraced Christ, the Pearl of the Godhead, the Hidden One. O Mary, thou chosen one, our Mother of angels and men."[8]

Lest we question that writer's detailed focus, a comparable litany of salutations is attributed to Christ himself. Bridget of Sweden (c.1303–1373) reported a "revelation" in which Christ told his mother: "Your head was like gleaming gold and your hair like sunbeams, because your most pure virginity ... pleased me and shone in my sight with all humility."[9] He went on to comment on each part of her body, beginning with her ears and ending with her womb. Of that last he declared: "Your womb was a spiritual and physical space so desirable to me and your soul so pleasing to me that I did not disdain to come down to you from the highest heaven and to dwell in you."[10] Perhaps we can discern here a reference to the *Shekinah* of rabbinic Judaism.

Bridget reported that in one vision Mary wore "a priceless and inestimable crown on her head, with her wonderfully beautiful hair hanging down over her shoulders, a golden tunic gleaming indescribably bright, and a mantle of the color of azure on a calm day."[11] At Guadalupe, Mary wore a pink, patterned robe, covered by a deep-blue mantle emblazoned with stars.[12] At Lourdes she wore "a white dress, a blue girdle and a yellow rose on each foot."[13] At Fátima—and at Knock, Ireland, in 1879—she was dressed entirely in white.

Hodson described Mary during a visitation in 1945: "Our Lady ... appeared as a highly spiritual, wonderfully refined young lady of perhaps twenty-eight years. She spoke in a voice of compelling sweetness and beauty and with the most engaging charm."[14] Hodson did not mistake the sweetness of Mary's voice for any lack of authority; and perhaps therein lies a message to modern women seeking to project

377

Mary: Adept, Queen, Mother, Priestess

their own power. Perhaps, also, we can understand the sweet femininity of Theosophist Katherine Tingley's "Real Woman."[15]

Witnesses to the Medjugorje apparitions testified that Mary's face is long and oval; she has black hair; her eyes are blue with delicate eyelashes and thin black eyebrows. She has a small nose and rosy cheeks. She has reddish lips and her smile is "like some indescribable gentleness." Her simple dress is bluish-grey and falls freely all the way down to the cloud on which she stands. Her pure-white veil covers her head and shoulders and also reaches down to the cloud. She wears a crown of twelve golden stars on her head.[16] One witness, Mirjana Dragićević-Soldo, commented:

> A beautiful blueness encompassed the woman. Her skin was imbued with an olive-hued radiance, and her eyes reminded me of the translucent blue of the Adriatic. A white veil concealed most of her long, black hair, except for a curl visible near her forehead and locks hanging down below the veil. She wore a long dress that fell past her feet. Everything I saw seemed supernatural, from the unearthly blue-gray glow of her dress to the breathtaking intensity of her gaze.[17]

Dragićević-Soldo testified that on Christmas Day, 1981, Mary appeared in a different outfit: a golden dress of "unearthly brilliance."

Despite the flexibility in appearance at her disposal, Mary has maintained surprising consistency in apparitions over the last several centuries. In multiple instances Mary has appeared as a young woman, in her late teens or twenties. She has dark hair—though we do not hear of the auburn, or "reddish golden," hair of the historical Mary. Her head is usually veiled, and she wears flowing robes that fall to her feet. In a few cases her robes have been purely white, but more often she dresses in blue and white. Accessories may be of a contrasting color, like pink or yellow. On special occasions she may wear golden robes and a crown.

We must be cautious in reading too much into what seems to be Mary's consistency in appearance. Possibly it lay in the expectations of the cultures and institutions that recorded and "validated" the apparitions; Mary may have appeared in quite different ways in contacts that went unreported, were never investigated, or were wrongly dismissed as invalid.

Chapter 10. Synthesis and Reflections: The Celestial Mary

Witnesses to Marian apparitions frequently commented on Mary's beauty. After the eighteenth, and last, apparition at Lourdes, Bernadette Soubirous remarked: "I have never seen her [Mary] so beautiful before ... so lovely that, when you have seen her once, you would willingly die to see her again!"[18] The Medjugorje witnesses commented in a joint statement: "It is not our kind of beauty. It is something ethereal, something heavenly, something that we'll only see in Paradise."[19] One of them asked Mary, "How is it possible that you are so beautiful?" The response was "I am beautiful because I love. If you want to be beautiful, then love."[20]

The very nature of apparitions makes it difficult to distinguish Mary's attire, especially her robes and veil, from her aura. Hodson commented on one visitation:

> The glory of divinity is all about her.... Her splendid aura of soft yet brilliant hues forms a shining halo of glory all about Her, veiling and yet revealing Her immortal loveliness. Deep blue, silvery white, rose, golden yellow, and the soft green of young leaves in spring flow continually throughout Her lovely auric robes in wave on wave of color and of living light. And ever and anon Her rich deep blue pervades the whole, lit up by stars and bright gleams of silvery hue.[21]

And on another visitation: "Her shining blue aura seemed to enfold me for a moment, and its light to fill the room."[22] Dragićević-Soldo affirmed: "The 'color' of her dress ... is almost like light—but an ethereal sort of light that bends, flows, and undulates according to Our Lady's movements and the feelings she wishes to convey."[23] The golden Christmas robes may simply have expressed the heightened vibration of the season.

Anna Kingsford (1846–1888) did not claim to have seen her, but she declared that Mary "is represented as clad in celestial azure."[24] Mary told Raimondi: "I am the blue vibration of truth."[25] The color blue might place Mary on the Sixth Ray of Devotion, but her healing ministry strongly suggests the Second Ray of Love–Wisdom, which also has blue as one of its colors.[26] Hindu scholar and early Theosophist Tallapragada Subba Row (1856–1890) explained: "There is a Ray specially adapted to women; it is sometimes called the "body of love.""[27] He did not identify the ray, but its association with love points to the Second Ray.

According to Alice Bailey our Solar Logos, unambiguously a Second-Ray entity, is "concentrating on the love or blue aspect."[28] In esoteric teachings the Solar Logos is the expression of God revealed to, and perceived by, consciousnesses within the solar system. The seven rays are divine emanations that "color" every created entity; combinations of rays give the entity distinctive characteristics.[29]

Significantly, the star Sirius is blue-white in color. Esoterically, Sirius is known as the cosmic heart center, the center of love in our region of the galaxy. Moreover, Earth's advanced initiates become initiates of Sirius; our fifth initiation—which Mary attained—is said to be the first initiation of the Sirian system.[30]

Adept, Queen, Mother, Priestess

Mary as Adept and Queen

A crucial step in the progression from the historical Mary to the celestial Mary was her attainment of the fifth initiation—when, in the words of Charles Leadbeater (1854–1934), she "became, indeed, an adept."[31] Geoffrey Hodson reaffirmed Mary's adeptship: "She did Herself attain to Adeptship, took the Fifth Initiation in the Egyptian Mysteries."[32] As noted in Chapter 9, Mary most likely attained the fifth initiation on her deathbed, when Christ called her to "come forth to the eternal dwelling places, to unending peace and joy, to the treasure houses of my Father, so that you will see my glory and rejoice by the grace of the Holy Spirit."[33]

Adeptship represents completion of the phase of human development we are currently in. The adept no longer needs to incarnate in a physical body, though a *mayavirupa*, or "temporary" body, can be manifested for a specific mission.[34] A mayavirupa may be compared with the "spiritual body" referred to in *1 Corinthians* 15:44. Adeptship represents a state of "relative perfection," given that we shall never reach a stage where opportunities for further perfectibility are denied us. The closest equivalent to adeptship in traditional Christian teachings is *theosis*, or "deification," and Sergei Bulgakov (1871–1944) affirmed that Mary "achieved perfect theosis."[35]

Mary is also a queen. During the Davidic monarchy in ancient Israel the king's mother often enjoyed social and political preeminence over the king's wives. Not simply a revered dowager, she might be the most powerful woman in the land; she reigned as queen. For example

Chapter 10. Synthesis and Reflections: The Celestial Mary

we find Bathsheba sitting on a throne next to her son, King Solomon.[36] Christianity drew upon worthy precedents when it anointed Mary Christ's queen.

From early times Christianity accorded Mary royal status, as Queen of Heaven or Queen of the Angels. Maximus the Confessor referred to Mary as "Queen Theotokos."[37] The medieval Marian anthem *Ave Regina Coelorum* includes the lines: "Hail, Queen of Heaven. Hail, Lady of Angels." The coronation of Mary became a popular theme for artists from the Gothic period onward. A detail from the *Madonna of the Magnificat*, by Sandro Botticelli (1445–1510), is shown in Figure 10.1.[38]

Figure 10.1. *Madonna del Magnificat* ("Madonna of the Magnificat"), detail, by Sandro Botticelli (1481). Botticelli created some of the most beautiful sacred images of the Renaissance—or perhaps of all time.

Mary: Adept, Queen, Mother, Priestess

Mary told Bridget of Sweden: "I am the Queen of Angels,"[39] and "I am the Queen of Heaven."[40] In the revelation mentioned earlier, Bridget reported that Christ spoke of the "crown" of his own divinity, telling Mary: "And you, my most sweet Mother won this crown and drew it to yourself through righteousness and love.... Therefore, dear Mother, the crown that was held in my keeping ... should be placed on no one but you, for you are truly Mother and Virgin."[41]

French priest Louis-Marie de Montfort (1673–1716), canonized in 1947, referred to Mary as "this radiant, immaculate, loving, all-powerful queen."[42] Pope Pius XII declared May 31 to be the feast of the "Queenship of Mary[43]—a date that also celebrated the Visitation. The feast was later moved to August 22, the octave of the feast of Mary's Dormition/Assumption.

The Eastern Orthodox churches acknowledge Mary as Queen of Heaven but are more cautious in using the term. They tend to prefer the traditional *Theotokos*, which they leave untranslated.

In mainstream Christianity the title "Queen of the Angels" is understood in a devotional context. Esoteric teachings showed that the title has literal meaning. Leadbeater explained: "finding the seven paths open before her, she [Mary] chose to enter the glorious Deva evolution and was received into it with great honor and distinction."[44] We recall that the deva evolution embraces a vast range of ethereal lives, from nature spirits to the mightiest archangels. Mary really did become Queen of the Angels.

The "seven paths" refer to options available to a newly crowned adept.[45] Some options involve leaving the planet to serve elsewhere in the solar system or beyond. Another option is to remain on Earth to serve humanity; the Masters Morya, Kuthumi, Djwhal Khul, and Polidorus made that choice. Moving to the deva evolution is a less-common but not-unprecedented option. It may have been easier for Mary than for a male adept because the deva evolution has a feminine polarity relative to the human kingdom.[46]

Corinne Heline (1882–1975) commented: "Upon the completion of her earth mission, the holy Virgin was lifted out of the human stream and translated into the angelic evolution."[47] Leadbeater declared that Mary is now "a mighty Angel, having under Her a vast host of subordinate Angels, whom She keeps perpetually employed in the work which is especially committed to Her.[48] The Queen of the Angels does not just sit on a throne; we trust that she experiences great joy, but her position carries immense responsibilities and she works ceaselessly.

Although Mary moved to the devic kingdoms, she retained her concern for humanity. She cares for women and children, and especially for women in childbirth. In Leadbeater's words: "As Queen of the Angels, [Mary] is present through Her representatives at every birth that takes place in the world. Never a child is born anywhere but the World Mother's representative stands by to give such strength, and such comfort, as karma may permit."[49]

Mary has also expressed concern for animals and, probably through her relationship with the devas, for the higher ranks of the vegetable kingdom. Heline remarked:

> The Blessed Lady is known as Queen of the Angels because of her intimate relationship with these bright beings. During each month of the yearly cycle the angels infuse the body of the earth with a particular emanation that manifests in certain rhythms of tone and color. In this pulsating color-music are formed the celestial patterns of the flower kingdom.[50]

"Bright being" is a close translation of the Sanskrit word *deva*.

In her *Conversations* with Anna Raimondi, Mary affirmed: "I am the Queen of Angels and heaven." Mary explained: "I am here, as the other masters in spirit and the angels, to teach and enlighten my children and lead all to the kingdom. I pray that my messages will be heard and the world find love and peace."[51]

In Mary's queenship we see a remarkable convergence of traditional Christian and esoteric teachings. Esotericists might wish to join their Roman Catholic brothers and sisters in celebrating the feast of the Queenship of Mary on August 22.

Mary as Mother

Humanity has a primal need for a divine Mother, recognized not only for her creative potential but also for her comfort of the afflicted. Mother goddesses played major roles in antiquity. The title "Mother of the World" has a long tradition in the religions of South Asia. Its first known appearance in the West was in the Kabbalistic text *Sefer ha-Bahir* ("Brilliance"), attributed to the first-century rabbi Nehuniah ben HaKanah and published in Provence in the twelfth century.[52]

Institutional Christianity decreed that Mary was the mother of God in 431 CE but never officially identified her as our mother too. Formal titles like Mother of Humanity, Mother of the World, and Mother of the Church are fairly recent and have not attained dogmatic status. Yet from early times people saw Mary as a mother figure and turned to her in their sorrows and grief. Sometimes they just wanted a shoulder to cry on. More often they approached her with their petitions. The first known prayer to Mary, the third-century *Sub tuum Praesidium*, was an intercessory prayer.

Not only was Mary believed to be sympathetic, she was believed to have a measure of power over Christ to grant favors to those who prayed to her. The Second Council of Constantinople affirmed that those who "with sincere faith seek her [Mary's] intercessions" can have "confidence in her access to our God, since she bare him."[53] Appeal was made to *Luke* 2:51 to argue that Jesus was still in some way obedient to his mother. An Old Testament passage provided further support: when Bathsheba asked "one small petition," King Solomon's response was: "Ask on, my mother: for I will not say thee nay."[54]

The fifteenth-century prayer known as the *Memorare* (Latin: "Remember") expresses feelings of desperation and guilt, but also captures a sense of trust in Mary's help:

> Remember, O most gracious Virgin Mary, that never was it known that anyone who fled to thy protection, implored thy help, or sought thy intercession, was left unaided.
> Inspired by this confidence I fly unto thee, O Virgin of virgins, my Mother.
> To thee do I come, before thee I stand, sinful and sorrowful.
> O Mother of the Word Incarnate, despise not my petitions, but in thy mercy hear and answer me. Amen.[55]

Terms like "my Mother" and "Mother of us all" were accepted in a devotional context but, for many centuries, lacked authoritative or doctrinal support. High-level support finally came in the nineteenth century and has steadily grown in strength.

Cardinal Nicholas Wiseman (1802–1865) addressed Mary as "O Blessed Virgin Mary, Mother of God and *our* most gentle Queen and Mother."[56] Pope Paul VI, writing in 1964 as spokesman for the Sec-

Chapter 10. Synthesis and Reflections: The Celestial Mary

ond Vatican Council, described Mary as "the mother of the members of Christ," adding: "The Catholic Church, taught by the Holy Spirit, honors her with filial affection and piety as a most beloved mother."[57] In 1990, Pope John Paul II addressed Mary in a public prayer: "You who serve as Mother of the whole family of the children of God...."[58]

Pope Pius XII suggested that Mary's prayers secured the descent of the Holy Spirit "on the newly founded Church at Pentecost."[59] If he was right Mary could legitimately be called "Mother of the Church." Indeed a proposal was made during the pontificate of John Paul II to enshrine that title in a dogmatic decree. John Paul declined, yet "Celebration of the Blessed Virgin Mary Mother of the Church" was added to the Roman liturgical calendar in 2018, to be observed the day after Pentecost Sunday.[60] Jesuit priest Robert VerEecke commented on the feast and on Mary's presence with the disciples: "As Mary was once open to the Spirit in the conception of Jesus in her womb, she is here open to the Spirit again, giving birth to the Church in the upper room."[61] In Chapter 3 we noted that Mary became a mother figure to the disciples after the first "Christian" Pentecost.

Esotericists created their own depiction of the Mother of the World, drawing upon Hindu and Buddhist traditions. Charles Leadbeater described the World Mother as "a mighty Being who is at the head of a great department of the organization and government of the world."[62] He did not offer a suggestion as to where, specifically, she might fit into the organization chart of the Planetary Hierarchy. We saw in Chapter 7 that the Theosophists struggled to decide whether the World Mother is a being in her own right, or is an office held by a succession of entities.

According to Helena Roerich (1879–1955) the World Mother expresses both love and beauty: "We see the radiance of the Mother of the World!"[63] She also commented that the Mother is a figure of contrasts: "How beautiful is the Image of the Mother of the World! So much beauty, self-renunciation and tragedy is in this majestic Image!"[64] We are reminded of the contrast between the Christian titles "Our Lady of Victory" and "Mother of Sorrows"—though Roerich, who embraced Buddhism, never discussed a possible connection between the World Mother and Mary.

Roerich remarked on the World Mother's *playfulness*: "The play of the Mother of the World is in joy. She enfolds the enlightened ones in Her veil of joy."[65] While joy is often projected onto Mary, one wonders why playfulness is not more commonly considered one of her attributes. What mother does not play with her children? In children, and in the young of many other species, play is an essential element in the development of cognitive, social, and even survival skills.[66] Perhaps it is also an element in our spiritual development.

Annie Besant (1847–1933) identified the World Mother directly with Mary. In 1928 Besant declared March 25, the feast of the Annunciation, to be World Mother Day.[67] She commented on what we have called Mary's "obstetric" ministry: "Hers is the tender mercy that presides at the birth of every child."[68] Geoffrey Hodson emphasized Mary's compassion and reiterated the attention she pays to mothers in childbirth:

> The Blessed Lady Mary ... moved by purest compassion and love, holds the whole of humanity in Her arms and at Her breast, nourishing it with spiritualizing life for the purpose of quickening the evolution of all sentient beings. The World Mother shares Herself with every mother—human and animal—throughout the periods of the gestation and delivery of her offspring. Impersonally, She is also present and Herself helps the mother during her labor.[69]

Besant also spoke of Mary's healing ministry:

> The sacredness of Motherhood brings Her beside the bed of suffering. Her compassion and Her tenderness, Her all-embracing Motherhood, know no differences of caste, color or rank. All, to Her, are Her children—the tenderest of all human movements and, because the most compassionate, the greatest power in the civilization.[70]

Andrew Harvey (1952–), who was influenced by South Asian traditions independently of Theosophical teachings, believed that Mary was a manifestation of the "Divine Mother":

> In Mary the Divine Mother comes to earth and lives on earth and lives the passionate, strong, serious, simple and transforming life that shows us all how to live. Mary is the bridge between heaven and earth, between the human and the divine worlds, between human and divine justice.[71]

The reference to Mary's strength reminds us that the historical Mary was an assertive leader in the early church, though Harvey evidently saw her as an avatara ("comes to earth...."). Harvey added that recognition of the Mother would restore balance in patriarchal institutional Christianity:

> [S]eeing Mary as the Divine Mother would help us to see Christ too as every much the son of the Divine Mother as the Divine Father. Seeing that would release Christianity from its patriarchal stranglehold and restore the mystical purity of its passion for fraternity and sorority, for equality and social justice and service.[72]

Mary as Priestess

We have seen that an angel prophesied Mary's Eucharistic ministry while she was still in the temple. Later, she may have participated in the institution of the Eucharist. Through her suffering she participated in the Sacrifice of the Cross, and Chapter 9 cited statements by a number of prominent churchmen relating to Mary's priestly role at Calvary. When the body of Jesus was taken from the cross and laid in her arms, who—save the Lord himself at the Last Supper—was more worthy to say: "this is my body, this is my blood"? Mary's sacerdotal role continued into her post-Pentecostal ministry and then into the celestial phase of her life.

Artists in the early church, and later, remembered or envisioned Mary as a priestess. The illumination in the *Rabbula Gospels*, shown in Figure 9.2, depicts Mary with her hands raised in blessing. She is wearing the blue *maphorion*; from her waistband hangs the fringed *enchirion*, or "Eucharistic cloth," signifying high priestly status. A twelfth-century mosaic in the Duomo di Cefalù, Sicily, presents essentially the same image.[73]

Other artwork shows Mary wearing the *pallium*, a stole otherwise reserved for the Jewish high priest, or in the Christian church for senior bishops or the pope. A sixth-century mosaic in the Basilica of Parenzo, Croatia, and an eleventh-century mosaic in Ravenna, Italy, show Mary vested to celebrate the Eucharist. A fifteenth-century painting: *Le sacerdoce de la Vierge* ("Priesthood of the Virgin"), shows Mary vested in a chasuble. The painting, from the School of Amiens, France, is shown in Figure 10.2.

Inspiration for *Le sacerdoce de la Vierge* may have come from a vision Abbess Elisabeth of Schönau (c.1129–1164) had one day during Mass. Mary was "standing beside the altar, in a garment like a priestly chasuble ... and she had on her head a glorious crown."[74]

Mary: Adept, Queen, Mother, Priestess

Charles de Condren (1588–1641), French mystic and doctor of the Sorbonne, Paris, affirmed Mary's continued mystical participation in the Mass:

> A Mass ... will be celebrated every day ... to the intention of the very blessed Mother of God ... I place her Son, Jesus Christ, into the hands (of Mary) by this foundation in as much as I can, and I beg her with my whole heart to offer it herself to God in this daily sacrifice as she does offer it and has offered it, in time and in eternity, on earth as in heaven.[75]

Figure 10.2

Le sacerdoce de la Vierge ("Priesthood of the Virgin"), detail. School of Amiens, France. Early fifteenth century.

The painting may have been inspired by the vision of Elisabeth of Schönau (c.1129–1164).

Condren's contemporary, Spanish Jesuit priest Ferdinand Chirino de Salazar (1575–1646) gave Mary both priestly and royal status:

> Christ the Lord has passed on to Mary much better and much more abundantly than in any other soul or even in the entire Church, the signification of his name. He who is called "Christ" ... poured out

Chapter 10. Synthesis and Reflections: The Celestial Mary

the abundance of his ointment on Mary, and so made her a saint, a queen, a priest, and a governess for ever.[76]

Pope Pius IX wrote in 1873: "Mary united herself so closely to the sacrifice of her divine Son that she has been called the 'Virgin Priest' (*Virgo Sacerdos*) by the Fathers of the Church." Whether the title *Virgo Sacerdos* was actually used by the church fathers is uncertain,[77] but papal endorsement of the term was of some consequence.

Mary's priestly status has received brief but significant attention in esoteric teachings. The Master Polidorus told Geoffrey Hodson to "Meditate upon the mystery of the deific Feminine Principle and its triple function of Queen, Priestess, and Mother of aspiring souls."[78] He repeated the three titles to give them emphasis. Clearly Polidorus wanted "Priestess" to have a significance comparable with "Queen" and "Mother."

Sadly, neither Hodson nor any of his sources elaborated on the concept, or on Mary's own priestly role. But we note that priestesses served in the ancient mystery schools, and Mary was initiated into the Egyptian mysteries. "The Lady Mary," used in early Christian writings, would also have been the honorific of a Mary in the mystery schools.

A number of commentators have seen parallels, even direct connections, between practices in Christianity and in the ancient mystery schools. Annie Besant declared, approvingly, that the Christian sacraments are the successors of the Lesser Mysteries, the more elementary and less secretive of the two major segments of the mysteries.[79] Hodson described a vision in which he "was shown some comparative passages in both the Liberal Catholic Church Liturgy and very old documents, some of which consisted of unbound sheets rather resembling the *Dead Sea Scrolls*." He commented "I was informed that these were preserved rituals of the Ancient Mysteries."[80]

Identifying Mary as a priestess links her not only with the ancient mysteries but with the mysteries of the future. We understand that, along with the Reappearance of the Christ, the Greater Mysteries—the more advanced segment—will once again be enacted in religious or masonic-like settings.[81] The Greater Mysteries can be expected to include at least some of the major initiations discussed in esoteric teachings.[82]

The restored mysteries may incorporate and build on the Christian liturgy, especially the liturgy of the sacraments. baptism, confirmation, holy orders, and the profession of religious vows could serve as the basis for the initiatory mysteries. The sacrifice of the Mass may be elevated to an even higher level, perhaps with the appearance of the Christ, or Christ and Mary together, during the Eucharistic Prayer. Artwork from the early church, showing a priest holding the paten and a priestess holding the chalice, may be prophetic of what we shall witness in the not-too-distant future.

Importantly, we should remember that sacred ritual attracts devic entities.[83] Along with her angelic hosts Mary, the High Priestess, can be expected to participate actively in—perhaps even preside over—major sacred rituals in the coming age.

Mary and the Divine Feminine

Is Mary Divine?

When the Council of Ephesus (431) declared Mary to be the *Theotokos*—understood in the West to mean "Mother of God"—the concept of a human mother giving birth to a deity was not without precedent. Hercules was born of Zeus and the human mother, Alcmene. But Alcmene was the granddaughter of the demigod Perseus and consequently had some "divine blood." Moreover, Hercules' own divinity was not assured at the time of his birth but had to be earned through his labors.

The bold wording of the Ephesus decree exceeded the claims made on Alcmene's behalf. The decree could easily imply that Mary was herself divine. The institutional church denied her that status, but then precisely what was she? The Synod of Hieria (754) affirmed that Mary was "higher than every creature whether visible or invisible."[84] And the Second Council of Nicaea (787) recognized that she deserved a special level of reverence, later termed *hyperdulia* (literally, "above the level shown by slaves to their masters").

From late antiquity onward, influential churchmen tested the boundaries of hyperdulia. Cyril of Alexandria, architect of the Ephesus declaration, extolled Mary's magnificence: "It is you through whom the Holy Trinity is glorified and adored throughout the earth; through whom the heavens exult; through whom the angels and archangels rejoice.'[85] Eleventh-century Peter of Damascus affirmed: "we confess

Chapter 10. Synthesis and Reflections: The Celestial Mary

that you are the Mother of God ... more honored than the cherubim and incomparably more glorious than the seraphim."[86] Peter's contemporary, Bernard of Clairvaux (1090–1153), associated Mary with the "woman clothed with the sun," mentioned in *Revelation*. For her role in the Incarnation Bernard accorded Mary the very highest place in creation; and, since Christ might be out of reach, "we need another to mediate between Him and us."[87]

Twelfth-century abbess Hildegard of Bingen affirmed: "Mary, you are the bright matter through which the Word breathed all the virtues forth, as once he led forth, in the primal matter of the world, the whole of creation."[88] Fifteenth-century mystic Thomas à Kempis urged people to bow when they spoke or heard the name of Mary.[89] Louis-Marie de Montfort (1673–1716) went so far as to declare:

> To Mary, His faithful spouse, God the Holy Spirit has communicated His unspeakable gifts and He has chosen her to be the dispenser of all He possesses, in such wise that she distributes to whom she wills, as much as she wills, as she wills, and when she wills, all His gifts and graces. The Holy Ghost gives no heavenly gift to men which He does not have pass through her virginal hands.[90]

Christianity's struggle to decide whether or not Mary is divine stemmed in large measure from its adherence to a dichotomous distinction between "divine" and "human"—between creator and creature. By contrast, esotericists take the view that the whole of creation is divine, but the degree to which that divinity is manifested depends on an entity's level of consciousness. Mary, like every other member of the human lifewave, has—or at the very center of her being *is*—an individualized monad, a unique fragment of divine essence. Because of her progress on the initiatory path, she expresses her divinity to a far greater degree than does the great mass of humanity.

Paraphrasing Geoffrey Hodson, we asked the question in Chapter 8: "Shall we kneel before the throne of Mary and beseech the heavenly Mother, surrounded by Her court of queens, whence was She born, has She Herself a mother, or is the mighty scale of motherhood complete in Her?" The answer has to be: "no, it is not complete in her." Mary is not God—or, in esoteric terminology, the Logos. Above her lies a divine *principle*: Subba Row's "Cosmic Virgin," or Helena Blavatsky's "immaculate Virgin-Mother," whom they claimed is the

Mary: Adept, Queen, Mother, Priestess

first manifestation of the Godhead. Mary is an *expression* of that principle, a "tangible" expression of the Feminine Face of God.

Mary as an Expression of the Divine Feminine

In a communication with Geoffrey Hodson, the Archangel Bethelda encouraged worship of the Divine Feminine, explaining. "The states of consciousness brought about in those who thus respond inwardly can grow towards the more abstract Feminine Principle in Nature. This principle pervades all creation from the mineral of the dense world to the formless aspects of Solar Systems, Universes, and Cosmoi."[91]

Bethelda told Hodson that, as World Mother, Mary "is to be revered most deeply and humbly."[92] Mary is the living feminine archetype, expressing the qualities of the Feminine Aspect of Deity, whose "triple function" is "Queen, Priestess, and Mother."[93] Andrew Harvey affirmed that Mary serves as "the bridge between heaven and earth, between the human and the divine worlds."[94] Bernard of Clairvaux would have agreed with him.

Hodson declared that, in becoming Mother of the World, Mary established "a conscious union" between the archetypal woman and "the cosmic principle of womanhood."[95] He reached out to the term "hypostatic union" to describe that conscious union—comparing it to the union of the human and divine natures in Christ. Hodson described Mary as an "Embodiment on earth of the Feminine Aspect of the Deity ... in whom all the highest qualities of womanhood and motherhood shine forth in their fullest perfection."[96]

What precisely are those qualities? Two millennia of Marian devotion, and even descriptions of the Marian apparitions, gave us a demure image of Mary that fitted well with ideals built up in western society. The "perfect woman" of a century or more ago was envisioned as "a combination of purity, piety, submissiveness and domesticity."[97] In 1941 Hodson wrote in his diary: "Behind all womanhood exists the Eternal Woman, the one divine manifestation as femininity .... Within and through the feminine personality is made manifest the spirit of femininity, the archetypal woman."[98] He listed the archetypal qualities as follows:

> They are sacrifice, tenderness, graciousness, divine radiance, heavenly fragrance, beauty, and grace. They are wisdom, fathomless as a still dark pool of infinite depth, profound compassion and

Chapter 10. Synthesis and Reflections: The Celestial Mary

intimate concern for all living things, ministration, healing love. They are joyous radiant girlhood, graceful womanhood, creative, preserving, and transforming motherhood.[99]

Today we would paint a richer portrait of the perfect woman. From studying the world's mythologies psychologists conclude that the feminine archetype is quite complex; one list includes seven forms: the Maiden, the Mother, the Queen, the Huntress, the Wise Woman, the Mystic, and the Lover.

We now know that the historical Mary was a strong, assertive woman. She may not have been a huntress, but neither was she the Victorian "perfect woman" or even Hodson's "Eternal Woman." Andrew Harvey described Mary's life as "passionate, strong, serious, simple and transforming." [100] Dietrich Bonhoeffer (1906–1945) spoke of "the passionate, powerful, proud, enthusiastic" historical Mary who followed in the line of "the prophetic women of the Old Testament: Deborah, Judith, Miriam."[101] The celestial Mary could hardly be less.

The Divine Feminine and the Trinity

How does the Feminine Face of God fit into our understanding of the Trinity? Repeated attempts have been made to incorporate a feminine element into the framework of the Trinity. Theophilus, bishop of Antioch (c.117–c.181 CE) failed in his attempt to name Sophia as Third Person of the Trinity. But notions of the femininity of the Third Person continued down the centuries. In our own time Benedictine monk Bede Griffiths unhesitatingly proclaimed the Holy Spirit as feminine and identified Mary as her earthly instrument:

> It is in the Holy Spirit that the feminine aspect of the Godhead can be most clearly seen.... [S]he is the mothering Spirit in humankind, who receives the Word, the Wisdom of God, in her heart, of whom in the Christian tradition Mary is the figure, receiving the Word of God in her heart and bringing him forth in his earthly manifestation.[102]

Identifying the Third Person as God the Mother raises the issue of the order of procession of the Masculine and Feminine Aspects from the Godhead. In multiple traditions the Feminine Aspect is considered to be either the first, or at least an early, manifestation from the Godhead; that Feminine Aspect gave birth to deities as well as to much of what we call creation. We should note that the Trinity itself is a manifestation of the transcendent Godhead.[103]

Another approach to feminizing the Trinity was suggested by Pavel Florensky (1882–1937) and Sergei Bulgakov (1871–1944), both of whom invoked Sophia as their representative of the Feminine. Florensky proposed that Sophia forms a fourth, "junior," hypostasis—turning the Trinity into a quaternity. Bulgakov initially agreed, saying that Sophia forms "a fourth, creaturely, and therefore nonconsubstantial Person" of the Trinity.[104] She "enters into the interior of the Trinity ... into communion with Divine Love." Under pressure from his superiors to preserve the required "threeness," Bulgakov retreated to the position that Sophia is a "non-hypostatic" element of the Trinity as a whole.[105]

Yet another approach would be to view each of the three persons of the Trinity as masculine and feminine dualities. Paracelsus (c.1493–1541) suggested that the First Person of the Trinity is a Father–Mother duality.[106] Building on his suggestion, God the Son could be paired with a God the Daughter. Perhaps the latter will take human form one day—or has already done so. Canadian choral composer David Rain envisioned a second Nativity:

> A new mystery unfoldeth one winter's night. Three kings bring gifts most precious: incense, gold and myrrh. They come from far off lands, guided by a star.... Angels do sing in the heavens with divine choruses, and the people gather around in awe.... She is born in a manger, the humblest of births, in the presence of an ox and ass to comfort her. She cries like any child.... But her soul is aglow, her spirit shineth with radiant love, with love to all people. Surely, goodness and mercy shall follow her all the days of her life and she will dwell in the house of her brother for ever.[107]

Likewise the Holy Spirit could be viewed as a gender duality. To represent the hypostases as dual is not the same as regarding them as androgynous; nor would it turn the Trinity into a hexinity.

Although Bede Griffiths related the Third Person of the Trinity to Mary, "receiving the Word of God in her heart," incorporating Mary into the Trinity itself poses considerable challenges. Yet Lutheran theologian Ludwig Feuerbach (1804–1872) affirmed: "[T]he Virgin Mary fits in perfectly with the relations of the Trinity, since she conceives without man the Son whom the Father begets without woman; so that thus the Holy Virgin is a necessary, inherently requisite antithesis to the Father in the bosom of the Trinity."[108]

Chapter 10. Synthesis and Reflections: The Celestial Mary

Theologians, as well as esotericists, have rich opportunities to explore the incorporation of the Feminine into our concept of Deity. But they must be free to follow promising lines of inquiry without fear of immediate censure; new ideas should be allowed to acquire a degree of maturity before being subjected to critical evaluation. Digressions often bring us back closer to the established body of knowledge than was first anticipated; or they may take us in unforeseen directions. Truth must be trusted to manifest itself, and Wisdom should be our guide.

New dogmas are not the answer. To define the Feminine is to limit it, almost to destroy it. The Feminine Aspect must be experienced, loved and served. Part of the solution lies in Marian devotion, but the full richness of the experience of the Feminine has not yet been attained. The Master Polidorus urged us to "Meditate upon the mystery of the deific Feminine Principle and its triple function of Queen, Priestess, and Mother." The focus should be raised from the emotional to the intuitive levels, as the mystics of every religion have demonstrated; and the Beloved should be sought as a female figure.

A Pre-Existent Celestial Mary?

In Chapter 9 we examined and rejected a theory that the historical Mary was the manifestation of a higher being (other than her own monad). We reaffirmed the traditional belief that she was a spiritually advanced member of the human family.

Another question needs to be addressed: How are the historical Mary and the celestial Mary related? The simple answer is that the historical Mary evolved into the celestial Mary after completing her earthly life. But complicating, or might even undermining, that answer are claims that a "celestial Mary" existed long before the historical Mary was born.

The Claims

Theosophist Annie Besant placed "Mary, the World Mother" at "the dawn of the Day of Creation, of Manifestation, when ... God 'made the worlds.'" The Logos, she explained,

> by His own will limits Himself, making as it were a sphere enclosing the Divine Life, coming forth as a radiant orb of Deity, the Divine Substance, Spirit within and limitation, or Matter, without.

Mary: Adept, Queen, Mother, Priestess

> This is the veil of matter which makes possible the birth of the Logos, Mary, the World-Mother, necessary for the manifestation in time of the Eternal, that Deity may manifest for the building of the worlds.[109]

Clearly Besant placed "Mary, the World-Mother" at the dawn of what esotericists call the *manvantara*; she claimed that Mary was there at the instant when the universe and all life therein came into existence.

Pope Paul VI declared that Mary was "[p]redestined from eternity by that decree of divine providence which determined the incarnation of the Word to be the Mother of God."[110] His successor John Paul II affirmed: "In the mystery of Christ she [Mary] is present even 'before the creation of the world,' as the one whom the Father 'has chosen' as Mother of his Son."[111]

Abbess María de Ágreda (1602–1665) testified: "[T]he Mother of the Divine Word incarnate [was] conceived in the divine mind, in such manner and such state as befitted and became the dignity, excellence and gifts of the humanity of her most holy Son." Mary, was "formed and conceived in the divine mind from the beginning and before all the ages."[112] Anne Catherine Emmerich proclaimed that Mary was "prepared and purified and ordained and consecrated through all the generations of her ancestors.... She was preordained in eternity and passed through time as the Mother of the Eternal."[113]

Bernard of Clairvaux (1090–1153) affirmed: "Now, when the Creator of men willed to become man and to be born in the human way, it was necessary for Him to select, or rather to create for Himself, out of all possible women, such a Mother as He foreknew would be worthy of Him and deserving of His esteem."[114] Bernard went on to identify Mary as "a virgin not newly discovered, nor discovered by chance, but chosen from eternity, foreknown and prepared for Himself by the Most High."[115]

In *Isaiah* we read that "the Lord himself shall give you a sign; Behold, a virgin shall conceive, and bear a son."[116] According to Emmerich, an Essene elder prophesized that a more tangible sign would mark Stolanus' and Emeron's lineal female descendants, leading to the mother of the Redeemer.[117] Their great-granddaughter was Mary.

The *Infancy Gospel of James* testifies that Mary was born under unusual circumstances—possibly even the product of a virgin birth. Pope Pius IX proclaimed as infallible dogma that she was conceived

Chapter 10. Synthesis and Reflections: The Celestial Mary

without original sin.[118] The *Gospel of Luke* records that Mary was "highly favored" and "blessed ... among women," even before she agreed to give birth to Jesus.[119] Mary's consent: "[B]e it unto me according to thy word," was no more than a formality. She was predestined to bear the Redeemer.

Some of these statements could be interpreted simply to mean that a particular human monad was selected at an early date to incarnate in Palestine and give birth to Jesus. Others assign to an entity, whom they identify as Mary, status and qualities beyond what a human monad could have attained by that time. From its creation at the beginning of the manvantara, Mary's monad needed to pass through the mineral, vegetable and animal kingdoms before individualization into the human kingdom.[120] Thereafter, she may have made exceptionally rapid spiritual progress, but it would still have taken her countless lifetimes to evolve to the stage where she incarnated in Palestine. In the earlier stages neither her monad not her soul would have resembled the pre-existent celestial Mary envisioned in the various claims.

Possible Explanations

The statements may simply represent pious hyperbole and need not be taken seriously. Or perhaps the entity in question really was a pre-existent "celestial Mary," distinct from Mary's monad. Or perhaps another entity was mistaken for Mary. This last seems the most plausible explanation.

The descriptions of the supposed pre-existent celestial Mary, offered by the Christian writers, overlaps to a considerable degree with passages in the Old Testament Wisdom Literature relating to Chokmah/Sophia. For example, in *Proverbs* we find: "The Lord possessed me in the beginning ... before his works of old. I was set up from everlasting, from the beginning, or ever the earth was."[121] And in *Ecclesiasticus*: "He created me from the beginning before the world."[122] Did those writers mistake Sophia for Mary? Or did the combination of Marian piety and a desire to minimize Sophia's importance provide the incentive to attach Mary's name to Sophia's characteristics? Instances have already been noted in which Sophia and the later celestial Mary were confused or conflated.

Both the alleged pre-existent celestial Mary and Sophia share important characteristics with the World Mother, as described by Helena Roerich and the Theosophists. Perhaps Sophia and the World Mother

397

Mary: Adept, Queen, Mother, Priestess

are one and the same entity, and Annie Besant projected the image of Mary onto that entity. Alternatively, Besant may have projected the image of Mary onto Subba Row's "Cosmic Virgin," or Helena Blavatsky's "immaculate Virgin-Mother."

Disagreement among the esoteric teachers was noted in Chapter 7 on the issue of whether the World Mother is a being in her own right, or is an office in the Planetary Hierarchy held by a succession of individuals. Sophia could be that being or could be one of the office holders, perhaps Mary's immediate predecessor.

The notion that Mary is the latest individuality to hold the position of World Mother raises the interesting question of what happened to the incumbent when Mary took office. That has not been revealed. But typically, at the conclusion of a term of duty, an entity moves on to service at a higher level. Mary's predecessor may have accepted a new position in, or outside, the solar system. If her predecessor was Sophia, it is significant that the latter's earthly revelations have become infrequent. Vladimir Solovyov (1853–1900) claimed to have seen her, but he may actually have seen Mary.

When a World Mother's term of office comes to the end, it is unlikely that she simply "clears out her desk" and leaves. More likely there is a diligent transfer of wisdom and energy, giving the new office holder the utmost ability to build upon the accomplishments of the past. There may even be a period of overlap, in which the outgoing World Mother provides support to her successor. The incumbent World Mother may have "overshadowed" Mary during the latter's Palestinian lifetime, sharing wisdom, guidance and energy—without disturbing her monadic identity. Anthroposophist Robert Powell (1942–) clearly was exaggerating when he suggested that "the Virgin Mary [is] a complete embodiment of Divine Sophia on a spiritual level,"[123] but he may have glimpsed the truth.

Sophia has attracted much attention among modern feminist theologians seeking a goddess to serve western religion. In their view she has returned from obscurity to champion women's empowerment. But in almost every case the outcome has been to turn her from an entity into an impersonal presence, even an abstraction. To quote Susanne Schaup, for example:

> Her return has no traffic with theological hairsplitting. Whether created or uncreated, emanation or hypostasis, helpmate of crea-

tion or divine creatrix, projection of Jesus or the Virgin Mary or the Church—these intellectual differentiations and theological niceties have lost all meaning. The deeply ambiguous terminology concerning the nature of her divinity is of no interest any more. Sophia is here, a fully empowered presence.[124]

Sophia has become something resembling the Hebrew *ruach ha-kodesh*—perhaps to await re-personification as a future Holy Spirit.

Mary's Influence

Artist and motion-picture producer Alfred Eaker noted that "Being a woman in first century, patriarchal-ruled Judea, Mary is a symbolic outcast, a secondary citizen."[125] He complained that the Second Vatican Council once again made Mary an outcast and second-class citizen. Yet Eaker suggested more optimistically that "sophomoric attempts to appease protestantism hardly stops two millennia of Marian devotion among the laity.... Marian apparitions and pilgrimages to attributed sights of these apparitions are still vigorous forces of mystical inspiration to be reckoned with."[126]

After her death Mary rose again, like her son, and reigns in glory as Queen of Heaven and Mother of the World. She is revealing herself to the world, and her ministry cannot be derailed—even by fears that "Marian excess" and "gross exaggerations" might harm ecumenical outreach.[127]

Lifting the Veils

Helena Roerich declared that the World Mother was forced to veil herself when Atlantis was destroyed; since then she has never "manifested Herself on a planetary scale."[128] But the veil is being lifted allowing the Mother—or her distant successor—to emerge from the shadows. It will not be lifted completely, because the Feminine never gives up all her secrets.

On a smaller scale Mary, who now serves as World Mother, veiled herself for much of Christian history. In scripture she allowed herself to be defined by: "Be it unto me according to thy word."[129] Then she allowed herself to be portrayed in Marian devotion as a demure, submissive figure: eyes cast down, hands clasped in prayer. Perhaps it was appropriate for Mary to withdraw behind that veil; we cannot know either her will or the divine will for a particular era. The familiar image by which we recognized Mary supported the church's and society's subjugation of women; but it may also have served her purpose by making her more accessible to the masses.

Mary's veil is now being lifted too. Scholars have discovered that the historical Mary was more active and assertive than the gospels might suggest. She was a strong leader of nascent Christianity, carrying on her son's ministry of teaching and healing, encouraging his disciples, and helping to mold the emerging sacramental liturgy.

The celestial Mary is also revealing more of herself and reaching out to humanity. Beginning with Guadalupe, Mary's apparitions took on a new quality. She has been seen more frequently; for longer periods of time; and by larger, more diverse, groups of people. Medjugorje, where apparitions have continued for four decades, may be the last in the series. But it is unique in the level of detail of Mary's messages, and perhaps it represents a transition to a mode of contact that already has notable precedents.

Mary recruited individuals like Bridget of Sweden, Geoffrey Hodson, and Anna Raimondi to serve as scribes to disseminate her teachings. We trust that contacts of this nature will continue and expand, and that she will share more of her wisdom. When Christ reappears, and the masters emerge into the light of day, Mary may reveal herself "on a planetary scale" as World Mother.

Mary's primary message is that she wants her loving presence in the world to be known: "I am here, as the other masters in spirit and the angels, to teach and enlighten my children and lead all to the kingdom. I pray that my messages will be heard and the world find love and peace." She wants people of all social, ethnic and religious backgrounds to acknowledge her and come to her. Esoteric teachings stress her healing ministry, her ministry to women and children, and the participation of her devic helpers in childbirth in all the kingdoms of nature.

Anna Kingsford, Roerich, and Annie Besant were all feminist activists,[130] and they saw the reemergence of the Mother as inextricably linked to the empowerment of women. Roerich drew attention to the responsibilities—and opportunities—that would come with empowerment: "In the hands of woman lies the salvation of humanity and of our planet. Woman must realize her significance, the great mission of the Mother of the World; she should be prepared to take responsibility for the destiny of humanity."[131] Roerich also commented: "[T]ruly ... women must sacredly guard the chalice entrusted to them: the moving of the consciousness and the saving of the world." The approaching age is the "epoch of woman. Let our every day be dedicated to the service of the Great Movement."[132]

When Kingsford, Besant and Roerich were writing, the feminist movement was in its infancy. A century or more later, it is still questionable whether Roerich's "epoch of women" has arrived. Yet much progress has been made, and the early pioneers would be encouraged to see the shift in women's roles in the family, business, and the institutions of government. They might also be encouraged to see that at least some segments of Christianity welcome women into the ranks of the clergy—and have benefited greatly by doing so.

Some reactionary factions fear that the patriarchy of the past will simply be replaced by a new dominant matriarchy. More appropriately, the Aquarian Age is expected to bring sharing and balance between the masculine and feminine principles. Mary always deferred to Christ, just as he accorded her the highest honors. We look forward to a world in which men and women can contribute their respective strengths, and in which masculine rationality and feminine intuition can play complementary roles to move our world forward on its evolutionary journey. As Theosophist Katherine Tingley (1847–1929) declared: "We want ... the splendid, royal warriorship of men and women."[133]

Liturgy and Devotion

We also look forward to a spirituality that recognizes and rejoices in both the Masculine and the Feminine Aspects of Deity and in which priests and priestesses can play complementary roles in the liturgy. Neither should be denied any desired role but each should have opportunities to express the unique aspects of his or her gender in the liturgy.

Current liturgies in the "high churches" were designed by and for male clergy; they are based on rigidly scripted rites and rubrics. New liturgical forms should be developed, or old ones rediscovered, that give more expression to the Feminine. They need to be less rigid. Respect must be accorded to tradition, which embodies great energy and beauty, and ritual demands both clear intent and careful preparation. But flexibility is also needed to allow the feminine energy to flow; the

High Priestess in her Wisdom will guide it. The process should not be rushed; it must be approached tastefully and prayerfully. The development of new liturgies will take time, and patience will be needed; but experimentation should be permitted to identify forms with the most promise.

For two millennia, Christians at every level of education and every level of spiritual attainment, have prayed to Mary and offered her praise. Will Marian devotion continue to be important? Some Christians contend that they have moved beyond devotional practices on their spiritual paths.[134] They insist that study, service and activism distinguish "adults of God" from children of God. They argue that we should move from an emotional to a mental form of religion. Those arguments have merit. But before discarding Marian devotional practices as relics of an unsophisticated, sentimental past, perhaps we should look more closely at the nature and content of devotion.

Llewellyn Vaughan-Lee explained devotion as a means to align ourselves with one another, with God, and with the earth.[135] Greater emphasis on prayer that is purely devotional—that is, without an intercessory agenda—would be a beneficial development. Intercession is appropriate at times, but it reminds us of our needs and weaknesses; more generally we should remind ourselves that we are divine beings, with a divine destiny. To pray for the sheer joy of praying would bring us closer to Vaughan-Lee's ideal—and closer to the contemplative practices that grace all religions. Pure devotion would align us with the living, loving consciousness of Mary, Queen of Heaven.

As a Sufi, Vaughan-Lee promoted traditional devotions of his faith that invoke the names of God. We could use devotions that invoke the titles of Mary. Those titles are words of power—power to be used for her purpose, not ours. Marian litanies like the sixteenth-century Litany of Loreto would be suitable,[136] perhaps with "Pray for us" replaced by an affirmation such as "We praise you." In multiple apparitions and other contacts Mary encouraged use of the Rosary. In the Rosary, the words of the Lord's Prayer and Hail Mary can become a mantra, allowing the mind either to find rest or to soar to great heights.

In the years ahead intercessory prayer will progressively give way to invocation. We noted that Mary is opening up a new channel between humanity and the Feminine Aspect of Deity. Marian intercession offers a hint of its operation, though the new channel should not be expected to serve simply, or primarily, as a conduit for petitions. Instead of seeking favors, invocation works with universal laws and within the parameters of Divine Will. It operates on a soul, rather than a personality, level; on a group, rather than an individual, level.

Theosophist Charles Leadbeater commented that if we pray to Mary "it is not that She should intercede for us but we ask Her to use us in Her work, to pour through us the strength which She is spreading abroad on the world and principally on the women of the world."[137] Alice Bailey explained that the "Science of Invocation ... will grow out of the ancient habits of prayer as used by the masses, and the practice of meditation as developed by the mystics and occultists."[138]

When we bring ourselves into harmony with the universe many of our needs are met naturally and automatically. Higher beings are more mindful of our real needs than we are, and see the larger context in which those needs arise. Higher beings, including Mary, may also alert us to opportunities for service: meeting others' needs, protecting the planet, raising the general level of consciousness, or any other area in which we can make a positive difference.

Great opportunities exist for new Marian themes in art and music. Artists have been slow to respond to evidence that the historical Mary was far from demure and submissive—or that the celestial Mary pursues a powerful global ministry. How should Mary be portrayed? No artist, to this author's knowledge, has set aside her traditional robes in favor of modern fashion. A few have shown Mary bareheaded, and in some cases the results have been stunning, though perhaps the traditional "veil" is an essential element of her aura.

Interestingly, musical works inspired by Mary have not always presented a demure, submissive demeanor. For example, settings of the *Magnificat* by composers from Antonio Vivaldi and Johann Sebastian Bach to Charles Villiers Stanford typically have been powerful and dramatic. The comparatively recent setting by Herbert Howells (1945) is more prayerful. It will be interesting to see how future composers present the strong, assertive Mary now coming into focus.

The Future of Christianity

For generations people have predicted the demise of Christianity. Metrics like the decline in membership in mainline denominations, and the increasing numbers of "nones"—people who claim no religious affiliation—relate chiefly to Europe and the English-speaking world, and the trends probably could be reversed if the proposed liturgical developments were allowed to take place. Meanwhile Christianity is flourishing in Central and South America and Africa.[139]

Christianity has timeless value, and its survival is assured for the foreseeable future. Mary urged the continuation of well-established traditions. In one of the Medjugorje messages she said: "You will find strength in the Eucharist .... [L]ook at the Cross. Only in the Cross is salvation."[140] As already noted she promoted use of the Rosary.

Mary lamented the divisions within Christianity. She told Medjugorje witness Vicka Ivanković-Mijatović: "God did not divide people into different religions. Those people divided themselves." Ivanković-Mijatović remarked: "[E]ach one of us should worship God in our own way and pray to Him in our own way. There is only One God and we all believe in One God."[141] Mary told Anna Raimondi: "I am the Queen of Peace for all people. I don't speak peace for only a select few but for the world."[142] She insisted: "Any religion that focuses on sharing love and peace is good but there is no 'one perfect religion.' ... A religion should be welcoming of all people, for all people were created by God."[143]

Alice Bailey shared her vision of the future of Christianity, drawing attention both to its accomplishments and to possible new directions:

> Christianity will ... be transcended, its work of preparation being triumphantly accomplished, and Christ will again give us the next revelation of divinity.... What the new formulation of truth will be, who can say? But the light is slowly pouring into men's hearts and minds, and in this lighted radiance they will vision the new truths and arrive at a fresh enunciation of the ancient wisdom. Through the lens of the illumined mind man will shortly see aspects of divinity hitherto unknown. May there not be qualities and characteristics of the divine nature which are as yet totally unrecognized and unknown? Can there not be revelations of God utterly unprecedented, and for which we have no words or adequate means of expression?[144]

One of the "new truths" should be acknowledgement of the birthing of the universe by the Feminine Aspect of Deity. The concept of birthing, or emanation, was embraced by the Neoplatonists but rejected in the early church in favor of creation *ex nihilo* ("from nothing"). Instead of recognizing the world as an extension of the Divine,

Chapter 10. Synthesis and Reflections: The Celestial Mary

institutional Christianity chose to view it as separate from God. Theologians, from Meister Eckhart (c.1260–c.1328) to Karl Rahner (1904–1984), who preached notions of divine immanence were unfairly labeled "pantheists."[145] A return to the concept of emanation would facilitate renewed recognition of our divine essence and destiny—and the recognition of Mary's divinity.

Bailey continued:

> The fact that the historical Christ existed and walked on earth is the guarantee to us of our own divinity and our ultimate achievement.... The fact of the cosmic Christ, manifest as the urge towards perfection in all the kingdoms of nature, proves the fact of God and is our eternal hope. Humanity stands at the portals of initiation.[146]

The historical Mary served as a similar guarantor of our divinity. And her achievement on the path of initiation serves as a model for our own spiritual journeys.

Mary's Ashram

We understand that Mary works from the Department of the World Mother in the Planetary Hierarchy. But we do not know where it is located relative to the more-familiar departments that express the three Rays of Aspect: "Will and Power," "Love–Wisdom," and "Active Intelligence."[147] Those latter three are said to be on the "human side" of the Hierarchy, while the Department of World Mother presumably lies on the "devic side." Little has been revealed concerning the realms of the Hierarchy associated with the deva evolution.

Nor do we know what structures have been established within the Department of World Mother to coordinate the work of Mary's human and devic disciples. Presumably Mary has formed an ashram, or multiple ashrams, comparable to those of the "human" masters.

Upon her arrival in the deva evolution Mary found orders of angels waiting to serve her commands. She also needs human disciples to help achieve her mission and to make it a reality in the world of human affairs. Among the masters, Mary may be in the enviable position of having a billion or more devotees around the world, from whom to select a body—a network—of active disciples. Louis-Marie de Montfort urged his followers to become "slaves" to Mary—and in turn to Christ—and "to do everything through Mary, with Mary, in Mary, and for Mary!"[148]

Those who pledge themselves to Mary's service have a unique opportunity to serve alongside devic coworkers. Multiple esoteric teachers have predicted closer contacts between the devic and human kingdoms in the Aquarian Age.[149] This development may be a natural outcome of the increasing self-revelation of Mary, Queen of the Angels.

---

[1] Llewellyn Vaughan-Lee, *Return of the Feminine and the World Soul*, Golden Sufi Center, 2009, 3.

[2] Greek Orthodox Archdiocese of America, "The Akathist Hymn and Small Compline," stanza relating to the visit by the Magi and concluding hymn of praise.

[3] Sandra Hodson (ed.), *Light of the Sanctuary: The Occult Diary of Geoffrey Hodson*, Theosophical Publishers, 1988, 284. We should be open to the possibility that Mary might reveal herself to the world, or even to us as individuals, in new ways. How would we react, for instance, if Mary appear in street clothes, a pantsuit, or jeans?

[4] Anna Raimondi, *Conversations with Mary: Messages of Love, Healing, Hope, and Unity for Everyone*, Atria, 2017, 17.

[5] Similar comments could be made about the fair-skinned, blue-eyed Jesus of traditional western Sunday school materials.

[6] Ben Long's fresco *Mary Great with Child* (1972) in St Mary's Church, West Jefferson, North Carolina, provoked controversy because of its realism. For information in the fresco see https://www.spiritualtravels.info/spiritual-sites-around-the-world/north-america/the-ben-long-frescoes-of-north-carolina/. Last accessed February 20, 2020.

[7] The language was archaic even when the King James Bible was published in 1611. The translation used Tudor-era terms and phraseology from a century or more earlier.

[8] "Salutations to the Members of the Body of The Blessed Virgin Mary," E. A. Wallis Budge, *Legends of Our Lady Mary the Perpetual Virgin and her Mother Hanna*, Medici Press, 1922, 236-244.

[9] Bridget of Sweden, *The Revelations of Saint Bridget of Sweden: Books 1-5*, edited by Darrell Wright, CreateSpace Indep. Publ. Platform, 2016, book 5, revelation 4. (Pages not numbered.)

[10] *Ibid.*

[11] *Ibid.*, book1, ch. 31.

Chapter 10. Synthesis and Reflections: The Celestial Mary

[12] See for example D. A. Brading, *Mexican Phoenix: Our Lady of Guadalupe. Image and Tradition over Five Centuries*, Cambridge Univ. Press, 2001.
[13] See for example "Biography of Bernadette Soubirous." online: https://www.biographyonline.net/spiritual/bernadette-soubirious.html. Last accessed Sept. 29, 2019.
[14] S. Hodson (ed.), *Light of the Sanctuary*, 115-116.
[15] Katherine Tingley, *Theosophy: the Path of the Mystic*, 2/e, Theosophical Publ. Co., 1922, 125. "From a Lecture to Women Only, in a series delivered early in 1911."
[16] "The Image of the Queen of Peace." Online: https://www.medjugorje.org/vint1.htm. Last accessed Oct. 4, 2019.
[17] Mirjana Soldo, *My Heart Will Triumph*, CatholicShop, 2016, 28.
[18] "Biography of Bernadette Soubirous." Online: https://www.biographyonline.net/spiritual/bernadette-soubirious.html. Last accessed Sept. 29, 2019.
[19] "The Image of the Queen of Peace."
[20] Soldo, *My Heart Will Triumph*, 83.
[21] Geoffrey Hodson, *The Miracle of Birth*, Theosophical Publ. House, 1929, 63.
[22] S. Hodson (ed.), *Light of the Sanctuary*, 116.
[23] Soldo, *My Heart Will Triumph*, 128.
[24] Anna Kingsford & Edward Maitland, *The Perfect Way, or the Finding of Christ*, Field & Tuer, 3/e, 1890, 54.
[25] Raimondi, *Conversations with Mary*, 32.
[26] See Alice A. Bailey, *Esoteric Psychology*, vol. 1, Lucis Trust, 1936. No definitive assignment of spectral colors has been made to the rays, partly because the perception of color changes with level of consciousness. In one passage Bailey associates the color blue with Ray VI (pp. 121-122); in another passage she associates it with Ray II (p. 127).
[27] T. Subba Row, "Women Adepts," *Esoteric Writings*, Theosophical Publ. House, 1895, 568.
[28] Bailey, *Esoteric Psychology*, vol. 1, 127. For a discussion of the ray of the Solar Logos see Alice A. Bailey, *A Treatise on Cosmic Fire*, Lucis Trust, 1925, 40.
[29] The rays' archetypal names are Will or Power; Love–Wisdom; Active Intelligence; Harmony through Conflict; Concrete Knowledge; Devotion or Idealism; and Ceremonial Order.
[30] Alice A. Bailey, *Initiation, Human & Solar*, Lucis Trust, 1922, 182.
[31] Charles Leadbeater, *Christian Gnosis*, Theosophical Publ. House, 1983/2011, 193. The first edition appeared in 1983, nearly half a century after Leadbeater's death. Citations are from the edition published in 2011.

[32] S. Hodson (ed.), *Light of the Sanctuary*, 267.
[33] *Life of the Virgin* (transl.: S. J. Shoemaker), Yale Univ. Press, 2012, §111, 136.
[34] Bailey, *A Treatise on Cosmic Fire*, 761, 1193. Christ likely appeared to the disciples in a *mayavirupa* after the Resurrection. It has a degree of solidity but may not be subject to ordinary laws of physics.
[35] Boris Jakim, "Sergius Bulgakov: Russian *Theosis*," Michael J. Christensen & Jeffery A. Wittung (eds.), *Partakers of the Divine Nature*, Baker Academic, 2008, 253.
[36] *1 Kings* 2:19.
[37] *Life of the Virgin* §134, 158-159.
[38] The work is exhibited at the Uffizi Galleries, Florence, Italy.
[39] Bridget of Sweden, *The Revelations of Saint Bridget of Sweden*, book 1, ch. 7, edited by Darrell Wright, CreateSpace Indep. Publ. Platform, 2016. (Pages not numbered.)
[40] *Ibid.*, chs. 8, 9, 10.
[41] Bridget of Sweden, *The Revelations of Saint Bridget of Sweden*, book 5, revelation 4.
[42] Louis-Marie de Montfort, *The Secret of Mary* (transl.: E. Doherty), Montfort Publications, c.1708/2001, 31-32.
[43] Pius XII, Encyclical letter *Ad Caeli Reginam*, October 11, 1954, §§1, 6.
[44] Charles W. Leadbeater, *The Masters and the Path*, Theosophical Publishing House, 1925, 288. Leadbeater made a similar point in *The World Mother as Symbol and Fact*, Theosophical Publ. House, 1928, 17-18.
[45] See for example Bailey, *Initiation, Human & Solar*, 185-191.
[46] S. Hodson (ed.), *Light of the Sanctuary*, 268.
[47] Corinne Heline, *The Blessed Virgin Mary: Her Life and Mission*, New Age Press, 1971, 106-107.
[48] Leadbeater, *The World Mother as Symbol and Fact*, 1.
[49] Leadbeater, *Christian Gnosis*, 194.
[50] Heline, *The Blessed Virgin Mary*, 115.
[51] Raimondi, *Conversations with Mary*, 32.
[52] *The Bahir* §104, (transl.: Aryeh Kaplan), Weiser, 1998, 39.
[53] Second Council of Constantinople, Canon 15.
[54] *1 Kings* 2:20.
[55] Source: https://www.vaticannews.va/en/prayers/the-memorare.html. Last accessed April 21, 2021.
[56] Nicholas Wiseman, "Prayer for England." Emphasis added. See for example: https://vultuschristi.org/index.php/2010/09/prayer-for-the-conversion-of-e/.
[57] Paul VI, Dogmatic Constitution on the Church (*Lumen Gentium*), Vatican City, November 21, 1964, ch. VIII, §53.

Chapter 10. Synthesis and Reflections: The Celestial Mary

58. John Paul II, prayer before the Roman Icon of Our Lady, "Salus Populi Romani," December 8, 1990.
59. Pius XII, Encyclical letter *Mystici Corporis Christi*, ("The Mystical Body of Christ"), Vatican, June 29, 1943, §110.
60. Congregation for Divine Worship and the Discipline of the Sacraments, "Decree on the Celebration of the Blessed Virgin Mary Mother of the Church in the General Roman Calendar," Vatican City, Feb. 11, 2018.
61. Robert VerEecke, "Baptized in the Spirit," journal entry for May 24, 2021. Online: http://www.robertvereecke.org/journal. Last accessed May 24, 2021.
62. Leadbeater, *The World Mother as Symbol and Fact*, 1.
63. Helena I. Roerich. *Hierarchy*, book 4. Agni Yoga Society, 1931, 12.
64. Helena I. Roerich. "Mother of the World." *Letters of Helena I. Roerich*, vol. I, Agni Yoga Society, January 9, 1935.
65. Helena I. Roerich, *Fiery World*, vol. I, 663, Agni Yoga Society, 1933.
66. Caitlin O'Connell, "Why Animals Play," *Scientific American* (August 2021), 48-55.
67. Annie W. Besant, "The New Annunciation," Insert in *The Theosophist*, (vol. 49, June 1928).
68. *Ibid.*
69. S. Hodson (ed.), *Light of the Sanctuary*, 414-415.
70. Besant, "The New Annunciation."
71. Andrew Harvey, *Return of the Mother*, Tarcher/Putnam, 2001, 343.
72. *Ibid.*
73. The similarities are striking: Mary's hands are raised in blessing, the enchirion hangs from her girdle, even the color of her shoes and the placement of her feet are the same. For a photograph of the mosaic see: https://en.wikipedia.org/wiki/Cefal%C3%B9_Cathedral#/media/File:Mosaico_della_Cattedrale_di_Cefal%C3%B9.jpg. Last accessed Sept. 16, 2019.
74. Elisabeth of Schönau, *First Book of Visions*, ch. 5. Cited in Anne L. Clark, "The Priesthood of the Virgin Mary: Gender Trouble in the Twelfth Century," *Journal of Feminist Studies in Religion* (Spring 2002), 5-24.
75. Charles de Condren, *Lettres du P. de Condren publiées par P. Auvray et A. Jouffrey*, Paris 1943, appendix 1, § 6. Parenthesis in translation. Cited in http://www.womenpriests.org/charles-de-condren-died-in-1637/. Last accessed Aug. 29, 2019.
76. Ferdinand C. de Salazar, Canticum, vol. 2, 92, 94-95. Cited in https://www.google.com/search?client=firefox-b-1-d&q=Ferdinand+Chirino+de+Salazar. Last accessed Aug. 29, 2019.
77. Christopher Smith, *Mary and the Priesthood*, License Thesis, Pontificia Universitas Gregoriana, Rome, 2005, 25-26.

[78] S. Hodson (ed.), *Light of the Sanctuary*, 413-414.
[79] Annie W. Besant, *Esoteric Christianity or The Lesser Mysteries*, 2/e, Theosophical Publ. House, 1905/1966, especially 222ff. (The corresponding pages in the 2006 edition are 173ff.)
[80] S. Hodson (ed.), *Light of the Sanctuary*, 247.
[81] Writing for the Master Djwhal Khul, Alice Bailey predicted that the Christ will reappear sometime after 2025, and that the masters will once again assume leadership roles in society. See her *The Reappearance of the Christ*, Lucis Trust, 1948; and *The Externalization of the Hierarchy*, Lucis Trust, 1957.
[82] Bailey, *The Externalization of the Hierarchy*, 514-515. See also Bailey, *Initiation, Human & Solar*; Alice A. Bailey, *The Rays and The Initiations*, Lucis Trust, 1960.
[83] See for example Geoffrey Hodson, *Clairvoyant Investigations*, Theosophical Publ. House, 1984.
[84] Synod of Hieria, Canon 15. Online: https://sourcebooks.fordham.edu/source/icono-cncl754.asp. In the nineteenth century Pope Pius IX used similar language in his *ex cathedra* pronouncement *Ineffabilis Deus*.
[85] Cyril of Alexandria, "In Defense of the Theotokos," homily, Council of Ephesus, June 22, 431.
[86] Peter of Damascus, "A Treasury of Divine Knowledge," *Philokalia*, (transl: G. Palmer *et al.*), Eling Trust, 1977, vol. 3, 130.
[87] Bernard of Clairvaux, "Sermon for the Sunday within the Octave of the Assumption," *Sermons on the Blessed Virgin Mary*, Augustine Publ., 1987, 207.
[88] Hildegard of Bingen, Antiphon "O Splendidissima Gemma," *Symphonia*, (transl: M. Atherton), *Hildegard Selected Readings*, Penguin Books, 2001, 117.
[89] Thomas à Kempis, *Founders of the New Devotion: Being the Lives of Gerard Groote, Florentius Radewin and Their Followers*, English translation, Kegan Paul, 1905, 64.
[90] Louis-Marie de Montfort, *True Devotion to Mary* (transl.: F. W. Faber), Tan Books, 1712/2010, 11.
[91] S. Hodson (ed.), *Light of the Sanctuary*, 420.
[92] *Ibid.*, 419.
[93] *Ibid.*, 413-414.
[94] Andrew Harvey, *Return of the Mother*, Tarcher/Putnam, 2001, 343.
[95] S. Hodson (ed.), *Light of the Sanctuary*, 82. Hodson claimed that all women participate in this hypostatic union *in potentia*, 82.
[96] Geoffrey Hodson, *The Kingdom of the Gods*, Theosophical Publ. House, 1952, 244.

Chapter 10. Synthesis and Reflections: The Celestial Mary

[97] Catherine Gourley, *Gibson Girls and Suffragists: Perceptions of Women from 1900 to 1918*, Twenty-First Century Books, 2008, 9-10, 67. The "Gibson Girl," created by American illustrator Charles D. Gibson (1867–1944), was a reaction against the Victorian "true woman," helping to change societal expectations of women's potential.

[98] S. Hodson (ed.), *Light of the Sanctuary*, 81.

[99] *Ibid.*, 81-82.

[100] Harvey, *Return of the Mother*, 343. Hodson did list "transforming motherhood" among his list of archetypal qualities.

[101] Dietrich Bonhoeffer, Sermon on the Third Sunday of Advent, 1933. Online: http://locusthoney.blogspot.com/2011/12/sermon-on-magnificat-by-dietrich.html.

[102] Bede Griffiths, *Marriage of East and West*, Medio Media, 1982, 192.

[103] The Trinity must be considered a divine manifestation because it has attributes: Father, Son, and Holy Spirit. The unmanifest Godhead, by definition, has no attributes; it is utterly transcendent, unknown, and unknowable.

[104] Sergei Bulgakov, *Sophia: the Wisdom of God* (transl: P. Thompson *et al.*), Lindisfarne, 1993, 252. Italicization removed. The Son and Holy Spirit are deemed to be *consubstantial* with—or are of the same substance as—the Father; the creaturely fourth person enjoyed a lower status.

[105] *Ibid.*, 35-37.

[106] Andrew Weeks, *Paracelsus: Speculative Theory and the Crisis of the Early Reformation*, Albany, NY: State Univ. of New York Press, 1997, 83-84. There is speculation that Paracelsus reincarnated as Helena Blavatsky. See James M. Pryse, "Memorabilia of H.P.B.," *The Canadian Theosophist* (March 15, 1935), 1-5.

[107] David Rain, "A new mystery unfoldeth," 2017. Rain's musical setting is available at https://www.youtube.com/watch?v=KR0T_FbxigI. Last accessed May 8, 2021.

[108] Ludwig Feuerbach, *The Essence of Christianity* (transl: M. Evans), 3/e, 1893, Kegan Paul, *et al.*, 70-71.

[109] Besant, *Esoteric Christianity or The Lesser Mysteries*, 2/e, 140. (2006 ed., 109-110.)

[110] Paul VI, Dogmatic Constitution *Lumen Gentium*, ch. III, §61.

[111] John Paul II, Encyclical letter *Redemptoris Mater*: "On the Blessed Virgin Mary in the life of the Pilgrim Church," Vatican, March 25, 1987.

[112] María de Ágreda, *Mystical City of God*, vol. 1, §42 (transl.: F. Marison), Conkey, 1722/1902, 56.

[113] Clemens W. Brentano (ed.), *The Life of the Blessed Virgin Mary: From the Visions of Ven. Anne Catherine Emmerich* (transl.: M. Palairet), Tan Books, 1954/1970, 147.

Mary: Adept, Queen, Mother, Priestess

[114] Bernard of Clairvaux, Second Sermon on the Glories of the Virgin Mother" (transl.: "a priest"), *St Bernard's Sermons on the Blessed Virgin Mary*, Mount Melleray Abbey, 1987, 15.
[115] *Ibid.*, 18.
[116] *Isaiah* 7:14.
[117] Brentano (ed.), *The Life of the Blessed Virgin Mary*, 15-16.
[118] Pius IX, Apostolic Constitution *Ineffabilis Deus*, Rome, December 8, 1854.
[119] *Luke* 1:28.
[120] According to Theosophical teachings the monad manifests in multiple physical bodies—perhaps a strain of bacteria or pack of wolves—until it reaches the human kingdom. Entry to the human kingdom is marked by *individualization*, after which the monadic impulse is focused in a single physical body at any given time.
[121] *Proverbs* 8:22-23.
[122] *Ecclesiasticus* 24:9.
[123] Robert Powell, *The Sophia Teachings: the Emergence of the Divine Feminine in Our Time*, Lantern, 2001, 48.
[124] Susanne Schaup, *Sophia: Aspects of the Divine Feminine Past and Present*, Nicolas-Hays, 1997, 212.
[125] Alfred Eaker, "Our Lady: Catholicism's Diaphanous Adagio. Online: https://alfredeaker.com/2010/09/12/our-lady-catholicisms-diaphanous-adagio/. Last accessed April 29, 2021.
[126] *Ibid.*
[127] Paul VI, Dogmatic Constitution *Lumen Gentium*, ch. VIII, §67.
[128] Helena I. Roerich. *Leaves of Morya's Garden*, vol. II, §220. Agni Yoga Society, 1925, 69.
[129] *Luke* 1:38. Several translations have "be it *done* unto me...."
[130] Annie Besant was a close friend of British suffragette Emmeline Pankhurst, founder of the Women's Franchise League and the Women's Social and Political Union.
[131] Helena I. Roerich, letter, May 8, 1935. Online: http://agniyoga.org/ay_en/Letters-of-Helena-Roerich-I.php. Last accessed Nov. 30, 2019.
[132] *Ibid.*, March 1, 1929.
[133] Katherine Tingley, *Theosophy: the Path of the Mystic*, 2/e, Theosophical Publ. Co., 1922, 126.
[134] Esotericists generally fall into that category.
[135] Vaughan-Lee, *The Return of the Feminine and the World Soul*, 76-79.
[136] "The Litany of the Blessed Virgin Mary." Online: https://www.ourcatholicprayers.com/litany-of-the-blessed-virgin-mary.html. Last accessed Dec. 15, 2019.
[137] Leadbeater, *Christian Gnosis*, 195.

Chapter 10. Synthesis and Reflections: The Celestial Mary

[138] Bailey, *The Externalization of the Hierarchy*, 416. "Occultist" is used in esoteric writings to denote someone engaged in active forms of esotericism, contrasting with a passive mystic; the term does not have the dark meaning often ascribed to it in everyday usage.

[139] Philip Jenkins, *The Next Christendom: The Coming of Global Christianity*, Oxford Univ. Press, 2002.

[140] "Our Lady's Latest Second-of-the-Month Message." Online: https://www.medjugorje.com/medjugorje-messages/latest-2-message.html. Last accessed Feb. 19, 2020.

[141] Finbar O'Leary (ed.), *Vicka: Her Story*, Dufour, 2013/2017, 48.

[142] Raimondi, *Conversations with Mary*, 67.

[143] *Ibid.*, 93-94.

[144] Alice A. Bailey, *From Bethlehem to Calvary*, Lucis Trust, 1937, 20. This was Bailey's own work, not one written at the behest of the Master Djwhal Khul.

[145] Few people are pure pantheists, claiming that God can be *equated* to, or is no more than, creation. A superior belief—to which Eckhart, Rahner, and many others actually subscribed—is *panentheism*. The latter asserts that God is both within creation and beyond it: i.e., both immanent and transcendent. *Philippians* 2:6–8 is sometimes cited in support of divine immanence.

[146] Bailey, *From Bethlehem to Calvary*, 21.

[147] Bailey, *Initiation, Human and Solar*, 41ff.

[148] De Montfort, *The Secret of Mary*, 20.

[149] Intentional contacts are permitted only with the higher devas, not with the lower "builders," who construct our physical, emotion and mental vehicles, or the elementals who form the substance of those vehicles. See for example Alice A. Bailey, *Letters on Occult Meditation*, Lucis Trust, 1922, 176-177.

Mary: Adept, Queen, Mother, Priestess

Epilogue

So who is Mary? Her story has taken us on a journey from "the beginning," to first-century Palestine, to the present, and beyond. The historical Mary was raised in the temple, gave birth to Jesus, carried on his ministry after Pentecost, was acclaimed high priestess of the nascent Christian community in Jerusalem, and attained the fifth initiation in a female body. She was a strong woman, faithful to Judaic tradition.

After the Dormition, the "celestial" Mary emerged as the subject of Christian doctrine and devotion, and eventually of esoteric studies. Crowned as an Adept, she became Queen of the Angels and now holds the exalted office of Mother of the World.

Mary is revealing more of herself. She is seeking to be known more intimately and in new ways. We have listened to the testimonies of people with whom Mary has communicated. We learned of Mary's message of peace; her concern for human suffering, particularly of women and children; and her special concern for pregnancy and birth in the human and animal kingdoms.

As Queen of the Angels Mary has devic hosts at her command, but she invites human disciples to work alongside them to proclaim her message and help carry out her mission in the world. Becoming one of her disciples offers unique opportunities. In whatever way is appropriate we respond to Mary's message and express our profound debt to her.

Mary preaches the way to Christ and never misses an opportunity to defer to her son and to the Father. At the Visitation Mary exclaimed: "My soul doth magnify the Lord, and my spirit hath rejoiced in God my Savior."[1] And on her deathbed: "He is my God, and I will glorify and exalt him, the God of my father. He is my son, born from me according to the flesh, but the father is also God the creator of all things."[2]

Mary's and Christ's ministries are complementary. For example, in their Second-Ray ministry of healing, Mary soothes our pain, while

Christ says: "[T]ake up thy bed, and walk."[3] The one approach is characteristically feminine, the other masculine.

Even though Mary defers to her son she is worthy of adoration. She herself exclaimed: "[A]ll generations shall call me blessed." Cyril of Alexandria, Peter of Damascus, Bernard of Clairvaux, Hildegard of Bingen, Thomas à Kempis, Louis-Marie de Montfort, and Pope John Paul II all raised Mary to a level above any other human creature. The Collyridians offered her sacrifice. The Council of Ephesus declared her to be the mother of God. The ancient text known as the *Transitus Mariae* records that the whole company of heaven worshipped Mary as she was raised from the dead.

Mary is not God. But as an Adept she expresses, to a degree far surpassing our own, the divinity invested in every human monad. By virtue of her positions as Queen of the Angels and Mother of the World she serves as an expression of the Feminine Aspect of Deity. As Priestess Mary holds the mysteries in her heart and presides over sacred ritual—which may range from a Christian liturgy, in which male and female participants play complementary roles, all the way to the restored Greater Mysteries of the Aquarian Age.

We end our story of Mary with two quotes attributed to Christ himself. The first is from Mary's vision of her risen son on the evening after the Crucifixion:

> All Paradise rejoices in thee. I say unto thee, O My Mother, He who loves you loves Life. Hail, you who did sustain the Life of the Universe in your womb! .... I will give My peace, which I have received from My Holy Father, to My disciples, and to every one who shall believe in My Name and in Mary.[4]

The second is from Christ's blessing when he came to take Mary's soul to Paradise:

> O Mary blessed among women, for every grace and gift has been given to you by my heavenly Father, and every soul that calls on your name with holiness will not be put to shame but will find mercy and comfort both in this life and in the age to come.[5]

If Christ bestowed the highest praise on Mary, why should we hesitate to do likewise?

Epilogue

So much more could be said. Anyone writing about Mary would have to agree with Bernard of Clairvaux, who confessed, "whatever can be said on that ineffable subject ... does not fully satisfy, does not fully please, is not quite acceptable."[6] Mary can never be captured by words any more than statues can capture her beauty. The Feminine cannot be defined or possessed. When we try to touch her, she is out of reach; when we clasp at her, she slips through our fingers; but when she reaches out to us, her robe brushes against our face.

---

[1] *Luke* 1:46-47.
[2] *Life of the Virgin* (transl.: S. J. Shoemaker), New Haven, CT: Yale Univ. Press, 2012, §§105-106, 130-132.
[3] *John* 5:8.
[4] E. A. Wallis Budge, "Bartholomew the Apostle," *Legends of Our Lady Mary the Perpetual Virgin and her Mother Hanna*, Medici Press, 1922, xxxvii-xxxix. Cast in modern English.
[5] *Life of the Virgin* §111,136.
[6] Bernard of Clairvaux, "Fourth Sermon on the Feast of the Assumption," *Sermons on the Blessed Virgin Mary*, Augustine Publ., 1987, 200.

Mary: Adept, Queen, Mother, Priestess

Glossary

Absolute Primacy of Christ: see **Primacy of Christ**.

Active Intelligence: in esoteric teachings, the Third Aspect of the **Logos**, roughly equivalent to the Holy Spirit. See **Logoic Aspects**.

actual sin: in western Christian doctrine, a sin committed by an individual, deemed to involve at least some degree of volition. Contrasted with inherited **original sin**.

adept: an individual who has attained the fifth planetary **initiation**. **Masters** form a subset of adepts.

Advent: the four-week liturgical period before Christmas.

Ain Soph: the unmanifest Godhead, as envisioned in the Judaic theoretical **Kabbalah**.

akasha: subtle substance or essence believed to pervade the whole of space.

akashic records: records of every event in the history of the universe, believed to be accessible to people with relevant clairvoyant capability.

amanuensis (pl. *amanuenses*): a scribe who records statements by another. Used specifically to refer to an individual who records communications from a higher being.

Ancient Mystical Order Rosae Crucis (AMORC): one of the modern **Rosicrucian** organizations.

angel: (i) in Judaism, Christianity and Islam a divine messenger; (ii) in esoteric teachings a senior member of the **deva evolution**.

Annunciation: the incident recorded in scripture in which the Archangel Gabriel appeared to Mary to announce that she was to give birth to Jesus. The Annunciation is celebrated on March 25.

antahkarana: the conscious bridge that, through esoteric work, is built linking the 4th and 3rd mental subplanes and giving access to the soul. The antahkarana eventually extends to the 1st, or highest, mental **subplane**.

Anthroposophical Society: esoteric organization founded by Rudolf Steiner. (See **anthroposophy, Theosophy**.)

anthroposophy: term coined by Rudolf Steiner to denote the study of wisdom as it relates to humanity; c.f.: **theosophy, Theosophy**.

Antidicomarians: literally "adversaries of Mary"; a derogatory term applied to a group of early Christians who believed that Mary was the mother of several children.

Apocrypha: texts accorded a degree of authenticity but which are omitted from the **canonical** Old or New Testament.

apostolic constitution: the most solemn and authoritative form of pronouncement issued by a pope. The two Marian dogmas of recent times were decreed in apostolic constitutions. See also **papal bull**.

Arcane School: esoteric school founded by Alice A. Bailey to provide training in esoteric work.

ashram: a group of disciples who share the responsibilities of a master. Reportedly, there are seven major ashrams, each associated with one of the seven rays.

Aspects of the Logos: see **Logoic Aspects**.

Assumption: the belief that Mary was taken up, body and soul, at the end of her earthly life. Mary's Assumption is celebrated in Roman Catholic and other western churches on August 15.

astral plane: a popular but ambiguous name for the 6th **systemic plane** (counting from above). Otherwise known as the **sentient plane**, it is the plane of emotion and desire.

atman: in Hinduism, the fragment of divine essence at the heart of every human entity. Equivalent to the **monad** and *yehidah*.

aura: the glow around the body of a living being, seen by persons with clairvoyant ability.

avatar (fem. *avatara*): (i) traditionally the incarnation or manifestation of a deity; (ii) in the teachings of Alice Bailey the term may extend to a human being who carries out a divine mission.

Glossary

Benedictine: a monk living in a religious community following the Rule of St Benedict.

Binah: literally "Understanding;" the third of the ten **sephiroth** in the **Kabbalah**; the primeval feminine force.

Brahman, the: a Hindu term for the unmanifest Godhead; sometimes called the ***Para-Brahman***, or ***Parabrahm***.

canonical: literally "defined, or established, by canon (i.e., law)"; may refer to the selection of texts for inclusion in the Old or New Testament.

Celestial Mary: Mary as envisioned by Christian doctrine and devotion and modern esoteric studies, and who has revealed herself to individuals and groups in apparitions and other communications.

Chokmah: literally "Wisdom;" a feminine semidivine or divine personage who features in *Proverbs* and the Old Testament **Apocrypha**. Her Greek name is **Sophia**, and her Latin name **Sapientia**. A masculinized Chokmah is also the second *sephirah* in the **Kabbalah**.

Co-Redemptrix (or **Co-Redemptress**): the suggestion that Mary participated with Christ in the redemption of humanity. See **Redemption**.

Collyridians: a fourth-century (or earlier) Christian sect in which female officiants allegedly offered ritual sacrifices of cakes to Mary.

consciousness: (i) the universal sentience that pervades the whole of creation; (ii) an entity's awareness of its environment and possibly of itself.

consubstantial (adj.)**:** of the same substance.

deification: see *theosis*.

deva: literally "shining one"; a member of the vast **deva evolution** that includes entities ranging from nature spirits to the highest ranks of angels.

deva evolution: the totality of devic entities on the planet. The deva evolution and the human kingdom follow parallel, but distinct, evolutionary paths.

Divine Feminine: feminine attributes or archetypes projected onto, perceived in, or manifested by the Godhead.

doctrine: a body of teachings or set of beliefs.

dogma: a doctrinal formulation decreed by an **ecumenical council** of bishops, or by a pope in an *ex cathedra* pronouncement, claimed to be infallibly true and binding on all believers. See **Marian dogmas**.

Dogmatic Constitution: one of four official pronouncements issued during or after the Second Vatican Council (1962–1965).

Dominican: a member of, or pertaining to, the Order of Friars Preachers, the religious order founded by Dominic de Guzmán.

Dormition: the death of the historical Mary, as described in early Christian writings. The Dormition of Mary is celebrated in the Eastern Orthodox churches and elsewhere on August 15.

Dormition Literature: the body of early Christian writings that focus on the **Dormition** of Mary.

ecumenical council: a council of bishops, ostensibly from the whole world, whose decrees are believed by Christians to represent infallible truth. Four such councils—First Nicaea (325), First Constantinople (381), Ephesus (431), and Chalcedon (451)—are regarded as authentic by most major Christian denominations.

encyclical letter: a statement by a pope to members of the Church of Rome, concerning a matter considered important but not binding on the church.

esoteric: relating to matters beyond everyday experience. Esoteric contrasts with *exoteric*, which relates to the obvious, literal or external.

esoteric school: an institution offering training in esoteric work, particularly in discipleship work.

ether: in esoteric teachings, a rarified form of matter encompassing the first four **subplanes** of the **systemic physical plane** (counting from above). The fifth, sixth and seventh **subplanes** correspond, respectively, to gaseous, fluid and solid matter. The ether envisioned in esoteric teachings is qualitatively different from the ether envisioned in Victorian-era physics.

Glossary

etheric body: in esoteric teachings, the form comprised of etheric matter which penetrates throughout, and extends a short distance beyond, any living organism.

Eucharist: the sacred ritual involving the consecration of bread and wine, believed to invoke the presence of Christ.

ex cathedra: literally "from the chair (of Peter)." A term used in Roman Catholicism referring to the action of a pope issuing an infallible pronouncement. Other Christian denominations do not recognize a pope's authority to make such pronouncements.

extracanonical: a reference to texts possibly contemporary with the books of the New Testament, but not included therein.

form: a differentiated aspect of reality, contrasting with undifferentiated pure **spirit**. A form may serve as the vessel into which **spirit** flows.

Franciscan: a member of, or pertaining to, one of the several religious orders founded by Francis of Assisi. They include the Order of Friars Minor, the Order of St Clare, and the Third Order of St Francis.

Godhead: the most transcendent aspect of Deity. Pure "Being." Often considered the unmanifest, unknown, and unknowable divine essence or power. Christianity identifies the "Godhead" with God the Father, or with the Trinity. See ***Ain Soph***, **Brahman**.

grace: divine benevolence, freely bestowed on humanity, regardless of merit.

Guglielmites: followers of the medieval noblewoman Guglielma di Boemia, who elected a female pope and planned to establish a female college of cardinals.

Hermeticism: system of practical philosophy of Middle-Eastern origin, usually considered to include alchemy, magic, and astrology. The name refers to the god Hermes, otherwise known as Thoth or Mercury.

hexinity: a hypothetical divine manifestation involving six **hypostases** ("persons") or aspects.

Hierarchy: see Planetary Hierarchy.

high-church: a term designating a sacramental focus in certain western Christian denominations, churches, clergy or laity. It contrasts with "evangelical," or "low-church."

Historical Mary: Mary who lived in Palestine at the turn of the Common Era and gave birth to Jesus.

hyperdulia: the level of reverence the Church of Rome deemed appropriate for Mary—intermediate between *dulia*, accorded to the saints, and *latria*, accorded to Christ or God.

hypostasis (pl. *hypostases*): a term crafted in early Christianity to capture the distinction between the Father, Son, and Holy Spirit. Translated as "person."

hypostatic union: the doctrine that the human and divine natures are united in the single **hypostasis** ("person") of Jesus Christ. By analogy the term is also applied to other intimate unions.

Immaculate Conception: the belief that Mary was conceived without the stain of **original sin**. The Immaculate Conception is celebrated December 8.

incarnation: taking on physical form. Human entities are believed to incarnate multiple times on their way to spiritual perfection.

Incarnation: the unique event, foundational to Christian beliefs, that God the Son took human form in the person of Jesus Christ.

infallible, infallibility: the claim, primarily by the Church of Rome, that certain doctrinal formulations are true—and will be true for all time.

initiate: individual who has attained one of the major **initiations**.

initiation: (i) any significant expansion of consciousness; (ii) one of the several major expansions of consciousness, recognized by the **Planetary Hierarchy**, that mark progress on the advanced spiritual path. In esoteric Christianity the first five initiations are often referred to as the "birth," "baptism," "transfiguration," "crucifixion," and "resurrection."

Glossary

intercessory prayer: prayer addressed to Mary or a saint in the expectation that she or he will intercede with Christ or God the Father to grant a favor or petition.

Jesuit: a member of, or pertaining to, the Society of Jesus, the Roman Catholic religious order founded by Ignatius of Loyola.

karma: (i) the universal law of cause and effect; (ii) the positive or negative consequences of our actions.

Kabbalah: (i) a system of cosmological and psychological inquiry that developed from Judaic roots but became integrated into western esotericism; (ii) a larger, amorphous system of Jewish mysticism that includes the ecstatic Kabbalah.

kingdom: one of several kingdoms of nature, or major groupings of evolving beings; the 1st kingdom is the mineral kingdom, the 2nd the vegetable kingdom, the 3rd the animal kingdom, and the 4th the human kingdom; the 5th kingdom is the "kingdom of souls." The **devas** are said to comprise two separate **devic kingdoms**.

Lent: the six-week liturgical period before Easter.

Lex orandi, lex credendi: literally "the law of what is prayed [is] the law of what is believed." The notion, in Anglicanism and elsewhere, that doctrine emerges from the **liturgy**.

lifewave: a large number of monads, created by a single Logoic impulse and sent on their long evolutionary journey through the mineral, vegetable and animal **kingdoms** to the human kingdom and beyond.

liturgy: (i) public worship; (ii) the scripted language, gestures and rituals prescribed for public worship.

Logoic (adj.): pertaining to a **Logos**.

Logoic Aspects: the three expressions of the **Logos**: Will and Power, Love–Wisdom, and Active Intelligence—roughly corresponding to the Father, Son, and Holy Spirit of the Christian Trinity.

logoic plane: the 1st, or highest, **systemic plane**, on which the **Planetary Logos** resides in "physical" incarnation.

Logos: (i) a term with the sense of mediator, applied to Christ and translated as "the Word"; (ii) in esoteric teachings, the manifest God. See **Planetary Logos**, **Solar Logos**.

Love–Wisdom: in esoteric teachings, the Second Aspect of the **Logos**, roughly equivalent to God the Son. See **Logoic Aspects**.

Magnificat: the canticle: "My soul doth magnify the Lord...," uttered by Mary after her greeting by Elizabeth at the **Visitation**.

Malkuth: literally "the Kingdom;" the 10th and lowest **sephirah** in the **Kabbalah**; associated with the **physical plane**.

manas: the Sanskrit word for **mind**; *manas* is the root of the English word "man," the thinker.

Mariamites: an early Christian sect that allegedly believed in a trinity of God, Jesus and Mary.

Marian dogmas: the four dogmas concerning Mary. Two were decreed by **ecumenical councils** in the early church: the **Virgin Birth** and Mary's status as **Theotokos** ("Mother of God"). Two more were decreed by the Church of Rome: her **Immaculate Conception** (1854) and her **Assumption** into Heaven (1950). See **dogma**.

Mariology: the branch of theology concerned with Mary.

master: an individual who, upon attaining the 5th **initiation**, chooses to remain on Earth to serve humanity. All masters are **adepts**, but not all adepts are **masters**.

maya: manifest reality, as distinct from the Godhead, regarded in eastern philosophies as illusory but perhaps more usefully interpreted as "not eternal."

mayavirupa: literally, "body of **maya**"; the body of manifestation created by adepts in order to appear on the physical plane.

Mediatrix: feminine form of "mediator," applied to Mary, viewed as the mediator between humanity and God.

mental plane: the 5th systemic plane (counting from above), expressing thought.

mind: aspect of the human constitution that permits thought and introspection; mind sets humanity above the 3rd, animal, kingdom.

monad: the individualized divine spark or spirit present in each human entity; the source of human life and the locus of identity.

Glossary

Mother of the World: see **World Mother**.

Mulaprakriti: literally the "Root of Nature," often perceived as feminine. According to Vedantic teachings Mulaprakriti is the primordial cosmic substance, overshadowed—but possibly not impregnated—by the Brahman in the creation of gods and worlds. See *prakriti*.

Nativity: literally "Birth." Most often used to denote the birth of Jesus, and celebrated December 25. May also refer to the birth of Mary, celebrated September 8.

nature spirit: in esoteric teachings a junior member of the **deva evolution**, concerned with building **forms** in the mineral, vegetable, animal and human kingdoms.

Nicene Creed: a document originated by the Council of Nicaea (325) and finalized by the First Council of Constantinople (381) identifying the three Persons of the Trinity. It is regarded as one of the foundational documents of Christian belief.

nonconsubstantial: not of the same substance.

occult: literally "hidden;" a reference to **esoteric** knowledge or practices. **original sin:** the collective, inherited sin of Adam and Eve. Belief in original sin has pervaded much of western Christianity. See also **actual sin**.

ousia: "essence," or "substance"; used in Christianity to capture the divine nature that unifies the three **hypostases**, or "persons," of the Trinity.

papal bull: an authoritative pronouncement by a pope, used for a variety of purposes including the excommunication of a person accused of heresy.

patriarch: literally "father." (i) one of the fathers of the Jewish nation, like Abraham or Isaac; (ii) a bishop of one of the early Christian churches: Alexandria, Antioch and Rome—later extended to Constantinople, Jerusalem and Moscow.

Pentecost: (i) the Jewish Festival of Weeks; (ii) the Christian feast commemorating the descent of the Holy Spirit on Mary and the disciples.

perpetual virginity: the claim that Mary remained a virgin throughout her earthly life.

personality: (i) mental structure that integrates the physical, astral, and lower mental natures, providing coherence of consciousness and stability of identity; (ii) the image a human entity presents to the world.

physical plane: the lowest systemic plane, consisting of the three dense physical subplanes—the solid, liquid, and gaseous subplanes—and four etheric subplanes. (See **plane, subplane**.)

plane: level of reality or consciousness; there are believed to be seven "systemic" planes—i.e., relating to the solar system—each of which can be divided into seven subplanes.

Planetary Hierarchy: the several ranks of masters and other evolved beings concerned with the long-term evolution of lives—including humanity—on Earth,. Reportedly the work of the Hierarchy is organized around three "departments," corresponding to the three **Logoic Aspects** of Will and Power, Love–Wisdom, and Active Intelligence; and seven major **ashrams**., corresponding to the **seven rays**.

Planetary Logos: God manifesting through the planet Earth.

physical plane: the 7th, and lowest, systemic plane, consisting of the dense physical and etheric subplanes.

Pneuma Hagion: Greek for "Holy Spirit."

prakriti: the undifferentiated matter from which the universe was constructed. See also **Mulaprakriti**.

Predestination of Mary: the suggestion that Mary had already consented, or in some way was unable to refuse, to give birth to Jesus.

preordination: a situation in which the outcome is already determined when an event takes place.

presiding bishop: title of the **primate** in several national churches, including The Episcopal Church based in the United States.

Primacy of Christ: the doctrine that Christ was ordained to take human form, even before the Fall of Mankind. Also known as the **Absolute Primacy of Christ**.

primate: the senior bishop in a national church or similar jurisdiction. The primate may be termed an archbishop or a **presiding bishop**.

Protestant: a term applied primarily to the Lutheran and Calvinist/Reformed Churches, which "protested" against Roman authority. Whether Anglicanism should be regarded as Protestant is a matter of debate.

quaternity: a hypothetical divine manifestation involving four **hypostases** ("persons") or aspects.

Queenship of Mary: the belief that Mary reigns as Queen of Heaven or Queen of the Angels. The Queenship of Mary is celebrated August 22.

ray: one of the seven **rays**, which see.

rays, seven: streams of energy that "color" the whole of creation. The seven rays are known as: Will or Power, Love–Wisdom, Active Intelligence, Harmony Through Conflict, Knowledge or Science, Devotion or Idealism, and Ceremonial Order—but it should be understood that these labels do not capture the full richness of meaning.

Redemption: literally "buying back." Christian belief that Jesus Christ came to buy back humanity which had fallen from grace through the sin of Adam and Eve.

Reformation: the series of events in the sixteenth century in which a number of western national churches rejected Roman authority to form distinct Christian denominations.

Rosicrucian, Rosicrucianism: esoteric movement inspired by the Rosicrucian Manifestos of the early 17th century.

Rosicrucian Fellowship: one of the modern **Rosicrucian** organizations

ruach: literally "breath," or "wind," but often interpreted in biblical Judaism to mean "spirit."

ruach ha-kodesh: literally "the holy spirit." Interpreted in biblical Judaism as a divine force or presence. In Christianity the Holy Spirit became personalized.

sacerdotal (adj): pertaining to priests or the priesthood.

Sanat Kumara: a high entity who serves as the incarnation and representative of the Planetary Logos.

Sapientia: the Latin name of **Sophia**.

sephirah (plural *sephiroth*): a Hebrew word, literally meaning "number;" (i) one of ten divine emanations from the **Ain Soph**; (ii) one of ten experiences through which the disciple must pass on the way to enlightenment. The ten sephiroth are depicted schematically on the Kabbalistic Tree of Life.

self-consciousness: an entity's ability to distinguish itself from other entities and from the environment.

sentience: the basic quality of **consciousness** possessed by creation at all levels.

sentient plane: the 6th systemic plane (counting from above), expressing emotion, feelings, and desire; popularly as the **astral plane**.

seven rays: see rays.

Shamballa: (i) an etheric location in the Gobi desert where Sanat Kumara and a number of masters are said to reside; (ii) another term for the **Planetary Council**.

Shekinah: in Rabbinic Judaism and the Kabbalah, the indwelling presence of God, often personalized as feminine.

Solar Logos: God manifesting through the solar system. See **Logos, Planetary Logos**.

Sophia: literally "Wisdom"; the Greek name of **Chokmah**. Sophia attained the status of a semidivine or divine feminine personage in Hellenic Judaism and segments of Christianity, and has emerged as a goddess in modern feminist writings. Sophia's Latin name is **Sapientia**.

soul: (i) that which creates forms enabling **Spirit** to express itself as it descends into matter; (ii) the aspect of the human constitution that mediates between the **monad** and the **personality**.

spirit: (i) the undifferentiated divine essence present in all aspects of creation; (ii) the individualized divine essence of the human **monad**.

Glossary

spiritual: having to do with the higher aspects or purpose of human existence; relating to individual or group evolution. (See **spirit**.)

subplane: one of seven subdivisions of a plane, usually numbered downward from the highest "atomic" subplane; for example, the solid physical subplane is the 7th, and lowest, subplane of the systemic physical plane; the liquid subplane is the 6th, and the gaseous subplane is the 5th. (See **plane**.)

systemic plane: one of seven planes into which reality in the solar system is divided. The 7th or lowest is the **physical plane**, the 6th is the **sentient** or **astral plane**, and the 5th is the **mental plane**. The higher planes are the buddhic (4th), atmic (3rd), monadic (2nd), and logoic planes (1st). (See **plane**.)

theosis: the doctrine, primarily associated with Eastern Orthodox Christianity, that individuals can attain a state of "participation in the divine nature." Sometimes referred to as "**deification**."

Theosophical (capitalized): pertaining to the **Theosophical Society** or its teachings.

Theosophical Society; an international esoteric organization founded in 1875 by Madame Helena P. Blavatsky and Colonel Henry Olcott.

Theosophist: a member of the Theosophical Society.

theosophy: a term of Gnostic origin meaning intuitive encounter with the wisdom of God. More generally, theosophy can refer to either the western or eastern esoteric traditions. (See **Theosophy**.)

Theosophy (capitalized): the teachings of the **Theosophical Society** and its offshoots.

Theotokos: literally "God-bearer," but typically translated in the West as "Mother of God."

Tibetan Master: see **Djwhal Khul**.

Tiphareth: the 6th **sephirah** in the **Kabbalah**; beauty and harmony; often associated with the Christ, or Jesus.

Tractarian Movement: a 19th-century **high-church** movement within Anglicanism to restore elements of pre-Reformation English Christianity. Named for a series of 90 tracts written by faculty at Oxford University in the U.K. Often referred to as the "Oxford Movement."

Trinity: God as envisioned in Christianity. Defined as three *hypostases*, or "persons," in one divine *ousia*, or "essence."

Vedanta: philosophical movement within Hinduism, usually associated with the 8th century CE scholar Shankara, or Shankaracharya.

Virgin Birth: the dogma that Mary was a virgin at the time she gave birth to Jesus.

Visitation: The episode recorded in scripture when the pregnant Mary visited her cousin Elizabeth, who was pregnant with John the Baptist. The Visitation is celebrated May 31.

Western Esoteric Tradition (also referred to as the Western Mystery Tradition): the amalgam of esoteric Judaism, Gnostic Christianity, and **Hermeticism** that developed from the late Middle Ages onward.

Will and Power: in esoteric teachings, the First Aspect of the **Logos**, roughly equivalent to God the Father. See **Logoic Aspects**.

Wisdom Literature: a set of biblical texts that includes *Proverbs*, *Song of Songs*, *Wisdom of Solomon*, and *Ecclesiasticus*. Which other texts should be included in the set is debated.

World Mother (or **Mother of the World**): in **Theosophical** teachings, an entity of high spiritual status who expresses the archetype of motherhood and is particularly concerned with the welfare of women and children. Opinions differ as to whether the Mother is a divine being in her own right, or is an office in the **Planetary Hierarchy**, held over the eons by a succession of individuals. Christian **Theosophists** identify Mary as the (current) World Mother.

yehidah: in esoteric Judaism, the divine spark in each human being. Equivalent to **monad**.

yoga (literally "union"): system of practical spirituality, often associated with the Indian teacher Patanjali who lived sometime in the first millennium BCE. The familiar hatha yoga is just one of many forms.

Index

A

Aaron
  19, 33, 43, 346, 361, 371
abortion
  217, 237
Abraham
  9, 24, 43, 60, 105, 135, 140, 161, 278, 289, 346, 427
Adept, Mary as
  1, 2, 4, 5, 11, 224, 228, 237, 243, 249–254, 263, 264, 275, 313, 327, 362, 363, 373, 380, 382, 407, 415, 416
adeptship
  5, 9, 247, 251, 253–2 55, 263, 265, 287, 353, 362, 380
Advent, season of
  79, 155, 167, 172, 197, 200, 365, 411, 419
Agni Yoga
  278, 280, 365, 409, 412
Ágreda, Abbess María de
  135, 136, 153, 205, 396, 412
akathist, *akathistos* ("not sitting")
  173, 174, 198, 406
Allah
  20, 22, 23, 44, 118, 296, 329, 364
alma (Latin: "nourishing")
  167, 191
almah (Hebrew: "a young woman")
  32, 46, 236, 245, 340, 342
amanuensis, amanuenses
  205, 265, 419

Ambrose of Milan
 152, 191
Amos
 108, 293
Andrewes, Lancelot
 144, 145, 155, 182, 199, 338, 366
angel, angels
 18–23, 25, 26, 28, 29, 32, 40, 52, 57, 59, 64, 65, 67, 95, 98, 99, 113, 129, 132, 137, 177, 178, 182, 221, 254–256, 275, 328, 329, 334–337, 346, 353, 354, 362, 365, 382, 387, 419
angelic
 28, 40, 137, 161, 175, 247, 248, 255, 256, 262, 263, 269, 270, 273, 278, 280–282, 314, 324, 325, 337, 363, 382, 390
Angelus (prayer)
 152, 177, 178, 183, 187, 199
Anglican, Anglicans
 1, 2, 113, 114, 128, 143, 145–148, 155, 156, 182–185, 187, 192, 199–201, 206, 338
Annunciation
 11, 18, 20, 22, 23, 25, 57–59, 85, 113, 114, 123, 132, 167, 173, 177, 180–182, 190, 221, 242, 261, 268, 269, 274, 280, 282, 329, 334, 335, 338, 386, 409, 419
Anselm of Canterbury
 120, 150, 162, 165, 195, 296, 320, 328
Anthroposophical
 266, 267, 420
Anthroposophist, Anthroposophy
 266, 398, 420
Antidicomarians
 115, 148, 367, 420
Antioch
 92, 117, 149, 295, 306, 319, 359, 364, 393, 427
Aphrodite
 261, 310, 327
Apocrypha
 108, 292, 321, 369, 420, 421

Index

apparition
> 1, 4, 7–9, 17, 67, 108, 122, 167, 177, 203–220, 209–214, 227–231, 235–241, 247, 252, 253, 270, 275, 306, 315, 332, 348, 376, 378, 379, 392, 399, 400, 402, 421

archangel
> 8, 18, 85, 91, 95, 97, 99, 103, 105, 221, 242, 224, 249, 255, 257, 262, 268, 269, 271, 301–303, 311, 314, 315, 334, 351, 354, 382, 390–392, 419

Arimathea, Joseph of
> 67, 348

Artemis
> 118, 310

Asherah
> 9, 106, 161, 289–292, 317, 318

ashram
> 405, 420, 428

Assumption
> 7, 16, 45, 70, 83, 98, 105, 110–114, 119, 123–126, 128, 130, 131, 146, 147, 151, 153–155, 169, 179, 196, 199, 203, 223, 255, 268, 321, 354, 356, 369, 370, 376, 382, 410, 417, 420, 426

Athanasius
> 14, 15, 133, 152, 296, 319

Augustine of Hippo
> 120, 134, 150, 152, 183, 196, 199, 321, 410, 417

Ave Maria (See also "Hail Mary")
> 176, 177, 192, 335, 375

Ávila, Teresa of (see Teresa of Ávila)

B

Bach, Johann Sebastian
> 192, 403

Bahir, The
> 280, 408

Bailey, Alice A.
> 245, 248, 259, 265, 266, 279–281, 310, 311, 316, 322, 324, 340, 360–362, 366, 367, 371, 380, 403–405, 408–410, 412, 413, 420, 421

Balthasar, Hans U. von
> 184, 199, 339, 366

435

Baptism
  5, 86, 94, 98, 111, 119, 123, 146, 249, 343, 390, 424
Bartholomew, Gospel of
  39, 41, 48, 75, 97, 100, 111, 137, 153, 314, 325, 329, 353, 364, 369
Bartholomew, disciple of Jesus
  82, 91, 109, 348, 368, 370, 417
Bathsheba
  381, 384
Benedict of Nursia
  127, 128, 130, 151, 180, 199, 421
Benedict XV, Pope
  127, 128, 130, 151
Benedictine (religious order)
  132, 138, 204, 298, 393, 421
Bernadette Soubirious
  122, 210–212, 236, 239, 242, 379, 406, 408
Bernard of Clairvaux
  134, 153, 163, 164, 196, 198, 302, 321, 361, 371, 391, 392, 396, 410, 412, 416, 417
Besant, Annie W.
  248, 260, 261, 271, 274–276, 280, 282, 297, 308, 311, 323, 363, 372, 386, 389, 395, 396, 398, 400, 401, 409–412
Bethelda, Archangel
  249, 255, 262, 268, 271, 314, 315, 392
Bethlehem
  14, 26, 30, 42, 44, 45, 55, 57, 59–61, 64, 85, 96–101, 104, 110, 173, 330, 336, 337, 339, 352–354, 413
Binah
  257, 421
Blavatsky, Helena P.
  248, 258, 259, 307–309, 323, 391, 398, 411, 431
Bodhisattva
  251, 262, 371
Böhme (or Boehme), Jakob
  322, 305

Index

Bonhoeffer, Dietrich
   172, 190, 197, 336, 365, 393, 411
Botticelli, Sandro
   190, 200, 381
Brahman, The
   307, 421, 423, 427
Brentano, Clemens W.
   49, 50, 70–73, 110, 153, 201, 238, 363–365, 368, 369, 371, 412
Bridget of Sweden
   8, 49, 121, 122, 150, 205, 207, 220–223, 236, 238, 241, 242, 247, 335, 337, 344, 353–355, 365, 368, 370, 376, 377, 382, 400, 406, 409
Bulgakov, Sergei (Sergius)
   133, 152, 175, 198, 286, 297, 306, 316, 320, 323, 380, 394, 408, 411

C

Calvary
   36, 66–68, 140, 141, 157, 169, 210, 222, 343, 347, 387, 413
Calvinist
   17, 132, 145, 146, 429
Cambridge
   107–109, 181, 239, 321, 324, 364, 369, 370, 406
Canterbury
   120, 143, 147, 150, 156, 162, 181, 184, 189, 195, 199, 296, 328, 338
canticle
   23, 24, 29, 90, 103, 163, 192, 335, 426
Carmelite (religious order)
   185, 186, 204, 213
Caroline Divine
   144, 155, 182, 183, 199, 366
cathedra, ex
   122, 153, 321, 410, 422, 423
Catherine of Siena
   121, 122, 242
Catholic (see Roman Catholic)

437

Celestial Mary
 3, 5, 9, 10, 42, 105, 114, 138, 158, 232, 236, 255, 271, 306, 308, 309, 327, 354, 373–376, 379, 380, 383, 387, 393, 395, 397, 400, 403, 415, 421
celibacy
 32–34, 47, 116, 164, 194, 301, 340, 366
Chalcedon, Council of
 125, 149, 240, 422
cherubim
 79, 81, 91, 103, 105, 134, 162, 175, 199, 242, 302, 391
Chokmah
 9, 137, 158, 257, 261, 291, 292, 295, 303, 322, 397, 421, 430
clairvoyance, clairvoyant
 49, 50, 61, 223, 226, 231, 242, 272, 315, 410, 419
Cleophas, Clophas, Clopas
 36, 37, 47, 51–54, 266, 332, 357, 370
Collyridians
 158, 160, 161, 169, 170, 195, 197, 291, 302, 374, 375, 416, 421
contraception
 217
Coptic Church, language
 87, 149, 204, 206, 214, 215, 238, 240, 365
Co-Redemptrix, Co-Redemptress
 119, 127–130, 421
Corinthians, I and *II*
 47, 113, 148, 151, 324, 368, 369, 380
Crucifixion
 6, 11, 36, 37, 42, 51, 65, 66, 76, 89, 90, 95, 141, 169, 190, 222, 249, 252, 333, 337, 343, 345, 350, 357, 365, 367, 416, 424
Cyril of Alexandria
 117–119, 149, 198, 301, 321, 375, 390, 410, 416

D

Daniel
 48
Dante Alighieri
 299, 300, 320

Index

David, King
　21, 26, 29, 31, 55, 105, 117, 167, 380, 394
Deborah
　172, 336, 393
deification (see also *theosis*)
　5, 80, 133, 152, 224, 306, 339, 366, 380, 421, 431
deva, devic
　112, 223, 224, 242, 254–256, 260, 263, 264, 268, 272, 273, 321, 363, 382, 383, 390, 400, 405, 413, 415, 419, 421, 422, 425, 427
Diego, Juan
　209, 210, 236, 239
Divine Feminine
　8, 9, 277, 282, 285, 288, 293, 300, 307, 311, 315, 316, 390, 392, 393, 412, 422
Djwhal Khul, Master
　249, 259, 265, 340, 360, 382, 409, 413, 431
dogma
　7, 52, 66, 113, 114, 119, 122, 124–132, 136, 145, 157, 179, 212, 223, 225, 301, 328, 356, 376, 395, 396, 422, 426, 432
dogmatic
　7, 83, 122, 126, 128, 131, 136, 147, 150–153, 198, 376, 384, 385, 408, 411, 412, 422
Dolorosa, Mater ("Mother of Sorrows")
　89, 139, 169
Dominic de Guzmán
　177, 204, 422
Dominican (religious order)
　121, 133, 177, 187, 190, 204, 210, 239, 422
Dormition of Mary
　6, 9, 45, 70, 80–83, 98–100, 102, 110–112, 124–126, 146, 151, 154, 159, 169, 203, 305, 321, 323, 354, 369, 370, 382, 415, 422
Dragićević (-Soldo), Mirjana
　215–217, 219, 240, 241, 378, 379, 407
Duns Scotus, John
　121, 122, 132, 133, 152, 366

439

E

Easter
 14, 37, 152, 168, 269, 347, 425
Ebionite
 358, 371
Ecclesiasticus
 280, 292, 318, 397, 412, 432
Egypt
 8, 15, 30, 31, 44, 53, 64, 65, 79, 83, 85, 98, 169, 203, 206, 213, 214, 240, 242, 247–249, 252, 289, 338, 356, 363, 365
Egyptian
 19, 31, 107, 215, 243, 250–252, 289, 296, 338, 362, 363, 380, 389
El Shaddai
 161, 289, 290
Elisabeth, Abbess of Schönau
 138, 154, 204, 387, 388, 409
Elizabeth, cousin of Mary and mother of John the Baptist
 19, 21, 23, 24, 35, 53, 54, 58, 59, 62, 64, 85, 182, 335, 365, 426, 432
Emmerich, Anne Catherine
 5, 6, 49–58, 60–73, 77, 84, 85, 95, 96, 102, 108, 110, 135, 153, 201, 205, 221, 232, 236, 238, 244, 247, 328–333, 340, 343–345, 348, 352, 361, 363, 365, 368, 370, 396, 411
encyclical letter
 127, 128, 130, 149, 151–154, 180, 198, 367, 369, 371, 408, 411, 422
Enoch, I and *II*
 303, 322
Ephesus, city of
 42, 68–70, 73, 79, 94, 96, 97, 100, 110, 341, 352
Ephesus, Council of
 113, 118, 134, 143, 149, 160, 172, 240, 301, 321, 390, 410, 416, 422
Ephrem the Syrian
 79, 107
Epiphanius, bishop of Salamis, Cyprus
 82, 86, 108, 115, 140, 148, 160, 161, 195, 232, 244, 331–333, 341, 364, 367

Index

Episcopal Church, Scottish Episcopal Church
  1, 143, 145, 146, 156, 184, 278, 319, 428
Erasmus, Desiderius
  171, 181
Essene
  51, 55, 110, 328, 329, 340, 396
Eucharist
  4, 6, 40, 69, 88, 89, 100, 127, 131, 137, 139, 141, 186, 218, 219, 237, 247, 292, 329, 343, 346, 353, 387, 404, 423
Eusebius, bishop of Caesarea
  79, 106, 112, 167, 357, 370
ever-virgin (see also perpetual virginity)
  81, 144, 369, 370
externalization of the Hierarchy
  259, 279–281, 366, 367, 371, 410, 412
extracanonical texts
  4, 6, 13–16, 18, 27, 30, 35, 38, 39, 50, 53, 75, 76, 80, 97, 107, 124, 192, 230, 295, 314, 353, 358, 423
Ezekiel
  32, 46

F

Fátima apparitions
  206, 212, 213, 217, 230, 236–239, 376, 377
Feuerbach, Ludwig
  297, 320, 394, 411
Florensky, Pavel
  297, 306, 320, 394
France
  114, 122, 138, 163, 186, 210, 341, 387, 388
Franciscan (religious order)
  121, 132, 133, 152, 209, 210, 302, 366, 423
Freemasonry
  5, 248

G

Gabriel, Archangel
21–23, 28, 44, 57, 85, 95, 97–99, 105, 113, 168, 221, 242, 269, 301, 303, 334, 354, 365, 419

Galatians
39, 43, 46, 47, 371

Galilee
20, 21, 26, 29, 35, 47, 50, 55, 88, 343

Genesis
43, 45, 49, 136, 153, 282, 308, 317, 318, 323

gnosis
278, 279, 281, 282, 322, 371, 407, 408, 412

Gnosticism, Gnostic
3, 42, 46, 48, 83, 100, 111, 153, 201, 303, 318, 322, 325, 364, 369, 431, 432

goddess
3, 9, 48, 106, 108, 118, 157–159, 161, 162, 171, 195, 209, 250, 251, 257, 262, 268, 269, 281, 282, 288–293, 297, 302, 306, 308, 311, 314, 317, 318, 341, 364, 371, 374, 383, 398, 430

Godhead
8, 87, 117, 140, 285–288, 294, 298, 306–309, 311, 312, 316, 346, 377, 392, 393, 411, 419, 421–423, 426

Golgotha
89, 141, 347

Gregorian chant
191, 192, 196

Gregory of Nyssa
133, 296

Guadalupe apparitions
8, 193, 206, 209, 210, 227, 230, 237–239, 376, 377, 400, 406

Guglielma di Boemia, Guglielmites
299, 423

H

Hail Mary (see also *Ave Maria*)
118, 129, 174, 176–178, 183, 402

Index

Hannah (Hanna, Anne), mother of Mary
> 18, 19, 24, 43, 51, 52–54, 56, 57, 59, 60, 65, 71, 83, 84, 85, 87, 107–109, 226, 232, 252, 328, 330, 332, 335, 368, 406, 417

Heline, Corrine
> 255, 268–270, 279, 282, 382, 383, 408

Hierarchy of Masters (see Planetary Hierarchy)

high-church
> 144, 159, 182–184, 201, 424, 431

Hildegard of Bingen
> 134, 153, 162, 163, 165, 196, 205, 261, 302, 304, 312, 319, 321, 322, 324, 391, 410, 416

Hodson, Geoffrey
> 2, 8, 11, 223–231, 236–238, 205, 242–244, 247–256, 262–265, 268, 270–283, 311–315, 324, 325, 360, 362, 363, 371, 372, 376, 377, 379, 380, 386, 389, 391, 392, 392, 400, 406–411
> 429

hyperdulia
> 134, 159, 390, 424

hypostasis, hypostases
> 117, 149, 240, 295, 297, 319, 325, 394, 398, 424, 529

hypostatic union
> 117, 118, 313, 325, 392, 410, 424

I

icon
> 131, 152, 156, 173, 188, 189, 200, 305, 330, 364, 366, 375, 377, 408

Immaculate Conception
> 7, 27, 52, 113, 114, 119–123, 127, 131, 136, 145, 147, 150, 171, 211, 223, 242, 268, 279, 282, 310, 328, 376, 424, 426

individualization, individualized
> 245, 256, 286, 361, 391, 397, 412, 426, 430

infallible, infallibility
> 66, 122, 127, 150, 225, 328, 396, 422–424

initiate
> 173, 243, 380

initiation
   5, 9, 235, 249, 251, 252, 265, 268, 279, 281, 322, 324, 338, 340, 347, 361, 362, 371, 380,389, 405, 407, 408, 410, 413, 415, 419, 424, 426
intercession
   5, 7, 100, 157, 159, 164–167, 171, 174–176, 181, 184, 185, 187, 195, 196, 354, 375, 384, 402, 403, 425
intercessory prayer
   79, 160, 165, 166, 169, 176, 178, 184, 354, 384, 402, 425
invocation
   167, 362, 402, 403
Irenaeus of Lyon
   79, 107, 114, 115, 148, 150, 295
Isaiah
   25, 31, 32, 46, 92, 110, 293, 318, 340, 350, 396, 412
Islam
   5, 6, 13, 16, 27, 43, 200, 215, 248, 285, 419
Israel
   19, 20, 24, 26, 27, 29, 32, 76, 84, 96, 108, 136, 165, 197, 201, 290, 293, 301, 328, 329, 338, 352, 380
Italy
   46, 85, 89, 169, 206, 337, 387, 408
Ivanković (-Mijatović), Vicka
   215, 217, 219, 234, 241, 404

J

James, Infancy Gospel of
   6, 16, 18, 20, 22, 24–26, 31–35, 43–46, 51, 55, 57, 60, 61, 71, 75, 76, 80, 119, 232, 236, 328–330, 341, 364, 396
James, "brother of Jesus"
   34, 37, 77, 83, 94, 95, 102, 106, 233, 341, 357, 367
James the Just (Note: James the Just" and "James the bother of Jesus" may be the same man)
   38, 39, 77
Jeremiah
   46, 108, 195, 201, 293, 318

Index

Jeremiah (prophet)
  84, 160, 161, 170, 290, 291

Jerusalem
  9, 22, 23, 29, 30, 34, 37–39, 42, 48, 54, 56, 58, 59, 63, 64, 66, 68–70, 73, 75, 79, 80, 83, 86, 91, 92, 94–96, 98, 99, 101, 102, 104–106, 124, 125, 159, 160, 165, 172, 185, 195, 203, 250, 290, 291, 293, 301, 327, 328, 330, 337, 338, 348, 349, 352–359, 362, 371, 375, 427

Jesuit (see Society of Jesus)

Joachim, the father of Mary
  18, 19, 32, 43, 51–54, 56, 71, 87, 252, 328, 330

John, disciple of Jesus
  39, 67–69, 82, 83, 89, 91, 92, 94, 98–103, 105, 106, 109, 111, 112, 321, 341, 352, 354, 368, 370

John, Gospel of
  11, 15–17, 35–37, 42, 46, 47, 70, 92, 94, 133, 154, 266, 281, 336, 345, 347, 366, 367, 417

John Paul II, Pope
  126, 129, 130, 136, 139, 151–152, 154, 177, 179, 180, 210, 219, 241, 260, 343, 352, 369, 385, 396, 409, 411, 416

John the Baptist
  20, 21, 32, 47, 51, 54, 64, 77, 94, 243, 329, 335, 340, 350, 432

John XXIII, Pope
  131

John Paul II, Pope
  126, 129–131, 136, 139, 151–154, 177, 179, 180, 198, 210, 219, 241, 260, 343, 352, 367, 369, 385, 396, 408, 411, 416

Joseph of Arimathea
  67, 348

Joseph, Mary's husband
  18, 20, 21, 25–27, 29, 30, 32–35, 44–47, 55–62, 64, 65, 84, 85, 94, 102, 115, 117, 232, 330, 331, 336, 337, 340–342, 357, 365

Josephus, Titus F.
  45, 77, 94, 106

Judaea, Judea or Judah
  19, 20, 26, 45, 50, 59, 106, 160, 290, 291, 293, 336, 357, 358, 399

Judith and Judith
  158, 165, 172, 336, 393

445

Justin Martyr
  79, 107, 113, 115, 148, 295

K

Kabbalah
  248, 257, 278, 288, 307, 308, 321, 323, 366, 383, 419, 421, 425, 426, 430
Kali
  257, 317
karma
  271, 273, 383, 425
Kateusz, Ally
  84, 88, 89, 109, 110, 142, 198, 351, 364, 367, 369
Kempis, Thomas à
  164, 196, 302, 321, 375, 391, 410, 416
Khul, Master Djwhal
  249, 259, 265, 340, 360, 382, 409, 413, 431
Kings, I and *II*
  200, 290, 316–318, 408
koheneth
  94, 110
Kuan (Kwan) Yin
  3, 230, 251, 257, 263, 265, 271, 281, 282, 311, 327, 360, 371
Kuthumi, Master
  249, 274, 275, 382

L

Last Supper
  66, 88, 89, 139, 141, 192, 329, 343, 346, 353, 387
Lateran Councils
  115, 116, 148, 294, 319
Latimer, Hugh, Bishop
  143, 181
latria ("worship")
  134, 159, 424

Lazarus
  55, 329, 352
Leadbeater, Charles W.
  248, 251, 254, 261, 262, 264, 271, 278–282, 311, 362, 371, 380, 382, 383, 385, 403, 408, 409, 413
Lead (Leade), Jane W.
  305, 323
Leo XIII, Pope
  127, 129, 150, 151
Leviticus
  109, 370
Lewis, Agnes S.
  83, 108, 321
Lex orandi, lex credendi
  145, 156, 425
lifewave
  263, 286, 316, 359–361, 391, 395
litany
  81, 167, 183, 191, 199, 377, 402, 412
liturgical
  6, 16, 53, 93–95, 106, 122, 128, 131, 145, 146, 153, 154, 157, 159, 161, 162, 167, 180–182, 191, 193, 194, 200, 201, 223, 268, 353, 358, 366, 375, 385, 401, 419, 425
liturgy
  21, 38, 75, 77, 81, 93, 114, 125, 130, 145, 146, 156, 181, 182, 193–195, 198, 294, 305, 323, 329, 335, 343, 375, 389, 390, 400–402, 415, 416, 425
locution
  4, 7, 203, 224, 231, 242, 247, 376
logoic
  309, 419, 420, 425, 426, 428, 431, 432
Logos, Logoi
  28, 117, 162, 254, 260, 262, 263, 277, 279, 281, 287, 308, 309, 311, 314, 362, 380, 391, 395, 396, 407, 419, 420, 425, 426, 428, 430, 432
Lombard, Peter, Bishop
  294, 296, 297, 319

Lossky, Vladimir
:   123, 150, 319

Lourdes, apparitions at
:   8, 122, 141, 154, 200, 206, 210–212, 216, 227, 230, 237, 239, 368, 376, 377, 379

Love–Wisdom
:   304, 309, 379, 405, 407, 425, 426, 428, 429

Luke, Gospel of
:   11, 15, 18–24, 26, 28–30, 33–35, 37, 42, 44–48, 57, 64, 156, 176, 316, 321, 334–336, 346, 365, 367, 384, 397, 412, 417

Luke the Evangelist, author of *Luke* and *Acts*
:   188, 200, 330, 331, 364

Luther, Martin
:   15, 42, 121, 150, 171, 192, 197, 200

Lutheran
:   17, 128, 143, 172, 201, 206, 238, 297, 305, 336, 394, 429

Lutheranism
:   159, 172

Luxor, Egypt
:   249, 252

M

Magdalene, Mary
:   36, 37, 67, 90, 109, 347

Magi
:   26, 30, 62–64, 72, 85, 173, 337–339, 406

Magnificat
:   23, 24, 58, 94, 145, 171, 172, 182, 190, 192, 193, 197, 286, 335, 336, 375, 381, 403, 426

mantra
:   234, 402

manvantara
:   287, 396, 397

Maria Heli (allegedly Mary's older sister)
:   51, 52, 54, 69, 85, 328, 332, 370

Index

mariolatry
 106, 184
Mariology
 4, 7, 8, 79, 113–115, 143, 145, 148, 323, 375, 426
Marist (religious order)
 142, 186, 198, 352
Mark, Gospel of
 13, 15, 31, 33, 36, 37, 39, 46–48, 106, 115, 244, 336, 341, 344, 358, 367, 370
master
 8, 10, 18, 96, 224, 225, 229, 249, 250, 252, 256, 257, 259, 265, 269, 274–278, 370, 382, 291, 340, 354, 360, 363, 366, 382, 383, 389, 395, 400, 405, 408, 409, 413, 419, 420, 426, 428, 430, 431
mater, materia ("mother," "matter")
 162, 261
Matthew, Gospel of
 15, 18, 20, 25, 26, 30–33, 37, 39, 42, 44–48, 51, 63, 65, 75, 90, 109, 110, 115, 148, 196, 243, 245, 336, 337, 341, 359, 363, 365, 367, 370, 371
Maximus the Confessor
 80, 81, 84–87, 89–92, 94, 102, 104, 108, 116, 123, 148, 340, 344, 345, 348, 367, 381
mayavirupa
 380, 407, 426
Mediatrix
 66, 113, 119, 129, 130, 270, 426
Medjugorje, apparitions
 8, 203, 215–220, 228, 234–238, 240, 241, 256, 270, 282, 376, 378, 379, 400, 404, 407, 413
Memorare (prayer)
 176, 384
Messiah
 22, 23, 28, 29, 32, 63, 66, 85, 92, 299–301, 321, 329
Michelangelo Buonarroti
 141, 190, 292, 344
Mijatović, Vicka (see Ivanković-Mijatović, Vicka)

449

monad
   252, 253, 257, 264, 279, 280, 286, 287, 316, 317, 339, 360, 361, 363, 391, 395, 397, 412, 416, 420, 425, 426, 430, 432
monadic
   253, 255, 264, 280, 363, 373, 398, 412, 431
Montfort, Louis-Marie de
   127–129, 130, 151, 152, 175, 180, 186, 198, 200, 277, 328, 363, 375, 382, 391, 406, 408, 410, 413, 416
Morya, Master
   249, 250, 280, 382, 412
motherhood
   131, 232, 261, 263, 265, 272–274, 275, 288, 299, 310–313, 325, 386, 391–393, 411, 432
Moses (prophet)
   19, 27, 61, 90, 262, 290, 350, 351
Mozart, Wolfgang A.
   191, 200
Muhammad
   16, 75, 296
Mulaprakriti
   308, 314, 427, 428
music, musical
   7, 54, 157, 159, 187, 191–193, 335, 375, 403, 411
mysteries
   24, 53, 81, 88, 177, 193, 251, 252, 260, 280, 312, 323, 338, 341, 343, 362, 363, 371, 380, 389, 390, 409, 411, 416
mysticism, mystic
   4, 49, 121, 139, 154, 164, 173, 186, 204, 247, 269, 273, 287, 304, 305, 310, 314, 319, 324, 339, 366, 375, 388, 391, 393, 395, 403, 407, 412, 425

N

Nag Hammadi library, texts
   15, 32, 42, 43, 46, 47, 148, 195, 303, 322, 367
Naslian, Jean (see Nazlian, Jean)

Index

Nativity of Jesus
  11, 20, 26, 31, 33, 42, 57, 60–63, 85, 97, 115, 173, 177, 336, 353, 394, 427
Nativity of Mary
  167, 181, 427
Nazareth
  21–23, 26, 29, 30, 35, 44, 45, 53, 56–60, 64, 65, 79, 225, 279, 336
Nazarite
  47, 340
Nazlian (Naslian), Jean, Bishop
  141, 154, 346, 347, 368
Nestorius of Constantinople
  117, 118, 149
New Testament
  6, 13–18, 24, 31, 34, 35, 41, 48, 92, 147, 224, 294, 327, 334, 358, 371, 420, 421, 423
Newman, John Henry
  144, 145, 155, 156, 199
Nicaea
  109, 113, 115, 134, 148, 153, 158, 295, 302, 390, 422, 427
Nicene Creed
  103, 115, 145, 149, 152, 240, 247, 295, 296, 366, 370, 427
Northcote, James S.
  135, 136, 153

O

obstetric(s)
  71, 271, 386
occult, occultist
  242, 273, 278, 324, 371, 403. 406, 412, 413, 427
Old Testament
  17, 32, 147, 172, 279, 290, 292, 293, 318, 334, 336, 346, 350, 384, 393, 397, 420, 421
Origen of Alexandria
  243, 319

451

P

Palestine
   1, 3, 4, 6, 9, 13, 30, 49, 65, 77, 78, 93, 94, 158, 225, 232, 242, 243, 250, 252, 265, 310, 358, 360, 361, 397, 415, 424

Palestinian
   6, 51, 76, 114, 247, 251, 252, 267, 332, 347, 361, 362, 398

palimpsest
   83, 96, 97, 100, 112

palm tree
   27, 31, 65, 292, 337

palm-staff
   98, 99, 102, 354

Panagia ("The Most Holy One")
   172, 188, 189

Parabrahm, or Para-Brahman
   307, 308, 421

Paracelsus (Theophrastus von Hohenheim)
   296, 297, 320, 394, 411

Parvati (Parviti)
   263, 264, 281, 360

Passover
   34, 58, 88, 342, 343

paten
   89, 390

patriarch
   14, 67, 117, 125, 133, 135, 147, 149, 185, 319, 348, 427

patriarchy, patriarchal
   3, 77, 116, 270, 277, 289, 305, 387, 401

Paul, Apostle
   14, 31, 38, 39, 43, 46, 69, 102, 110, 113, 115, 124–126, 128, 150, 190, 286, 312, 347, 355, 356, 358, 359, 365, 371

Paul VI, Pope
   128, 136, 151–153, 156, 177, 179, 180, 198, 215, 384, 396, 409, 411, 412

Pavlović (-Lunetti), Marija
   215, 241

Index

Pentecost
    4, 6, 9, 37, 66, 68, 75, 77, 92, 109, 131, 169, 180, 268, 295, 349, 350, 352, 356, 362, 385, 415, 427
Persephone
    161, 195
Peter, *I* and *II*
    43, 133, 152, 316
Peter, Apostle
    38, 66, 69, 102, 103, 122, 125, 347, 356, 369, 423
Peter of Damascus
    81, 134, 153, 161, 175, 195, 302, 321, 390, 410, 416
Petrarch, Francesco
    300, 320
Philokalia
    148, 153, 195, 321, 410
Pilate, Pontius
    67, 78, 358
Pistis Sophia
    303, 322
Pius IX, Pope
    122, 127, 136, 142, 150, 153, 239, 321, 328, 389, 396, 410, 412
Pius X, Pope
    127, 142, 155
Pius XII, Pope
    125, 128, 130, 141, 151, 152, 154, 179, 349, 362, 369, 371, 382, 385, 409
plane, systemic (see also subplanes)
    244, 262, 267, 310, 420, 422, 425, 426, 428, 430, 431
Planetary Hierarchy, Hierarchy of Masters,
    10, 175, 223, 247, 249, 255, 259, 262, 266, 270, 271, 276, 278–281, 311, 315, 340, 359, 363, 366, 367, 371, 385, 398, 405, 409, 410, 412, 424, 428, 432
Planetary Logos
    277, 281, 287, 309, 362, 425, 426, 430
Plato
    43, 242, 294, 363

453

Pleroma
    100, 303
Pliny the Younger
    78, 107
Pneuma Hagion (Greek: "Holy Spirit")
    295, 428
Polidorus, Master
    249, 252, 257, 274, 276, 277, 363, 382, 389, 395
Postel, Guillaume
    300, 321
prakriti
    427, 428
predestination, predestined
    7, 114, 123, 132–136, 302, 339, 376, 397, 428
preordination, preordained
    7, 58, 113, 114, 123, 131, 132, 135, 136, 302, 339, 361, 396, 428
Priestess, Mary as
    1, 2, 4, 5, 7, 11, 94, 114, 140–142, 160, 195, 227, 228, 243, 249, 250, 271, 327, 346, 347, 362, 373, 380, 387, 389, 390, 392, 395, 402, 402, 415, 416
priesthood, priestly function
    4, 7, 19, 77, 93, 94, 96, 113, 114, 127, 128, 137–139, 142, 143, 154, 155, 250, 271, 320, 329, 340, 346, 347, 351, 361, 371, 387–389, 409, 429
Primacy of Christ (, Absolute)
    7, 132, 134–136, 152, 302, 339, 419, 428
Priscilla Catacombs
    93, 159
prophet
    25, 31, 33, 159, 160, 188, 290, 291, 300, 323, 350
prophetess
    19, 29, 43, 94, 192, 252, 338, 361
Protestant, Protestantism
    7, 17, 121, 144, 159, 171, 175, 373–375, 399, 429
Proverbs
    137, 153, 158, 195, 261, 280, 291, 292, 303, 306, 318, 397, 412, 421, 432

Index

Psalms
 30, 46, 93, 110, 182, 191, 318, 338

Pulcheria, Empress
 125, 364

Q

Queen, Mary as
 1, 2, 4, 5, 11, 42, 81, 87, 92, 95, 105, 128–131, 138, 139, 161, 164, 168, 169, 178–180, 183, 222, 228, 234, 236, 240, 243, 247, 249, 250, 254–257, 263, 271, 277, 288, 289, 291, 302, 309, 316, 327, 341, 373–375, 380–384, 389, 392, 395, 399, 402, 404, 406, 407, 415, 416, 429

queenship
 4, 7, 114, 130, 254, 262, 353, 362, 382, 383, 429

Qur'an
 6, 13, 16, 19, 22, 27, 31–33, 43–46, 75, 118, 149, 215, 230, 296, 320, 329, 346, 361, 364

R

Rabbula Gospels
 351, 369, 387

Raimondi, Anna
 8, 11, 205, 229–238, 241, 244, 245, 247, 250, 252, 256, 270, 279, 280, 282, 329, 330, 332, 333, 345, 364, 368, 376, 379, 383, 400, 404, 406–408, 413

Rain, David
 411

Ravenna, Italy
 85, 89, 108, 337, 365, 387

rays, seven
 68, 254, 264, 371, 380, 405, 407, 410, 420, 428–430

Reappearance of the Christ
 259, 389, 410

Rebecca, Rebekah
 90, 135, 153, 305

Redemption
 1, 7, 19, 29, 42, 88, 113, 114, 121, 133, 136, 141, 327, 328, 337, 338, 376, 421, 429

Reformation
  7, 106, 116, 122, 144, 157, 171, 174, 176, 177, 181, 182, 184, 192, 197, 299, 320, 321, 411, 429

reincarnation
  224, 234, 235, 237, 243, 252, 272, 275, 279, 411

Renaissance
  28, 188, 190, 191, 200, 296, 299, 353, 381

Resurrection
  9, 11, 37, 39, 76, 91, 125, 126, 151, 249, 341, 347, 348, 350, 369, 371, 407, 424

ritual
  6, 19, 52, 56, 62, 63, 78, 88, 89, 96, 157, 159–161, 170, 183, 188, 256, 290, 291, 332, 343, 353, 354, 362, 389, 390, 401, 416, 421, 423, 425

Roerich, Helena
  11, 248, 250, 251, 259, 260, 278, 280, 333, 342, 365, 367, 385, 397, 399–401, 409, 412

Roman Catholic
  2, 49, 52, 84, 126, 127, 129–131, 135, 140, 142, 147, 150, 153–155, 175, 178, 179, 184, 187, 188, 199, 204, 215, 217, 220, 223, 226, 229, 234, 241, 242, 250, 261, 274, 276, 278, 309, 344, 346, 352, 383, 385, 420, 425

Roman Catholicism (see also Church of Rome)
  7, 122, 128, 144, 145, 147, 157, 175, 178, 181, 184, 194, 198, 258, 276, 278, 310, 423

Rome, Church of; (Catholic Church)
  7, 8, 16, 17, 66, 77, 83, 113, 114, 119, 123, 124, 126, 127, 136, 137, 139, 171, 172, 177, 194, 205, 208, 215, 219, 223, 237, 239, 240, 242, 320, 374, 376, 422, 424, 426,

Rome, City of
  64, 78, 93, 97, 110, 131, 141, 150, 153, 159, 188, 305, 306, 323, 344, 352, 359, 366, 409, 412, 427, 429

Rosicrucianism, Rosicrucian
  248, 255, 268, 281, 419, 429

ruach (Greek: "breath" or "spirit")
  9, 293, 295, 296, 299, 399, 429

Ruach ha-kodesh (Hebrew: "the Holy Spirit")
  9, 293, 295, 296, 399, 429

S

sacrament
    4, 5, 142, 152, 155, 186, 194, 195, 199, 271, 276, 353, 389, 390, 408
sacrifice
    9, 18, 29, 55, 56, 59, 66, 71, 88, 89, 93, 109, 113, 114, 135, 139–142, 159–161, 185, 186, 218, 250, 252, 271, 290, 291, 294, 313, 315, 343, 346, 353, 362, 364, 387–390, 392, 416, 430, 421
Sanat Kumara
    283, 430
Santos, Lúcia
    212, 213, 236
Sapientia
    137, 304, 322, 421, 430
Sarah (Sara)
    18, 43, 90,
sephirah, sephiroth
    257, 421, 426, 430, 431
Septuagint
    32, 46, 261, 318
sepulcher
    69, 70, 90, 95, 99, 104, 345, 356
seraphim
    81, 91, 103, 105, 134, 162, 175, 242, 302, 319, 391
Shamballa
    340, 430
shekinah
    3, 9, 163, 196, 293, 306, 318, 377, 430
Simeon
    29, 55, 64, 85, 169, 173, 338, 365
Society of Jesus (Jesuit)
    88, 139, 176, 187, 201, 367, 385, 388, 425
sodality
    157, 185, 187, 230
Solar Logos
    254, 262, 281, 287, 309, 314, 380, 407, 425, 430

457

Soldo, Mirjana; see Dragićević (-Soldo), Mirjana
Song of Solomon
   163, 165,
Solomon, King
   290, 318, 381, 384
Solovyov, Vladimir
   306, 323, 398
Sophia
   3, 9, 42, 84, 137, 158, 261, 267, 268, 281, 285, 291–293, 295–297, 303–306, 318, 320, 322, 323, 393, 394, 397–399, 411, 412, 421, 430
spirituality, spiritually
   171, 180, 186, 191, 196, 197, 219, 242, 261, 351, 395, 401, 432
Steiner, Rudolf
   201, 266–268, 281, 305, 323, 420
stigmata, stigmatic
   6, 49, 50, 135, 238
Subba Row, Tallapragada
   307, 308, 323, 324, 379, 391, 398, 407
subplane
   244, 420, 419, 422, 423, 428, 431
Sufism, Sufi
   198, 374, 402
synagogue
   33, 92, 356, 358

T

Tacitus, Publius Cornelius
   78, 79, 107
Taylor, Jeremy
   144, 145, 155
Teresa of Ávila
   186, 204, 319
Theophilus of Alexandria
   149

Index

Theophilus of Antioch
  295, 306, 319, 393
theosis
  5, 80, 107, 133, 144, 152, 224, 243, 286, 287, 306, 316, 339, 346, 380, 408, 421, 431
Theosophical Society, Theosophical teachings
  8, 223–225, 248, 251, 255, 257–260, 266, 268, 272, 281, 285, 307, 308, 312, 317, 324, 359, 386, 407, 412, 431, 432
Theosophist
  8, 226, 232, 254, 257, 258, 260, 261, 263, 276, 280, 297, 311, 359, 363, 378, 385, 379, 395, 397, 401, 403, 409, 411, 431, 420, 432
Theotokos, Mary
  27, 45, 79, 81, 88, 97, 101, 111, 114, 117–119, 134, 147, 149, 160, 171–175, 185, 188, 189, 198, 240, 267, 301, 309, 321, 331, 356, 370, 373, 381, 382, 390, 410, 426, 431
Thomas, *Gospel of*
  38, 42, 358
Thomas, *Infancy Gospel of*
  35, 47, 75, 86, 342
Thomas, disciple of Jesus
  69, 102, 104, 105, 320, 355
Timothy, *I* and *II*
  43, 102, 195
Tingley, Katherine
  312, 313, 324, 378, 401, 407, 412
Tractarian Movement, Tractarians
  145, 156, 183, 199, 431
Transfiguration
  236, 249, 424
Trans-Himalayan teachings, masters
  249, 254, 304
Transitus Mariae
  83, 95–98, 100, 101, 105, 106, 108, 110–112, 321, 352, 354, 369, 370, 416

459

Trinity, trinitarian
    9, 33, 49, 53, 68, 111, 119, 134, 135, 173, 175, 212, 264, 270, 285, 288, 294–299, 301, 306, 308, 319, 349, 350, 390, 393, 394, 411, 423, 425–427, 432

U

Underhill, Evelyn
    339, 366
unmanifest
    294, 307, 309, 411, 419, 421, 423
Upanishads
    248, 307, 323
Uppsala, Sweden
    143, 151

V

Vatican Council I
    122, 150, 242
Vatican Council II
    126, 128, 129, 131, 136, 179, 180, 385, 399, 422
Vaughan-Lee, Llewellyn
    374, 402, 406, 413
Vedanta, Vedantic
    8, 248, 288, 307, 308, 427, 432
Vedas
    248, 307
Venus
    289, 310, 315
Vespers
    174, 191, 192
vestments
    55, 96, 138, 204, 329, 353
virginity
    31–34, 37, 71, 85, 113–116, 143, 144, 148, 221, 236, 293, 305, 340–342, 374, 376, 377, 428

Index

W

Walsingham, apparition site
    155, 167, 181, 184, 204, 206
Water (element)
    262, 263, 268, 314, 315
Will and Power
    405, 425, 428, 432
Wisdom of Solomon
    280, 292, 432
womanhood
    11, 227, 236, 258, 275, 311, 313, 392, 393
womb
    21, 23, 24, 27, 32, 35, 52, 90, 91, 117, 119, 121, 140, 144, 163, 169, 174, 176, 182, 184, 221, 254, 261, 298, 301, 305, 308, 310, 334, 335, 337, 347, 348, 374, 377, 385, 416
World Mother
    11, 131, 247, 249, 257–266, 268, 271–273, 275–277, 279, 281, 282, 285, 309, 311, 313–315, 359, 363, 383, 385, 386, 392, 395, 397–400, 405, 408, 409, 427, 432

X

Y

Yahweh
    289, 290, 291–294, 303, 317
yehidah
    287, 420, 432
yoga
    248, 278, 280, 365, 409, 412, 432
York
    153, 279, 320, 322, 411

Z

Zachariah (Zechariah), father of John the Baptist
    19–21, 23, 54, 55, 58, 59, 329
Zebedee, father of James and John
    39, 78, 82, 89, 109, 347, 368

Zeitoun, apparitions
    8, 203, 206, 213, 215, 228, 236–238, 240, 376
Zephaniah
    293, 318

CPSIA information can be obtained
at www.ICGtesting.com
Printed in the USA
BVHW040215031221
623153BV00015B/1054